Bird-by-Bird Gardening

The Ultimate Guide to Bringing In Your Favorite Birds—Year after Year

SALLY ROTH

RODALE
LIVE YOUR WHOLE LIFE™

Every day our brands connect with and inspire millions of
people to live a life of the mind, body, spirit — a whole life.

Printed in the United States of America

Rodale Inc. makes every effort to use acid-free ♾, recycled paper ♻.

Book design by Joanna Williams
Illustrations by Elayne Sears

Library of Congress Cataloging-in-Publication Data

Roth, Sally.
     Bird-by-bird gardening : the ultimate guide to bringing in your favorite birds—year after year / Sally Roth.
          p.   cm.
     Includes index.
     ISBN-13: 978-1-59486-620-3   (direct mail hardcover)
     ISBN-10: 1-95486-620-1   (direct mail hardcover)
     1. Bird attracting. 2. Gardening to attract birds. I. Title.
     QL676.5.R6684   2006
     639.9′78—dc22   2006004797

ISBN-13: 978-1-59486-311-0 (trade hardcover)
ISBN-10: 1-59486-311-3 (trade hardcover)
ISBN-13: 978-1-60529-825-2 (trade paperback)
ISBN-10: 1-60529-825-5 (trade paperback)

Distributed to the book trade by Macmillan

2   4   6   8   10   9   7   5   3   1   hardcover (direct)
      4   6   8   10   9   7   5   3   hardcover (trade)
2   4   6   8   10   9   7   5   3   1   paperback

RODALE
LIVE YOUR WHOLE LIFE™

We inspire and enable people to improve their lives and the world around them
For more of our products visit **rodalestore.com** or call 800-848-4735

For my family

Contents

Part 3: Birds Across America

Family Ties

Even though we're almost a generation apart in age, my sister Marie and I are best friends. She's the oldest of the six of us; I'm the baby of the family.

My sister loves beauty as much as I do. But, from the early days, her interests leaned toward art and antiques, while I could always be found outside, generally with grubby fingernails.

Her house is warm and cozy, filled with honey-colored wood, hundred-year-old baskets, her own oil paintings, and beautiful old pottery — décor that belongs in a country-style magazine.

Mine is decorated with, um, natural objects. Or, as a first-time visitor said recently, "This stuff looks like what you pull out of your pocket when you're a kid."

What's in our heads is just as different as what's in our houses. While I "collect" the names and habits of birds and plants and everything else under the sun, my sister can recognize just about any piece of china, silver, pottery, or furniture made in the last 200 years.

Still, she's always thrilled to report the latest robin nest in her yard in eastern Pennsylvania, or the mockingbird that sings on moonlit nights, or the wren that sometimes comes in through her open kitchen door and perches on an antique teacup.

Marie has lived in the same house for decades. Her yard wasn't planted with birds in mind, but it does have a gracious weeping willow, an old-fashioned privet hedge, and a few grand old mock orange and lilac bushes.

With plenty of protective cover, plus a feeder and birdbath, her place is a great example of how the general principles of attracting birds work out. You'll get enough birds to keep life interesting, you may find a nest or two, and sometimes you'll get a jaw-dropping surprise, like the huge, hungry night heron that showed up at my sister's feeder during a snowstorm.

My sister's happy with her birds, but she also likes to hear which birds I have at my place, here in western Washington. Some of them are birds that never turn up in Pennsylvania. But many of them — waxwings, vireos, tanagers, and orioles, for starters — are birds that anyone, anywhere, has a good chance of attracting.

"Ohh, an oriole," she said with longing, when I told her about the pair weaving a nest in my yard. "I haven't seen an oriole in years."

That's when it dawned on me. We all have our favorite birds, birds we want to see right in our own yards, and a feeder is a great place to start. But a feeder can only go so far. To really bring in birds, and to keep them coming back, you need the plants they like best.

All my life, I've been watching birds, in backyards and in the wild. I've learned where they feel at home, and which plants they can't resist. And I've put those lessons to work in every place I've lived, to bring the birds I like best to my own backyard.

"Want that oriole?" I asked Marie. "All you have to do is plant a mulberry tree. Remember how Mom used to get so mad when they'd eat mulberries and she had the sheets on the wash line?"

We both laughed, remembering our mom's indignation over the purple streaks on her clean sheets.

"Or you could plant a chokecherry. I bet you've been weeding them out of your yard, haven't you? Let a couple grow; orioles love 'em. And those Juneberry trees, some people call them shadblow, the ones that bloom when the shad are coming up the Delaware? And strawberries are good. Oh, and grapes—you could put up an arbor and you'd have grapes next summer; they're really easy to grow."

I was on a roll now. "And flowers, because orioles eat a lot of butterflies. And caterpillars. Oh, darn, if you lived out West, you could plant agaves, they love those flowers, they drink the nectar out of 'em. But you can put up an oriole feeder, sugar water, it's like a hummingbird feeder but bigger, with orange plastic because they love oranges, oh yeah, and you can put out oranges, too, or maybe some grape jelly. And white string—"

"Stop, stop!" she said, laughing. "That's like 5 years' worth of projects."

Exactly. And that's the great thing about gardening bird-by-bird. You can start with just one of the ideas you'll find here for your favorite birds, then add others whenever you want. You'll discover exactly what particular bird families like best, in terms of natural habitat and food, so you can create a backyard that's best suited to their needs. And you'll find that gardening bird by bird will not only bring in your favorites, but beautiful birds that may have never before visited your backyard, as well.

"How'd you learn so much about what orioles like?" my sister asked, when I finally ran out of steam.

"Watching 'em," I said.

"I'll have to try some of those things," she said. "Wouldn't it be neat to show Robert an oriole?"

Sure would. Sharing birds with a grandson—or a sister—only makes them more special.

Like I told Marie, it's the birds themselves that taught me everything I know. Every recommendation you find in this book is based on behavior I've seen myself.

A lifetime of watching birds, from one end of the country to the other, has been the best education I could have ever dreamed of.

And the best part? I'm still learning.

PART 1

Welcome, Friends!

Q UICK, NAME YOUR FAVORITE BIRD. The perky chickadee that greets you like a friend? The outrageously orange oriole that makes your backyard feel like the tropics? The gentle bluebird, with his quiet manners and breathtaking color?

This book takes a new approach to attracting your favorite birds to your own backyard. The key is to focus on bird families, the groups of species that include your particular pals.

In Chapter 1, you'll learn how science sorted out the birds into families. A classification system sounds like the worst kind of dull, but it's more like Sherlock Holmes in action. The big clues to bird families are eating habits and behavior, and the detective work spells out a perfect case for gardening bird-by-bird.

Knowing which birds you have a chance of bringing to your yard starts with a quick look around the neighborhood—not for birds, but for the places they might live. In Chapter 2, you'll learn how to figure out which birds you may get bragging rights to in your own yard. And you'll discover some potential new friends you might not even have on your wish list.

Chapters 3 and 4 will help you brush up on bird gardening, so you have the basics under your belt before you dive into the specifics of your favorite bird families.

Why even bother to garden for the birds, you might ask? For starters, many bird species are dwindling in numbers. Any small steps we take to make a haven for them can help. That's a great reason to do what we can in our own yards.

But the biggest reason for bird-by-bird gardening is that it's so much fun. What were those favorite birds again? Get ready to welcome them, and more, to a backyard that's focused on your favorites.

Chapter 1

Birds of a Feather

S o, you say your favorite bird is the bluebird? Welcome to the club. Bluebirds are so beloved that there are whole organizations devoted to them. They're beautiful, well-behaved, and quick to accept a helping hand.

If bluebirds live near your home, you'll find that it's easy to attract them to your own yard by planting to suit their habits and their appetites. For eastern bluebirds, start with a winterberry bush (*Ilex verticillata*); for western bluebirds, plant Nevin's barberry (*Mahonia nevinii*) and other mahonias (*Mahonia* spp.). In fall, the berries on these bushes will catch the eye of any bluebird scouting for food in the area.

Uh-oh! What are those brown birds doing, eating the berries you planted for bluebirds? And, hey, isn't that a robin?

Those interlopers are just doin' what comes naturally. Bluebirds are members of the Thrush family, and their cousins, the brown birds and robin at your "bluebird" bush, share the family's love of berries. Your eastern bluebird may share the branches with a wood thrush or gray-cheeked thrush. In your western garden, a hermit thrush or Swainson's thrush may keep the bluebirds company.

Each family shares some similar eating habits and behavior, and that's the simple trick to making a bird garden that welcomes them. It's also the basis that scientists depended on when they sorted out birds. You'll see why, when you consider just what "birds of a feather flock together" really means.

A Grain of Truth

Look out your window on a winter day, and you're bound to see birds of a feather, flocking together. Maybe it's a crowd of cardinals at the feeder, or a gang of evening grosbeaks cracking sunflower seeds side by side. And just look at all those perky little chickadees; why, there must be a dozen at least.

A few weeks later, when you're wondering whether spring will ever arrive, you're likely to look out your window and spy a batch of robins investigating your lawn. Yay, you've made it—daffodil time will soon be here!

◀ *The same plants you use to attract bluebirds to your yard may also grab the attention of a hermit thrush, a veery, or a gang of robins—all members of the fruit-loving Thrush family.*

A flock of spring harbingers, a flock of winter holdovers—it sure *seems* true that birds of a feather flock together.

But, like all old sayings with a grain of truth, this one can use a bit of fine-tuning.

For starters, let's look at those feathers. A scarlet tanager is as red as any cardinal, but you'll rarely see the two species side by side. Blue jays and bluebirds? Never together. As for the tufted titmouse and the mockingbird—both are gray, but these birds are as mismatched a pairing as Albert Einstein and Marilyn Monroe.

At first glance, the red feathers are what you notice about a male cardinal. But when it comes to classifying birds into families, color doesn't count.

It's plain to see that feather color can't be the characteristic that decides which birds are in a flock.

The word *flock* creates some problems, too, because not all birds are fond of the crowd scene. You'll never see a batch of brown creepers, for instance, unless they're fresh out of the nest. Instead, this diminutive brown bird hitches up and around tree trunks with nary another creeper for company. And many of the birds that appear to be a flock at the feeder go their own individual ways when they're done with dining.

It's nice to contemplate a happy, buzzing crowd of hummingbirds, too. But as anyone who keeps a nectar feeder knows, the reality is that these birds-of-a-feather are usually highly aggressive. The word *share* doesn't seem to be in their vocabulary. Many hummingbirds won't even tolerate other species of birds in their personal space. I once watched a tiny ruby-throated hummer singlehandedly chase away an entire flock of cedar waxwings, when the much larger waxwings inadvertently wandered too near the wildflowers that the hummingbird had claimed as its own.

But when we look a little deeper at that familiar saying, beyond the words we can all quote, we get to the truth of it: Birds with similarities do indeed hang out in the same kinds of places.

And that's the key to fashioning a yard that welcomes the birds you like best. By learning what those similarities are, and why they're so important, your garden and your feeding station will be brimming with birds—of all kinds of feathers.

Notice how different this tanager's beak is from that of the cardinal. Scientists put cardinal and tanager into distinct families, and one look at their beaks will tell you why. They're both red birds, but their diet and habits are totally different.

Sorting It Out

Oh, boy, it's time for my favorite household chore—sorting socks! Dump your laundry basket here, next to mine, and let's match them up. I'll bet you can do most of the sorting in a flash, because deciding what category your socks belong to is second nature by now. If you have a big pile, you probably begin by separating the white socks from the dark ones. It's easy to pull out the distinctive socks, the thick wool hiking socks, the fuzzy blue socks you wear around the house, and make them into pairs.

But often, the selection isn't as automatic. Then we sort them further—black or navy blue? Anklet or calf-high? We have to take a closer look, so we don't match up a white sock with a gray toe to a white sock with a white toe.

By the time you get to the bottom of the pile, you're left with socks that are almost identical. Then you may do what I do, hold them up beside each other to see whether they match. And sometimes—not that I ever would do this—you may pair up a leftover sock with another that's similar but not exactly the same.

That's exactly what scientists do when categorizing birds.

Deciding what's a bird and what's a cat, say, is as easy as pulling the misplaced T-shirt out of the sock pile. But figuring out how to organize the rest requires a closer look.

Imagine trying to sort out a few thousand socks, er, I mean birds, of all colors, shapes, and sizes. That was the mess that the early bird scientists faced.

Just like sorting the laundry, they started by

Don't try to pair up the perky little tufted titmouse with a sleek mockingbird or a hyperactive kinglet. Although all of the birds are gray, their beaks and behavior put them into three totally different families.

grouping birds with general similarities. Knee socks with knee socks, ducks with geese.

Color is an undependable clue when it comes to classifying birds, as we've seen with Mr. Titmouse and Miss Mockingbird. So these organizers, or taxonomists, as they're called, didn't look for "birds of a feather," those that share the same color of plumage.

The clues they used to decide which birds are related were similarities of shape and behavior.

Take It from the Top

No matter how different a hummingbird looks from a heron, they both belong to the most general bird category of all: the class *Aves*. Every bird in the world belongs to this class.

After that is where the fun starts.

Ever wonder why toddlers can play for hours with a shape-sorting game? Organizing by recognizing similarities, even those as simple as squares, circles, and triangles, seems to be a basic human instinct, and one that gives us a sense of satisfaction, too. We're making order out of what looks like a jumbled mess.

Once taxonomists started looking for similarities among the vast assortment of birds, they had a pretty easy time sorting out the birds to the next level, which scientists call their "order."

You can do it, too, even if you're a beginner at watching birds. Ducks and geese, it's easy to see,

Sez Who?

You might think that classifying birds is pretty dry stuff. Quiet, polite taxonomists, laboring away in dusty offices. . . . Not hardly. This is a lively bunch, and their arguments get pretty heated. Not to mention obsessive. How about 14 subspecies of Bewick's wren, each championed by experts who knew that *their* wren was different?

The *Check-list of North American Birds* produced by the American Ornithologists' Union (AOU), is the standard used in this book and many others, but even this venerable institution doesn't have the last word.

A real firestorm was touched off back in the 1970s, when Charles G. Sibley (1917–1998) challenged some of the long-accepted classifications, based on his studies of bird DNA. Most of the changes occurred in exotic birds, such as toucans, and in seabirds and some waterfowl. Scientists are still arguing about his findings. And even after such diligent genetic study, some birds still stump the experts. You can wow your birder friends, or maybe bring nonbirders to their knees with laughter, by quoting Sibley on one such bird: "The broad-billed sapayoa *Sapayoa aenigma* remains an enigma."

Research into DNA examination continues. But what I find the most interesting part of Sibley's research is the fact that about 75 percent of bird classifications—including nearly all of our backyard birds!—stayed exactly the same. To me, that's great evidence that watching bird behavior and looking at body and beak shape are just as good as examining genes with the latest high-tech equipment.

As for those dry, dusty taxonomists, this line from Sibley's obituary gives us a glimpse into what really goes on in those hallowed halls of science: " . . . Critics were baited with an acid tongue, and, in fits of temper, he could be a cruel mimic." Kind of makes you wish you'd been a fly on the wall, doesn't it?

are pretty similar. But hummingbirds are nothing like them. And neither are turkeys. And woodpeckers don't look or act like ducks or hummingbirds or turkeys.

There you go—that's four orders of birds already, and you're just getting started.

May I Take Your Order?

The first steps may be simple, but sorting all those birds into groups, according to their similarities, isn't as black and white a matter as matching socks.

The vast majority of birds belong to only one

Wings and feathers are about all these two birds share. It's easy to see why they belong to two wildly different bird orders.

order, the Passeriformes, or perching birds. No matter what size or color they are, or what beak shape they have, most of our familiar friends have feet made for grasping a twig or other perch. Cardinal, chickadee, jay, song sparrow, bluebird: All are passerines (say "PASS-uh-rine," with a long *i*).

Most of us are likely to see birds from only four to five different orders in our yards. But depending on where you live, you may also spot birds from a dozen or more other orders, too, such as waterfowl (Anseriformes), kingfishers (Coraciiformes), or wild turkeys and other chickenlike birds (Galliformes). *Whooo* is calling at night? Maybe a member of the order Strigiformes, or owls. And, if you live near an ostrich ranch, you can count the order Struthioniformes if one of those long-legged feather-dusters happens to stray into your yard.

Meet the Family

Most field guides, bless their helpful little hearts, are organized according to the orders of birds. No need to page through the gulls or the owls when you're trying to identify a woodpecker.

But field guides can still be frustrating, especially when you're trying to pinpoint a passerine. That's when a further classification of birds—the family—comes into play.

Remember that unpaired pile of athletic socks, the ones that need extra care to match up because their differences are so slight?

Same deal with birds.

Just as we peer at our socks to see which one has the gray toe, which the white, scientists had to peer more closely at birds to separate them into more finely tuned groups, or families.

If it looks like a duck, and walks like a duck, it's a duck. According to order, that is. Simple as separating the athletic socks from the dress socks!

But if it looks like a duck, and is really a goose, then it must be in a distinct family.

Easy enough. For ducks and geese, anyway.

When it comes to the passerines, the huge order of perching birds that includes more than half of all the bird species in the world, the similarities were a little trickier to sort out.

All perching birds have the same general body shape and the same structure when it comes to feet. They're built for grasp-and-go perching.

But you and I know that a chickadee looks way different from a robin. And not only do the birds look different, but they also behave differently.

So how did scientists sort out those mismatched socks?

Birds of a beak, so to speak.

The kind of bill a bird has is the key to what it eats. And what it eats is the clue to how it behaves when finding food.

By sorting out the birds according to their beaks (and dozens of other not-so-obvious physical characteristics, such as number of tail feathers), as well as by behavior, taxonomists had a great trick for separating the birds in each order into a more fine-tuned arrangement, called families.

Birds spend much of their time searching for food. So, by focusing on their families—on what they eat and where they find it—we backyard bird lovers have a great trick for making our yards welcoming to the families we like best.

Kissing Cousins

I've always been a fan of those children's picture books with the pages sliced in half so that you can create weird animals by matching an alligator's head, say, to a hippo's body. Alligators and hippos are odd enough animals to start with, but mix 'em up, and the incongruous result always makes me laugh.

Imagine a hummingbird's head on a chickadee's body, or a heron's head on a robin's body. Not only is it a pretty silly picture, but the poor bird would have to change its entire way of life.

That's because a bird's beak is the tool it uses to eat. And because birds eat all kinds of different things, the shape and structure of the beak varies from one bird family to another.

A hummingbird needs a needle beak to sip nectar from flowers. But a chickadee would be at wit's end trying to pick tiny insects from leaves with that appendage. And while the massive beak of a great blue heron is perfect for snapping up fish, frogs, snakes, and other squirmy critters, it's way too clumsy for pulling worms out of the ground.

Bill of Fare

Next time you have a lively crowd at the feeder, pull out your binoculars and take a close-up look at the beaks of those birds. You can bet that birds with bills of a similar style will be busily eating the same kinds of feeder foods.

Take a look at the suet block first. That high-fat food mimics the appeal of insects, so that's where you'll find birds with bills made for gobbling up bugs. You'll spot the small, sharp bills of

Fast-action fliers, kinglets often flutter among foliage to snatch small insects with their tiny, quick bills.

titmice and chickadees, both of them built for quickly picking off small insects. And you can't miss the strong, dagger beaks of woodpeckers, tailored for prying insects out of wood. If you have a Carolina or Bewick's wren in the neighborhood, you might notice a third distinctive bill at your suet block—the long, curving trademark of the Wren family.

Meanwhile, you're bound to see birds with wider, shorter beaks, such as cardinals or grosbeaks, and their smaller cousins, the house finches and goldfinches, at your sunflower seeds. Small seeds, such as millet, will be favored by sparrows and juncos—birds of a beak, so to speak.

Checking out feeder eaters for similarities of bill and bill of fare is a great game to play at the window, but it's not as reliable as watching birds in the wild. Beaks and other physical characteristics are only part of the story.

Behavior is the other big clue to classification.

Insect eaters, for instance, could be focusing on foliage, as kinglets and chickadees do; or probing into bark, à la nuthatches and brown creepers; or flipping over leaves on the ground to expose edibles, as thrashers and grackles do.

At the feeder, all of these insect eaters will sample the suet. But in the wild, their very different behaviors when finding natural foods, as well as their beak shapes, are why they're classified into different families.

Beak or Bill?

Either term is correct. Those who consider themselves serious birders often use the word *bill*; backyard birdwatchers tend to stick with *beak*. As my Pennsylvania Dutch forebears would say, "*Machs nichts*"—it doesn't matter. Whether you call it a beak or a bill, it all means the same thing. Besides, I think the distinction is a bit of snobbery, like the ongoing split between the American and the British pronunciations of clematis. Are you a better gardener because you adopt the currently fashionable English version and call it "KLEM-uh-tis"? Not in my book!

Let's Be Specific

Figuring out the families isn't enough for taxonomists, who have organized birds down to the last detail, sorting out all the members of a family into genus and, finally, into species.

It's easy enough to tell which birds are in the Woodpecker family, for instance. But that bunch of hammerheads can be distinguished even further. All woodpeckers hammer on trees to find insects, but each genus of woodpeckers adds its own trademark touch to that basic trait. Behavior—it's the key to who's who in the family.

- Woodpeckers that drink sap are grouped, naturally enough, into the sapsucker genus (*Sphyrapicus*).
- Those that often fly out from a perch to catch insects and also have a habit of storing food—such as the acorn woodpecker or red-bellied woodpecker—go into another genus (*Melanerpes*).
- "Classic" peck-peck-peckers that pick at bark to get at the bugs, get their own group (*Picoides*), which includes our familiar friend, the downy woodpecker, and its relatives.
- Flashy flickers, with their habit of eating on the ground, get put into another genus (*Colaptes*).
- And, last but not least in the five genera of woodpeckers, there is the genus (*Dryocopus*), which includes the humongous pileated woodpecker—which digs out big, rectangular holes in trees and pries apart dead logs—and the recently rediscovered and even bigger ivory-billed woodpecker.

Within those genera, woodpeckers number only 22 species. Not too overwhelming. But across North America, species of all birds total somewhere around 654, a number that fluctuates as official checklists are updated. It's a good thing all the species in a family share the same general eating habits; it's much simpler to think about tailoring our yards to the tastes of 20 or so families of backyard birds than to the 600-plus species within them.

This gilded flicker isn't dining at this anthill—he's bathing. Letting ants crawl through his feathers, or smashing them to wipe over his body, helps to deter lice and other pests.

Family Matters!

Organizing birds into genus and species is just neatening up the sock drawer, making sure everything matches. And since I'm the type who will pair up a black sock with a navy blue one if

Then and Now

Long before the AOU stepped in to make names official, birds were called by common names. What we now call a goldfinch (or American goldfinch, if we're being official) used to be known among country people as a "wild canary," because its looks and song were similar to the cage bird. Some folks, especially in rural areas, continue to use the old names that were handed down but never made official. If you want to be official, use the AOU names, but be warned: Like bird classifications and Latin names, even these garden-variety monikers undergo updating. And old habits are hard to change: I still say "green heron" when I spot the bird now updated to green-backed heron.

Former Official Name	Current Official Name	Reason
Green heron	Green-backed heron	More accurate description
Louisiana heron	Tricolored heron	More descriptive
Eastern pewee	Eastern wood-pewee	To differentiate from Western species
Catbird	Gray catbird	To differentiate from Mexican species
Scrub jay	Florida scrub jay	Reorganized
	Island scrub jay	Reorganized
	Western scrub jay	Reorganized
Gray-breasted jay	Mexican jay	Reorganized
Plain titmouse	Oak titmouse	Reorganized
	Juniper titmouse	Reorganized
Short-billed marsh wren	Sedge wren	More descriptive of habitat
Long-billed marsh wren	Marsh wren	More descriptive of habitat

they're the only two left, I'll happily leave the fine details of bird classification to the experts.

Besides, when it comes to attracting birds to the yard, it's the family that matters. Despite the small differences among members of a family, that bunch of relatives has many traits in common.

And it's the behavior of a family group that gives us the clues we need to make them feel at home in our backyards. Since birds spend most of their lives looking for food, that's the best place to start.

By focusing on the menu, eating habits, and habitat of different bird families, you're on your way to better birdwatching, and better birds to watch, right in your own backyard.

What's for Dinner?

Ask a tree swallow, and the answer is insects, preferably on the wing, thank you. "Seeds! Seeds! Seeds!" chirp the sparrows. Meanwhile, cedar waxwings are like the diners who can't decide what to order: Fruit

That heavy-duty bill means business for an evening grosbeak. Its heft is tailor-made for cracking tough seeds, including those of trees. The large, oil-rich seeds of sunflowers are another favorite; they disappear fast when grosbeaks come to call.

will get their attention fast, but maybe an entrée of tasty insects would be better.

Whatever the specifics, the main foods of nearly all backyard birds fall into four general categories: insects (including arachnids, such as spiders, and arthropods, such as sow bugs), seeds (including nuts), fruits and berries, and nectar.

Most birds depend mainly on one or two of these categories. Swallows are insect eaters; sparrows are seed eaters; waxwings eat fruits and berries plus plenty of insects.

There's also plenty of crossover going on. Nearly all of our backyard birds make up their menu from two or three categories, sampling some insects, some seeds, and some berries, say, in the course of a season.

Only a very few birds, all of them insect eaters, are so specialized that they stick to just one category. Even hummingbirds, which we think of as nectar drinkers, nab an occasional insect, too.

Table Manners

I keep waiting for a new version of the food pyramid to be released—one with chocolate as the foundation, say. But, for some reason, that never seems to happen. Still, no matter how you fiddle with the food pyramid, three square meals a day, not to mention coffee breaks and midnight snacks, is the way most of us eat.

For backyard birds, it's more like nonstop snacking from dawn to dusk. Most daily bird activity is dedicated to finding food. Sure, there are plenty of times when birds pause to sing, or splash, or weave a nest. But for a huge part of the time, birds are on the lookout for food, fluttering from one place to another as they seek out seeds, insects, and other quick bites.

Each bird family has its own way of doing things. By looking at how birds get their food, you can tailor your yard to attract birds with all kinds of table manners. Treetop feeders, such as vireos and tanagers, can search among the leaves of your shade trees, while nuthatches and creepers examine the bark. Towhees can scratch under the shrubs, while native sparrows and juncos patrol your perennials. Bluebirds and waxwings can fly in to pluck berries from your bushes, while thrashers and catbirds duke it out over the leftovers on the branches.

In the family profiles that begin on page 70, you'll learn about the feeding behavior of each family, and you'll discover lots of tips for putting those natural instincts to use in your own yard. You'll also find plenty of suggestions for specific plants that each family finds irresistible, and feeder foods to bring them right up to your window.

Thinking about each family's table manners makes it easy for us to make our yards appealing. Once you have a handle on where a bird family finds its foods, you'll know what kind of tweaking to do to your yard. Here's just a sampling of the info we can glean:

- Woodpecker beaks are sturdy chisels, flattened to a tip that's tailor-made for jabbing and prying into wood. Want to see a woodpecker? Keep your eyes on tree trunks and dead branches.
- Bluebirds, robins, and other thrushes seek out soft food for their thin beaks, which aren't very strong. You'll find these birds wherever there's an abundance of juicy caterpillars and other soft-bodied insects or fruit, which generally means near ground level or in the bushes.

- Wood warblers, kinglets, and bushtits all have itty-bitty beaks, tiny pointed tools made for rapidly picking small insects from the foliage. Fans of these little, quick-moving birds know that the best place to see them is in the leafy treetops or shrubbery, where they can put those fast-action beaks to best use.
- Cardinals and other members of the Grosbeak family have big, heavy bills made for cracking through tough-shelled seeds. When they're not feasting on your sunflower spread, they're seeking out tree seeds, giant ragweed seeds, and other tough customers.
- Native sparrow beaks look like miniature versions of the cardinal's bill, so that tells us they're used as seed crackers, too. But these smaller beaks are best suited to smaller

A niche for every bird: It's a plan that guarantees a good meal to birds by preventing overcompetition. The eastern towhee forages near ground level for its favorite insects and fallen seeds.

seeds, so you'll find song sparrows, white-throated sparrows, and other small finches at home in grassy, weedy places, which are chock-full of the small seeds they're best adapted to eat.

• Jays and crows have multipurpose beaks that can slice, stab, yank, or gulp just about anything. No wonder this family is known for eating just about anything that isn't nailed down. With such a varied diet, you may spot a jay or crow just about anywhere, from backyards to garbage dumpsters to farm fields.

To whet your appetite, take a look at the possibilities of your yard from a bird's-eye view. Maybe you have a patch of lawn, a few flower beds, an herb or veggie garden. If yours is an older neighborhood, you may have a shade tree

in the front, or a hedge along the back. Congratulations—you have a great start!

That simple yard is a solid foundation for attracting bird families that feed on the lawn, in treetops, at flowers, among shrubs, and in the air. A little fine-tuning, to include specific plants for specific families, and many of your favorite friends will soon come to check it out.

You'll also want to adjust the accommodations so that birds feel safe when they're visiting your yard. Include some of the elements of each family's natural habitat, and you'll have the final key to a yard that's brimming with birds who find it irresistible to visit—and a welcoming place to stay.

Feels Like Home

Fruit for the fruit eaters, seeds for the seed eaters, insects for the insect lovers, and that fancy koi from your garden pool for the fish eaters. (Or not, on that last one.) Tailor the menu in your yard to the tastes of the birds you want to attract, and you're likely to tempt every bird family you like best.

The right foods will get them there, but unless birds feel at home, they won't linger any longer than it takes to grab a quick bite.

"Regulars" in your yard are even more gratifying than regulars at the feeder. I love knowing that the winter wren will trill his song from the shady glen of ferns behind my house, and that the towhee hangs out under the overgrown rose bush year-round. I get a kick out of seeing the song sparrows carrying grass to fashion a nest among the sprawling stems of the 'Powis Castle' artemisia on my hillside. And I'll never forget the year a hummingbird decided to plaster its tiny eggcup of a nest to the branch right outside my desk window. I'm still waiting for a violet-green swallow pair to adopt one of the nest boxes I put up for them last year, but in the meantime, I've been watching a red-shafted flicker hollow out a home in the dead branch of the maple. Okay, so I could live without the flicker's ear-splitting drumming on the chimney cap, but I figure that's a small price to pay.

My yard was nothing but raw dirt with one mid-size maple and one fir left standing, not much different from other yards in this subdivision. It was a far cry from my previous places, where old shade trees graced the yard and peonies planted a hundred years before still sprouted every spring.

Still, even starting from scratch, it doesn't take long to make a yard, any yard, into a real haven for birds.

What's the trick? Nearly all members of each bird family prefer the same kind of homeland—open spaces, brushy fields, shady woods. Don't worry; you won't need to let your yard go wild to attract the families you like best. Instead, the garden plans you'll find for each family in this book use simple tricks that capture the appeal of the places each family prefers—their natural habitat, scaled to fit your yard.

You'll find plenty of suggestions for making your yard a real haven for birds in the next two chapters.

Chapter 2

Great Expectations

You may know how chickadees behave when they're pecking at the suet or dashing in to snitch a sunflower seed. They're active, friendly, and fun to watch. But just wait until you see them doin' what comes naturally—working at hemlock cones, splashing in the bath, or raising a fuzzy-headed family. Branching out beyond the feeder means that you'll get better acquainted with your feeder friends. Even better, you'll also meet fabulous birds that never set foot at a feeder (did somebody say waxwings?).

When was the last time you saw a cedar waxwing at your feeder? Yep, me neither. These sleek birds with the mysterious wing tips of red wax—will some scientist please figure out what that's about? I've given up trying to puzzle it out—are well known for scorning bird feeders, no matter how temptingly they're stocked. Even mealworms, the latest feeder-food sensation, don't catch the eye of the haughty waxwing clan that roams my neighborhood.

I did have some success luring waxwings to almost-feeder status by pinning cherries to a tree branch in the dead of winter. Okay, so the waxwings were mighty hungry, and the cherries were pricier than prime rib, so I guess it doesn't really count.

Waxwings will probably never be feeder regulars. Neither will vireos or flycatchers. Nix, too, for just about all of the tiny birds called wood warblers. You probably won't see swallows at your feeder spread, either.

I haven't hosted any of these birds in forty-some years of feeder keeping, but I won't say "never." Maybe someday those waxwings will realize that the dried cherries in the feeder taste even sweeter than fresh ones.

There's no denying that some birds are simply more partial to feeders than others. You'll see a lot more chickadees at the feeder than you do wrens. You'll count more visits by juncos than by thrushes. Maybe you'll get a brown thrasher—or maybe not.

Tailoring your feeder menu to the birds you want will boost your chances of seeing your favorite birds, which is why you'll find tips and recipes for feeder favorites in this book.

But gardening bird-by-bird works even better. It's the combination of new behavior and new birds that makes it so much fun.

Those cedar waxwings that scorned my feeder changed their tune in a hurry as soon as I planted a red elderberry bush. When the berries ripened, they stayed all day for more than a week, until they'd gorged themselves on every last one. The best part about their visit was that these birds are so naturally tame that I could approach within arm's-length of them. I settled on a comfortable rock and enjoyed their feast, listening to their sweet, wheezy calls and feeling like I was an honored guest. Okay, at least a tolerated one.

So what can you expect to see in your own

Gardening for birds pays off big-time when you get to see beautiful birds that might never come to a feeder. Add fruit and berry plants like this juniper to your yard, and sleek cedar waxwings, which rarely frequent feeders, may drop in for a visit.

Old Birds Learn New Tricks

About 20 years ago, indigo buntings and rose-breasted grosbeaks were feeder rarities. Now, these vivid birds are a regular spring treat at feeders everywhere within their range. More recently, it's orioles that are showing a change in habits. Baltimore, Bullock's, and other orioles have begun to adopt feeders in many areas of the country. Seems like once a few orioles figured out that there might be grape jelly or oranges waiting for them, the word spread like wildfire. Sugar water's no secret anymore, either, even though it was only in the 1960s that hummingbird feeders came on the market. Nowadays, hummers take to feeders instantly, and house finches, downy woodpeckers, pine siskins, and a long list of other birds have learned to seek out the sweet stuff, too.

The glorious rose-breasted grosbeak was once a rarity at feeders. Now, these striking birds are often spotted cracking sunflower seeds at feeders in spring.

A New Side of Old Friends

Even birds that are so common you rarely give them a second thought can surprise you with behavior that's brand-new to you. Take the American robin, for instance, a bird so familiar that nearly everybody can identify it. Robins hop on lawns, splash in birdbaths, and eat worms—sure, we know all about them.

One day, I happened to wonder who was singing that pretty song outside my bedroom window every morning at the first lightening of the sky. It turned out to be a robin, one of the best backyard singers. Once I knew the song, I felt like I had a better connection to the bird. Still, I wasn't ready for the biggest robin surprise when it came along a few years later.

Termites are so common in southern Indiana, where I once lived, that many mortgage companies insist on a termite inspection just to make sure the house isn't ready to fall down.

One spring day, I stepped outside just as a huge swarm of termites started taking off from a long-dead stump in my neighbor's yard.

"Hurry! Get boiling water!" she urged me, fearing that the wood-munching pests would invade our houses.

Before the kettle ever whistled, a dozen robins had arrived on the scene like a SWAT team swinging into action. In minutes, they completely decimated the swarm, picking off termites on the ground and in the air until there wasn't a single pest to be seen. Then they retreated to nearby shade trees, to pick their teeth, I presume, while I watched to see what would happen next.

As soon as another batch of termites left the stump, the robins descended from the trees to snatch up every one in that swarm.

For hours, the birds kept it up, until not a single termite was left.

Meanwhile, my neighbor and I sat on the shady porch, sipping the mint tea we'd made with the boiling water we hadn't needed after all. Robins: termite control on the wing. Who would've guessed?

yard? That depends on where you live. Not in the big picture of geographic ranges (you'll find details on that in Chapter 25), but in the smaller scale of your own neighborhood.

Backyard Potential

Any yard can be a good yard for birds. Any yard!

Sure, a yard that's measured in acres instead of feet can host a lot more birds, and it may already be bird heaven. Or then again, it might not: A sweeping stretch of acres of manicured lawn,

weeded and feeded and pesticided into unnatural perfection, will have way fewer birds than a suburban lot with a smaller lawn that's dotted with weeds and worms, or a tiny in-town backyard with lots of bushes.

Your yard, wherever it is and whatever size it is, will become bird heaven when you supply the elements that birds like best. You'll find general tips for doing just that in the next chapter, plus plenty of specifics in each bird-by-bird chapter. But before you dig in, let's take a look at what kinds of birds you may draw in—and why.

An underpinning of violets (common violet, *Viola sororia*, and Confederate violet, *V. sororia* var. *priceana*) gone wild beneath shrubs creates inviting habitat for foraging thrushes. Violets attract egg-laying fritillary butterflies, adding a crop of caterpillars to the bird attractions.

The Nature of the Neighborhood

Most birds that belong to the same family prefer similar habitat. Oh, there are a few independent sorts (unlike other members of the Thrush family, the robin spends a lot of time on lawns), and plenty of room for variation, but in general, the same kinds of surroundings will satisfy nearly all members of a family.

The wild places and open spaces near you, such as parks, cemeteries, or golf courses, will determine which birds are apt to call your place home. To get a hint of the possibilities, start by taking a look at what's around you.

- Live near a city park or greenspace? You can expect to attract birds that seek the gracious old trees, dense shrubbery, and green lawns that are usually part of a park. That may mean an influx of orioles, tanagers, vireos, titmice, woodpeckers, and other birds.
- If your house or neighborhood is near farm fields or grasslands, you can count on coaxing in some of those birds of the fields and hedgerows. Meadowlarks, quail, pheasants, red-headed or red-bellied woodpeckers, field sparrows, grasshopper sparrows, buntings, and a host of blackbirds may come calling.
- Is that a woods at the end of your block? Your chances of tempting thrushes, vireos, warblers, grosbeaks, towhees, chickadees,

Taking Stock

When I moved to a new home, my first order of business was to set up a feeding station to begin taking stock of the local birdlife. Within a few days, I had a loyal crew of chestnut-backed chickadees, Steller's and scrub jays, spotted towhees, black-headed grosbeaks, golden-crowned sparrows, purple finches, and red-shafted flickers. Other birds, including Oregon juncos and the gregarious bushtits, took a little longer to arrive.

By setting out a variety of foods, in a variety of feeder styles, you'll find out in a hurry who's living near enough to make your yard a destination. Once you have a basic cast of characters, you can start planning your yard to make them feel more at home.

titmice, kinglets, and even wild turkeys just went up.

- If there's a lake, large pond, river, or creek within walking distance, you may spot some surprising guests in your own backyard. Yellow warblers, cedar waxwings, swallows, purple martins, flycatchers, and red-winged or yellow-headed blackbirds may check out your appealing yard.
- Nothing much but roadways or parking lots in your part of town? Don't despair. The shrubby landscaping put in along highways, in parking lots, and in commercial or industrial areas also attracts birds. Then it's just a hop, skip, and flap of the wings for these native sparrows, common yellowthroats, mimic thrushes, and other birds of the bushes to find their way to your yard.
- Yards, yards, and more yards, on every side? Not a problem. Shade trees attract orioles, tanagers, vireos, and grosbeaks; lilacs (*Syringa vulgaris*) and other common shrubs are perfect homes for cardinals, mocking-

Fill part of your yard with garden-worthy prairie plants, including big bluestem grass (*Andropogon gerardii*) and yellow coneflowers (*Ratibida pinnata*), and grassland birds such as bobwhites and field sparrows will feel right at home.

Winging It

Whether it's meadow, desert, chaparral, or towering trees, wild places are brimming with birds. Your proximity to such abundance determines what kinds and how many birds you may get in your yard. Natural woods right next to your property line will contribute lots of forest-loving birds to your list of backyard possibilities, even if your yard has only a tree or two and some shrubs. All birds have to do is travel a few short wingbeats to get to your place.

But what if the nearest natural area is at the end of the block, or a half-mile away? Or what if you live on a city street or in a large subdivision, where natural areas are few and far between?

Ah, that's the beauty of wings. Most birds will routinely travel from a few blocks to about a half-mile to reach a good source of food or water. Some birds fly even farther on their daily rounds. The great horned owl that swoops in to check out your feeder at night, in hopes of mice, may cover several square miles on its nocturnal tour.

Most birds don't follow the crow's example of taking the shortest distance between two points. Instead of traveling as the crow flies, in a straight and direct route, they take such a convoluted path that you may not even notice that they're trying to get from Point A to Point B.

Dash and dart, twist and turn, start and stop, skulk and hide—it's all part of the bag of tricks birds use to avoid being eaten. Most birds try to stay as much out of sight as they can when they travel, whether it's to cross your yard or to cross the country. They move along "corridors" of plants, flying or hopping from one shrub or tree to the next.

The more handy pit stops there are along a path, the more birds will be inclined to use it.

If your neighbors have planted hedges or shrubs, or if there are shade trees and street trees, birds will make use of the cover to move from one yard to another. They'll also use these travel paths, or corridors, to get from a wild place to your yard.

The short story is that most birds don't like to travel across big areas of unsafe territory unless they're desperate. You may have noticed that winter storms often bring unusual visitors to your feeder or your yard. Hunger is a prime incentive for birds to overcome their desire to stay out of sight.

Wherever you live, corridors for bird travel are the main clue as to what birds you can regularly expect to see. When birds feel safe traveling about, you'll see more of them in your yard.

birds, robins, and song sparrows, among others. Wrens also like the civilized life. And all that open space may make your place a good site for nest boxes for swallows or purple martins.

City Life

City birds seem like a limited cast of characters. Pigeons, doves, English sparrows, starlings—you see these few species on the streets and at your feeder.

The big limitation to city birdlife is the lack of vegetation. Solid blocks of shops, office buildings surrounded by concrete plazas, and streets that lack curbside plantings are signatures of city life, and none of them hold much hope for birds. But city parks and residential areas with even tiny backyards can add the greenery that attracts birds, and increase the bird-sighting potential for your own piece of the city.

New York City is mostly a concrete desert, but there's quite an oasis in it—the 843 acres of Central Park. More than 300 species of birds have been spotted there!

Your city yard is way smaller than Central Park, but you can still create an inviting bit of green in the middle of all that gray. Care to add hummingbirds, orioles, and dozens of others to your list of backyard guests? It's easy, once you start gardening bird-by-bird.

Prime Times

Spring and fall migration will be the best seasons for your yard. Migrants spread out over wide areas when they travel. If your city yard is an appealing rest stop, you can bet they'll stop for a spell.

Easygoing zinnias thrive in city yards and containers. Grow them from seed or start with inexpensive plants. They'll bloom for weeks, advertising your inviting yard to hummingbirds.

Many of them become casualties of collisions with the glass windows of skyscrapers and other city buildings. In Allentown, Pennsylvania, where I was a regular patron of the library, I could tell who was passing through by doing a quick check of the pitiful feathered bodies at the foot of the building. Cerulean warblers, Cape May warblers, wood thrushes, vireos, and many other migrants—as many as a dozen birds per week during the height of the season—met their fate at just that single building.

We can't put up detour signs to help migrants get safely past city buildings. But you can make your own city yard a nurturing place along the way.

Follow the bird-by-bird gardening suggestions for the Mimic Thrush and Thrush families, the Vireo and Warbler families, the Blackbird and Oriole family, and the Tanager family, and you'll have a good chance of delighting in "city" birds such as orioles, scarlet tanagers, red-eyed vireos, and lots of other beautiful creatures. For weeks at a time, your city yard can be alive with birds that normally seek a much different habitat.

One sad note in the migration song is the danger that city buildings pose to traveling birds.

Catch the Buzz

Hummingbirds are migrants, too, and they're year-round treats in the South. Stock your yard with plenty of early-blooming flowers to catch the spring wave, and add some late-blooming nectar favorites for the autumn rush. You'll find more specifics in the Hummingbird family chapter.

Hummers often make their homes in cities, as long as there are plenty of flowers and some sheltering shrubs and trees. Keep a nectar feeder

Get Wet

Water can be a scarce commodity for city birds, once the rain puddles dry up. Add a birdbath to your yard and you'll see a constant stream of visitors sipping and splashing during the dry times.

A reliable source of fresh, clean water will bring city birds to your yard even when water isn't scarce. Birds are creatures of habit, and a refreshing dip in your birdbath is likely to become a regular part of the routine. Who knows, you may even change your attitude about starlings, once you see how endearing they look with wet heads, and how much they enjoy a bath. It's easy to feel fond of a goofball!

hanging, and fill your yard with hummingbird flowers, and your yard may be abuzz even in the middle of a city.

Older Neighborhoods

Trees and birds go together like peanut butter and jelly. Orioles and elms or sycamores, tanagers and oaks, evening grosbeaks and pines or firs—wherever there are trees, there are bound to be birds. Older neighborhoods usually have a wealth of older trees, and that means great bird habitat.

The lovely flower of the well-named tulip tree (*Liriodendron tulipifera*) often blooms unnoticed by human admirers, but birds will visit the blooms for insects. The flower ripens into an upright "cone" of seeds, a favorite of goldfinches, evening grosbeaks, and other birds of the Small and Large Finch families.

Trees That Please

Trees serve up a huge variety of superb bird food, much of it insect in nature. Most of us never notice the millions of insects supported by trees, but birds sure take notice. Depending on the feeding habits of their family, they gobble everything from big, juicy caterpillars to teeny, sticky aphids.

Tree flowers attract plenty of birds, too, and so do the acorns or seeds that follow. Even in winter, when the trees are bare, insects still lurk in bark crevices or elsewhere on trees. That's when you'll see chickadees, titmice, nuthatches, and brown creepers ferreting out the goodies. It's a giant feeding frenzy above our heads, so don't forget to look up.

You'll find an abundance of tips for bringing treetop birds closer to eye level in the bird families chapters. Check out the advice for the Waxwing, Vireo, Warbler, Blackbird and Oriole, Tanager, and Large Finch families, for plenty of practical suggestions for both your yard and your feeder.

Super Shrubs

Established shrubbery and flower gardens are two more boons for birds in older neighborhoods. These plantings offer plenty of food, abundant cover for travel corridors, and great nesting sites.

All common backyard nesting birds, including cardinals, jays, robins, wrens, hummingbirds, catbirds, mockingbirds, and native sparrows, are possible nesters in older neighborhoods. In my not-very-big backyard in southern Indiana, about

40 by 70 feet square, I often found at least six nests of different birds each year.

To win the seal of approval for your own place, increase the temptations for nesting birds by using some of the tips in the Crow and Jay family, the Wren family, the Mimic Thrush family, and the Small and Large Finch families. Oh, and don't forget the Hummingbird family— you may never spy the itty-bitty nest, but it might be there!

Welcome to Suburbia

The housing developments rising across the country have created their own kind of bird desert, thanks to the building practice of bull-dozing to bare ground. I'm happy to see that style is shifting, with many developers now taking pains to protect large trees and tuck in "green-space" areas for walking trails. In a decade or two,

after newly planted trees and landscaping have some time to grow, subdivisions can be transformed into decent bird habitat. Still, suburban yards can be a challenge to make bird-friendly.

Wild Neighbors

Suburbia sits between town and country, and that's the good news. The natural habitat that's still likely to exist outside the land of cul-de-sacs holds many birds who can be coaxed into investigating the new yards on the block.

In a brand-new development, your best bet is to start by planting a generous number of shrubs, because they grow fast into good bird cover. Add

Fast-growing shadblow (*Amelanchier canadensis* and hybrids) is a graceful small tree that's just the right size for suburban yards. Its berries are delicious—but wrens, waxwings, and a crowd of other birds will probably beat you to them.

Barricades to Progress

Tall, solid fences enclosing the backyard are a standard sight in subdivisions. They're great for privacy. But they're bad for birds. That unadorned wall of wood or masonry can stop some birds right in their tracks. While jays, cardinals, and others will fly over it without a second thought, birds that stay on or near the ground, such as towhees, native sparrows, and juncos, may find it a barrier.

Luckily, there's an easy and quick way to make a privacy fence a plus instead of a minus. Plant vigorous vines along the fence, so that they cloak it in greenery and spill over the top. Foraging birds will consider it part of the feast and a welcome way to get from place to place. Try these fast growers for bird-friendly foliage and maybe a bonus of fruit or flowers:

- Sweet autumn clematis (*Clematis terniflora*)
- *Clematis montana*
- Virgin's bower (*Clematis virginiana*)
- Hops (*Humulus lupulus;* 'Aureus' has golden green leaves)
- Grapes of any kind (*Vitis* spp.)
- Honeysuckle vines (*Lonicera* × *Americana*, *L.* × *heckrotti, L. sempervirens*)
- If your fence is extra sturdy, you may want to try rampant-growing trumpet vine (*Campsis radicans, C. grandiflora, C.* x *tagliabuana* 'Madame Galens') or wisteria (*Wisteria* spp. and hybrids). Prune them back heavily in early spring, before growth begins, to keep them in bounds.

Sometimes, a vine refuses to climb a new fence, perhaps because of wood stains or paint. If your vine is reluctant to cozy up to the fence, just attach a strip of chicken wire with hooks to give it an initial grip.

fruit trees, shade trees, and conifers, too, as soon as you can. Look for quick payoff suggestions in the Chickadee and Titmouse family, the Crow and Jay family, and the Wren, Waxwing, Blackbird and Oriole, Large and Small Finch, and Hummingbird families.

Depending on what kind of natural areas are nearby, you may also be able to attract field-loving birds and birds that like to be near water or woods. If your neighbors are like-minded, so that your yards function as travel paths to and from those wild places, you all can benefit.

Country Cousins

Congratulations! If you live in the country, your backyard bird list is going to be a big one. Just about any of the birds whose range or migration puts them in your area are possibilities (you'll find details on exactly which species you can expect in every part of the country in Chapter 25, near the end of this book). Hawks and owls are more likely to frequent your yard in the country, and so are birds that need large wild areas to feel at home, such as wild turkeys, pheasants, quail, and grouse. Lucky you!

Birds will move seamlessly from wild areas through your yard. So the only trick will be getting them to stick around. A well-stocked feeder is the first step. Then, focus on any bird families you like, and add some of their favorite plants to your place. Since natural habitat is conveniently nearby, it makes sense to begin by adding food plants to your yard. Fruit trees are a guaranteed source of temptation.

Win Favor with Fruits

Fruit bushes and trees grow wild in the country, so you may wonder whether there's any point to planting them in your yard. Yes, yes, yes!

Seems like there's never enough fruit to go around (except for wild blackberries in the Pacific Northwest; they've engulfed so many acres that birds simply can't keep up with the crop). Wild fruits are quickly stripped when they're ready to eat. Fruit in the backyard is always popular, too, which is why many gardeners who want a taste for themselves cover some of the plants with antibird netting.

Winter Respite

Keeping birds in your country yard when there's so much natural appeal nearby calls for sneaky

Fruit Lure

Two alluring fruits are tops with birds in all areas: cherries and mulberries. Both are absolute magnets for birds of every fruit-eating family—and that includes all our favorite birds. These fruits are easy to pluck, soft, and juicy, so any fruit-eating bird can enjoy them. Plus, they're super-easy to grow, and it costs only about $20 for a tree that will produce fruit the same year.

Sour or sweet cherries are equally welcomed, so plant whichever kind you like best. Cherry trees are pretty, and dwarf cultivars are perfect for nestling into a flower bed—or wherever you'll have a good view of the birds that come to the feast.

Birds go crazy over mulberries, which is why mulberry trees grow wild in many areas. Mulberries were a lot more popular in days gone by, when yards were bigger and their messiness wasn't considered a problem. The fruit stains any surface it drops onto, or any surface where the semi-digested remains are deposited, courtesy of birds. If neatness counts in your yard or neighborhood, it's best to stick with cherries.

If your country yard is big enough to make room for a mulberry, give it a try. The bonus of orioles, tanagers, vireos, waxwings, and dozens of other beautiful birds may be worth those purple splashes on your pickup truck.

tricks. Here's another one: Plant evergreens for winter shelter.

Many birds seek out evergreens for nighttime roosting places, especially in winter. Those sheltering branches also keep birds warm and dry during snowstorms or freezing rains.

Plant a grouping, to help birds get the hint. Aim for a mix of larger conifers, if you have room, and broad-leaved evergreens, which are great at shedding rain and snow. Plant them where they'll be undisturbed by human or pet traffic, so birds feel safe to snuggle in for the night. You'll find more details on planting for shelter in Chapter 3.

Wide Open Spaces

You know who you are—your backyard is surrounded by grassland or sagebrush or farm fields. It's wide-open spaces that stretch for long distances without being interrupted by patches of woods, or by many trees at all. Bring on the grassland birds!

Interesting birds from several families will be pleased to call your yard home. You might see birds from the Swallow and Crow families. And you'll definitely host birds from the blackbird branch of the Blackbird and Oriole family, too. Birds of the Small Finch family and Gallinaceous family, including those endearing bobwhites and quail, are also high on the list of possibilities.

Eat, Drink, and Be Merry

Food and water are the double prongs of your best-bet approach. Welcome your neighboring birds with a banquet of the seeds they like best, set out in low-level feeders where they can easily access them. Water near the ground is highly appealing, but these birds will also adjust to pedestal-type birdbaths.

Create beds and borders or other areas of your yard that mimic your nearby wild spaces. Flower gardens of mostly annuals, including zinnias (*Zinnia* spp.) and sunflowers (*Helianthus an-*

Forest soil is loose and crumbly and smells delicious. That enviable black soil is nature's own compost, the remains of decades' or centuries' worth of fallen leaves. It's also home to a plethora of tasty tidbits for birds, thanks to the myriad of insects, worms, and spiders that hides among the fallen leaves and their composted remains.

Just what I love best: a good reason to be lazy. Put away that rake, let the fall leaves settle where they will, and enjoy the birds that come to feast on your living mulch. Keep your eyes open for woodland thrushes, towhees, native sparrows, juncos, and other forest dwellers digging in to fill their bellies. It's all part of the grand plan of Mother Nature. Follow her lead, and you're not being lazy—you're being smart.

nuus), hold great appeal year-round. After the blossoms are done and the plant stems die, many will remain standing. That's just the sort of cover grassland birds appreciate. Oh, and don't forget the grasses! Clumps of ornamental grasses or native species are just what the doctor ordered. Investigate native grasses for turf, and you'll improve your bird outlook even more.

Woodland birds won't mind at all if you sit a spell, as long as your yard offers undisturbed areas, too. To give birds more foraging potential, go for the layered look, snuggling in shorter plants beneath taller ones.

Into the Woods

A shady, woodsy yard in an area of forest gives you the chance to attract some shy citizens of these areas. Imagine being serenaded by the gentle, fluting song of the wood thrush, or watching the hyperactive antics of tiny golden-crowned kinglets in the branches.

Make the most of wooded surroundings by using the suggestions you'll find for birds of the Woodpecker, Flycatcher, Chickadee and Titmouse, Nuthatch, Thrush, Gnatcatcher and Kinglet, and Vireo families, in their respective chapters. Oops, almost forgot the wild turkey and grouse of the Gallinaceous family. Whew, that's a long list. But it gives you a hint of the amazing potential of a wooded backyard.

Build on the riches of your surroundings by coaxing the birds to where you can see them more easily. Groups of shrubs and shade-loving plants will extend the woodsy feel.

Down to Size

An old set of brightly painted Russian nesting dolls has been part of my home décor since I was a teenager. I love fitting the dolls together, closing the halves over smallest, next-biggest, all the way up to the matriarch of the clan, who encloses all of the others. My daughter likes to play with them, too. But she prefers to separate them, close each doll individually, and line them up in order of height.

Her approach is the key to creating a satisfying bird garden in a wooded area. By lining up your plants from lowest-growing, to knee-high, to waist-high, all the way up to those already existing trees, you'll increase the kinds of birds you'll see. You'll find ideas for layered plantings in many of the bird family chapters. A big part of the payoff of attracting birds is actually being able to watch them, so bring those birdies down to size by coaxing them to eye level or below.

Chapter 3

Basics of Bird Needs

For insight into what's important to birds, think about your favorite restaurant: Is it that little Italian place with checkered tablecloths, luminous candlelight, and long-simmered marinara sauce? Or are you a bistro lover, preferring clean lines, cozy seating, and the latest foodie treats? Or maybe your hangout is Mom's Diner, with belly-warming breakfasts and endless coffee, in a cushy booth.

Whatever style of dining suits your pleasure, it's bound to be a place that combines the perfect ambience with good food. And that's exactly what birds need. Without ambience *and* good food, our feeders would be nothing more than a pit stop for birds. Birds would simply drop in and depart as soon as they'd filled their bellies.

Think of bird-by-bird gardening as your chance to create a topnotch dining destination for your feathered friends. That means making your patrons feel right at home and serving food that's suited to their tastes.

Bon Appetit

After twenty-some years together, my husband and I can pretty well guess which dishes on a restaurant menu will catch the other's eye. He'll probably order the fish, or possibly the penne pasta, while I'll go for anything with the word *eggplant* in it. And no penne for me, please; I prefer my pasta shaped like bowties. As for dessert, make mine chocolate; he'll take the fruit cobbler.

At home, we're not nearly as picky. We have a repertoire of maybe a dozen dishes that we both enjoy, and that's what we rely on, changing them with the seasons to take advantage of fresh fruits and veggies. Sometimes, we depart from the usual and try out a new coffee cake recipe for Sunday breakfast, or stop at the bakery for fresh bread. But we're pretty darn predictable in our tastes.

I'll bet your family is pretty much the same. Chances are, your kids (if you have them) share your eating habits because that's what they know and like.

Birds operate that way as well. The regular menu is all in the family.

Adding bird-favored plants to your yard invites birds to spend time foraging for natural food in between bites at your feeder. Shrub roses provide cover and winter food, and a flowering crabapple offers insects at flowers and foliage. The flower bed provides more cover plus insects, including butterflies, and, later, seeds. A grapevine gives additional cover and tempting fruit, while the pussy willow near the birdbath offers a place for preening, insect food, and potential nesting material from its soft catkins.

To Each Its Own

Year ago, scientists studied birds' diets by painstakingly taking inventory of the contents of their stomachs. I've never been able to get any bird to hold still long enough for that kind of exam (just joking—the experts dispatched the birds in the interests of science), but I have spent a lot of time watching them fill their bellies. What I've seen matches the scientific evidence: Each bird family has its own everyday menu, just as your family has its standard dinner dishes.

Day in, day out, a basic selection of seeds, insects, or fruits goes down the hatch.

And just like at our own dinner tables, bird meals vary with the seasons, depending on what's available in the great outdoor market. Plus, each bird family takes advantage of extra-special goodies, whenever it can find them.

As I mentioned in Chapter 2, four major food groups satisfy the needs of nearly all backyard birds: insects, seeds and nuts, fruits and berries, and nectar. A handful of other foods, including sap, snails, and lizards, fills in the gaps for some species. Exactly which of those food groups are on the menu for a bird family depends on the beak and behavior of the family, as seen in Chapter 1.

By tailoring your yard to bird-by-bird tastes, you have the secret weapon for attracting birds of the families you like best. Stocking your feeders with the favorite foods of your favorite birds, which you'll find detailed in the family chapters, is a quick and easy start.

After that is where the fun of gardening bird-by-bird begins.

Insect Fare

Insects are the number one food choice for birds, simply because nearly all birds eat bugs. With thousands of insect species, each one with habits of its own, the possibilities for birds are just about endless. No matter where a bird lives or how it gets its food, there's a banquet of bugs that will fill the bill.

Pity the poor periodical cicada—years spent living underground, only to emerge in full bug-eyed glory and get gobbled up by birds. Woodpeckers, cardinals, grosbeaks, and even house sparrows all make a meal of cicadas, whose loud buzz makes them easy to find.

Insect Aficionados

Although nearly all birds eat insects, birds from these families rely heavily on them:

Woodpecker	Kinglet
Flycatcher	Waxwing
Swallow	Vireo
Nuthatch	Warbler
Wren	Tanager
Thrush	

Tiny chickadees, for instance, are big fans of equally tiny aphids. Big-beaked cardinals usually don't bother with the fine points of eating aphids, but they do take advantage of the periodical crop of meaty cicadas. When ants swarm up from underground, flickers are quick to alight at the six-legged smorgasbord.

It's a great natural system because for each kind of insect, you can bet there's a bird family that preys upon it. Naturally, there's a lot of overlap, with many insects eagerly gobbled up by more than one bird family. But because of those varied bird habits and beaks, there are also clear favorites: Swallows and martins, for example, never touch a cicada or a grasshopper; their niche is gnats and other airborne insects.

Bird families that eat mostly insects will be devoted visitors to your delicious garden. Watch for thrashers, mockingbirds, catbirds, thrushes, bluebirds, robins, orioles, vireos, warblers, and kinglets to scour your backyard for an insect feast. They'll glean beetles and ants from the foliage of your plants, collect a host of wasps, bees, and other insects from the flowers, and uncover insects in the mulch below the plants.

The suggestions for plants and planting in each bird family chapter are designed to encourage the kinds of insects each family prefers. Wood warblers, for example, migrate in spring, when many ornamental and fruit trees are in full bloom. Those clouds of blossoms attract swarms of small insects. Right on their heels will be Cape May warblers, Tennessee warblers, Wilson's warblers, yellow-rumped warblers, and others, snapping up insects at the flowers. So, you'll find that planting a flowering crabapple tree is a top suggestion in the Warbler family chapter.

More Bugs, More Birds

You don't need to worry about figuring out exactly which bugs your birds are eating. But you do need to take a hands-off approach to pesticides, if you want to be a good bird host. Most pesticides kill several kinds of bugs, both the targeted pest plus others that happen to be in the way of the spray. As far as birds are concerned, the more insects in your yard, the better. Get rid of the bugs, and you're downgrading the appeal of your yard.

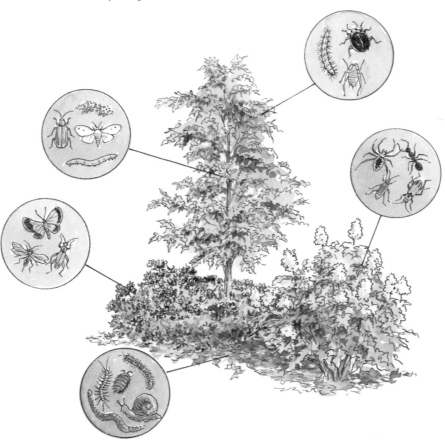

Planting a variety of shrubs, trees, and flowers provides a diverse menu of insect food for bug-eating birds—and that's every single bird species in your backyard.

Leaving the Trees

Chickadees, titmice, and downy woodpeckers tend to stick to the trees. But when a tempting treat of insects calls them to lower levels of your garden, they won't hesitate to leave the bark and branches behind.

Chickadees and titmice are small and agile, so they can zero in on insects on just about any tree, shrub, or flowering plant. But downy woodpeckers seem to like flowering plants that remind them of trees. Look for one of these dapper black-and-white birds pecking away at the stalks of hollyhocks (*Alcea rosea*), mulleins (*Verbascum* spp.), sunflowers (*Helianthus annuus*), or other extra-tall flowers with stout stalks that may harbor an insect within (and provide a prop for a woodpecker's tail).

The opportunity for an insect feast also draws other tree-dwelling species, including orioles, vireos, and warblers, to lower levels of shrubs and flowers. Tempt these birds out of the trees by using layered plantings in your yard.

Flavor of the Month

The insect scene changes with the season, just as the birds themselves do. Aphids, caterpillars, Japanese beetles, and other delectables run in cycles in your yard, but there's always something for birds to eat. As birds move through the branches, they'll vacuum up the goodies with a quick peck here, a sharp nip there.

Insects begin to hatch in big numbers right at the time of spring migration. As temperatures warm in spring, birds move northward, snapping up multitudes of emerging insects along the way.

Some migrants, such as swallows, are so dependent upon insects that they'll retreat if a cold snap makes their main food unavailable.

When insects are at their peak in spring and summer, you may see just about any bird in the neighborhood investigating your garden, including thrashers, vireos, tanagers, buntings, and orioles.

Why the big surge in interest? Because all of a sudden, there are hungry mouths to feed. Nesting birds need lots of insects to stuff those hungry beaks at home. Now you'll see who's raising a family in your area because the parent birds will show up for a fast meal for themselves and a take-out bag for the kiddies.

Insect appeal lasts right into winter, even though many bugs drop dead when cold weather comes in. That's because insect eggs, cocoons, or overwintering larvae are still on or in your plants. Some adult insects, including the beautiful mourning cloak butterfly, stick out the freezing temps by going into a sort of hibernation. It's a good trick, and one that means a few extra bites of winter food for the birds in your garden.

The short, pointy beaks of chickadees, titmice, and kinglets are ideal for tearing through flower stems or into cocoons to reach these last little tidbits. Woodpeckers, too, seek out insect "leftovers" by drilling holes or flicking off bits of bark to get at them.

Butterflies and Moths

Flowers in your garden add a bounty of other bugs, many of them drawn by the nectar or pollen of the blossoms. As usual, birds won't be far behind.

Butterfly gardens are a big draw for birds. You can plant caterpillar host plants, such as parsley, dill, and violets, to invite a crop of caterpillars. And—brace yourselves, kind hearts—butterflies themselves are prime fodder for many birds; those dainty butterflies we admire for their grace and beauty are just another insect to birds. If it makes you feel any better, bluebirds are big fans of butterflies, especially the white cabbage butterflies that dance over the veggie garden.

I like to snuggle in a few broccoli or mustard plants among my flower gardens. They're flowers, too, with big, loose clusters of tiny yellow blossoms that attract butterflies big and small. As a bonus, they also attract egg-laying butterflies.

Moths are prime menu items, too. An eastern phoebe visited the area around our porch light every summer morning for years, collecting moths that had been drawn to the light at night and then settled on the wall or nearby foliage. If you plant a patch of night-fragrant flowers to draw in moths, such as evening primrose (*Oenothera biennis*) or petunias (*Petunia* cvs.), your birds may find leftovers the next day, too.

Seed Specialists

Birds from these families rely heavily on seeds:

Dove	Large Finch
Chickadee	Small Finch
and Titmouse	Gallinaceous
Nuthatch	Birds
Blackbird	
and Oriole	

Beetle Mania

Insects have taken the feeder world by storm in recent years. Suet blocks and treats that include dead fruit flies and other insects are a real lure for wrens, bushtits, and other birds.

The larvae of certain beetles make a terrific treat for bluebirds, orioles, and lots of other great birds. Roasted versions, including one with the appealing name of "Beetle Mania," are available, too, as are seed mixes that include the tasty larvae. Even live larvae are gaining popularity fast at the feeder, thanks to the amazing results you'll see. If you can get over your squeamishness, you'll discover that bugs at the feeder are as irresistible as insects *au naturel* to birds.

Ready to catch this wave of the feeding-station future? You can shop for supplies with the aid of the Resources section (see page 372).

Seeds

Close to 200 bird species in America depend on seeds for a major part of their menu. That's a lot of busy beaks to feed.

Seeds are perfect little packets of nutrition. They're chock-full of carbohydrates, protein, and life-giving oils. They also supply an alphabet soup of vitamins and many minerals. That's why we grind seeds of various sorts for bread, eat them in our cereal bowls, and make snacks out of them. And that's why so many birds depend on them for a big part of their diet.

Feeder Seeds

Even the most dedicated feeder hosts depend on two seeds for the bulk of their menu:

sunflower seed and proso millet. These are the standard offerings for feeder birds, because they're so widely accepted by backyard birds.

Tiny black nyjer is another staple seed to keep on hand, because it's irresistible to small finches.

If you read the label on a bag of premium birdseed, or check the offerings at your local bird store or online, you'll find a handful of other specialty seeds, including rapeseed or canola, canary seed, flaxseed, and German millet. These seeds aren't grown as widely as sunflower or proso millet, so they cost more.

Check the fine print on cheaper mixes, and you'll find a few other seeds, including cracked corn, oats, wheat, and milo. All of them are much less popular with many desirable birds and in many regions, go uneaten. If you live in the Southwest, or near grasslands, you may get takers for those seeds, particularly milo: Quail, doves, some native Southwestern sparrows, and other birds of open areas are fond of it.

Garden Seeds

Many seeds that don't make it into bird-feeder mixes, including those of zinnias (*Zinnia* spp.), bachelor's buttons (*Centaurea cyanus*), impatiens (*Impatiens* spp.), and other flowers, are just as nutritious. No wonder cardinals, grosbeaks, buntings, sparrows, juncos, blackbirds, meadowlarks, and many other seed eaters seek them out in the garden.

It's easy to grow a banquet of birdseed in your yard, because overabundance is the name

Big and beautiful, the eastern fox sparrow is easy to attract to a garden with plenty of small seeds.

Indigo buntings, goldfinches, and native sparrows are big fans of bachelor's buttons (*Centaurea cyanus*), and not because they're hoping to get hitched. Nope, what they seek is seeds. Each "floret" of the blossom matures into a seed, so a single flower holds dozens of delicious seeds for fall and winter flocks.

Willowy flax flowers (*Linum* spp.) mature into a myriad of flat, shiny, brown seeds. Many of them drop to the ground for towhees, doves, native sparrows, and other birds to forage for all winter.

of the game when it comes to the seeds of the flowers called annuals. Nearly all annual flowers produce enough seeds in a single blossom to grow dozens of new plants, and many go way beyond that—into the hundreds. Why so many seeds? Excessive seed production helps ensure that at least a few escape the birds, so a new generation of flowers can sprout from the seeds of the parent plant. That ample supply of seeds will keep birds flocking to your garden as long as they last.

Tree seeds, including those of ash trees (*Fraxinus* spp.), maples (*Acer* spp.), tulip trees (*Liriodendron tulipifera*), and hemlocks, firs, pines, and other conifers (*Tsuga* spp., *Abies* spp., *Pinus* spp., and others), are popular with some birds, too. You'll find lots of suggestions for seed plants of

all sorts, tailored to taste and habits, in the bird family chapters.

Birdseed Gardens

I buy my sunflower seed by the 50-pound sack, but I also plant sunflowers all over the yard, poking a few seeds from the feeder into any sunny space. Even expensive specialty birdseed, such as finch mix, is budget-priced for planting. The cost can be even less if you shop the bulk bins at health food or grocery stores.

Every fall, I buy a pound or two of flaxseed (*Linum* spp.)—less than 50 cents per pound at my local supermarket—and scatter it around my garden, without covering it with soil. The seeds sprout fast, and they stay green all winter. In spring and summer, the plants are topped with sky blue blossoms that sway in the slightest breeze.

The happy faces of sunflowers are charming in your garden, and other bird seeds grow into good-looking plants, too. Millets and canary grass (the annual species found in birdseed mixes, not the pesky perennial called reed canary grass) add grace to a flower bed. Rapeseed, or canola, is a mustard, with cheerful yellow blossoms and a plethora of seeds in long, skinny pods. All of the birds that enjoy the seeds at your feeder will happily serve themselves in your garden.

If you can't find specialty seeds in bulk, or if you only want to plant a small area, just sow some of that bag of birdseed. It's fun to get to know the plants that provide the daily bread for your birds, and adding more seed supplies on the stem will bring more birds.

Nonsprouting Nyjer, or the Thistle That Isn't

Nyjer seed, also known as niger seed, was originally marketed as "thistle seed." It's not a thistle and never was. It's a pretty plant, full of small golden daisies that mature into tiny, skinny black seeds.

Goldfinches love nyjer seeds. They also adore real thistle seeds so much that they were once known as "thistle birds" (or *distelfink*, in the Pennsylvania Dutch dialect). So maybe the "thistle seed" name for nyjer was a misguided marketing attempt to trade on the reputation of real thistle seed for attracting goldfinches.

Just as you might expect, the name set off a wave of unease among feeder hosts because we all know how vigorously sunflower and millet seeds sprout below the feeder—and who would want to bring home the makings of a thistle patch? Apparently, whoever was involved in introducing so-called "thistle seed" to the birdfeeding market didn't think about that aspect at first. After a few years, though, the name was changed to niger seed, and recently to nyjer. Still, the old name of thistle seed hung around, and folks worried about sprouting a crop of "thistles."

To allay those fears, nyjer distributors adopted the practice of heating the seed to prevent it from germinating. Unfortunately, that treatment will also keep you from growing your own patch of nyjer (*Guizotia abyssinica*) to enjoy its bright yellow daisies and bird fans. Don't bother trying to grow nyjer seed from a bag of birdseed; it's rare to have any sprout. But sometimes, a sproutable seed happens to sneak through the heat treatment and come up on its own near the feeder. If that happens, collect a few of the seedheads and save them for future crops.

By the way, you may have noticed that the spelling of *nyjer* has changed in recent years. For decades, it's been spelled *n-i-g-e-r*, like the country of Niger and the river of the same name that flows through the African home of the plant. But in recent years, the bird-feeding industry has waged a campaign to change the spelling to *n-y-j-e-r*, a phonetic spelling, in an attempt to prevent the name from being pronounced incorrectly. In Ethiopia, where in 4 short years the seed has become the top export (zero tons exported in 2000; 27,000 tons sent to the United States in 2004), and in other nations that produce this black gold, it's still called "niger"—or "noug" or "neug." No matter what you call it, this is one great seed.

Swinging Singers

Some birds swing back and forth between the treetops and the lower levels when foraging for food. They're opportunists that seek out a snack wherever they can find it. Look for house finches, goldfinches, purple finches, cardinals, chickadees, grosbeaks, and the occasional band of redpolls to take a break from the trees and swing down for your seeds.

In the garden, you're likely to see lots of these swingers searching for seeds of taller garden flowers, such as cosmos (*Cosmos bipinnatus*) and sunflowers (*Helianthus* spp.). Unlike bird families that eat on or near the ground, they won't usually stoop to ground level. Luckily, other bird families eagerly fill that niche. That's why juncos, native sparrows, towhees, doves, and quail, which share the habit of foraging on or near the ground, are loyal customers for low-level seeds in the garden.

Field Fans

Meadowlarks, red-winged blackbirds, horned larks, buntings, and other birds of open fields

Weed Appreciation

I know, I know; it sounds like complete craziness to encourage weeds in your yard and flower gardens. For years, I dutifully pulled every weed I spied, long before it set seed, in hopes of reducing the sprouts next year. But there's always a few that sneak through, it seems. And when I realized how much my birds loved weed seeds, I changed my whole attitude.

Weed seeds are a big hit with all seed-eating birds, and the seeds are so abundant, they bring in birds all the way through winter. Overlooking a few weeds, which I now do intentionally, is one of the best ways to attract birds to your yard. Each family has its own favorites, which you'll find in the family chapters. Figure out which ones you can live with, too, and you may gain a whole new appreciation for lowly weeds.

Blue chicory and Queen Anne's lace are rich with bird-attracting seeds, and they're pretty enough to fill a flower garden. Queen Anne's lace brings in a bounty of insects, too—another bonus for birds.

often resort to visiting backyards in winter, especially if a seed-filled flower garden awaits.

For these birds, neatness counts—in the negative column. Plenty of grasses and dead flower stems for shelter are just their style, rather than a garden that's been neatly tidied up. These birds of the field often forage low to the ground in open places, and they depend on those plants for cover. A weedy patch suits them even better, which is why I let a discreet corner of my yard grow up in lamb's-quarters (*Chenopodium* spp.), pigweed (*Amaranthus* spp.), chickweed (*Stellaria* spp.), and other good-looking weeds. If your flower garden looks more like the brushy edge of a field, you've found the key to their hearts.

Seed-Eater Seasons

Fall migration is the busiest season in the seed garden. Scores to hundreds of native sparrows and juncos will crowd in to feast on the fresh crop of seeds, many of which they glean from the ground. The mob will thin out as many of these birds move on, but dozens will linger into winter, joined by other daily visitors, such as finches and ground-feeding mourning doves, towhees, and quail.

If you delay cutting back the dead stems in fall, you'll find that winter brings flocks of seed seekers, including pine siskins, white-throated sparrows, redpolls, finches, and doves, to the flower garden. They'll pull out any seeds that are still on the plants, and some of them will scour the ground below to pick up any bits that may have fallen during the fall feasting.

By spring, the seeds are mostly gone, and most of the seed eaters disperse. In late summer, the cycle starts again as new seeds of sunflowers (*Helianthus*, annual and perennial spp.), cosmos (*Cosmos bipinnatus*), purple coneflowers (*Echi-*

nacea purpurea) and others ripen. They'll entice grosbeaks, cardinals, and finches, which prefer to feed on seeds that are still on the plants rather than those on the ground.

Nuts

Nuts are simply big seeds. Plant an acorn, an oak will grow; plant a walnut, and guess what you'll get. Meaty, oily nuts are an alluring morsel of nutrition for birds, which are highly tempted by any nuts within reach.

All of the birds that eat seeds, and many that eat soft foods, will gladly eat nuts—as long as they can get their beaks around them. In nature, only a few bird families have the kind of beak that allows them to pluck nuts from the tree or peck through the shell to get at the meat. The Crow and Jay family, the Woodpecker family, the Nuthatch family, and the Chickadee and Titmouse family are the prime eaters of nuts from the branch.

Once the nuts fall to the ground, they're fair game for wild turkeys and other members of the Gallinaceous family, who eagerly seek them out. Bits of nutmeat are adored by all kinds of small birds, including the Small and Large Finch families, the Wren family, the Mimic Thrush family, and many others.

If you already have a nut tree or oak in your yard, consider yourself lucky, as these large trees can be tricky to shoehorn into a small or medium-size yard. If you don't have an existing tree, you may want to stick to serving nuts at the feeder. There, you can chop them or serve them whole in various styles of feeders, to suit the birds you want to attract.

Fruit and Berry Fans

The top takers for fruits and berries are birds that eat mainly soft foods, especially insects. That means you'll meet many new friends that don't ordinarily come for seeds at the feeder. Look for lovely vireos and flycatchers, waxwings and warblers, tanagers and thrushes, and even a flurry of tree swallows. Since most bird families include several species, you might add two dozen new birds to your backyard list.

Our old reliable feeder friends enjoy fruits and berries in the natural state, too. Expect to see cardinals, jays, chickadees, titmice, finches, grosbeaks, juncos, mockingbirds, catbirds, Carolina wrens, and even woodpeckers getting in on the action. Native sparrows may seek berries in fall, when large numbers are passing through during migration. Rock doves (pigeons) and band-tailed doves nibble on berries, too, but mourning doves don't seem to show much interest.

Betting on Berries

Plant nearly any berry, and you'll attract birds. Success is a sure thing, because so many species of birds love berries.

Fruit and Berry Eaters

Fruits and berries are a treat for birds of nearly all families, no matter what other foods they depend on. For members of these families, a large part of their menu consists of fruits and berries:

Mimic Thrush	Vireo
Thrush	Tanager
Waxwing	

Fruit or Berry?

The lingo of fruits and berries can get confusing, because berries are technically fruits. But bird families that prefer what most of us call fruits don't necessarily adore what we call berries, and vice versa. To try to keep things clear, I've used a few simple rules to separate them:

- The words *fruit* or *fruits* describe juicier crops, such as mulberries, cherries, apples, oranges, and plums. You'd never call an apple a berry, and neither would I. Most "fruits" are good people food, too.
- *Berry bushes* or *berry plants* mean the berry bushes or plants with fruit that we eat, too, such as blueberries, raspberries, elderberries, and strawberries.
- I've used plain old *berries* to describe the fruit of trees and shrubs that aren't usually eaten by humans, such as holly berries (*Ilex* spp.), dogwood berries (*Cornus* spp.), and bayberries (*Myrica* spp.).

But not all birds are attracted to the same berries. So, which birds will your berries attract?

Just to whet your appetite, let's say that your goal is to bring a breathtaking red-and-black scarlet tanager to your backyard. Plant a flowering dogwood (*Cornus florida*), and when the berries ripen in fall, you've got him—and his friends and family. Oh, it's eastern bluebirds you're yearning for? Add a deciduous holly (*Ilex americana*) to your backyard menu, and you're

Native or Not?

Native plants are those that have grown in your area since before it was disturbed by civilization. They can be shrubs, trees, flowers, or grasses. Some of our favorite garden plants are natives, including flowering dogwood (*Cornus florida*), hemlock (*Tsuga canadensis*), and black-eyed Susan (*Rudbeckia* spp.). Native to your region, that is: If you plant that dogwood in Tennessee, where the woods foam with dogwoods in spring, it's considered a native; in California, it's as much a foreigner as a palm tree would be on the streets of Memphis.

Native plants are ideal for birds because they've grown up together, so to speak. Birds are already familiar with these plants. They're accustomed to using them for nesting, nest materials, food, and cover. Many native plants, especially native trees and shrubs, also host the insects that birds like best. And nearly every native fruit or berry is a big hit with birds, while "improved" nursery varieties may go uneaten.

You can't go wrong with natives. But birds will also eagerly make use of nonnatives, a giant category that includes many beloved bird plants—from that Eastern dogwood in Texas to the Himalayan blackberries in Oregon.

It's fun to get to know the natives of your own area, which are showing up more and more in local nurseries. You can also track them down through specialty catalogs and on the Internet. But a mix of plants from anywhere in the world is just fine for backyard birds, as long as it satisfies their needs for food, cover, and nesting niches.

likely to have bluebirds clamoring for a perch at the table. You'll find lots of other specific best bets for berries, as well as fruits, in the family chapters for your favorite birds.

Berries and fruits are such a hit with birds that they often draw a gang of gluttons. Instead of spotting only a single dainty eater, you'll often see half a dozen cardinals, plus 20 cedar waxwings, plus as many woodpeckers as can weasel in. A bird can fill its belly without much effort and without much competition, either. A large tree loaded with berries may easily host a hundred birds—all at the same time. No wonder the crop vanishes in no time.

Buyer Beware

I love to watch the birds that come to gorge. But, apparently, many people would rather see the berries than the birds. So plant breeders have tinkered with some bird favorites to make their berries or fruits distasteful to birds, thus staving off the disappearing act.

A berry-laden bush of pyracantha (*Pyracantha* cvs.), for example, was once a guarantee of seeing cedar waxwings. Not any more. Some cultivars are now touted as pyracanthas that birds won't eat. Crabapples, too, either by accident or design, have had the good taste bred right out of them; many cultivars hold their fruit until it simply falls off the branches, with nary a bird showing up to share a bite. Winterberry (*Ilex verticillata*) may be the next victim: I've noticed heavily berried plants in nurseries that remain untouched by even the mockingbirds that call the place home.

The cultivars recommended in the bird family chapters are those that I know birds like to eat. If you branch out, read the label and do some research, or you may wind up with berries that please only your eye. And if you end up with fruit hanging heavy and no takers, remember that the plant will still serve as cover in your garden, and its flowers will still attract insects—both a benefit to birds.

Seasonal Support

Berries and berry plants are great for attracting a crowd of birds to your yard. But the crop is so tempting that it's devoured quickly, usually in 2 weeks or less. When the berries are gone, so will be most of the birds.

Fruits can disappear just as fast as berries, but, generally, fruit trees have a more limited appeal to birds, and thus hold their crop a lot

Free Trees

Here's a secret for you penny pinchers: Keep your eyes open for tree seedlings sprouting in your yard, especially around your bird feeder or anywhere else birds usually congregate. The seeds in berries often pass through a bird's digestive system without harm. If you're lucky, you may harvest the benefits, including cherry, dogwood, holly, hackberry, and other tree seedlings. It's fun to nurture them along to blooming size. That usually takes about 5 years, but I don't mind the wait when I'm growing freebies. That progeny may look or taste different from its parent, being closer to the species form than to a cultivated variety, but birds are guaranteed to approve.

longer. Bite-size cherries and mulberries will get snatched up quickly. But apples and crabapples will feed birds through fall and often into winter.

Since our goal is to make our backyards appealing in all seasons, you'll find suggestions for fruits and berries with a longer season of appeal in the bird family chapters. But you'll also find those that serve as magnets for the birds you want, even if the harvest lasts only a short time.

Many fruits and berries ripen in summer. But others are at their peak in fall, and some hang on through winter. A few are ready for eating in spring. Planning for a seasonal spread of berries means a big crop of birds in every season. Here's what you can expect to see as the seasons change through summer, fall, winter, and spring.

Summer romance. Blueberries, strawberries, raspberries, cherries, and other tasty treats are bursting from the branches in summer. Both summer resident birds and year-round friends are here, so why not seduce them all with summer berries? Look for summer-resident buntings, flycatchers, vireos, warblers, tanagers, orioles, thrashers, catbirds, wrens, and rose-breasted grosbeaks—if you can find them among the bluebirds, cardinals, mockingbirds, jays, finches, sparrows, towhees, waxwings, woodpeckers, and other year-round birds. Time to pull out the field guide, and prepare to fall in love.

Fall migration. Stock your yard with fall fruits and berries, such as dogwoods (*Cornus florida, C. mas*), burning bush, and barberry (*Berberis* spp.), and you, too, can enjoy the surprise of some unexpected company during fall migration. Migrants such as warblers, swallows, vireos, and thrushes will show up in places far from their usual haunts, dropping in overnight from their nocturnal flights. What a feast of birds to greet you in the morning.

Winter windup. By the time cold weather arrives, birds are settled on their winter ranges, ready to forage until spring. Any lingering berries or fruit get cleaned up now, because they make a welcome change of pace from the usual menu of seeds and occasional insects. Chickadees, woodpeckers, titmice, finches, cardinals, grouse, evening grosbeaks, crossbills, and any other winter bird in the area may come in search of any berries still on the bush or fruits on the tree. An isolated catbird, brown thrasher, house wren, or warbler may try to eke out a living in cold climes; they'll appreciate the lingering fruits and berries of apple (*Malus* cvs.), holly (*Ilex opaca*), or roses (*Rosa* spp.).

Spring leftovers. In cold-winter areas, plants don't have enough time to produce berries by springtime. That's when hangers-on, such as sumac (*Rhus typhina* and other spp.) and bayberry (*Myrica pensylvanica*), grab the spotlight. Any berries that are still on the branches will be a target of early arrivals, such as robins, blackbirds, catbirds, wrens, tree swallows, and maybe even a migrating meadowlark. By late spring, early-ripening strawberries draw towhees, sparrows, robins, and wrens for a juicy bite of berries.

Nectar

A steady stream of hummingbirds is all the reason I need to plant plenty of nectar flowers. But there's always the possibility of orioles, too. And, of course, I get to enjoy the beautiful flowers, even when they're not attended by beautiful birds stopping to feed.

The nectar season starts in spring, when many flowers haven't yet begun to bloom. Here's where your nectar feeder is worth its weight in gold. Augment the sugar solution with spring-blooming nectar flowers, and your garden may become a rest stop on the highway of hummingbird migration.

Hummers migrate one by one as they zip along, but when they reach a sumptuous food source, they pull off to take a break. Before you know it, your flowers are hosting a crowd of buzzy wings. That's why I make sure to include spring nectar flowers in my garden, such as wild red columbines (*Aquilegia canadensis* or *A. formosa*) and the red-flowering currant (*Ribes sanguineum*). They're always a hit with those early arrivals.

Your choices in nectar flowers reach a peak in summer and early fall, when hummingbirds are at their most active. Once the babies are out of the nest, the whole family will be visiting your garden, and so will other hummers from around the neighborhood. Keep the nectar flowing by planting salvias (*Salvia* spp.), weigela (*Weigela* × *florida*) and other long-blooming nectar flowers that will nourish these busy birds right into fall migration.

In warm climates, hummingbirds stick around all winter, and so do fuchsia flowers. But even in the coldest, snowiest regions, these frost-tender perennials are worth investing in for a single season, because hummingbirds find them irresistible. And they'll continue blooming without letup until cold weather stops them in their tracks. Hang a basket of fuchsias on your porch, and you'll hear the whirr of wings right above your head until the hummers say, "See you later."

The sturdy stalk of this yucca supports a Scott's oriole as he maneuvers his way to its nectar.

Oh Is for Oriole

Orioles everywhere are becoming regular users of feeders, where they may sample nectar, or-anges, and jelly. But it seems that only western oriole species regularly visit flowers for nectar. Eastern orioles don't seem to have gotten the

Sweet Success

One of the sneakiest plants on the noxious weed list in some states is Himalayan impatiens (*Impatiens glandulifera*), a giant-size cousin of the familiar garden impatiens. This 6-foot-tall annual spreads rapidly by seeds, but that's not the only reason why it's such a problem: Its nectar is so sweet that humming-birds, butterflies, bees, and other pollinators forsake other plants and feed only at its flowers. The not-so-sweet flowers that *don't* get pollinated won't set seeds to start the next generation, which can cause a decline in native species.

Natural plant nectar varies in sweetness from one kind of plant to another, and it can even change with the weather. No wonder hummingbirds and orioles seek out our feeders: There, the sweetness is guaranteed. The usual formulas are also sweeter than plant nectar, which is why feeders are so popular. Here's how to concoct two basic bird favorites.

Hummingbird nectar: Mix 1 part granulated sugar, 4 parts water.
Oriole nectar: Mix 1 part granulated sugar per 6 parts water.
Heat the water in a pan or in a microwave oven, then stir in the sugar. I usually drop in two or three ice cubes to cool it down after the sugar has dissolved, so I can refill the feeder fast.

message yet. Though they may drain a nectar feeder dry, they rarely visit flowers for anything but insects.

The West has more hummingbird species—and thus more nectar flowers. Maybe that's the reason that western oriole species are more accustomed to sipping nectar from flowers. Eastern orioles seem to prefer to eat the insects attracted to the blossoms.

As far as I'm concerned, what the orioles are eating at my flowers isn't important. I just like seeing those fancy feathers. If you want to see whether yours drink nectar, catch their eye with agaves (*Agave* spp.), aloes (*Aloe* spp.), and other nectar flowers with tall, sturdy flower spikes, where these bigger birds can get a grip. Unlike hummingbirds, they can't hover while dining.

Cover

Spend a little time watching what the birds at your feeder do after they've grabbed a bite to eat, and you'll see that they head for cover in a hurry. Once sheltered by branches, they can crack their seeds or clean their beaks, out of sight of predators. Although food is foremost for bird appeal, your customers are looking for that all-important ambience, too. Before they'll linger in your yard, they need to feel safe.

Hermit thrushes, which live in the shady

Fringe Benefits

Any birder worth her binoculars knows that the best places to look for birds in the wild are along the brushy edge of a woods, field, or road. That mix of grasses, shrubs, and trees provides plenty of hiding places, so it's always brimming with birds in every season. Not only will you see plenty of birds of the bush, you'll also see birds that live in the habitat bordering the brush. It's a transition zone, where birds step up from the fields or step down from the treetops.

Call me a slow learner. I used to think that the best place to find birds was way off the beaten path. So I'd hike deep into the forest, settle myself against a stump, and wait for the birds to arrive.

It was a long wait. All I ever saw was a handful of forest dwellers, the species that skulk about in the dim light of a deep woods. Oh, it was definitely a treat to watch a wood thrush hunting for snails on the forest floor. And if I craned my neck long enough, I could catch a brilliant Blackburnian warbler moving through the trees during spring migration. But as for masses of birds? Few and far between was more like it. Often I spent more time watching box turtles than I did watching birds.

Eventually, it dawned on me that I saw far more birds on the fringes than in the forest. The brushy edges held white-throated and white-crowned sparrows galore, and in winter, dozens of cardinals—count 'em, dozens—hung out there. Finches flocked to the fringes, white-eyed vireos nested there, and towhees scratched on the ground. Even the elegant Cooper's hawks were more plentiful along the edges than deep in the forest—because their chances of nabbing a bird for lunch were a lot better where there were more birds.

I see that lesson in action every day in my own backyard. With a mix of young trees, clumps of shrubs, and a tangle of blackberries, plus big stretches of naturalistic flower beds and ornamental grasses, I get the best of the bunch. Natural food is plentiful, inviting cover is everywhere, and so are the birds.

woods, have earned their name; these gentle brown birds are secretive souls. But many other birds, including the dozens of species of native sparrows that range across the country, also live out of the limelight. And even the birds that we think of as bolder characters, such as the robin hopping on the lawn and the cardinal at the feeder, spend a lot of their time in leafy hideaways.

Most birds see open areas like your feeder as danger-ridden, so they don't linger. Supply them with cover where they can stay half-hidden, and they won't have to fly very far to feel safe. They'll spend more time in your yard instead of high-tailing it out of there.

We stick to the open spaces when we cross the yard, but birds use plants as stepping stones to travel in safety. When you group shrubs, trees, and flower beds into "corridors," you're creating natural paths for birds to follow as they move about.

Multilevel Marketing

To transplant that natural appeal into your own backyard, focus on supplying plenty of cover, with plants of different heights.

The "layered look" mimics the appeal of natural places. Birds hang out at different heights depending on family habits. By planting a mix of trees, shrubs, and lower-growing plants, including flowers, grasses, and groundcovers, you'll improve the appeal of your yard. You'll find many ideas for combining multilevel plants in the garden designs in this book, and even more suggestions for plants of all sizes in each family chapter.

Planting a mix of heights creates travel corridors, too. Pathways of plants allow birds to move safely from one side of your yard to the other. And when the plants go from ground level to sky's-the-limit, birds can safely travel up and down, too. With layered plantings, you'll see bird traffic flowing in all directions. That Baltimore oriole in your backyard, for instance, will feel comfortable coming down to pluck up the white strings you've laid on the grass and carry them high up to its nest in the making.

Although you can turn your small to medium-size yard (say, 15,000 square feet or less) into a jungle for the birds, ultra-dense plantings probably won't make using the yard very pleasant for you. Instead of planting every square inch, invest in the edges. There, you can use plantings that step down in height to invite all kinds of birds to your place. Start with small trees, then plant shrubs in front of them. Finally, step down to a flower bed in front of the shrubs. Birds will move freely from one height to the next, making themselves at home. And your yard will look much better than a jumbled jungle. You'll find many planting designs that follow this style throughout the bird family chapters.

Secret Weapon: Shrubs

Shrubs are the fastest way to achieve good cover. They're the secret to coaxing birds to give up their grab-and-go eating habits, because they offer the cover that birds crave.

A newly planted tree can take years to settle in, but a shrub takes off like a racehorse. In just a year or two, many shrubs can double or even triple in size. Be sure to read the label to discover the plant's mature height and width: Your new oak tree can take 50 years to reach its mature height, but that cute little shrub you brought home with it might be rubbing shoulders with its neighbors next year. Get educated by reading the fine print before you dig the hole, so that your new shrubs have enough space to spread out.

All shrubs provide quick cover, insect food, perching places, and possible nest sites—almost as soon as you put them in the ground. In a year or two, many shrubs will reach 3 to 4 feet tall and wide. They're hardy, hearty plants that need no extra care to look good. Try these ideas for making the most of them:

- Plant groups of shrubs like stepping stones in your yard, safely leading birds from one area to the next. Allow about 6 to 15 feet of space between groups. You'll have plenty of room to walk between the groups, and the distance won't be too daunting to birds.
- Group shrubs and trees in the corner of your yard, where they'll remain fairly undisturbed. Birds appreciate privacy.
- Choose flowering shrubs and berry bushes, so you'll have the extra draw of seasonal food.
- Snuggle shrubs into flower beds and borders, to add cover and nest sites.
- Plant shrubs and smaller trees beneath mature trees, to multiply the appeal of the planting and add cover for bird families of different habits.
- Plant a hedge along at least one of your

property lines. A hedge along two sides is even better, and three beats two. Already have a fence? Plant shrubs in front of it.

Panic Attack

Any shrub is a good shrub when birds need to make a quick getaway. They'll dive for the closest cover and hide out there until the coast is clear. Add shrubs to your yard, and birds will recognize that your place offers protection.

Any kind of bush is eagerly embraced when a bird needs to save its neck. When you plant shrubs in groups or hedges, birds can retreat from one bush to the next if a hawk happens to show interest in the place where they were perched.

If cats, raccoons, or slithery snakes are pests around your place, put thorny shrubs at the top of your list. Spiny branches are like armed guards, adding an extra layer of protection from predators. Ultra-thorny barberry bushes (*Berberis* spp.) are widely available, grow fast, and fit into just about any style of garden. Try fancy golden- or purple-leaved types for a dash of color among your greenery.

Grasslands Cover

Adding shrubs is a good idea even in grassland areas, chaparral, or desert. Ground-dwelling birds such as quail will use them as travel corridors, even if their natural haunts aren't as full of inviting shrubby vegetation as your yard. Instead of planting a solid hedge of shrubs, though, intersperse the shrubs with stretches of grasses, especially native species, and annual flowers, to better imitate the natural habitat of your local birds.

Hedge Your Bets

To birds, a hedge looks like Easy Street: A row of closely spaced shrubs lets birds cover a lot of territory without being exposed to predator danger. Hedges are a practical way to add a lot of good bird cover to your yard, and they make a good-looking frame of greenery, too.

You may not notice the birds in your bushes, because laying low is part of the game plan. But take a closer look and see who turns up. Depending on where you live, you might see any of these characters: cardinals, jays, robins, towhees, thrashers, catbirds, mockingbirds, bluebirds, chickadees, titmice, wrens, bushtits, warblers, vireos, kinglets, sparrows, juncos. Whew! That's a lot of birds—and all of them visit hedges daily. And all you have to do is plant a row of love-'em-and-leave-'em bushes because hedges can take care of themselves.

Cover, with a Bonus

Hey, birds, come on down! Vireos, orioles, tanagers, great crested flycatchers, and waxwings generally stay in trees, rather than hopping about in shrubs. That's why I make sure to include some shrubs with berries and small fruit trees among my plantings, along with the shade trees and evergreens. When the bright berries and juicy fruits ripen, they draw birds right down from the tallest treetops.

Tough, fast-growing, and cheap to boot—weigela (*Weigela x florida*) is a bargain for hummingbird lovers. It blooms for months. Perfect for hedges!

One of the big reasons we're gardeners to begin with is because we love beauty. That's why I like to grow flowering shrubs, such as weigela (*Weigela × florida*), butterfly bush (*Buddleia davidii*), lilacs (*Syringa vulgaris*), and other bushes with blossoms. I like their look and scent, and my birds appreciate the insects drawn to the blooms or the nectar hidden within. You'll find plenty of suggestions for flowering shrubs and shrubs with berries in the bird family chapters, so that your cover plants can make birds feel more at home in other ways, too.

Popularity Contest

Go to any garden center in the country, especially those at big-box stores, and it seems you'll find the same plants over and over in each region. Barberry, burning bush, arborvitae, azaleas, non-native viburnums, flowering crabs and flowering cherries, 'Stella d'Oro' daylilies, and a few dozen others seem to form the backbone of the inventory at many garden centers, with a bit of regional variation.

These plants are popular, say the staff. And there's no doubt that plant outlets sell a lot of them.

But are they popular because they're the only things available? Popular because they're familiar, and many of us feel safe planting things we see in every yard on the block? Popular because they're easy to propagate and grow fast to saleable size, cutting costs for producers?

And what happens when we all buy the same thing, and later, widespread problems become evident? Bradford pears are being cut down in many areas, thanks to their habit of suddenly keeling over at a certain age. Viburnums may be next on the list, due to various blights, including sudden oak death (*Phytophthora ramorum*), and the viburnum leaf beetle, a European pest, which are making inroads.

Planting for Posterity

Some readily available plants are fine for birds, but often there are better choices. To get the most out of your bird-by-bird garden, you'll have to withdraw from the popularity contest. Step away from the rows upon rows of "popular" plants, and seek out more bird-appealing selections like those recommended in the bird family chapters.

I look for bird-plant bargains at big garden centers. But I buy much more at locally owned nurseries, where the staff are usually thrilled to talk plants and happy to special-order anything I ask for. Sometimes I buy through the mail, from suppliers I've learned give good value for the money. (You'll find my favorites in the Resources section, starting on page 372.)

Native plants of your area are a great place to begin because local birds are accustomed to making use of them. I long for the day when I can visit a garden center and find a good selection of natives of that region—priced reasonably, not at a premium because they're the latest thing. Until then, I make a treasure hunt of ferreting them out. I ask for them at nurseries, shop at plant sales run by conservation groups, or buy through mail-order sources.

The plants you select are going to be with you for a long time. So, start with the best of all possible picks, even if they don't win the garden center popularity contest. You'll find specific suggestions in each bird family chapter in this book.

Added Attractions

Food and cover will bring in nearly all of the birds you're yearning to see in your yard. Once you have those two biggies, ahem, covered, then you can add the finishing touches that will make your backyard *the* place to be.

Now is the time to consider what birds need when they're not busy eating. Easy answer: Same as us, they need a safe, dry place to sleep; a refreshing place to drink and bathe; a good spot to raise the kids; and a helping hand with home construction. Top it all off with a mint on the pillow—or should we say, crushed eggshells in the feeder?

Shelter for Roosting and Bad Weather

You can't see the birds that spend the night at your place, but it will still give you a warm feeling to know you've supplied lots of places where they can cozy up for a good night's sleep. Nighttime roosting places may also serve as shelter when snowstorms blow in or when ice blankets the landscape. Birds seek shelter during extra-cold weather as well. Rain usually doesn't deter birds from going about their daily business of finding food, though they may spend more time perched in sheltering branches.

We know a lot about the habits of birds during daylight hours. But when it comes to nighttime arrangements and times of severe weather, much is still a mystery. Generally, most birds seek shelter in places that reflect the habits of the family.

A Cozy Cavity

Birds that nest in natural cavities or in birdhouses often spend the night or wait out bad weather in those same cozy spaces. Expect birds of the Woodpecker, Chickadee and Titmouse, Nuthatch, and Wren families to make use of such shelter. Some members of the Swallow family, and everybody's favorite bluebirds from the Thrush family, will also roost or shelter in bird boxes. Often, these birds share the space, roosting in groups.

You can help them by adding a roosting box to improve the accommodations. It looks like a bird house, but it has perches inside so the birds don't have to jockey for space.

Ever-Ready Evergreens

Evergreen shrubs and trees make super shelter at night or in bad weather. The thin needles of conifers may not look like they would shield birds within, but this foliage actually does a super job of shedding snow and rain, as well as breaking the force of wintry winds. During winter storms or sudden summer deluges, you may see birds of almost any family seeking respite from the weather in a conifer. Rhododendrons (*Rhododendron* spp.) and other broad-leaved evergreens are also adopted for shelter during bad weather. They're popular with some members of the Warbler family, as well as with thrushes and other birds.

Junipers (*Juniperus* spp.) supply bird-approved berries and safe, prickly shelter at night.

Conifers, especially prickly ones such as junipers (*Juniperus virginiana* and others), often serve as group roosting spots for birds that live at lower levels, including members of the Small Finch, Mimic Thrush, Thrush, and Dove families. These birds may roost singly, or in groups. Large conifers, such as Douglas fir (*Pseudotsuga menziesii*) or pines (*Pinus* spp.), often serve as shelter for far-ranging members of the Crow and Jay family.

Canopy Bed

Birds that spend most of their time in the treetops, including members of the Flycatcher, Waxwing, Vireo, Tanager, Blackbird and Oriole, and Large Finch families, often find shelter or a sleeping spot in the branches of deciduous trees, such as sycamores (*Platanus* spp.), maples (*Acer* spp.), oaks (*Quercus* spp.), and many others. By the time the sheltering foliage of the leafy canopy has fallen, most of these birds have already gone to warmer climes. Wild turkeys also roost in trees, both deciduous and evergreen.

Some of these birds roost singly or in small numbers. But the Blackbird family can sometimes try the patience even of bird lovers. Grackles are particularly notorious for gathering in communal groups that can reach pest status, usually during migration times when the birds congregate in vast flocks.

Summer Sleepover

When I was a kid, one of my favorite things to do was to watch the birds come from all directions to settle into our "hedge bushes" for the night. I know now that the bushes were good old-fashioned privet, never touched with pruners, so they were 10 feet tall and thick with dead branches as well as leafy ones. And even though they covered only about 6 feet on either side of a walkway, they were magnets for birds settling down to roost. Lots of little brown birds, the native sparrows and house sparrows, made themselves at home, but so did cardinals, robins, and my special favorite, the big brown thrasher. By the time the lightning bugs started flashing, dozens of birds were safely tucked inside—and you'd never know it unless you'd seen it happen.

The dense cover of hedges—deciduous, evergreen, or a mix—makes an inviting place for many backyard birds to spend the night. Hedges are a hit during bad weather, too, thanks to their interwoven branches, which protect birds from rain, snow, and wind. Cats that may be creeping about usually aren't motivated enough to brave the branches, so birds can sleep undisturbed.

Many species of the Small Finch, Mimic Thrush, and Thrush families look for a perch deep inside hedges when dusk sets in. Cardinals and doves may join them. These birds often roost in groups with companions of all kinds. At twilight, stand quietly near a hedge and listen: You're likely to hear the soft peeps of birds settling down to sleep.

Water

Both feeder birds and birds that don't visit feeders take advantage of a reliable source of fresh, clean water. Thirsty birds will adapt to

All of our fancy birdbaths are just an attempt to match the attractions of a good old puddle. Supply shallow water, and songbirds will splash daily.

whatever water source they can find. I used to watch the bluebirds that lived up the road line up along the rim of a 3-foot-deep horse trough to daintily dip their beaks.

For bathing, birds need a shallow puddle with a bottom that's not slippery. They'll happily use a natural puddle at the corner of a street or wherever they find it, or they'll use the "puddle" in your birdbath.

Suitable Styles

An old-fashioned pedestal birdbath is all you need to catch the eye of dozens of species. Add a low-level saucer, a drip tube, or a misting device, and you'll get even more. You'll find recommendations for supplying water in the family chapters.

Investing in fancier features, such as ground-level baths with multiple shallow pools and a trickling pump, will pay off hugely if you like to watch birds at the bath. These natural-looking baths draw in colorful tanagers, wood warblers, goldfinches, and many others, who happily share the generous space. During migration, when a refreshing bath is just what a tired traveler craves, naturalistic birdbaths really draw a crowd.

Garden pools are good for drinking but too deep for bathing. If you have a pool, pile rocks in one end to create a stable, shallow area where birds can bathe.

Creative birdbaths made of glass, glazed ceramic, smooth plastic, or metal are less popular with birds than run-of-the-mill concrete. It's all about feeling safe. If you've ever tried to take a shower while using a slippery lotion or soap, you know how unsettling it is to feel like your feet are sliding out from under you. If birds only sip from your basin, and rarely stand and splash, try these tricks:

- Set a low, flat rock in the bowl.
- Apply stick-on nonslip bathtub decorations.
- Cut a section of a suction-cup bath mat to

Help birds get a grip in your slippery glass or metal birdbath by recycling an old nonslip bath mat.

A Birdbath That Blooms

One of my best bird surprises happened in my southern Indiana backyard, where I had a bed filled with native prairie plants. I was strolling around the yard when I heard the definite sound of water splashing—and I had no birdbath set up. I had to look twice before I believed my eyes: A Carolina chickadee was bathing with abandon on my cup plant (*Silphium perfoliatum*), splashing water out of the small cup that forms on the plant where each leaf joins the stem. It had rained the day before, and each leafy cup had become a mini-birdbath.

Once I started looking for bird activity on the plant, I also spotted ruby-throated hummingbirds, wrens, and vireos making use of the little puddles. It turned out to be a regular activity whenever rainwater refilled the leaves.

The tall, stout cup plant (*Silphium perfoliatum*), an American prairie native, is an intriguing perennial for a big garden, or to punctuate a fence. Water collects in its leaves, making mini-birdbaths for hummingbirds and other small sippers.

fit, and stick it in place. (Remove the mat and give it a scrubbing as needed or toss in your washing machine with an old towel.)
· Add gravel (just make sure you dump it and replace it every time you clean the bath).

Water, Water Everywhere

My two shaggy dogs make keeping a birdbath a challenge. They lap from low-level saucers, they wallow in garden ponds, and they tip over pedestals willy-nilly. I keep trying. But, meanwhile, unless it's a period of drought, I've noticed that my birds do perfectly well finding water on their own.

Vireos, warblers, chickadees, hummingbirds, and other small birds often take a bath right on a leaf. They rub against the water collected on the leaf's surface, fluffing their feathers and rustling their wings just as they do in a birdbath. Trees with big leaves, such as maples (*Acer* spp.), seem to be the most popular spot for leaf-bathing.

Nesting

Bringing nesting birds to your yard isn't as straightforward as luring them to your feeders and food plants. Birds build their nests in many, many places and plants. Where they nest depends on the height at which they spend most of their time, protection from predators, food sources, and the birds' other habits. Even those that stick to one or two choices for nest sites generally have to have all the other pieces in place, too: The habitat must make them feel at home, the food selection must be up to their standards for family raising, and who knows what other fine points birds consider before they say, "Here! Here's where I'll build my nest!"

I've had a lot of success attracting nesting birds by planting trees and shrubs that I've seen them choose for nesting in the wild or in someone else's backyard. But success is never guaranteed. Sometimes, the birds choose my yard; often, they don't.

The bird family chapters will give you ideas for planting possible nesting places for birds. Regardless of their favored plants, though, nearly all birds demand privacy around the nest. Most backyard birds nest in undisturbed areas of your yard, and they're highly secretive when entering or leaving the nest site—with a few exceptions, such as that house finch in your hanging basket and the robin at eye level in your doorstep lilac. Once a pair of birds has nested in your backyard, there's a good chance they'll come back next year. Birds return to their particular breeding territories year after year. Of course, next time they may set up house 10 feet away from the previous year's site—just enough to put the nest on the other side of the property line, in your neighbor's yard.

Niches for Nests

No matter how pricey gasoline gets, I still like my Sunday drives in the country. In winter, when the leaves are down, I like to look for bird nests in trees and shrubs along the route, to see who was living where.

I spot some nests in tall trees. But many more

are in the bushes or the smaller trees, roughly 20 feet or less above the ground. That's because there are more birds that live at mid- to low levels than high overhead. You can check my theory in your own neighborhood by comparing the number of sparrows and robins in the bushes with the number of orioles in the treetops.

Come spring, all those birds need a place to make a new nest, and it just might be in your yard.

When you add shrubs to your yard, you're likely to soon see an increase in nesting birds as well as visitors. There's a big market of tenants for low-level nest sites, including native sparrows, buntings, catbirds, cardinals, towhees, and many other birds.

Of course, you'll want to plant a young tree or two or 20, for future nesting needs. If your yard is already graced with mature trees, the nesting real estate is even better. In the bird family chapters, you'll learn which plants your favorite birds usually choose to support their precious nests.

Birds in a Box

No matter how cute that birdhouse is that you picked up at the craft sale, it will only appeal to a

The Well-Built Birdhouse

"Sure," I said to the woman who'd just told me that she loved birds and wanted to sell birdhouses. "I'll buy five of them: two chickadee boxes, two swallow boxes, and one flicker box."

Too bad I didn't think to ask to see a sample first. When I went back to pick up the birdhouses, I discovered they were totally unusable. The holes were the wrong sizes, the boxes were the wrong sizes, they had only a flimsy loop of wire for mounting (meaning they swung in the breeze), and the roofs were made of two pieces of wood attached to a round dowel (inviting leaks). Live and learn!

It's worth spending the typical $20 or so to buy a well-made birdhouse that will last for years. Natural unpainted wood is fine. Experts have determined what size box, what size hole, and what kind of mounting best suits each type of bird. Look for boxes endorsed by the Audubon Society or other reputable organizations, and check the illustration below to see which details matter, and why.

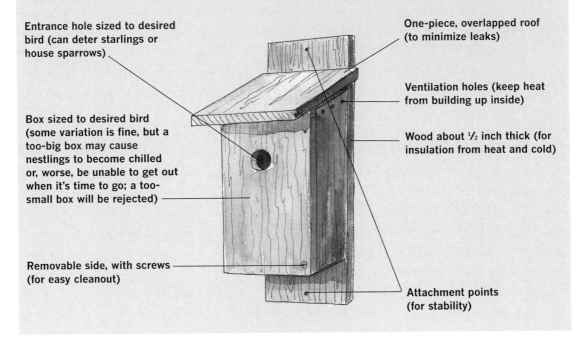

Entrance hole sized to desired bird (can deter starlings or house sparrows)

One-piece, overlapped roof (to minimize leaks)

Ventilation holes (keep heat from building up inside)

Box sized to desired bird (some variation is fine, but a too-big box may cause nestlings to become chilled or, worse, be unable to get out when it's time to go; a too-small box will be rejected)

Wood about ½ inch thick (for insulation from heat and cold)

Removable side, with screws (for easy cleanout)

Attachment points (for stability)

limited number of birds. Most species build their nests out in the open air, not in a box.

The good news is that putting up birdhouses, or nest boxes as they're also called, gives you a great chance of attracting a tenant. Birds that nest in cavities adopt manmade homes just as eagerly as the do-it-yourself kind pecked out of dead wood. You'll find advice about choosing and mounting a house in the family chapters for the cavity-nesting birds.

Birdhouses attract starlings and house sparrows, too, which may not be your tenants of choice. If you'd rather not host what many consider pest birds, stick to birdhouses with smaller entrance holes, such as those sized to fit chickadees and wrens.

Special Needs

Some birds have habits that are so specific, yet so easy to satisfy, that you'll need another bag of tricks to bring them to your yard. Here's a sampling; you'll find the specifics of special needs in the bird family chapters.

- Nesting materials. Birds work hard to gather natural materials for their nests. By adding plants that they make use of, such as grapevines, to your yard, or by setting out feathers or fibers they treasure, you may attract homemaking birds such as orioles, swallows, chickadees, and purple martins.
- Mineral sources. Salt and calcium are simple to supply in the form of salt blocks and crushed eggshells, and they're eagerly sought by finches, grosbeaks, purple martins, and several other birds.
- Grit. Doves and some other birds swallow frequent helpings of grit to aid in their digestion. A box of cage-bird grit will take care of this special need.
- Mud. Nest-building robins, swallows, and other birds need mud for their building projects. Make your own mud puddle, and birds may check it out when the need arises.

Creating a Safety Zone

When I think of all the indignities birds suffer, I figure that turning my yard into a bird haven is the least I can do. After all, it can shelter those smaller birds who have been displaced by human activities or natural forces. And birds need all the help they can get. In 2000, the Audubon Society announced the alarming results of a study: More than one-quarter of all US bird species (including those of Hawaii and Puerto Rico) are in decline. Even worse, some species' numbers are dropping like a rock. Henslow's sparrow of the Midwest and the tiny and beautiful cerulean warbler of the eastern half of the country have both declined in number by 70 percent since the 1960s. There's only half the number of California thrashers, with their dramatic curved bills, and

Belling the Cat

It seems like such a good solution, fastening a bell to Kitty's collar. And many cat owners do just that, then let their pet outside to roam, thinking they're doing their part to keep birds safe.

Maybe it would work if cats trotted along like horses pulling a sleigh, so the bell went jingle-jingle-jingle. But the reality is that cats are slow stalkers, and they lie in wait. By the time the bird hears the bell ring, it's signaling dinner for the cat who's pouncing upon it.

The only good use for a belled collar is to let *you* know when a cat is on the prowl in your yard. Then you can chase it away.

half as many painted buntings of the Southeast as there were in the 1960s.

Destruction of habitat, both in the United States and in birds' wintering grounds in Central and South America, is a major factor. So are pesticides, herbicides, and other chemical contaminants, which may affect birds directly or affect their food sources. Even acid rain can affect birds: It dissolves the shells of snails so that their numbers decline, as do the wood thrushes that feed upon them.

The good news is that for many of these species, creating backyard bird havens can help. Of course, I want the birds that find sanctuary in my yard to stay safe. That calls for a little planning to alleviate the dangers.

Cats? Not in My Backyard

If only. Nope, I regret to report that cats simply love my yard. None of them are mine, which only makes it a harder problem to solve.

Keeping your own kitties indoors is the first step. Birds are most vulnerable at night, when cats love to hunt. Nesting season, from April through late June, is another especially vulnerable time. But there's really no good time for cats to be out and about. Experts agree that pet cats and cats gone wild are the worst predators of birds, by a mile. They kill billions every year.

I'm constantly trying to discourage my neighbors' cats, and the campaign seems to be working, though it's not a total success. Three years ago, when I first made my yard bird-beguiling, there were nine felines prowling my place. Now, only two sneak over, and only now

and then. (Fuzzball and Pooty-Poo, if you're reading this, SCAT!)

Here's my arsenal of anti-cat devices:

Motion-activated squirter. At nearly $60, this was an expensive investment, but worth it at the feeding station. Install a battery, figure out where to aim the motion detector, stick the device in the ground, and attach a garden hose—the setup takes 5 minutes. As soon as a cat or other critter trespasses within range of about 20 feet, the squirter instantly lets loose with a blast of water. It's very, very effective, and the only thing that keeps my feeder birds from becoming dinner themselves. By occasionally moving it to another area, I keep the cats guessing. Drawbacks? I keep forgetting about it and get spritzed in the legs myself.

Squirt guns. I keep big and little squirt guns ready and waiting on the deck, on the garden bench, and in my hand when I'm outside. A good shot of water, and the target takes off running for home. It's a low-tech solution, but repeated use definitely has an effect. Sneak attacks are best, so that those wily kitties don't connect you with the Discourager.

Clapping, yelling, running, and generally acting like a madwoman. This works, too, but only when I'm outside. Those darn cats learned fast to avoid the yard when I'm in it, but otherwise they prowl with impunity. Still, it has helped downsize the cat presence.

Dogs. Man's best friend is a surefire anti-cat device, but unfortunately not for me. One of my dogs is totally uninterested in chasing cats, and the other doesn't roam free. They do guarantee, though, that no cats enter their fenced part of the yard. Dogs can also scare birds away, even though they don't stalk them as cats do.

Why go to all this trouble when I could just ask the neighbors to keep their pets at home? Because there's no way to make that request without arousing resentment. To most people, roaming free is simply what cats do. They're not on the same scale as straying dogs, or kids who don't stay in their own yard. Cats are just cats, prowling around wherever they please. And anyone who complains must be, um, a bird nut. That's enough reason to stop being neighborly right there.

Hawks and Owls

Ample food, and a reliable supply of it, is such a huge factor in bird life that some backyard birds have changed their time-honored patterns of migration and range, thanks to the availability of feeders year-round.

Some hawks have also taken notice of the popularity of bird-feeding. They've altered their behavior, too, to take advantage of this generous buffet.

When I started birdwatching seriously, some 30 years ago, Cooper's hawks and sharp-shinned hawks were birds of the forest. Now, these species are common visitors to backyards, even in towns and cities. Feeding stations are what brought them out of the woods.

Give your birds a corridor of dense cover, so they can escape the steely gaze of a sharp-shinned hawk.

Red-tailed hawks, too, were once birds of the countryside, not the city. Nowadays, one can show up anywhere there's a well-stocked feeder—stocked with birds to eat, that is.

Kestrel, merlin, peregrine falcon, broadwing hawk: Just about any bird of prey may show up to prey on your birds.

I'm looking forward to the time when the elegant white gyrfalcon of the Far North makes its move and becomes a regular in my backyard.

Jays and Other Bird Predators

Jays, crows, grackles, and a few other birds sometimes prey on the eggs or nestlings of other birds. It's a natural habit to them but an unsavory one to us. There's nothing you can do to stop it. Chalk it up to the ways of nature, and try not to hold it against the birds whose natural diet includes these foods.

Well, until it grabs its first chickadee, that is. Hawks don't take nearly as many birds at feeding stations as cats do. But I still think it's unfair to invite birds to dinner, only to have them find out that they are on the menu.

I haven't found a foolproof solution yet. But these ideas can help:

- You can empty your feeders when a hawk becomes a regular. However, feeder birds will still come to the area, and they'll be even more vulnerable as they try to find a few leftovers that may still be lurking.
- Adding extra cover beside your feeder, such as a young fir or spruce, can help birds make a safe getaway. Connect it to other plantings as part of a corridor, so they won't be sitting trapped in a single bush.

Nuisance Birds

Whenever I start thinking of certain birds as pests in my yard or at my feeder, I like to play a little game.

"What if there were only one of them?" I ask myself.

Funny how fast that changes my perspective.

If house finches were as rare as purple finches at the feeder, we'd celebrate when a pair of them showed up. If only a single starling ever came to call, we'd make sure to have all his favorites on hand. And what if a blue jay was only an occasional treat instead of an everyday screamer?

Sometimes, beauty or good manners is enough to override the sheer numbers. Can you ever have too many sunny yellow goldfinches? Even when the flock builds into the hundreds on a migration stopover, I happily keep ladling out the sunflower seed and filling the nyjer tubes.

But I can see my own biases at work, because I don't feel nearly as generous when the equally abundant but dowdy brown pine siskins show up. Must be those cheery yellow feathers, uncomfortable as the thought is.

Feeder hogs are no fun, either. Jays land on my not-appreciated list when they cart off every nut I put out, stuffing their throats with six at a time, before the other birds can take a bite.

Which birds you consider a nuisance is a matter of personal taste. But when you garden bird by bird, you can rest easy knowing that all the birds in your yard will get their fair share.

Start with Starlings

Starlings sure are hard to love. They're big, they're not exactly beautiful, and they're noisy. Worst of all for most folks, they're messy and they eat a lot. Plus, they arrive en masse, shouldering aside other birds to grab a seat at the table.

I know I'm in the minority, but I admire starlings for how cleverly they have adapted to living with humans. They make nests in the letters of store names on the side of the flagship store at the mall. They make nests in street lights and traffic signals. They clean up barnyards and feedlots—and fast-food parking lots.

In the natural world, starlings have earned their place. Those long, sharp beaks spear many larvae of Japanese beetles, European craneflies, and other pests from our lawns. And when it

Starlings aid other birds by driving away hawks. When the flock spots a redtail or other hawk perched or flying, the group instantly goes into tight formation around the predator, wheeling and diving in unison. The harassment is highly effective, and most hawks quickly give up and make their getaway.

comes to driving off hawks, starlings do other birds a big favor. They mob any flying hawk they see, flying in tight formation around it until it flies away in confusion.

Starlings do compete with flickers and other cavity nesters for homesites in trees and nest boxes. But modern farming methods and the continued destruction of natural places are more to blame for the problem than the starling, which never ventures far from civilization.

At the feeder, though, starlings can quickly wear out their welcome, even at my house. Like dogs under the dinner table, they'll eat just about anything with gusto. A block of suet can disappear in a couple of days under a starling onslaught, and so can lovingly made bluebird treats or other soft foods. The constant presence of the starlings, whose motto seems to be "Gulp 'til it's gone," discourages other birds from trying to get their share.

I've learned a few tricks to make it less frustrating to deal with starlings at the feeder and in the yard. Try these ideas for peaceful coexistence:

- Keep a decoy feeder for starlings, away from other feeders. Stock it with their favorite foods. I use the cheapest brand of dog kibble softened with water; it goes a long way and they love it. Old bread, crackers, or cereal, meat scraps, and other people foods will hold their attention, too. Chicken feed, sold at farm stores, is another money-saving way to feed a crowd.
- Serve soft foods for other birds in feeders that starlings can't use. Suet feeders within an outer cage of starling-excluding bars work great for suet blocks and homemade recipes.
- In winter, when starlings are likely to sample the birdseed, put millet and other small seeds in starling-proof feeders, such as those sold by the sources listed near the back of this book.
- Serve black oil sunflower seeds in tube feeders, which are tricky for starlings to use.
- In open feeders, offer striped sunflower seeds instead of black oil; starlings usually won't eat them.
- Fruit trees and bushes are fair game for starlings. Don't begrudge them their share;

there's plenty to go around and enough perches for any bird that's interested.

- Stick to nest boxes for smaller birds, including chickadees, titmice, nuthatches, wrens, and downy woodpeckers. Starlings won't be able to enter them.

House Sparrows

House sparrows, also called English sparrows, were imported here, just like starlings were. And, just like starlings, they made themselves at home just a little too well.

These chirpy, gregarious birds aren't in the same classification as our very own American sparrows, the native white-throated sparrows, song sparrows, fox sparrows, and other species that we look forward to seeing. They're actually related to the African weaver finches you may have seen on nature shows on TV. Like weavers, house sparrows build huge nests, stuffing in everything but the kitchen sink. I've seen scraps of plastic wrappers, tissues, and lots of other flotsam in the constructions, which may be in a shrubby tree, in dense vines on a wall, or in a birdhouse.

Nesting habits are a big reason why house sparrows are considered nuisances. Bluebird boxes are just the right size for them, and they wage vigorous battles to claim such houses as their own. That doesn't win them many friends.

At the feeder, house sparrows behave very much like native sparrows, dining on small seeds such as millet. The only problem is that they usually show up in vociferous groups, which may crowd out more desirable birds. Their only "bad" behavior is being too common.

If a house sparrow has adopted a birdhouse as its own "Home Sweet Home," you can bet there'll be some grasses or other materials hanging out the entrance hole.

I don't bother trying to outwit these birds. Any feeder that would exclude them would also exclude other feeder regulars. So I just pour out some extra birdseed right on the ground, where they seem to like it best, to take the pressure off of other feeders. They like bread and baked goods, too, and they're big fans of cracked corn and chicken scratch.

Competition for houses with bluebirds can be enough to make you see red. Often, the house sparrows don't make their move until the bluebirds have already settled in, which is really disheartening for both the bluebirds and the bluebird lover.

I've tried putting up extra houses and "anti-sparrow" designs, and neither was effective. Until an ideal bluebirds-only house is invented, here's food for thought:

- Human activities and the weather have done far more to affect bluebirds than house sparrows have. Destruction of woods and hedgerows, agriculture that relies on immense fields and clean edges, the switch from wooden farm and ranch fence posts to metal ones—all have had a huge effect on bluebird homesites. Brutal winters, spring storms, and cold snaps can devastate adult and nestling bluebirds, causing them to freeze or starve to death. If house sparrows plague your backyard bluebird house, you may want to focus on making sure that bluebirds have plenty to eat, and let them find their own home. I stick to feeding bluebirds instead of putting up nest boxes, and I let them settle their housing battles themselves. Sure, I'd love to host bluebirds in a birdhouse in my yard—for my own pleasure. But I also love the thrill of seeing them flutter down to a tray of food I've prepared just for them. At the feeder, house sparrows and bluebirds peacefully coexist because the birds have different preferences.
- House sparrows are less inclined to use natural cavities in trees than they are a birdhouse. Over the years, I've watched many bluebirds expertly search for and select a tree hole that I had completely overlooked. Look around, and you'll see that living trees as well as dead branches are riddled with holes, such as knotholes where a branch fell off, plus holes previously excavated by woodpeckers, nuthatches, or other feathered carpenters.
- House sparrows are not "bad"; bluebirds are not "good." They're simply birds. Bluebird fans who make statements about the relative benefits of both species are guided by their hearts or by human interests.

Making the List

Several other birds may fall into the nuisance category at the feeding station or in the yard. Here's how to deal with them.

Grackles and Other Blackbirds

Grackles are among the largest of feeder visitors, and they may show up in big flocks. Red-winged and other blackbirds may descend en masse on your yard or feeders, too. Usually, they're a seasonal problem because the flock disperses as the nesting season gets underway or migration continues. If you want to uninvite them, invest in feeders that exclude large birds.

In the yard, grackles may dine on the eggs and young of other birds. It's a natural habit to them but an unsavory one to us. Mortality is built into birds' lives; if every egg survived to adulthood, there'd be too many birds.

Jays

Jays make a commotion when they come to a feeder, and other birds often flee until the jay is gone. Jays can also vacuum up a lot of your more expensive treats, such as nuts, in a hurry. Serve nuts in a jay-proof feeder, such as a wire mesh tube. Switch to feeders that exclude large birds. Or expand your feeding station by adding

Gadzooks, It's Grackles!

Next time you visit the Dallas–Fort Worth area, mention the word *grackle* and watch how fast people start to sputter. *Grackle* is a dirty word in many parts of Texas and other places in the South, thanks to the blackbirds' habit of roosting together by the thousands.

Great-tailed grackles flock in huge numbers to certain areas, filling trees and building ledges with what many Texans consider a "black plague." The birds spend the night, then fly out in search of food, often in surrounding grain fields.

Repeat and repeat for weeks on end, and we're talking about quite an accumulation of bird droppings, which quickly adds a certain stench to the clamoring scene. Oh, and did we mention that grackles are highly vocal?

Using scare tactics barely makes a dent in the tide of blackbirds, once they fixate on a roosting spot. Some folks advocate putting up nest boxes for owls, a natural predator, in hopes of sending the grackles a message. Usually, it doesn't work. One Texas institution even cut down trees so the birds would depart—a measure so desperate that it shows what a problem communal roosts can be.

Thankfully, such flocks rarely look for a long-term roost in backyards. Flocks of grackles and other blackbirds may, however, drop in during migration, to flip over leaves and otherwise scout out food at your place. I enjoy them while they're here. And when they go, I wave goodbye with a touch of relief.

feeders for small birds and putting the jays' daily allotment of nuts in an accessible tray.

Like grackles, jays eat eggs and young birds. But they also save the necks of many birds by acting as the neighborhood alarm, screaming their heads off when a cat, snake, or hawk appears.

House Finches

House finches can grow to nuisance numbers, reason enough for many feeder hosts to consider them pests. The species is also vulnerable to an eye ailment, avian conjunctivitis, which eventually blinds the bird in one or both eyes. Any feeding station that's overrun by too many birds runs the risk of spreading disease. Although avian conjunctivitis seems to be mainly confined to house finches, other maladies may take hold if an infected bird is part of a lingering flock.

You can't deter house finches without blocking many desirable species. But if you're determined, you can switch to upside-down tube feeders and suet feeders only, preventing house finches from free access to the seeds they like.

In the yard, house finches aren't usually a problem. They do have a fondness for nesting in hanging baskets, though, or in door decorations. But for most people, the fun of hosting the growing family outweighs any damage it causes.

Cowbirds

Cowbirds eat calmly side by side with other birds. But it's their nesting habits that make them a pest to many birds.

These birds have the unique habit of letting other species raise their young. Cowbirds don't build nests or care for nestlings themselves.

Cowbird flocks arrive in spring, just in time to prance and preen and pair up before other birds begin nesting. Later the female cowbird sneaks into a nest when another bird isn't looking and lays her eggs.

No parenting chores—and big competition for the natural nestlings, who may not survive. Plus, the poor surrogate parents—often, birds that are much smaller than cowbirds—have to work much harder than normal to keep that cowbird "child" well fed.

Some parent birds have been known to push cowbird eggs over the edge when they notice them. But most bird brains aren't very good at recognizing the interloper in the family. They'll treat the cowbird nestling with the same dedication as they would their own brood. Interfering with a nest to remove cowbird eggs may cause predators to take interest in it, too. So all you can do is stand back and hope for the best.

Snakes and Lizards

Doin' what comes naturally: For these critters, eating bird eggs and birds is just part of the plan. Birds that nest on or near the ground are at high risk from these reptiles. But even those in trees aren't safe because some snakes can climb.

Birds do a pretty good job of defending their nests against these critters, unless they're taken by surprise. Jays are often the first line of defense: They start making a loud racket whenever they spot a snake. Nesting birds in the area join in, with all of the birds either hollering or flying at and threatening the reptile.

To deter reptiles from reaching into bird-

houses, install a predator guard on the post or pole. This wide collar makes it difficult for a slithery creature to climb any farther.

Raccoons and Opossums

'Coons are cute, all right, but they're happy to make a hearty meal of bird eggs and nestlings. Not too many folks are fond of 'possums, although I find them utterly endearing.

Originally country dwellers, both animals have adapted very well to living around people. They thrive in towns and cities. In areas where cars are their only enemy, they can grow so plentiful that they become pests, especially in a yard that's filled with tempting bird nests.

Window Treatments

Windows don't look like windows to birds. They see the reflections of the sky and their surround-

Many of the species that are declining in numbers, including the Blackburnian warbler shown here, suffer fatal collisions with windows, buildings, or towers during their daily doings or on migration flights.

ings in the glass, instead of taking note of the curtains or knick-knacks on the ledge inside. Head-on collisions are far too common, and sometimes they're fatal. There's no surefire solution, but a grab bag of tricks may help save the necks of your backyard birds.

Break It Up

Large expanses of glass, undivided into panes, are the worst. To birds, they're simply invisible. The number of victims can break your heart.

When we moved into a house that was blessed—or from the birds' viewpoint, cursed—with a picture window, the body count in just 1 week in spring included wood thrushes, Swainson's thrushes, veeries, ovenbirds, warblers, and others. I covered the outside of the window with a large piece of black plastic bird netting, sold for protecting fruit crops. It wasn't pretty, but it worked.

I've used a modified version of that solution on sliding glass patio doors: I cut 2-foot squares of the same plastic netting and used suction cup hooks to stretch them here and there on the outside of the glass. Even uglier, but also effective.

At one point, I wondered whether it was just a coincidence that no birds had collided with the glass since I put up the devices, so I took them down.

Ouch! Ouch! Ouch! Three pine siskins, in rapid succession, bounced off the glass. A fluke, I figured.

An hour later, *Bang!* There went a mourning

A trio of screw-in hooks will guide a vine into a graceful swag across the top of a window. Let the side stems trail downward over the glass to help reduce the danger of the window to birds.

dove. Feathers drifted across the deck while the stunned bird gathered its wits.

Back up went the nets.

Maybe we can start a new fad of using lace curtains on the *outsides* of windows? Until that kicks into gear, you may want to plant a group of shrubs a few feet in front of the window. They won't interfere with the view, and they'll give birds a place to pause. Anything to slow them down, so that they don't hit the glass full steam ahead, will help.

Planting a tree or tall shrub in front of the window will also help, but few of us are willing to block the view. At my current house, I've grown a vigorous *Clematis montana* vine on a trellis beside a large window. When it topped the height of the window, I trained it along the top of the window and let tendrils hang down. Whatever you can come up with to break up that deadly reflection will help diminish the number of accidents.

Come a Little Bit Closer

Those panic flights, when everybody leaves the feeder in one frantic rush, often cause birds to hit windows that don't usually take a toll.

It sounds like reverse logic, I know; but in this case, the best solution may be to move the feeder *closer* to the window. A foot away is far enough. The birds get accustomed to entering and exiting the feeder area in other directions, not via the window. If any do collide with it, the bump is apt to be slight, because there's not enough distance for the bird to gather much forward force with one or two wingbeats. There's always a chance that birds will forget that that's a wall of glass be-

side them, not a getaway route, when a hawk swoops through or a jay causes a stampede, but the collisions will most likely be kept to a minimum.

Pesticides and Herbicides

Pesticides, herbicides, fungicides, and other "-cides" don't fit into a bird-friendly yard. They may or may not directly affect the health of the bird, but they *definitely* kill off the insects that birds depend upon. They can also alter the balance of organisms in the soil and affect natural cycles.

Banish the bottles from your yard care routine, and your birds will thank you.

Years ago, kids on bikes followed the cloud spewing from the mosquito truck as it fogged the streets and alleys of towns across America. Nowadays we shudder at the thought of what they inhaled. But insecticides still sell like hotcakes, even though they are known to be neurotoxins, to disrupt the endocrine system, and to have other negative effects. Let swallows and other birds be your bug control, and we'll all be healthier.

PART 2

Family by Family

Now that you've learned how birds are divided into families according to beak and behavior, it's time to see how that works in the real world—your own backyard.

Get ready for a new look at old friends. Gardening for the birds will introduce you to a whole new side of your feeder friends, the way they behave in nature.

And get set to greet a whole flock of new friends. Gardening bird-by-bird will bring in beautiful birds that you might have missed, even if you have the best feeding station in town.

Each chapter in this section focuses on a particular family of birds and tells you exactly what it likes best. You'll learn how to create a backyard version of the habitat that each family prefers, and how to serve up the natural foods that will tempt it to linger in your yard.

Whether it's a chipper little chickadee, a tuxedo-clad nuthatch, or a virtuoso thrush that catches your fancy, you'll find them all in the chapters that follow. You'll also find vireos, warblers, and other birds that rarely visit feeders, but which are surprisingly easy to attract to your yard if you pay attention to their family habits.

As you meet the families, you'll see how easy it is to accommodate them by supplying the natural foods they prefer in the surroundings that make them feel at home.

The best news? Once your favorite birds discover that your backyard is tailored to their tastes, they'll come back year after year.

Chapter 4

The Family Plan

So, who was at *your* feeder this morning? Chickadees, you say? And a whole clan of tufted titmice. The usual juncos and white-throated sparrows, a couple of cardinals, oh, and don't forget that big flicker that flew in to the suet holder.

Or maybe you had a bevy of quail come to call. Or saw an oriole pecking at an orange. Or thrilled to the sight of the first black-headed grosbeaks of the year—or the first robin.

However we answer the question of who's at the feeder or in the yard, I'm sure none of us would say, "Oh, I saw two members of the Woodpecker family, some birds of the Gallinaceous family, a half-dozen species of the Small Finch family, and a member of the Thrush family."

Birds are as particular to us as our own family members. We call each one by name, instead of identifying it as part of a clan.

That's why thinking in terms of bird families seems a little odd at first.

But the family that chickadee, junco, or robin belongs to is just as important as the bird's individual name. By learning the habits of a bird family, you'll have a whole bag of tricks for making your yard appealing to *all* members of the family.

The Families

A robin and a bluebird seem very different at first glance. Robins are as common as, well, lawn grass, and bluebirds are elusive beauties that many of us yearn for.

But they're both members of the Thrush family. And that means they share a similar style of beak, body, and behavior. So do their cousins, the veery, hermit thrush, varied thrush, and other velvet-voiced members of this family.

So, if you include plants that are a special treat for robins, you boost your chances of attracting all thrushes in your neighborhood—including fabulous bluebirds.

◀ *Add garden treats for the black-capped chickadee, and his titmouse cousins will come to visit, too.*

Apple trees are famed for hosting nesting bluebirds in spring. The fruit pulls in other thrushes, too.

Alive with insects and rich with seeds, a rustic meadow beckons to quail, flycatchers, and other birds that favor open spaces.

That's the principle behind the bird family approach. Garden for one member of a family, and you have a good chance of attracting its relatives.

How to Use the Family Chapters

Attracting birds is a combination of creating the kind of habitat they feel most at home in and supplying the foods they like best. In the family chapters, you'll find everything you need to bring in the birds of each family.

Each chapter starts with a list of family members, and a rating for how easy the family is to attract. Then you'll be introduced to the family, so that you can identify its members when you see and hear them.

You'll learn when and where to watch for them, too, so that you're not straining your eyes for birds that don't venture into your territory or looking for birds in seasons when they aren't at home in your area.

You'll discover what kind of natural habitat best suits the family, so that you can look around your area and gauge your chances of drawing birds from nearby wild places. Then you'll find out how to match that habitat in your own backyard, to make your friends feel more at home.

Each family chapter will tell you what birds like to eat in the wild, and how you can take advantage of those tastes by adding favored natural food sources to your own yard. If you keep a feeder, you'll also find a quick rundown of the feeder foods that help turn backyard birds into loyal visitors.

Finally, we'll finish the big picture with the extras that have high appeal for some birds, such as water, nesting places, and nesting materials.

Focus on Planting

Throughout the family chapters, you'll find hundreds of recommended plants and other ideas for bringing your favorite birds to your backyard.

Putting all those pieces together can make you wonder where to begin: a dozen favorite plants for this family, another dozen for that family, and so on until you're ready to slam this book shut and take up knitting.

That's why nearly all family chapters include a garden design that will appeal to the family.

"Simple and easy" are the guidelines for the garden plans in this book. Each design is one you can plant in an afternoon, and each one includes some of the top favorites for that family.

Think of the plans as a starting point. You can substitute or add other plants that you like better. And, most important, you can tie the plans together in a way that pleases your eye and suits your own yard.

My Take on Hardiness Zones

The hardiness zone listings you'll find in the plant tables in the bird family chapters are those supplied by the *American Horticultural Society's A–Z Encyclopedia of Garden Plants,* and plants are bound to flourish in those regions. That doesn't mean that you won't have good luck with them outside of those zones. Take northern bayberry (*Myrica pensylvanica*), for instance. According to the reference book, this shrub is suited for USDA Zones 3 through 6. Well, here

(continued on page 77)

Multipurpose Plants

Although each bird family prefers certain plants, many plants attract more than one family. Include some of these crossover plants in your yard, and you'll broaden the appeal.

Firs (*Abies* spp.)
Maples (*Acer* spp. and cvs.; not Japanese maples)
Serviceberries (*Amelanchier* spp. and cvs.)
Birch (*Betula* spp. and cvs.)
Dogwoods (*Cornus* spp. and cvs., including shrub types)
Hawthorns (*Crataegus* spp. and cvs.)
Sunflower (*Helianthus annuus*)
Tulip tree (*Liriodendron tulipifera*)
Apples and crabapples (*Malus* spp. and cvs., including flowering crabs)
Mulberries (*Morus* spp. and cvs.)
Bayberry (*Myrica pensylvanica*)

Prickly pear and cholla cactus (*Opuntia* spp.)
Spruce (*Picea* spp. and cvs.)
Pines (*Pinus* spp.)
Mesquite (*Prosopis* spp. and cvs.)
Cherries (*Prunus* spp., including wild cherries)
Oaks (*Quercus* spp. and cvs.)
Blackberries and raspberries (*Rubus* cvs.)
Willows (*Salix* spp. and cvs.)
Elderberries (*Sambucus* spp. and cvs.)
Hemlocks (*Tsuga* spp.)
Blueberries (*Vaccinium* cvs.)
Grapes (*Vitis* spp. and cvs.)
Zinnias (*Zinnia elegans*)

Invasive Implications

Invasive plants are those that spread to where they aren't wanted.

In the garden, the word *invasive* is sometimes used to refer to a plant that's an aggressive spreader. It goes too far, too fast, taking over garden beds or seeding itself to areas of the garden where it isn't wanted. Many goldenrods (*Solidago* spp.), bee balms (*Monarda* spp. and cultivars), horsetails (*Equisetum* spp.), mints (*Mentha* spp.), and Jerusalem artichoke (*Helianthus tuberosus*) are a few of the plants that multiply fast by spreading roots; bachelor's buttons (*Centaurea cyanea*), California poppies (*Eschscholtzia californica*), columbines (*Aquilegia* spp.), and cosmos (*Cosmos* spp.), among others, seed themselves with abandon. How much of an annoyance such plants are depends on your particular climate and conditions, and your sense of aesthetics. If you like cosmos sprinkled around your gardens, you'll cherish every seedling; if not, you'll yank them out, muttering, "Weeds!"

Plants can also be invasive in a larger sense, and this is the hot-button issue that can set off feuds among plant people.

According to the USDA, which maintains lists of invasive plants across the country, plants are considered invasive if they have been introduced into an environment where they did not evolve. Many have been with us since the first Europeans set foot here: Queen Anne's lace, thistles, and dandelions, for starters. Others were actually distributed by the USDA to supply wildlife food and habitat or halt erosion: Japanese honeysuckle, multiflora rose, Russian olive, and kudzu, to name a few. They were appealing to wildlife, all right, and birds and animals spread the seeds far and wide. And kudzu did its job of erosion control a little too well, soon blanketing vast areas.

Today, many folks are eager to attack the plants on these USDA lists as "invasives" and advocate against their use in backyard gardens. They talk about the plants as if they're mortal enemies of nature. The usual reason for the scorn? They're said to "choke out natives."

But let's take a closer look.

First of all, those lists were determined by the Department of *Agriculture*—so the plants on them were included because they caused problems for farmers and ranchers. How the plants interacted with native plants wasn't even considered, let alone studied, at first. More research into this aspect is taking place today, but usually it's limited to competition with native species on land that's already been changed by human activities, such as western rangeland.

In fact, many native plants are actually on the USDA lists of problematic plants because they can cause problems for agriculture, such as sprouting in pastures.

Most of the nonnative "invasive" plants on these hit lists have spread by way of the wind and wildlife, which carry their seeds to new locations. But in most cases, it's already-disturbed land that has become infiltrated by the plants. Multiflora roses, for example, rarely grow very deeply into the woods, but they do colonize pastures and roadsides. Bush honeysuckles, such as Morrow's honeysuckle (*Lonicera morrowii*), may find a niche along the edge of a woods, but they're mostly confined to highway interchanges and other open areas.

A danger to native plants? Not much. But definitely an aggravation for farmers, who don't have time to spare for weeding their pastures.

Invasives can, however, be a serious problem in mild climates, such as the Southeast, Florida, California, and Hawaii. There, they can quickly overwhelm less vigorous natives. If you live in such a place, it's a good idea not to tempt fate with these plants. Wetlands and waterways can also be overwhelmed by invasives.

But in many other areas, the situation isn't as clear. More science is needed—not research driven by agricultural and other economic interests, but research that weighs the effects of invasives on the ecosystem as a whole, and that factors in the damage caused by attempts to control or eradicate them. For example, we still need to learn a lot more about the effects of herbicides. But we already know that they can harm insects, fish, birds, and other wildlife, not to mention us. Is it worth spraying a pasture full of multiflora roses and destroying the balance of insects and soil life in the process? We simply don't know enough to say.

I've seen a bit of such collateral damage firsthand in a nearby national wildlife refuge, and it was heartbreaking. For weeks, my family had watched a pair of Virginia rails, an unusual marshland bird. Sitting silently for hours, we got to know the birds as they engaged in courting, mating, and nest-building—in the middle of a small patch of an "invasive" purple nightshade

My family had the honor of watching a pair of Virginia rail as the birds courted, coupled, and nested among the stems of a nonnative nightshade.

(*Solanum* spp.). Just as the female rail was sitting on her nest full of eggs, a machine was brought in to uproot the nightshade. It destroyed the nest.

Most invasives are here to stay, and eradication is impossible—how would you like the job of getting rid of every dandelion in America? Natural controls, such as the foreign beetles that were set free to prevent purple loosestrife from setting seed, keep many of them at tolerable levels. Of course, how that nonnative beetle will affect the natural balance of wetland ecosystems remains to be seen.

USDA authorities try to keep invasive plants from proliferating. States keep lists of noxious weeds and invasive plants, which include plants whose cultivation is prohibited. Since different invasive plants are problematic to different degrees in different areas, you'll find quite a bit of variation in what's listed as invasive or outright prohibited. Fountain grass (*Pennisetum* spp. and cultivars, especially 'Moudry') is on the outs in California—but a beloved garden character in the East.

Personally, I think the issue has been blown way out of proportion in most areas. With the exception of several notorious bad actors, such as purple loosestrife, reed canary grass, and English ivy, which do infiltrate deep into wild areas, most "invasives" stop quick when they run up against a healthy natural habitat.

(*continued*)

Most of these plants gain a foothold only where we ourselves have altered the natural state of affairs. Building a road, making a path, letting cattle graze on wild land—all of our many human activities open the door to invasives. But we've already altered the habitat. And a bulldozer, or a hungry herd of cattle, can destroy more native plants in a few days than invasives could crowd out in years. So can the chemicals used to control the invasives, which have damaging effects on other plants as well as on all the other life forms that get in their way.

I'm all in favor of native plants, and my yard is filled with many of them. But I'm not a "natives-only" purist. Maybe if we didn't cause so much damage ourselves, with chemicals and pollution and clearing of land, I'd feel different. But I believe that nature is ever-changing, and that there's room for many of those species that are officially called "invasives" or even "noxious weeds" in various areas. Except for a few well-known thugs, I've rarely come across invasives that have crowded out native species. In most cases, the plants manage to find a way to coexist.

Birds make excellent use of plants that may be considered invasive. They eat their berries and seeds, use the plants for cover or nesting material, and even choose them as a place to build a nest. Which is another reason I stick up for many invasives: We've destroyed so much bird habitat, so many native plants, and such multitudes of insects, that I believe birds deserve some extra help.

Sure, I long for the day when I can visit a garden center and find a wide selection of native trees and shrubs at reasonable prices. But until that happens—and also just because I'm a gardener—I'll be adding nonnatives to my yard, and some of them may be considered invasive in other areas.

Generally, if a plant is available at your local garden center or nursery, it's not a problem. Although I did find pots of purple loosestrife—in 2005, long after the plant had established its notorious reputation—at an independently owned nursery in my neck of the woods! To find out for sure, call your local USDA extension agent; you'll find the number in the blue pages of your phone book. Or visit the USDA Web site on noxious weeds and invasive plants, at http://plants.usda.gov/cgi_bin/noxious.cgi; it's fascinating reading, and you'll find many of your favorite garden plants, such as grape hyacinth, yarrow, Shasta daisy, and forget-me-not, on the list for some areas.

In this book, I've steered clear of the worst of the invasives, those that infiltrate deeply into wild lands, or whose seeds spread by water to quickly become unstoppable. We all agree that those are bad actors.

But I have included a handful of plants that may be considered invasive in some areas, including hawthorns (*Crataegus*, nonnative spp.), privet (*Ligustrum* spp.), barberries (*Berberis* spp.), burning bush (*Euonymus* spp.), and bush honeysuckles (*Lonicera* spp.), as well as natives such as switchgrass (*Panicum virgatum*), red pokeweed (*Phytolacca americana*), chokecherry (*Prunus virginiana*, which is a species of "special concern" in Tennessee, due to declining numbers, but an "invasive" in the Northeast), and others that show up on official invasive lists.

Feel free to eschew these plants and substitute a noninvasive plant, if you prefer. But next time someone tsk-tsks about an invasive plant, you might ask them: Why do you think that plant is so "bad"? What effects does it have on a natural, unadulterated ecosystem? Will its usefulness to wildlife help offset habitat destruction? And are the methods used to control it more harmful than the plant itself?

in Zone 8, it's a mainstay of gardens and commercial plantings.

Why the discrepancy? It's due to the hardiness zone map itself, which you'll find on page 392. It's a great idea, but it definitely needs fine-tuning. The divisions of the map are based solely on minimum winter temperatures, and plants are sensitive to lots of other factors besides, such as summer heat, rainfall patterns, salt air, and winter wind, to name a few. My Zone 8 in the Pacific Northwest is significantly different from Zone 8 in the Southwest, and a plant that flourishes in my yard won't necessarily do well in the desert.

So, even though zone info looks nice and tidy, it's really only an approximation.

The listings in the tables in the following chapters supply the range of zones in which some species or cultivars of that plant will thrive. If you're not sure whether a plant will thrive, refer to a regional gardening guide. Then you can see if bayberry, for instance, will actually thrive in your area, or whether it will suffer through summer begging, "Water! Water!"

The Bit-by-Bit Approach

Years ago, I used to tackle large areas of my yard all at once. I'd spend hours turning the soil, and I'd haul home carloads of plants. And I'd end up feeling overwhelmed, cranky, and frustrated that I'd worked so hard and achieved not much of anything.

Now, instead of biting off more than I can chew, I tackle small, doable projects that gave me satisfying results in a hurry. Bit by bit, I work on my yard, transforming one small section at a time.

I think of it as making a patchwork quilt—I combine small pieces to make one finished "block," then stitch the blocks together.

Even while my yard is still in progress (and it probably always will be), the effect of my garden "pieces" is more like a work of art instead of a construction zone. I can stroll around and enjoy looking at small gardens that just get better, and bigger, with time.

Think of each plan in the bird family chapters as a piece of your own patchwork quilt. Each plan is designed to tie together with any other plan, in whatever arrangement looks good to you.

For instance, you might decide to plant the Thrush family garden plan next to the Chickadee and Titmouse family plan, perhaps with the Flycatcher family plan in front. The eventual design of your yard will depend on which "pieces" you decide to stitch together. And of course you'll want to add your own touches, too!

You'll notice that each garden plan is designed for a small space. If you have a very small yard, one or two of these plans may use up most of your space. In that case, snuggle in a few of the plants recommended for other families you like, to widen the appeal. Many plants appeal to more than one family of birds, so you can do a lot even in a small space.

You can accomplish each suggested plan in an afternoon or less. It will look good from the time you put the shovel away, and it will only get better over time.

Ready to dig in? Let's meet the families.

Chapter 5

The Woodpecker Family

BIRD FAMILY: Picidae
EASE OF ATTRACTING: ★★★★★ (practically guaranteed)
BIRDS IN FAMILY: Woodpeckers · Flickers · Sapsuckers

Meet the Woodpecker Family

Don't you love it when birds have a name that makes it easy to identify them? Woodpeckers are exactly that: They peck at wood.

Within the family, genera are sorted out just as clearly. Every woodpecker species pecks at wood, but flickers show a flickering patch of white when they fly, and sapsuckers—okay, take a wild guess—yep, they sip up sap. Couldn't be simpler.

If you keep a suet feeder, you've already met at least one member of the woodpecker family. Now, by gardening for woodpeckers, you'll really get to know this crew of clowns. You'll see them doing things you never imagined—like "bathing" with ants, perhaps, or playing peekaboo with their mates, or finding dinner in ways you've never dreamed of.

Look and Listen

Like all other birds, woodpeckers' bodies go hand-in-hand with their eating habits. Pounding into a tree requires not only a strong, straight beak but also a sturdy system of support. That's why these birds have stiff, pointy tail feathers, to prop them up when they're clinging to tree trunks. Their legs are short, and their feet have long, strong toes with good-size claws: All the better for clinging to bark, thank you.

Excavating insects is a downy woodpecker's signature style. This family also adores berries and nuts and has a taste for nectar, too.

Inside a woodpecker's beak is a remarkable tongue that the bird can stick out fast and far. Bad news for bugs!

Drumroll, please. There   you've just made the signature sound of all members of this family. Believe it or not, you can learn to tell woodpeckers apart just by listening to their drum solos.

I like to track down drumming woodpeckers to hear who's who. One muggy afternoon, I clawed my way through briers and poison ivy toward the tree where I was sure that a pileated woodpecker was sounding off. The drumming was so loud and deep, it simply had to be the crow-size pileated, a bird I'll grab any opportunity to see.

Doing my best to be sneaky, I finally got to the tree, wiped the steam off my glasses, and pinpointed the bird. I couldn't believe my eyes. It was a cute little downy woodpecker. What I learned that day, and have to keep reminding myself every time I think "Pileated!," is that the resonance has more to do with the drum itself than with the drummer. And this guy must've had himself a bass drum branch.

Each species does have its own variations of tempo and length of effort. With practice, you can learn who's sounding off just as you learn the songs of passerines, or songbirds. The sapsucker is one of my favorites to ID by ear, no doubt because it's so easy. To me, these birds sound like jazz artists, with an almost syncopated rhythm.

Woodpeckers also vocalize, as well as pound away. These aren't songbirds, and you wouldn't call it singing. Most have loud, raucous or harsh calls and chirrs. Many are pretty easy to mimic, and it's fun to call back. In spring, your efforts could draw a territorial male to see the new "bird" in his neighborhood.

When woodpeckers are flying rather than sticking tight to a tree, they're easy to identify even when they're so far away that you can't see any colors. All share a distinctive undulating pattern of flight, like the scalloped edge of my kitchen curtain.

Range of Woodpeckers

Every part of the country has its woodpeckers. Some, such as the familiar downy, are commonly seen just about everywhere. Other widespread species, including the spectacular red-headed woodpecker, occur only in limited neighborhoods within their range, so they're a treat to see. (Ready to go try our luck with ivory-billed woodpeckers in the Big Woods of Arkansas?)

The eastern half of the country is home to only a handful of woodpeckers, including one flicker and one sapsucker—the much-mocked yellow-bellied version. Counting the eastern species of the Far North, the possibilities number about nine.

But in the West, nearly double that number of species make their home. Seems a little unfair, I know, but most of these birds stick to separate niches: gila woodpeckers in the saguaro desert, acorn woodpeckers near oaks, and red-naped sapsuckers toward aspens and cottonwoods.

This family is famed for straying outside the lines. No matter how carefully scientists try to plot their range, the birds often disregard it and show up elsewhere. Weather is often a factor, with the birds getting off base in storms.

After a blizzard swept across the country into eastern Pennsylvania one year, I went outside to clear off the feeders and made a sad discovery. Buried under the snow was a hybrid red-shafted northern flicker, a bird whose range begins in the Great Plains—a thousand miles away from where I found him.

Best dressed? The regal red-headed woodpecker is common only in limited areas of its wide range.

Now You See 'em . . .

Most woodpeckers are year-round birds. They don't take seasonal vacations to warm climates or depart for faraway nesting grounds when spring rolls around. Some individual birds may make short trips in winter, but incoming birds quickly fill the gap, and others, even of the same species, don't relocate at all.

That's one reason why woodpeckers are so rewarding to tempt to your yard. When your yard is full of the plants they like, plus a well-stocked feeder, you're likely to see them year-round.

A few woodpeckers do migrate beyond short hops. All sapsuckers go to milder areas in winter. The red-bellied and Lewis's woodpeckers leave the colder parts of their range in winter, and the northern flicker withdraws from some northern areas. But everybody else pretty much stays put, so they're possible customers for the winter handout in your yard. If migrants leave your area for the winter, you can count on them coming back in spring, hungry and hopeful.

Family Habits of Woodpeckers

Got any couch potatoes in the family? Then you'll already be familiar with the sedentary habits of woodpeckers. Compared to energetic chickadees and other birds, woodpeckers are slowpokes. They stay in one location for long periods of time rather than frenetically covering ground, because that big bag of Doritos, so to speak, is close at hand.

But that doesn't mean they're not industrious. Woodpeckers are constantly and tirelessly searching for food; they just don't cover as much ground to do it. It's kind of like walking from the sofa to the kitchen, instead of flitting from one restaurant to the next.

The best place to look for woodpeckers? Clinging to a tree. Woodpeckers spend hours hitching around the trunk or working at an excavation. Sometimes they move to another tree, or occasionally they fly a longer stretch to another area to look for food.

When flying insects are active, woodpeckers come alive. Their habits switch from sit-and-peck to behavior that's more like that of a flycatcher. They perch on a good lookout branch, fly out to nab a passing insect, return to the perch, and do it again, over and over. That's one of the best ways to spot woodpeckers, especially the red-headed—just look for a bird "flycatching" from the tip of a tree.

As a general rule, the bigger the woodpecker, the more secretive it is. The downy, for instance, has very little fear of humans. But its larger lookalike cousin, the hairy, is likely to fly off when you come near.

Still, all of the Woodpecker family, except the giant ivory-billed, are likely to turn up in an inviting backyard, if you live within their range.

Woodpeckers often join roving groups of foragers in winter, tagging along with a mixed batch of chickadees, nuthatches, titmice, and kinglets.

At-Home Habitat of Woodpeckers

Trees. That's the short answer to what makes woodpeckers feel at home. Most members of this

A yellow-shafted northern flicker threatens a rival.

family live in areas with good-sized trees, whether it's a city park, your backyard, or a national forest.

Woodpeckers not only eat in trees, they nest in them, too. These are cavity-nesting birds, and they peck out a home to fit their needs in a dead or living tree. Members of this family also leave the trees to scout out other favorite foods. Flickers often get right down to ground level to enjoy a helping of scurrying ants.

The Wild Side

Most woodpecker species aren't fussy. They make use of whatever trees grow within their natural range, whether they're natives or nursery types. As long as there are plenty of insects to be found by pecking into tree trunks and branches, woodpeckers are right at home. And, by the way, the classic saguaro cactus of the Southwest, with its stout trunk and arms, serves perfectly well as a tree.

The acorn woodpecker definitely needs oaks to supply the food it collects for eating later. Its storage areas look like an odd Chinese checkers game board, with an acorn stuffed into each hole.

Backyard Matchup

Since woodpeckers spend much of their time in trees, no matter what's growing at their base, it can be a cinch to attract them to your yard. If you are lucky enough to have an older shade tree of any kind, you've got the makings of a woodpecker garden.

If you live in an area dotted with larger street trees or shade trees, woodpeckers are probably already regulars at your place. If your yard has no trees or only very young ones, try a two-part approach: Plant fruit and nut trees for a fast crop of enticing food, and plant a dead tree.

Well, more like a dead branch, since few of us have the brawn to maneuver an entire dead tree into place.

Planting a dead tree will instantly catch a woodpecker's attention. I like to pick out real branches with graceful curves that look like garden art to my eye. Driftwood is my favorite find. First of all, it's free! It's also interestingly

Secondhand Homes

It's thanks to woodpeckers that lots of other cavity-nesting birds have a home. The beaks of chickadees, titmice, and others aren't stout enough to do heavy construction work on a nesting cavity. So they often adopt a woodpecker's home after the woodpecker is finished using it.

The bufflehead duck, an adorable black-and-white butterball, is one of the duck species that, incredible as it seems, nests in holes in trees. Buffleheads depend mainly on flickers for their housing needs. A flicker's nest cavity is just the right size for this small duck and its brood. When the ducklings hatch, they hop out and tumble down to what we hope isn't too hard of a landing, then skedaddle after their mother to reach water.

Acorn woodpeckers, another striking species, have the peculiar habit of turning trees and poles into their pantries.

shaped, and it's usually sturdy enough to last a few years after "planting."

I've also planted larger limbs that came down in a storm. Right now, I have my eye on a dying snag at the top of a bigleaf maple (*Acer macrophylla*) in the neighbor's yard. I'm hoping that the next time we get a good stiff wind, it may land in my yard.

Go for the biggest branch you can maneuver. Remember that you'll need to bury about 3 feet of it in the ground, to hold it steady. I'm not Hercules, by any stretch of imagination, but I've discovered that I can lift and transport a branch as big as 8 inches in diameter and 12 feet long if I

balance it just right. Of course, a helper makes things a lot easier!

If you don't want to plant a dead branch, or can't find one, try an unpainted wooden fence post or a piece of 4 × 4 lumber.

Trees, dead or alive, and the utility poles around your house make great stepping-stones for woodpeckers on their daily travels.

But you don't need to turn your yard into a woods to attract woodpeckers. Although woodsy yards are appealing to this family, a sunnier backyard with a shade tree or two, a few young fruit trees for extra allure, a patch of lawn, and flower or vegetable beds will suit them just fine.

Watch those woodpeckers in open spaces, and you'll see that they use nearby trees, poles, arbors, and other sturdy perches as staging sites: They fly from them and return to them after visiting your lawn or garden.

Bad Press

Woodpeckers take plenty of interest in nonnative trees—sometimes a little too much so. Orchardists and nut growers often consider the birds as pests. They devour nuts and fruits by the bushel.

Sapsuckers, especially, are often maligned as undesirables, because some growers believe that their feeding habits weaken orchard trees.

It's simply not true. In healthy trees, the bark soon heals, although the rows of scars will remain.

Personally, I like to see those neat lines of little holes, the evidence that sapsuckers have been sipping at my trees. And I've never seen a loss of vigor in a tree, no matter how heavily woodpeckers have been working at it.

(continued on page 88)

Happy Landings

With chisel beaks and a sweet tooth, woodpeckers will come for the wood and stay for the fruit.

This planting starts with a dead branch or wooden post, to offer woodpeckers a secure landing site when they come to investigate. The plums are fast-growing small trees, good for any size yard. They're beautiful in spring, with a drift of sweet-smelling spring flowers.

The fragrant blossoms of plum trees, usually white but occasionally soft pink, attract multitudes of insects for woodpeckers and other birds. And wait'll you see how many plums a plum tree produces! Any plum variety sold as a fruit tree will produce bushels of tasty fruit, so pick whichever one sounds good to you. To maximize bird appeal, steer clear of purpleleaf plum (*Prunus cerasifera* 'Thundercloud' and other cultivars), an ornamental tree with moody, dark foliage and lovely flowers, but with little or no fruit.

You can plant this garden in a sunny spot at the edge of your lawn, digging up only as much turf as you need to make planting holes. Or place it near a vegetable or flower bed that will also interest woodpeckers. It's ideal near your feeding station, too, where woodpeckers can move from treats in feeders to treats in trees. (For extra temptation, nail a suet feeder to the dead branch or post.)

Plant List

1. Plum trees, any cultivar; for a bargain, buy bareroot trees, available in early spring for as little as $10 (3 trees) (Hardiness Zones 5–10)

2. Dead branch or wooden post, about 4 to 6 inches in diameter and about 8 to 12 feet long (1 dead branch)

3. 'Carlton' or 'Ice Follies' daffodils (12 bulbs) (Hardiness Zones 4–8)

Garden Size
20' × 10'

Scale of Plan
1/4" = 1 1/2'

When you're planting fruit trees for the birds, you won't have to worry about pruning, pests, or perfect fruit. Just enjoy the trees as their flowers and fruit attract woodpeckers, warblers, vireos, and other birds.

Surefire Plants to Attract Woodpeckers

Insects are the main menu item of woodpeckers, but that doesn't mean the birds don't like some variety in their diet. This family can't resist nuts and fruit. Try these plants for future crops of fruits, berries, nuts—and woodpeckers.

Plant	Type of Plant	Description	Zones
Apple (*Malus,* any cultivar)	Deciduous tree	Small to medium size trees, depending on cultivar	4–8
Virginia creeper (*Parthenocissus quinquefolia*)	Deciduous vine	To about 30 ft, with gorgeous red fall leaves	3–9
Oak (*Quercus,* any species or cultivar)	Large deciduous tree	To 80 ft; columnar forms available for smaller spaces	4–10
Staghorn sumac, species form *not* cutleaf (*Rhus typhina*)	Single or multi-stemmed deciduous shrub	To about 10 ft, with vivid red fall foliage and fuzzy clusters of small berries	3–8
Saw palmetto (*Serenoa repens*)	Evergreen shrub	Like a small palm, with fans of sharp-edged leaves creating a large clump about 6 ft tall, with a cluster of berries that ripen to black	9–10
Common mullein (*Verbascum thapsus*)	Biennial	Rosette of soft gray leaves at ground level, from which emerges a flowering stem about 4 ft tall in the second year	3–9

Used for	Comments	Other Birds Attracted
Fruit	If you want a few apples for yourself, try disease-resistant cultivars such as 'Liberty' or 'Yellow Delicious.'	Warblers, vireos, tanagers, and orioles are attracted to small insects at the flowers; finches, jays, thrushes, and mimic thrushes enjoy the fruit, especially any that remains in winter.
Berries	Grow on a wood arbor so that wood-peckers have an easier time getting to the berries.	Thrushes, mimic thrushes, gros-beaks, and others also eat berries.
Insect food; acorns; insects in bark; with age, possible nesting sites	Useful to birds even when the trees are young, because of the insects attracted to them.	Warblers, vireos, tanagers, gros-beaks, and many other birds use oaks for insect food and nesting; jays, titmice, nuthatches, chicka-dees, and wild turkeys adore acorns.
Berries	Sumac berries attract woodpeckers in winter.	Bluebirds and other thrushes
Berries	A native plant of the American Southeast. Grows well under pines and in sandy soil. Avoid brushing against it; it's earned its name. Waxy coating on leaves fuels wildfires in the Southeast.	Warblers, vireos, and other birds visit the flowers to collect insects; wild turkeys, quail (and black bears!) also eat the fruits; Florida scrub jays and native sparrows collect fibers for nest building.
Insect food	Downy and hairy woodpeckers visit mullein stalks in winter to eat insects and possibly seeds. Self-sows moderately. Transplanting can be difficult, because of the taproot; move only young plants.	Native sparrows, finches, humming-birds, and other small birds use the flowerstalks for perching places.

Natural Foods for Woodpeckers

Insects, fruits and berries, and nuts are the big three for woodpeckers, with insects making up about two-thirds to three-quarters of the menu. Add a sampling of seeds on the side, and woodpeckers are happy.

Most woodpeckers dig for insects buried in the wood or hidden beneath the bark of trees. But sapsuckers have a sweet tooth: They drill a series of small holes, just enough to puncture the tree so that sap seeps slowly into the holes; then they return to drink the sap and snatch up insects that have also been attracted to it.

Main Menu: Insects, Berries, and Nuts

Late at night, when our 100-year-old family home was especially quiet, I would often hear a steady, rhythmic gnawing noise. It was way too soft to be a mouse, but it was definitely the sound of something chewing.

My mother and father couldn't hear it.

"Put your ear against the wall," I suggested. "It sounds louder then."

A red-breasted sapsucker leaves its calling card: rows of small holes where sweet sap collects.

They tried, but they couldn't detect anything.

Months later, my father was poking around in the cellar, two stories below my bedroom, and stumbled across a tidy pile of fine sawdust. He hurried for a brighter light and his big pock-

Snacking on the Siding

Wood siding on your house usually attracts woodpeckers for the same reason that trees do—there are bugs in your belfry. Or, to be more exact, some kind of insect has moved into your wood siding and is beginning to eat you out of house and home.

If the hammering is annoying, or if you fear that it's damaging your house, check your Yellow Pages for a pest control company that specializes in woodpecker antidotes. Using safe pest control measures, such as replacing the insect-infested wood, should restore your peace and quiet. Once the insects are gone, the woodpecker will quickly lose interest.

Adding shrubs such as vivid staghorn sumac (*Rhus typhina*) among your flowers adds beauty and bird value. Sumac berries draw woodpeckers in winter.

etknife. When he poked the knife into one of the floor joists, the wood crumbled away, revealing the tunnels of a busy colony of powder-post beetles, a scourge that does exactly what the name says—turns posts to powder.

My parents ended up replacing beams. But I was enthralled by the notion that I had actually heard the beetle larvae chewing.

For humans, those tiny noises are easy to miss. But for woodpeckers, they're a clue that food is nearby. When their sharp ears pick up the sound of insects active in the wood or beneath the bark, it's time to hammer away to get at the goodies.

Many kinds of insect larvae, insect eggs, and insects themselves are the target, including cicadas, caterpillars, wood-boring beetles, aphids, and other critters. On the ground, woodpeckers zero in on ants, grasshoppers, crickets, and beetles.

The berries of native plants, especially hackberry (*Celtis occidentalis*), blueberry, staghorn sumac (*Rhus typhina*), and Virginia creeper (*Parthenocissus quinquefolia*), are a big hit. Poison ivy and poison oak berries (*Rhus* spp.) are favored, too, which is one of the reasons these plants pop up all over the place from the seeds that pass through birds.

Acorns, beechnuts, pecans, and all other nuts are eagerly sought. So are corn and giant ragweed (a plant you won't want to invite into your yard, no matter how much birds love it!), by some species.

Woodpeckers are at a disadvantage when it comes to eating the seeds of many plants, because they need a secure perch for their big bodies. The seeds they eat in the wild are usually on plants with stout stems, where they can get a grip without bending a delicate stem to the ground.

But when food is the draw, woodpeckers can be surprisingly acrobatic. They contort themselves into amazing positions, often using their tails as counterbalances, so they can reach the prize.

Backyard Fare

Insects are a given in a yard that's not sprayed with pesticides, so your woodpeckers will find plenty of natural fodder in your trees and gardens. Besides hammering on your trees, you may see them

The fruits of saw palmetto, a common Southeast native, are too big for small birds to eat, but red-bellied woodpeckers visit these and other palms.

or native plums (*Prunus* spp.), which you can find at specialty nurseries or through mail-order catalogs, send up suckers that expand the planting. They make a good hedge or naturalistic thicket, with clouds of fragrant white flowers followed by bite-size fruit.

Let Virginia creeper (*Parthenocissus quinquefolia*) cover a freestanding trellis that has room for a woodpecker to get a grip, or let the vine scramble up a tree to add a flash of red fall color and a built-in perch. Or try an arbor of grapes, such as hardy, trouble-free 'Concord'.

Stout-stemmed mulleins (*Verbascum* spp., especially common mullein, *V. thapsus*) are beautiful in a flower garden, thanks to their rosettes of soft, felted gray leaves. Let the finished flower stalks stand through winter, and you're likely to see woodpeckers examining them for hidden insects.

In desert gardens, cactus fruit, including that of prickly pear (*Opuntia* spp.) is popular with gilded flickers and other woodpeckers. Woodpeckers also approve of figs. In the Southeast, saw palmetto fruit (*Serenoa repens*) will tempt them to your yard.

Even your vegetable garden can be a hot spot for woodpeckers. You may see red-headed and red-bellied woodpeckers checking out the corn or tall sunflowers, or giving you a hand by picking off beetles and caterpillars or cabbage butterflies in flight.

Your lawn is an inviting place for flickers. Take a closer look when robins, starlings, or grackles are poking around in your grass, and you'll often spot a big brown flicker or two—or a dozen, during spring or fall migration. They're ex-

plucking off caterpillars and beetles, or catching butterflies, grasshoppers, and wasps in flight.

You can plant a butterfly garden to provide snacks on the wing or juicy caterpillars. My mother's big clumps of heavy-headed peonies drew flickers every spring, thanks to the ants on the flowers—a favorite flicker food.

Fruit is a major motivation for woodpecker visits, so why not add a fruit tree, or two or three? Cherries (*Prunus* spp.), mulberries (*Morus* spp.), apples and crabapples (*Malus* spp.), and plums (*Prunus* spp.) are popular. Elderberry (*Sambucus nigra*), staghorn sumac (*Rhus typhina*), and wild

Woodpecker Harvest

Some years ago, I thumbed off a few kernels from a leftover ear of Indian corn into a back corner of a flower bed, just to see what would come up. What came up were sturdy plants with foliage tinged with purple and red, a statuesque backdrop to the zinnias in front.

When a few ears started to form, I got pretty darn excited. I was dying to know what colors were hidden under those husks, but I didn't want to wreck them before they ripened, so I left them alone.

Then I got distracted by other garden goings-on, and I forgot all about the Indian corn for a while. I was looking out the window one morning when I saw a red-bellied woodpecker fly into the patch and make himself at home, bracing his tail against a cornstalk. Bending over, he grabbed a piece of husk and firmly pulled it away from the ear. While I wavered between watching and running out to chase him away, the bird extracted one kernel after another from my lovely red-and-purple ear of Indian corn, which was now looking pretty moth-eaten.

Corn is a beautiful plant, adding an almost tropical feel at the back of a flower garden. If you can shoehorn a few corn plants into your yard, woodpeckers may visit the ears from the time the corn is still fresh until it's hard and dry. They'll come back all winter, until every last kernel is eaten.

That kind of entertainment makes it worth buying your own Indian corn for decorations at the farmers' market, and leaving the garden corn to the birds.

The red-bellied woodpecker is a suet regular—and a corn snitcher.

---

tracting grubs of Japanese beetles, plus the larvae of other insects.

Feeder Foods for Woodpeckers

Woodpeckers are reliable visitors at feeders. Even if your yard isn't exactly Deadwood City, they'll keep coming back if you stock these favorites at the snack bar:

Suet
Insect foods, including mealworms, waxworms, and bug-enriched suet
Nuts and nut spreads, including peanut butter, almond butter, and others
Corn
Sunflower seeds

Nesting Needs of Woodpeckers

One of the easiest ways to get woodpeckers to your yard is to put up birdhouses, or nest boxes. Choose the size of the box according to the kind of woodpeckers you want to attract. The small downy, for example, feels more at home in a box tailored to its size than in a large flicker box.

You'll need a ladder to mount the box. Attach it to a tree, about 15 to 25 feet from the ground.

Little Extras for Woodpeckers

When I see ants swarming out of a crack in the sidewalk, I don't rush for the kettle of boiling water. Instead, I watch for woodpeckers to arrive—flickers, to be exact. They not only eat ants, they also "bathe" in them. If you catch them in the act, it's an amazing sight.

You may see the bird settle in the midst of the ants, raising its wings and fluffing its feathers to allow the ants to crawl all over it. Or you may see a woodpecker with an ant in its bill, wiping the insect over its own body like a bath sponge.

What's the point? Ants contain formic acid—that's what makes their bite so irritating—and scientists theorize that the substance repels or controls bird lice and other feather pests.

A Good Word for Short-Lived Trees

Oaks, maples, and other classic shade trees require decades to gain size—and even longer to sport some dead wood. But a Lombardy poplar (*Populus nigra* var. *italica*), a notoriously short-lived tree, can be just the ticket for woodpecker fans.

Lombardies are columnar trees that grow super fast from cuttings or rooted plants. Three to five years after planting, the trees may be 30 feet tall. And that's the beginning of the end. Their weak wood is attacked by insects (read: woodpecker food!) and disease, and before you know it, dead branches and dead trunks are poking up amid the surviving greenery.

You can buy Lombardy poplars at reasonable prices, but why waste even a few bucks? Cut a few live branches in early spring from a neighbor's tree, strip off the bottom foot of leaves, and stick the bare ends in moist soil. Keep them watered, and they'll root fast and take off like lightning. Of course, you'll want to plant these soon-to-be sad sacks away from parking areas and streets. But they make a great fast hedge, or a single specimen. And, before you know it, they'll be attracting woodpeckers to chomp on bugs and chisel out homes.

Chapter 6

The Flycatcher Family

FAMILY NAME: Tyrannidae

EASE OF ATTRACTING: ★★★ (moderately easy)

BIRDS IN FAMILY: Flycatchers · Pewees · Phoebes · Kingbirds

Meet the Flycatcher Family

Next time you come across a cloud of swarming gnats, give yourself a little test: See if you can isolate one of the insects and follow only its movements with your eyes.

Like watching a snowflake in a blizzard, isn't it? Following a flying insect is just about impossible for us to do. But it's child's play for a flycatcher.

Flycatchers are the bane of flying insects. They're fast and agile in the air, and turn on a dime when they're in pursuit. All of the more than three dozen species in this big family share the same style of feeding: perch, pursuit; perch, pursuit. A flycatcher sits alertly on a perch, then darts after a flying insect, grabs it, and returns to a perch. Repeat until the belly is full!

Look and Listen

When I was in junior high, my most dreaded class was Home Ec, where a dragon lady of a teacher screamed at us over stitches that weren't fine enough, or popovers that were soggy in the middle. Years later, when I came back to sewing and cooking on my own, I was surprised to find out they were actually fun to do, even if the results were less than perfect.

I can't say the same for the posture lessons that were part of those classes. At the end of the class, we'd stand in a line and settle a heavy book just so on our heads. Then we'd walk around the room, gliding like queens. Or at least that was the idea. My book invariably landed on the floor with a loud bang—until I figured out that if I wore my ponytail really high on the back of my head, I could cheat and rest the book against it.

What does perfect posture have to do with flycatchers? Every species looks as though it'd spent years under the tutelage of my home ec teacher, getting that regal bearing just right.

Flycatchers can be small, medium, large, or extra-large, but all sit erect and alert when perched. Most are greenish or grayish, and many are so hard to tell apart by looks that birdwatchers listen for their voices to make sure of who's who. On the other hand, some species, such as the vermilion flycatcher of the Southwest and the Say's phoebe of the West, are spectacularly colored.

Most flycatchers have unexciting songs, often a repeated pair of syllables that blends into the general symphony of birdsong. A few, including the kingbirds and great crested flycatcher, are attention grabbers, with sharp whistles or whoops. And a few species, including the phoebes and the peewees, very kindly say their own names—well, if you use your imagination.

Flycatchers, like this Say's phoebe, seek a conspicuous perch from which they can dash out after insects, then return to wait for the next.

Range of Flycatchers

Flycatchers blanket the country, occurring just about everywhere flying insects are found. Each species has its own range, with some covering half the country and others limited to a tiny corner of a single state.

Nearby habitat affects which flycatchers you

Faux Flycatchers

Once you start looking for flycatching behavior, you'll notice that it's a habit with other birds, too.

When mayflies or other insects are hatching and rising from a stream or lake, a flock of cedar waxwings often settles in trees along the water, taking turns darting out and snatching a bite on the wing, then returning to a perch until the next mayfly comes along.

Red-headed woodpeckers display the same behavior from the top of a utility pole or other perch. So do kinglets, warblers, gnatcatchers, bushtits, chickadees, hummingbirds, and others.

These birds are "flycatching." But they're not flycatchers.

True flycatchers depend on this style of feeding most of the time, while other birds flycatch only now and then.

Many birders depend on their ears to identify flycatchers. This willow flycatcher will say "FITZ-bew"; the look-alike alder says "reeBEEuh."

The eastern phoebe is as reliable a spring harbinger as the robin. Its mossy nest is often plastered over the door of a garden shed.

might see at your own place. If you live on a ranch in the West, or next to a forest, or beside a lake, your chances of seeing flycatchers are far better than someone who lives in a city.

Most small species hang out in brushy areas, some haunt the woodlands, and many stick to the rich hunting grounds near water. Some are birds of open country, such as the dapper kingbirds and the incredible scissor-tailed flycatcher that trails a deeply forked tail that's nearly twice as long as its body.

Of all the many flycatchers, only a few are likely to show up in backyards. The phoebes, the great crested flycatcher, and the eastern and western kingbirds are top candidates.

Now You See 'em . . .

Flycatchers survive almost entirely on insects, with a small helping of fruits and berries on the side. So, when cold weather nears, spelling the demise of their diet, the birds hightail it to warmer areas, from Mexico southward.

When insects once again are active in spring, flycatchers move northward.

Family Habits of Flycatchers

You know those chases on the nature channel, with the cheetah or lion tearing after big game, zigging and zagging close behind? (The ones when I usually switch the channel before the denouement.)

On a small scale, that's the same drama of a flycatcher chase.

When flycatchers are catching flies—or bees, wasps, dragonflies, butterflies, and a horde of other flying insects—they're just as focused as any cheetah. Of course, it helps to have a mouth that works like a dustpan and broom. Flycatcher beaks open w-i-d-e, and special short, stiff feathers around the beak help sweep the insect right in.

Flycatchers aren't particularly secretive, but they're definitely "background" birds. Most species are easy to overlook, even though they usually perch in conspicuous places—the tip of a tree, or a dead branch, say. When you spot a perched bird with good posture, watch its tail: Most flycatchers share the habit of raising and lowering their tails while perched.

Many species erect their head feathers when they get excited. Some flycatchers can be aggressive birds—to each other, and to other birds or predators in their area. Top candidates for temper? Kingbirds and the genus known as tyrant flycatchers, of which the great crested is one species. They'll attack snakes, cats, hawks, and other flycatchers that stray into their territory.

At-Home Habitat

Where are multitudes of flying insects most likely to be found? Near water, when mayflies, mosquitoes, and other insects that have spent their early life stages underwater become adults, and break through the surface into the air. And over grassy fields, where grasshoppers and crickets abound. Flycatchers are common in both places.

You'll have good luck finding flycatchers if you watch for them on exposed perches in the shady brush along water. That's the preferred habitat of many members in this family. But with

The delicate wings of a hairstreak butterfly are only an impediment to a flycatcher. They're quickly stripped before the plump body is swallowed.

Alert posture, always on the lookout, is a trademark of flycatchers. This western kingbird coasts gracefully to a landing, with wings spread wide.

such a number of species, just about every niche in nature is covered by these birds.

The Wild Side

Within the flycatcher family, the genera have distinct preferences for habitat, even though their eating style is the same.

For many species, a brushy habitat near water is the preferred place. Kingbirds and phoebes, however, are birds of open country, and so is the gotta-see-it-to-believe-it scissor-tailed flycatcher.

Flycatchers also patrol the forests; that's where you'll find the ash-throated, brown crested, and great crested flycatchers. Desert species are found in sagebrush and chaparral, flycatchers of the Great Plains in fields or in trees or bushes along watercourses.

Despite these differences, flycatchers share a need for perches from which to mount their attacks. Depending on the region, that can be a barbed-wire fence, a tall tree, a rock, or the branch of a shrubby willow.

Backyard Matchup

An ordinary yard, with a mix of trees, shrubs, and open spaces, suits most flycatchers, as long as there's plenty to eat. If you have a garden pool, you can fringe its edge with shrubby willows, to recreate a smidgen of naturalistic habitat. Or you can plant a hedge of mixed fruiting shrubs and trees to supply food and create good habitat.

But it's the combination of perches and flying insects that really make a yard attractive to these birds. You'll learn more about supplying bugs and fruit later in this chapter. For now, let's focus on perches.

Trees and shrubs of any kind may serve the purpose. Open branches, dead limbs, or an inviting tree tip allow a flycatcher to settle on the exposed perch it prefers. Flowering cherries (*Prunus* cvs.) and willow trees (*Salix* spp.) are ideal as perch plants, because their foliage is fairly sparse and the top of the plant invites a good grip.

But manufactured objects in the midst of shrubbery, trees, and open space are even better. Ever notice how your eye goes right to the man-made objects in a garden? Flycatchers respond just as fast to nonnatural perches.

You can easily incorporate some of these into your yard:

- Iron shepherd's-crook-type hooks
- Metal or wood arbors and arches
- Metal or wood trellises
- Stand-alone posts with a decorative finial that's securely attached, and a suitable shape for a bird to grip onto. A fleur-de-lis is fine; a ball is not.
- Bamboo teepees, such as a bean tower
- Wire or twig structures, such as tuteurs
- Wash lines

Keep in mind that the purpose of a flycatcher perch is to allow a clear view of flying insects and an unobstructed takeoff when a tasty morsel flies into sight. In most cases, a tall perch—6 feet high or better—is preferable to a shorter one of only 3 or 4 feet because it affords the bird a better view.

(continued on page 102)

Flycatcher Flower Garden

Catch a flycatcher's fancy with fluttering butterflies and a place to perch.

Flycatchers follow the insects to this flower garden, but many more birds on the block, from cardinals to goldfinches, will find something to crow about in this flower-filled oasis. It will attract insects, butterflies, and other nectar seekers in summer. And in fall and winter, it will appeal to small seed-eating birds, such as goldfinches and juncos, and rose hip eaters, such as jays and mimic thrushes.

This plan is easy to tuck into a sunny spot of about 5 by 8 feet.

Since we want our gardens to please us as well as the birds, this one relies on extra-long-blooming flowers that will make this a bright spot of color for months, from early summer until frost. Let the sunflowers and coneflower stems remain standing after they die in fall, to supply cover for feeding birds. The rose will hold its leaves well into winter, and the low-growing alyssum will bloom even through several frosts.

Plant List

1. Purple coneflowers (*Echinacea purpurea*) (3 plants) (Hardiness Zones 3–9)

2. 'Pink Knockout' shrub rose (1 plant) (Hardiness Zones 4–9)

3. 'Vanilla Ice' sunflowers (*Helianthus* 'Vanilla Ice') (1 packet of seed)

4. White sweet alyssum plants (*Lobularia maritime*) (1 six-pack)

5. 'Lemon Gem' marigolds (2 packets of seed)

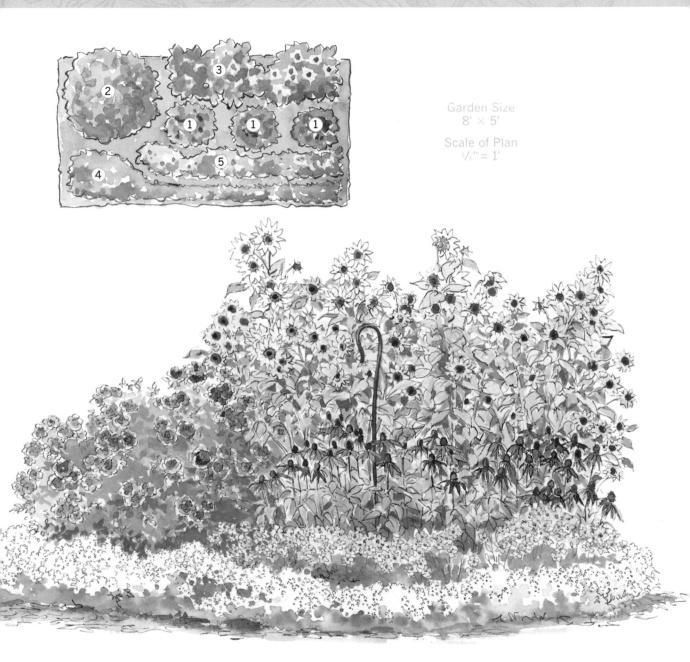

Garden Size
8' × 5'

Scale of Plan
3/8" = 1'

The black shepherd's hook is more than a punctuation point here—it's an inviting perch from which flycatchers can sally forth to catch the butterflies and other insects drawn to the flowers.

Surefire Plants to Attract Flycatchers

These plants attract butterflies and other flying insects, or supply fruit, nesting materials, and perching places for flycatchers in your neighborhood.

Plant	Type of Plant	Description	Zones
Milkweeds (*Asclepias* spp.)	Perennial plants to 4 ft tall	Varies according to spp., but all form clumps and many spread by roots; flowers are complex and deliciously fragrant, mature into seedpods filled with silken seed "parachutes."	3–9
Thornless blackberries (*Rubus* × 'Chester')	Deciduous, suckering shrub, to about 6 ft	Fast-growing stems supply perches; bountiful, juicy fruit	5–9
Willows (*Salix* spp., *not* corkscrew type)	Shrubs to medium-size trees, depending on species	Long, thin leaves; deciduous; twigs become colorful in late winter; catkin flowers mature to fuzz.	3–9
Elderberries (*Sambucus* spp. and cultivars)	Deciduous shrubs or small trees, to 15 ft tall, depending on spp.	Fast-growing, multistemmed; large white flower clusters ripen into small, juicy berries.	3–9
Goldenrods (*Solidago* spp. and cultivars)	Perennial plants, most 3 to 4 ft tall	Clusters of tight-packed, small yellow flowers	5–9

Used for	Comments	Other Birds Attracted
Nesting material; flowers attract butterflies and other insects for flycatchers to eat.	Take a look through a magnifying glass at the unusual flowers.	Orioles eat insects; hummingbirds seek nectar.
Larger flycatchers, including great crested, eat the fruit.	Why worry about wicked thorns when you can have smooth canes?	Thrushes, mimic thrushes, jays, wrens, and other birds eat berries; mimic thrushes may nest.
Nest sites, nesting material	Experiment with species that are native to your region.	Warblers, orioles, vireos, chickadees, and titmice glean insects and may collect nest material.
Food from insects at flowers; food from berries; nest sites	To keep the bush vigorous, cut some of the older stems down to the ground each year in late winter.	Orioles, tanagers, thrushes, mimic thrushes, woodpeckers, and wrens eat insects at flowers and may eat berries.
Flying insects travel to and from flowers.	Many goldenrods are aggressive spreaders, best in a naturalistic garden.	Vireos, warblers, and other insect eaters

Natural Foods for Flycatchers

Insects win by a mile in the flycatcher world. Fruit comes in a distant runner-up, with only some species dining upon it.

Main Menu: Insects

A smorgasbord of insects fills the beaks of flycatchers. Gnats, flies, bees, wasps, butterflies, moths, tree hoppers: Seems like anything with wings is fair game. Spiders go down the hatch, too. Even giant cicadas aren't safe; the larger flycatchers are happy to make a meal of them.

Many of the insects are nabbed on the wing. But flycatchers also pluck them from plants. When a 17-year-cicada brood hatched near my home in southern Indiana, the hapless bugs were snatched up by great crested flycatchers as soon as they began to sing. Sometimes it just doesn't pay to advertise.

When berries ripen, many flycatchers make a beeline for the fruity change of pace. Wild blackberries, elderberries, mistletoe berries, honeysuckle berries (*Lonicera* spp.), and other small, soft berries are favored.

I saw my first scissor-tailed flycatcher in unusual conditions: hundreds of miles off course, and drunk as a skunk. The bird showed up in eastern Pennsylvania one autumn, far from its usual haunts in Oklahoma and Texas. He'd taken refuge in a roadside hedgerow that was thick with wild cherries. The fruit was past its prime—so far past that it had started to ferment. Didn't bother Mr. Flycatcher in the least. Although he was already a little too wobbly to fly, he kept on swilling down the fruit.

Backyard Fare

A butterfly garden is one of the best ways to attract flycatchers to your yard. If you plant flowers and host plants that butterflies find attractive, you'll have a good chance of catching the attention of a flycatcher, too.

Your vegetable garden can be a good source of flying insects as well, especially if cabbage butterflies are fluttering around. These white butterflies are easy to see from a distance, which may be why they're so popular with flycatchers and other insect-eating birds.

Thanks to their myriad of small blossoms, herbs are ideal for attracting butterflies big and small. Common oregano is a favorite of swallowtails.

Bird-Planted Plantations

Seeds of berries and fruits pass unharmed through the digestive tracts of birds, which is why they sprout like weeds wherever fruit-eating birds hang out.

In open countryside, you'll often see the airy ferns of asparagus growing wild in tidy straight lines that look like they were planted and then forgotten. It was birds doing the "planting," no doubt when they perched on a long-gone fence after eating red, ripe asparagus berries, making a deposit before they flew away.

Beneath my clothesline in Indiana, a popular perch for robins, bluebirds, mockingbirds, and flycatchers, was another bit of fertile ground for bird plants. I found seedlings of all sorts there: hackberry trees, dogwoods, wild cherries, but especially pokeweed (*Phytolacca americana*).

Pokeweed (*Phytolacca americana*) is a common native that birds have helped spread far and wide.

Pokeweed is a peculiar plant with fantastic fuchsia-colored stems and thick, tenacious roots. In one growing season, it reaches large shrub size, with strings of purple-black berries that the birds can't resist. Yet the whole thing keels over and turn to mush when frost hits.

English gardeners call it "architectural" and grow fancified varieties.

I suppose they've never tended a clothesline, or they'd have second thoughts. While those birds were planting the next generation of their berries, they were decorating my sheets and shirts with splashy purple stains.

If you have a wild corner, pokeweed is a great plant for attracting flycatchers and other fruit-eating birds. It's simple to grow from seed.

Also be sure to plant some plants with small, soft berries to catch the eyes of flycatchers. Bush honeysuckles (*Lonicera korolkowii* var. *zabelli,* also known as Tatarian honeysuckle; *L. maackii, L. morrowii,* and other spp.) are easy-care, fast-growing plants that flycatchers appreciate. Try ever-popular elderberries, blackberries, raspberries, mulberries, or Cornelian cherry (*Cornus mas*). Wild cherries often sprout in bird-friendly backyards from seeds that pass through birds.

Nurture them along, or shop for native wild cherries, and in a few years you'll have a good crop of small fruits.

During fall migration, you'll have a good shot at catching the eyes of passing flycatchers via food, even if you don't see them at other times of the year. I make sure to include plenty of late-blooming flowers in my garden, such as asters (*Aster* spp. and cultivars), sneezeweed (*Helenium* spp. and cultivars), and goldenrod (*Solidago* spp.

and cultivars), to keep those butterflies, wasps, and other insects flying.

Many soft, small berries ripen naturally right about the time that flycatchers are stocking up for migration or passing through on their journey. Arrowwood viburnum (*Viburnum dentate*), silky dogwood (*Cornus amomum*), and redtwig dogwood (*C. alba*) bear fruit that's just the right size for flycatchers.

Feeder Foods for Flycatchers

No matter how tempting a spread I put out, flycatchers would rather find their own, it seems.

You won't have to wait long for elderberry to amount to something: In just one season, it'll reach shrub size, with abundant bird-approved fruit.

I haven't given up entirely. I still hope to see a flycatcher sampling my dried fruit mixes, or maybe the mealworms or crumbled suet–bug mix. Until then, I'll make do with watching flycatchers help themselves to butterflies and other insects I've "provided" in the garden.

Water Wishes of Flycatchers

Flycatchers don't usually visit birdbaths. Focus on planting fruits and flowers instead, and supplying perches and nesting needs.

Nesting Needs of Flycatchers

Ah, now here's a way to win favor with flycatchers!

Although these birds may scorn our feeders and birdbaths, they're ultra-fond of our handouts of nesting materials. And some species may even become tenants in birdhouses. Supplying favored nest-site plants is a long shot, but it's worth a try, since the plants are useful in other ways, too.

Nest Materials

Flycatcher nests are beautiful creations. The dainty, woven cups include many soft materials in the mix. And that's where you come in. Although these birds are perfectly capable of collecting their own building materials, they may also investigate treasures that you supply. Bird

Some flycatchers pluck the "fur" from willow catkins (many *Salix* spp.) when building their soft nests. The plants themselves may be used as nest sites.

A scrap of snakeskin is a real treasure to the ash-throated flycatcher, which adds these crinkly strips to its cavity nest.

supply stores and catalogs have made it easy by selling pre-filled containers of such materials. But I still like to gather my own. Here are some good materials to try:

- Fresh moss—the long-fibered types that often grow in shady spots
- Dried sphagnum moss, bought at craft stores or recycled from florists' arrangements
- Easter-basket grass
- Spanish moss, collected naturally or bought at craft stores
- Twists of natural cotton, from natural—not synthetic—cotton balls
- Short sections of cotton twine that you've untwisted
- Milkweed fluff, from inside the seedpods
- Cattail fluff
- Soft feathers
- Pet fur
- Onion skins
- 1-inch-wide, 6-inch-long strips of clear cellophane; cellophane sheets are available at craft stores

The last two items on that list may be selected by the great crested flycatcher, which has the unusual habit of adding cast-off snakeskins to its nest, perhaps to scare off predators, or maybe because the birds just like a little flash and crackle—no one really knows for sure. Apparently, dry, crinkly onion skins and shiny cellophane strips are close enough to the real thing, which can be hard to come by.

Nest Boxes

A few species of this family seem to have an independent streak when it comes to nesting. Instead of building a nest in a shrub or tree, they seek out a cavity to call home.

The great crested flycatcher is the most likely species to adopt a nest box. But you may also have luck attracting an ash-throated, olivaceous, sulphur-bellied, or western flycatcher as a tenant, if you live within their nesting range.

The western kingbird, black phoebe, Say's phoebe, and eastern phoebe often build their nests on or around houses and outbuildings, supporting the nest on a doorsill or other small ledge, or plastering it to an eave. Try a nesting shelf for these birds.

The cavity-nesting flycatchers, including this great crested, are quick to adopt a nest box that accommodates their big bodies and brood.

Little Extras for Flycatchers

I discovered one of the best tricks for attracting flycatchers totally by accident: the porch light.

I'm just as fascinated by bugs as by birds, and sometimes I leave the porch light on at night, to see what insects it attracts. It's a standard 60-watt bulb, but that's enough to bring in great bugs.

So far, I've seen ethereal luna moths, huge cecropia moths, pastel rosy maple moths, fantastic beetles big and small, craneflies, midges, and a bevy of other weird and wonderful insects.

One night I forgot to flip off the switch before heading to bed. The first thing I saw when I stepped outside the next morning was a tattered cecropia wing. Then I spotted other moth wings. As I was kneeling to take stock, a phoebe came zipping in over my head and grabbed a leopard moth from the wall near the light.

The leopard moth, a common species that often rests during the day near a light that lured it in at night, falls prey to backyard flycatchers.

I took a step backward and stood quietly. For more than an hour, the phoebe breakfasted on bugs that had been drawn to the light at night and had settled to sleep nearby.

I try the porch light trick every now and then, just to see what flycatchers are in the area. When I leave the light on all night, moths and other insects settle nearby and stay there until morning comes—or until a flycatcher arrives. The impromptu buffet has attracted wood pewees, a kingbird, great crested flycatchers, eastern phoebes, willow flycatchers, and, once, an olive-sided flycatcher that was passing through.

Try, Try Again

Cavity-nesting flycatchers may pick oddball sites for their homes. House gutters often attract their efforts, and all you can do is keep your fingers crossed that there's not a deluge until the birds are done nesting. They've built nests in the buckets of bulldozers, in pipes stuck in the ground, and in exhaust pipes. And we worry about whether our birdhouses are good enough!

But the prize for originality goes to a pair of ash-coated flycatchers in Escondido, California, nearly 100 years ago. Fred Gallup, writing in *Bird-Lore,* way back in 1917, related this tale of determination:

> [I] hung an old pair of overalls on a line to dry; a pair of these birds began carrying in nesting material through a hole in one leg, but it fell out of the bottom of the leg as fast as they carried it in; they kept at the hopeless job for about an hour, until Mr. Gallup tied up the bottom of the leg. They finally succeeded in filling up the leg with material, lined the nest with feathers, and raised a brood of young.

Chapter 7

The Vireo Family

FAMILY NAME: Vireonidae

EASE OF ATTRACTING: ★★★★ (very easy)

BIRDS IN FAMILY: Vireos

Meet the Vireo Family

The name *vireo* comes from the Latin word for *green,* and that's a pretty good description of these small songbirds. About a dozen species live in North America. Once among the most common of birds, many of them are declining in numbers, due to the destruction of the woodsy places they favor both here and in their winter homelands in Central and South America.

Look and Listen

These small songbirds stay within concealing foliage. They're fast movers, pausing only to sit still for a quick break, then they're on the go again.

Worse yet, they're perfectly colored to blend in with the trees and bushes where they live. Most are greenish or greenish gray on top, with paler undersides often tinged with yellow. For a truly diabolical twist, the gray vireo, a very well-named species, is found in equally gray junipers.

During spring migration, vireos are singing everywhere along their route. They have musical voices that lend themselves to rapid, warbling songs that can continue for minutes at a time. The white-eyed vireo is a talented mimic, adding the calls of thrushes, towhees, and the great crested flycatcher to its own loud song of rapid notes. Even the sharp "*Peek!*" of a downy woodpecker may be borrowed for its repertoire.

Among the songbirds, only warblers are more difficult to observe and identify. At least vireos sit still every once in a while: Warblers are more like perpetual-motion machines.

Range of Vireos

Two vireos range across most of the country: the red-eyed vireo and the warbling vireo. Bell's vireo has a big range, too, covering the midsection of North America, and the Southwest. The white-eyed vireo covers most of the eastern half of the United States.

Other species are much more limited. The thick-billed vireo, for instance, is found only on the tip of Florida, while Hutton's vireo stays mainly along the Pacific coast, east of the mountains.

Now You See 'em . . .

Like other bird families that eat mainly insects, vireos are a seasonal treat. In fall, most of them head southward into Central and South America.

In the mild Pacific area, Hutton's vireo sticks around all year. And the white-eyed species lives along the Atlantic and Gulf coasts in winter, as well as in Florida.

During migration in spring and fall, vireos may pop up anywhere along their flight path. That's what led to the name of the Philadelphia vireo. This bird never nests anywhere near Philadelphia; it spends the breeding season far to the north, in the topmost edge of the United States and into Canada. But during migration,

The red-eyed vireo rarely sits still. Even when singing, the bird keeps moving through the foliage.

it's a frequently seen tourist in the City of Brotherly Love and Really Good Cheesesteaks.

Family Habits of Vireos

There! Right there! See that little greenish bird, up there in the green leaves? Oh, wait, he's gone. Oh! There! There he is again! He's sitting right on that branch! Oops, sorry, gone again.

Vireos spend most of their time gleaning insects and caterpillars from the leaves. They're super-quick at their job, constantly moving through the foliage of one tree, then flying to the next. Like flycatchers, vireos have bristlelike feathers around their beaks, to aid in catching insects.

I usually content myself with listening to the pretty songs of vireos, instead of driving myself crazy trying to focus my binoculars on their busy bodies. Or at least that's what I say now; when the moment comes, I'm out there looking hard for greenish feathers against green leaves. Especially after a rain, when vireos often attend to their washing-up by rubbing against a wet leaf. Thank goodness I have a reliable chiropractor to ease my aching neck!

At-Home Habitat

You can find vireos anywhere there are deciduous trees, whether it's a single maple in your backyard or an entire forest full. Some species rarely leave the canopy, so you'll need to crane your neck to get a glimpse.

The vireos that live in trees are plain colored birds without stripes or bars on their wings. But some vireos spend their time at a lower level, in brush or small trees such as mesquite and shrubby willows—and, interestingly, these species have light-colored bars on their wings.

The Wild Side

Deciduous trees and shrubs, plus juniper in the West, are the preferred habitat for vireos foraging for insects in the wild. The foliage hides many a beetle, ant, spider, caterpillar, tree cricket, and moth, plus a host of other insects.

Vireos visit the flowers of wild plants to pick off insects. They eat a lot of fruit, too, which is why they're often seen in wild fruit and berry bushes and trees.

No other vireo has an eye like this, so it must be the white-eyed vireo. Eye color and head decorations are big clues when identifying vireos.

Unseasonable snowfalls can wreak havoc on insect-eating birds. That's when vireos switch to berries, such as these abundant barberries (*Berberis*).

Trash or Treasure?

"Trash trees" are fast-growing, not classically beautiful like an oak, often short-lived, and have little or no dollar value for lumber. They're the chokecherries, poplars, hackberries, boxelders, and other trees that spring up in unattended areas almost as soon as your back is turned.

When I first heard the term years ago, I didn't argue. I could see that the trees in those brushy hedgerows weren't nearly as beautiful as the graceful dogwood that held a place of honor in my yard—and for which I'd paid a pretty penny. Sniff! Trash trees, who needs 'em?

Oh, how young and dumb I was.

Eventually it dawned on me that just about every bird that landed in my dogwood came from the trash trees. Maybe we can't make boards out of them, and maybe they aren't classic beauties, but "trash trees" are hugely valuable to birds. They offer ideal nesting sites, they're great cover, and the mixed thickets create corridors for birds to safely move about. And that's not even considering all the insect food and fruit they offer up, let alone their use as nesting material.

"Weedy" trees along fences and in other overlooked nooks and crannies are rich with insect food for this warbling vireo and other species.

One of my most successful bird gardens ever was a 6-foot-wide strip that we simply stopped mowing, along one side of our country yard. Goldenrod and asters soon moved in, followed by blackberries, wild grapes, and saplings of all sorts. Sumacs, pincherries, chokecherries, wild plums, and lots of other fast-growing native trees—"weeds," in other words—sprang up and grew like lightning.

In just a few years, I had a great natural hedgerow that was burgeoning with vireos, flycatchers, orioles, bluebirds, wrens, robins, flickers, native sparrows, even quail.

Trash trees? I don't think such a thing exists. Trees that volunteer, grow 6 feet tall in a year or two, and provide super bird appeal are more like true treasure.

Backyard Matchup

To make vireos feel at home, keep in mind that these birds prefer their privacy. You'll do best by planting trees and shrubs in groups, to create a naturalistic thicket that takes care of itself. An undisturbed group of shrubs or a hedge may attract this interesting bird to your yard.

Focus on fruiting plants, too, especially if you have limited space, so that your plants attract vireos looking for both insects and fruit.

Like other migrants, vireos often show up in larger numbers in your yard when they're traveling through in spring or in fall. Listen for their pretty voices to help pinpoint their presence in your yard; those slender, greenish bodies can be tricky to see among the foliage.

And don't forget to look up when your flowering trees are in bloom: Vireos may be dining on insects drawn to the blossoms.

(continued on page 116)

Native Viburnum Sampler

Fast-growing shrubs are the next best thing to nature for viburnum-loving vireos.

Native viburnums make beautiful backyard plants, and they're real magnets for insect- and fruit-eating birds such as vireos. Their clusters of tiny, fuzzy flowers draw zillions of insects, and their fruit is so popular that birds will strip it as soon as it ripens. Native viburnums are tough and adaptable: This garden will grow well in part to full shade, or in a sunny area, in Zones 3 to 9. You won't find these plants at discount garden centers—yet—but they're worth tracking down at native plant nurseries, such as those listed in the Resources section on page 372.

You'll need an area about 10 feet by 12 feet for this planting. As the viburnums grow, the garden will eventually expand to about 18 feet wide; it's easy to cut them back if you prefer to keep the planting smaller. Use decorative rocks for accents if you wish.

Spread 2 to 3 inches of bark mulch or chopped fall leaves around the plants. In subsequent years, fallen fall leaves will form their own mulch. This garden pretty much takes care of itself—another plus for birds, which prefer undisturbed areas of your yard. Many viburnum fruits need to go through a few freezes and thaws before they become palatable, so don't be discouraged if the berries linger on the bush. Early spring migrants will take care of any leftovers.

Plant List

1. Black-haw viburnum (*V. prunifolium*) (1 plant) (Hardiness Zones 3–9)

2. Arrowwood viburnum (*V. dentatum*) (1 plant) (Hardiness Zones 3–8)

3. Maple-leaved viburnum (*Viburnum acerifolium*) (3 plants) (Hardiness Zones 4–8)

Like all of the gardens in this book, this one provides cover as well as food, so that birds feel safe in it. Native viburnums offer insect-attracting flowers and small fruits, both sought by vireos.

These fast-growing shrubs and this vine offer inviting cover to foraging vireos as they ferret out insects among the abundant foliage and flowers. All of these plants also supply a later offering of fruits or berries, and some may even be selected as nest sites—as long as you keep your distance.

Plant	Type of Plant	Description	Zones
Barberry (*Berberis* spp. and cultivars)	Deciduous shrub to about 5 ft	Thorny branches; yellow, 5 to 9 insect-attracting flowers; small berries	3–9
Bayberry (*Myrica pensylvanica*)	Evergreen shrub or small tree to about 10 ft	Glossy, aromatic leaves; waxy grayish-white berries	3–6
Roses (*Rosa* spp. and cultivars, with small hips)	Deciduous shrubs to about 6 ft	Fragrant flowers mature into colorful rose hips.	3–9
Native viburnums (*V. acerifolium, V. dentatum, V. lantanoides, V. nudum,* and other native spp.)	Deciduous shrubs to about 6 to 10 ft	Usually multistemmed, forming a clump or small thicket; large clusters of tiny, insect-attracting flowers, followed by small, soft berries	3–9
Grapes, especially native spp. (*Vitis riparia, V. labrusca, V. rubra, V. rupestris,* and many other native spp.)	Deciduous vines	To 20 ft or more, depending on spp.	4–9

	Used for	Comments	Other Birds Attracted
	Food; nest sites	Let the plant grow naturally rather than shearing it.	Thrushes, mimic thrushes, wrens eat berries; warblers eat insects at flowers.
	Food, cover	Berries persist into spring, so they're available to spring migrants.	Tree swallows, thrushes, wrens, warblers eat berries.
	Food	Look for cultivars or species with small hips; most small-flowered roses have small hips.	Thrushes, mimic thrushes, woodpeckers, flycatchers, jays, and others eat fruit; mimic thrushes and cardinals may nest in plant.
	Food; nest sites; cover	Native viburnums are fast-growing and beloved by birds; they're worth tracking down at native plant nurseries. Many species are widely adaptable, or you can ask a nearby nature center which species are native to your area.	Thrushes, mimic thrushes, woodpeckers, flycatchers, native sparrows, and gallinaceous birds eat berries.
	Food	Native grapes are highly popular with birds and trouble-free for gardeners.	Thrushes, mimic thrushes, woodpeckers, flycatchers, warblers, jays, orioles, tanagers, and others eat fruit.

Natural Foods for Vireos

Insects, insects, insects, with a side dish of fruits. That's the extent of the vireo menu. Oh, and perhaps an occasional snail or lizard.

Main Menu: Insects

Sometimes I feel a little creepy, thinking about all the millions of bugs that live in my yard. Most of them go without notice, leading their busy insect lives right under our noses. Until a vireo comes along, that is. Not much escapes those sharp eyes—or sharp beak.

Vireos grab up all sorts of insects from the trees and shrubs they patrol. Just about any insect is fair game. Here's a mouthwatering sampling of what might be the Special of the Day for vireos:

Waste not, want not: Where small lizards are available, vireos snatch them up just as they would a cicada or grasshopper.

Ants	Grasshoppers
Aphids	Gypsy moths
Bees	Ichneumon flies
Beetles	Moths
Butterflies	Scale insects
Caterpillars	Spiders
Cicadas	Spittlebugs
Craneflies	Stinkbugs
Crickets	Treehoppers
Dragonflies	Walking sticks
Flies	Wasps

In summer, vireos turn to wild fruits such as mulberries (*Morus* spp.), native viburnums (*Viburnum* spp.), wild blackberries or raspberries, and native grapes (*Vitis* spp.)—any soft fruits that they can find near the hedgerows, thickets, and trees where they live. The aromatic red

Goldenrod flowers (*Solidago* spp.) are ambrosia to wasps in early fall. Migrating vireos may take notice.

Arrowwood viburnum grows fast and bears a crop of blue berries within a year or two after planting. Native viburnums like this are popular with vireos.

berries of spicebush (*Lindera benzoin*) are a great favorite. During fall migration, fruits remain a mainstay in the diet of most vireos, augmented by insects, of course.

Backyard Fare

Avoiding pesticides is the first step toward making your yard inviting to vireos. These feathered vacuum cleaners do a great job of controlling insects in trees and shrubs. All of the leafy greenery of your backyard plants, no matter what kind of plants they are, holds a smorgasbord of six-legged snacks. A garden pool, with shrubs on the side, may attract vireos, thanks to the dragonflies, mayflies, and other insect possibilities near the water.

Bring vireos to eye level with fruiting shrubs. You may spy vireos at backyard brambles, such as black or red raspberries and blackberries. Elderberries in the backyard are just as tempting as elders in the wild. And good old barberries, that landscaping staple, offer small berries that vireos find delectable.

Vireos are a great excuse to explore the vast array of native shrubs with berries. You can find an interesting selection of natives for your area, no matter where you live. I'm partial to viburnums (*V. acerifolium, V. dentatum,* and *V. lantanoides,* to name just a few). These hardy shrubs and small trees get short shrift in most gardens, and I don't know why. They're beautiful, easy to grow, and beloved by birds and butterflies, and they have a lovely range of fall color. Here's your chance to be the first on your block to start a collection. When the berries ripen, you can expect dozens of bird species to drop in to share the fruits of your labor.

A flower garden is always popular with insects—and thus with insect eaters such as vireos. Herb gardens may be of interest to vireos, too, because the flowering herbs attract a myriad of insect creatures great and small. But to attract vireos to your flower or herb gardens, you'll need to make a few improvements to the usual bed of low-growing plants.

Incorporate a few small trees or large shrubs in or near your flower or herb beds, such as flowering crabapples (*Malus* spp. and cvs.), Vanhoutte spirea (*Spirea × vanhouttei*), elderberries, or dogwoods (*Cornus* spp. and cvs.). Insects at the blossoms will attract foraging vireos, and the taller height and leafy branches will supply the cover that helps make them feel safe.

Deep pockets—that's the kind of nest that vireos make. Here, red-eyed vireo nestlings stay cozy within the woven fiber walls of this creation, which is suspended from slender twigs.

Strong, sticky spider silk is a prized material for vireo nests. A web may be used, but the thick layer of silk that protects spider eggs is even better.

Feeder Foods for Vireos

Vireos aren't feeder birds; they do just fine getting their own food. But you can try your luck at attracting them with mealworms or waxworms.

Nesting Needs of Vireos

The shrubs, trees, and fruiting plants in your yard may be selected as a vireo home, which you'll probably never notice until the leaves come down in fall. These birds hang their nest from a forked branch, at heights from 3 to 30 feet or more, depending on species and on individual habits. Look for gray plant fibers and spider silk on the outside walls for one clue to the former homeowner.

Nesting Materials

Being a litterbug on your own lawn may catch the eye of red-eyed vireos or other species. These birds sometimes use bits of paper from wasps' nests in their own homes, and they may accept bits of paper as a substitute.

To give it a try, just tear a few short strips from a cheap newsprint tablet and scatter them on the grass under a shade tree, or drape them on shrubs. I've had some interested vireo "lookers," but only once did I see a vireo actually carrying off the paper. More often, robins snatch them up first.

Birds can be mighty picky when it comes to using our litter. Printed newspaper strips don't seem to have the appeal of plain newsprint paper. But you can tear off short, narrow strips from the unprinted side margins of your newspaper, if you don't have a newsprint tablet handy. (One of the oddest bird nests I ever came across was a red-eyed vireo nest that incorporated pieces of thin onionskin-type paper—from a Bible. The bird didn't seem to be particular about the content: I recognized bits of Job and Revelations as well as the Psalms.)

Vireos may select their own plant fibers right from your compost pile or a corner of your garden. When I cut back the dead stems of my flowers in late winter, I pile them in a separate area for nesting birds to take their pick. Fibers from the weathered stems of milkweeds (*Asclepias* spp.) and goldenrods (*Solidago* spp.) are popular, along with many other common garden flowers and weeds, such as lamb's-quarters *(Chenopodium album)*. It's easier for birds to pull off thin fibers from dead plant stems that are still anchored in the ground, but they don't seem to mind working a little harder to get the goods. As for the spider silk that strengthens the walls of the nest, watch for vireos collecting silk-wrapped egg sacs as well as webs from your yard.

Chapter 8

The Crow and Jay Family

FAMILY NAME: Corvidae

EASE OF ATTRACTING: ★★★★★ (practically guaranteed)

BIRDS IN FAMILY: Crows • Ravens • Jays • Magpies • Clark's Nutcrackers

---

Meet the Crow and Jay Family

Big, smart, loud, and hungry: That's the Crow and Jay family, or *corvids,* as they're also called.

Corvids throw their weight around when there's food, which tends to cause resentment among feeder watchers. When a jay comes screaming in, all the smaller, less aggressive birds take off. Even in the wild, other birds yield when these big guys decide they want first dibs on whatever food is at stake.

But these birds are worth inviting as visitors to your yard for a couple of big reasons. First of all, they're fascinating to watch, because of their intelligence and awareness. And they do a great job of warning other birds about prowling cats, snakes, hawks, and owls. They flash to the attack when a predator shows up, doing their best to drive it off.

Look and Listen

The first time I saw a magpie, in a yard next to the little restaurant in New Mexico where I'd just eaten my first *sopapilla* (a light-as-air fried pastry dusted with powdered sugar), I thought it had to be some kind of exotic tropical bird that had somehow ended up living in North America.

That super-long tail, those striking pied markings, that beautiful blue-green iridescence—how could this beautiful bird be a cousin of plain old crows?

Then the magpie opened its mouth. Various shrieks and loud, harsh, guttural noises poured forth as the bird took wing. Hmm. Sounded something like the honking ravens I'd just been watching in the mountains, not to mention the raucous blue jays back in my Pennsylvania yard.

And where was this beautiful bird heading? To a Styrofoam take-out container that somebody had dropped in the parking lot. As I watched the gorgeous magpie cleverly open the lid and rip into the leftovers, the family resemblance was clear as a bell.

You won't have to look hard to spot birds of this family. All of them are unafraid of humans, and they don't seem to mind being in full view. Besides, they're the biggest birds in your backyard (not counting the occasional wild turkey or hawk).

Next time you see a jay, crow, or magpie, try taking a closer look instead of just a glance. You'll see that the family members share big, stout beaks, strong legs and feet, and wide wings that carry them long distances.

Crows and ravens are black, magpies black and white with iridescence, and Clark's nutcracker a workmanlike gray with black trim. Except for the gray jay, the jays are various shades of blue. If you visit the birding hot spot of Brownsville, Texas, where Mexican birds often show up, you may spy the fantastic green jay, as bright as a parrot—but with the same kind of screaming, croaking, querulous voice as its cousins.

Range of Crows and Jays

Every part of the country is attended by at least one of these species. And many of them are on the move, showing up far outside their traditional ranges. The blue jay, a bird that once

Like other crested jays, the Steller's jay telegraphs its attitude with its head feathers. This bird is normally alert, not alarmed. A bolt-upright crest would signal warning, threat, or intense curiosity.

With a range covering much of the West, the black-billed or American magpie is a familiar sight—and sound!—to many. Exotic plumage and a harsh, nasal, repeated call announce its presence.

Clark's nutcracker isn't as flashy as other members of its family, but it's just as much of a loudmouth. Like its relatives, it's an intelligent bird that quickly learns to look to humans for a handout.

sentatives. Oddly, the western scrub jay has an almost lookalike relative clear across the country: the Florida scrub jay.

Now You See 'em . . .

Years ago, around daffodil time in my yard, I got a letter from an acquaintance who lived far to the north, in snowy Minnesota. "The crows are here," she wrote excitedly. "Saw seven today. Spring must be on the way!"

Except for those harbinger crows in the Far North, nearly all members of this family live year-round in the same areas. The American magpie (formerly the black-billed magpie) is another exception. For some reason, in winter, the birds move into the western half of Minnesota from neighboring North Dakota. I'm sure they have a good reason for it. Better bird feeders, maybe?

stayed east of the Rockies, is now seen in Washington, Oregon, and other western states. Just for fair play, the lovely Steller's jay of the West is sometimes spotted in Plains states. Clark's nutcracker, a bird that's familiar in western mountain states, makes forays to the Mississippi River.

The western part of the country, including the Southwest, gets the lion's share of this family. Magpies cover a huge portion of ground from the Plains westward. And several varieties of jays, as well as Clark's nutcrackers, can be found in the West, too.

In much of the East, the American crow, fish crow, and blue jay are the most common repre-

Family Habits of Crows and Jays

All of these birds have an alert, bright-eyed look, like an eager first-grader just waiting for a chance to raise her hand in class. They're cunning and adept at solving problems.

Birds of this family behave differently from others, in ways that are fun to watch. For one thing, they vary their habits to make use of whatever food is at hand—like the magpie that had learned to open a take-out container.

I like to watch these birds master unfamiliar foods. But even more, I like to watch them play. Crows and ravens fool around in the air like pilots at an air show. I've often watched them doing death-defying dives just for the thrill of it, pulling up at the last second as if to say "Ha-ha! What a rush!" And I've seen them actually turning complete somersaults and even multiple flips in the air. Performance? A perfect 10.

They're practical jokers, too, as our elderly dog never quite figured out. He spent a lot of time sleeping in the shade, and the jays saw their opportunity. A pair of them would perch overhead, staying totally silent—the first clue that they were up to something. Then they'd take turns flying down and tweaking the end of his long tail. By the time he woke up, they'd be back in the tree overhead. At first I thought they might be collecting hair for a nest, but nope, they were just playing. I swear I could hear them laughing.

Birds of this family aren't homebodies like the house wren or song sparrow that sticks close to your backyard. They're strong fliers, and they can easily cover miles every day in their search for food or diversions.

During breeding season, these birds show their tender side. They share quiet, intimate songs, and they often caress their partner's feathers and beak. In fall and winter, crows and ravens roost together at night in flocks.

Nuts to you, crows and jays! Why, thanks, say these big birds, which you can bet have already spotted these ripening pecans. They'll eat some and carry off others to hide away for a rainy day.

IQ Test

Scientists who study the intelligence of crows get excited when the birds master some human skill, such as using a tool, opening a lock, or mimicking human speech. They point out, too, that crows have their own language, with different calls for different purposes.

I love reading about the latest tricks. But I think these studies miss the mark. What they do is judge another species' intelligence by its ability to master skills that we value in ourselves.

Sure, crows are the smartest birds—by human standards. Cunning, clever, problem-solving? Definitely. Able to adapt to a world that humans have changed drastically? Sure. And that's where this human-based intelligence standard pays off. Crows will probably continue to thrive long after less-adaptive birds die out.

Dozens of native oak species cover this country, and every one of them is ideal for birds. They're popular with jays for food and nest sites.

At-Home Habitat of Crows and Jays

If you live within the range of any of these species, your chances of seeing them in your own yard are practically guaranteed. Their far-ranging daily habits are highly likely to include your backyard.

Many jays live in the forests or in brushy areas in their range. But they often leave the trees behind and hang out in backyards.

Crows and ravens may live in mountains, in forests, at the coast, in open farmland, and often, anywhere in between. Generally, ravens tend to be found in more isolated areas than crows, farther from human habitation. But that's not always the case.

Clark's nutcracker, which looks and behaves like a combination of a woodpecker and a crow and often soars like a hawk, is a bird of high elevations. After the brood is out of the nest, nutcrackers often move down to lower levels.

Magpies, which spend more time on the ground than other members of the family, prefer open space with scattered bushes and trees, whether it's the farming valleys of California or your own yard.

Backyard Matchup

Magpies prefer thick clumps of brush, with plenty of open ground for foraging. They're not built for getting airborne in a hurry, so you can make them feel safer by including clumps of dense shrubbery in the yard. Junipers (*Juniperus* spp. and cultivars) and willows (*Salix* spp. and cultivars) are popular for cover with these big, bold birds.

Most of the other members of this family quickly take to conifers, which they use for cover and food and for moving from place to place.

Clark's nutcracker, the gray jay, and Steller's

Watch for the characteristic hop-hop-hop these birds do before taking off, or when traveling on the ground. Although they can and do walk left-foot, right-foot, they also bounce along with both feet together.

jay prefer wild places—or backyards near those natural haunts. A yard with conifers near the woods they call home is likely to attract them. A single older conifer native to your area, such as a pinyon pine (*Pinus edulis*) in nutcracker territory, or a fir (*Abies* spp.), western redcedar (*Thuja plicata*), or hemlock (*Tsuga* spp.) in Steller's or gray jay range, makes an inviting destination when one of these birds ventures out from the woods. If you don't have an existing conifer, a group of three young trees can make a suitable substitute. But these birds may also visit a more open yard, with nary a Christmas tree in sight. In winter, they expand their ranges and may drop in to forage at your place as long as there's food to be had.

The other members of the family, such as blue jays, scrub jays, and magpies, have much looser standards. These birds are likely to be regular visitors to your yard, no matter what kind of habitat your place holds. Because they're so skilled at ferreting out food of all different kinds, they can find something to interest them in just about any kind of habitat, from deep woods to mall parking lots.

Even though jays will readily visit your yard as long as it offers some sort of food, you'll miss out on some fascinating, fun-to-watch behavior if you stick to watching them only when they're eating. Creating comfy habitat for these birds will give you a look at an entirely different side of their personality—the tenderness with which they treat their mate and family.

During courtship and nesting, jays make a sudden switch from being brassy loudmouths. Oh, sure, they'll still kick up a fuss whenever

If you live in the North or West, watch for incoming jays as they roam the neighborhood and make a beeline for your conifers. Even aggressive birds appreciate cover as they move from place to place.

there's an alarm to be raised—or peanuts to grab. But in their private moments, you'll see a bird of another color.

Jays are so secretive when it comes to courting and nesting that you may never know there's a nest right in your own yard. They sing quiet, murmuring love songs to each other, instead of shrieking like banshees. And to approach their nest site, they alight well away from it, then sneak through the foliage, utterly silent, to reach it.

More than once, I've been oblivious to a nest—even when it was just a few feet overhead. Until the young got big and hungry, that is. Then, it's hard to miss those "Feed me!" cries.

(continued on page 130)

Garden of Eatin'

Entice an entertaining troupe of jays in fall and winter with a strip of extra-large seeds.

The way to a jay or crow's heart? Via its appetite. While you're waiting for your conifers to get growing, tempt these intriguing loudmouths with a hearty crop of corn and plump sunflower seeds. You won't want to add a scarecrow to this patch—unless you want to see how smart these birds are. As gardeners learned generations ago, even the scariest scarecrow doesn't fool these brainy birds for very long. When corn is ripe for pecking, jays and crows will probably use the scarecrow for a perch.

This fast-growing planting provides quick cover for birds in your yard, and is pretty enough for any sunny spot. It will fit in an area about 6 feet by 10 feet, or you can lengthen it if you want to use it as a privacy hedge. The sunflower and zinnia blossoms may attract hummingbirds with their nectar, plus wrens and other birds to feed on the insects the blossoms attract. As the corn ripens, you may see woodpeckers, quail, pheasants, and other corn lovers, plus a bonus of cardinals and other finches, blackbirds, nuthatches, chickadees, and other friends to the sunflower and zinnia seeds. Not bad for less than 10 dollars' worth of seeds!

Plant List

1. Tall sunflower (*Helianthus annuus*, such as 'Russian Giant') (1 packet)

2. Sweet corn, any cultivar (I'm partial to 'Butter and Sugar', if I can grab a few ears before the birds do) (1 packet, about 1.5 ounces, or 150 to 200 seeds per packet)

3. Strawberry popcorn (1 packet; about 100 seeds per packet)

4. 'Persian Carpet' zinnia (or any other low, bushy cultivar) (1 packet)

Garden Size
10' × 6'

Scale of Plan
¼" = 1'

This is a rewarding garden for little birdwatchers because the seeds sprout just a few days after they're poked into the ground. Of course, who doesn't appreciate big, sturdy seedlings that grow like lightning?

Surefire Plants to Attract Crows and Jays

These plants appeal to the crows and jays in your neighborhood with a varied selection of seeds, nuts, and insects.

Plant	Type	Description	Zones
Firs (*Abies* spp.) and Douglas fir (*Pseudotsuga menziesii*)	Evergreen conifer trees, to about 100 ft	Short needles and dense branches; multitude of cones with age	Firs, 3–8; Douglas fir, 5–7
Pecan (*Carya illinoensis*)	Large deciduous tree, to about 100 ft	Pecans bear delicious nuts, but you'll have to patient; it takes several years for the first crop.	5–9
Annual sunflower (*Helianthus annuus*)	4–8 ft or taller	Extra-large daisy faces in sunny gold or russet shades on stout stems	Annual
Pines (*Pinus* spp.)	Evergreen conifer trees; many spp., from about 25–100 ft	Long-needled, relatively open-branched pines produce a bounty of cones.	3–10
Oaks (*Quercus* spp. and cultivars)	Large deciduous trees, to about 80–100 ft	Stately, slow-growing trees with catkinlike flowers and acorns	4–10
Corn (*Zea mays*)	4–8 ft tall	Fast-growing corn comes in heights that will fit any flower garden.	Annual

Used for	Comments	Other Birds Attracted
Seeds and insects; cover	Appealing to birds even when trees are young, because of dense cover and insect food. Jays may use as nest site.	Kinglets, bushtits, chickadees, and others eat insects from foliage; chickadees, titmice, and nuthatches eat seeds; gallinaceous birds eat buds, fallen seeds; many use as cover or roost.
Nuts	The best nut for attracting a variety of birds. No bite of nutmeat goes uneaten.	Many, many birds—scores of species, big and small—adore pecans. Even the ivory-billed woodpecker was known to be a fan.
Seeds; used by other birds for insects and cover	Classic sunflowers with a single large head are guaranteed to attract birds; other cultivars with fancier flowers or multiple flowerheads will also appeal.	Wrens, chickadees, and warblers visit flowers to eat insects; hummingbirds may drink nectar. Dozens of seed-eating species, from chickadees to wild turkeys, dine on the plant or on dropped seeds beneath it.
Seeds from cones; insects from bark and twigs; nest sites.	Pines look gawky when very young, but they grow fast into beautiful specimens.	Kinglets eat insects from foliage; chickadees, titmice, and nuthatches eat seeds; gallinaceous birds eat buds, investigate fallen seeds; many birds use as nighttime roost.
Acorns; nest sites	Scout out your local nursery and you may find an oak that already has a few acorns on it, for a head start. White oaks have tastier acorns than red oaks, and are highly popular with birds.	Woodpeckers, chickadees, titmice, gallinaceous birds, doves, small finches including juncos, and many other birds eagerly eat acorns. Tanagers, orioles, vireos, warblers, and flycatchers eat insects from foliage or at flowers.
Seeds	Corn is simple to grow; just poke seeds into the ground, water, and stand back. In order to get a good crop, plant several rows side by side so that the wind can carry the pollen from the tassels to the silks of the developing ears.	Woodpeckers, cardinals, red-winged blackbirds, and other birds eat corn while it's still on the cob; wild turkeys, pheasants, and others will search for kernels near ground level.

Natural Foods for Crows and Jays

Omnivorous: That's the word for these birds. Their big, heavy-duty beaks can eat just about anything and everything. Seeds, nuts, fruits, insects, meat: It's all eagerly devoured. Only berries and small seeds seem to be uninteresting to these birds.

Main Menu: Anything That's Not Nailed Down

Just about anything that can be wrested into submission is fair game for these birds. Their stout beaks are suitable for almost any task: cracking nuts, gobbling acorns, tearing into fruits, choffing down insects, gorging on grains, and ripping into meat and fish. Nectar seems to be the only edible they can't access.

Speaking of meat, these birds enjoy it in any form, living or dead. Carrion forms a major part of their diet. So do alive-and-kicking mice, moles, turtles, lizards, smaller birds, salamanders, snails, clams, mussels, sea urchins, crabs, crayfish, frogs, fish, and bats. No wonder old-timers called them "meat birds," "meat hawks," and "camp robbers."

All members of this family may engage in occasional nest-robbing, but blue jays and crows are the worst. You'll often see one of these birds being chased or mobbed by other birds during nesting season, and no wonder: They frequently plunder other birds' nests. Other jays rarely or only occasionally stoop to such habits.

This unsavory habit is part of Mother Nature's grand plan. "Extras" are built into the

"And on ze menu tonight, Monsieur Jay, vee have frog legs, frog belly, in fact, ze whole frog." The Crow and Jay family is famed for its appetites, which sure aren't picky.

habits of birds, so losing one of their young helps keep the population of, say, robins in balance. Jays and crows aren't the only birds that engage in stealing eggs or young; grackles, meadowlarks, and other birds also occasionally engage in the practice, and wrens have been known to puncture the eggs of rivals.

In many years of watching birds, I've seen that jays save the lives of far more birds than they ever consume. Their alarm calls and courageous attacks on predators protect every nesting bird in the area. Not only the eggs and young are saved by the jays' alertness: So are the parent birds, which might have been the victim of that cat or snake the jays drove away.

Backyard Fare

As you've probably guessed by now, you won't have to try very hard to put out an inviting spread for this family—since they eat just about anything that's not nailed down.

The birds will help themselves to insects in your yard, plus they'll grab a share of fruits, seeds, and nuts.

Nuts are definitely a top pick, which means I still haven't had a taste of the filberts I planted a couple of years ago. Invariably, just before I decide the nuts are ready to sample, the jays have already plucked them. At my former home in Indiana, they beat me to the pecans, too, although the beech trees produced such a heavy crop that we all got a share.

Acorns are just as alluring as nuts, so count your blessings if you have an oak in your yard. If you don't, why not try one? It'll take a few years before the crop comes in, but in the meantime, the young tree will provide a bounty of insects for all birds.

Butterflies are particularly popular at nesting time in fact, they peak at the same time. The jays in my neighborhood seem to follow the rule of "One for me, one for the kids." They carry plenty of butterflies to the nest, but in between those trips, they eat the insects themselves. After removing the wings, of course.

These birds will also scout out snails, frogs, mice, and anything else that seems tasty at the time. Harmless garter snakes are abundant in my rocky yard, but only until the baby jays hatch. Then the parent birds hunt down the young snakes to carry them home for dinner. Six inches seems to be the limit for this catch; when the

Jays to the Rescue

Whenever jays make a commotion in my yard, I hurry to see if I can help. A trespassing cat may be hard for jays to chase away, but it'll run when I come clapping and hollering.

I also have an ulterior motive: I want to see who is nesting nearby. When a jay raises the alarm, every parent bird that has a nest in the area joins in. Other birds aren't as brave at close combat as jays, but they'll add their voices and anxious flutterings to the general ruckus. By watching a warning jay, I've discovered vireos, thrushes, and other shyer birds that I wasn't aware were nesting nearby.

One sultry June afternoon, I hurried to see what the jays were screaming about now. The birds were agitatedly flying and screaming at a 6-foot-long black snake that had climbed perhaps 60 feet up in our big old silver beech tree. The snake had been making its way out a horizontal limb, no doubt to reach a bird's nest, when the blue jays spotted it.

I couldn't lend a hand, so I stood underneath, watching the battle. Joined by brown thrashers, robins, Baltimore orioles, summer tanagers, and other furious birds, the jays led the charge in harassing the snake on the smooth-barked limb.

Just about the time I wondered, "How does that snake stay glued to the branch?" the slithery thing seemed to loosen all its muscles. In the split second before I put two-and-two together, it dropped full force—on me!

You think jays are noisy? I bet my shrieks were heard in the next county.

The bigger the better when it comes to food, says the Crow and Jay family. Giant silk moths like this cecropia are a target, thanks to their plump, meaty bodies.

berries don't seem to have much appeal. Think juicy, and you have the key. Grapes, mulberries, strawberries, and other fruits that we like ourselves are popular with this family.

Feeder Foods for Crows and Jays

It doesn't take much effort to attract attention at the feeder. You'll have good luck with:

Nuts, shelled or whole
Peanuts
Corn, whole or cracked
Baked goods
Mealworms
Sunflower seeds
Meat scraps
Suet

snakes get bigger, the jays switch to snatching up basking lizards for their babies.

Fruit attracts this family, although small, hard

Peanut Plantation

The first summer after planting a perennial garden on what had been a hillside of weedy annual grass, I was plagued by a plant that I couldn't identify. I hesitated to pull it out, since I had hopes it might be a Northwest native wildflower that I'd enjoy. The plant was a legume of some kind; that was clear from its pea-shaped yellow flowers. But I couldn't match it up to any of the native lotuses or vetches in my field guide.

The plants seemed to sprout up everywhere in the layer of mulch around my young perennials, and they grew fast. Finally, I pulled up one of them that was threatening to smother a lavender plant. The roots were full of nice, plump peanuts!

Raw peanuts in the shell had been a mainstay at my feeder. And the scrub jays had shoved the nuts into the mulch, to save for a rainy day. Well, that rainy day had come and gone, and now I was the proud owner of a peanut plantation. My crop wasn't quite as satisfying as those boiled peanuts I love to buy at roadside stands in the South, but it was still a treat to nibble raw peanuts out of my own yard.

Since then, I've also found young filbert trees, walnut sprouts, and oak seedlings in the garden—and in the flower pots on the deck. It's a habit that ensures a continuing supply of the food plants that jays depend on. And it gives me lots of free trees, so I'm not complaining.

Members of this family soon become so accustomed to your presence that they're easy to tame, if you'd like to give it a try. An acquaintance told me about her father's magpie, which would follow him like a dog at his heel on his morning stroll around the yard. It wasn't because the bird was friends with the fellow—it was because he took a tortilla along on his daily walk and tossed pieces of it to the magpie as they made the rounds.

Water Wishes of Crows and Jays

A classic pedestal birdbath suits these large birds well. Make sure the basin is settled well on its base, so it doesn't tip. Or you can also set out a low saucer or basin of water.

My birdbath has been well attended by jays, but only once did I have any luck getting a crow as a customer. I'd thrown out a big hunk of fancy bakery bread that had become hard as a rock in its paper bag. Sparrows and other birds had been pecking at the chunk for days, without making much headway. Then a crow arrived to investigate. The gleaming black bird took the hard hunk of bread to the birdbath, where he dunked it like a day-old cruller in a cup of coffee. A few gulps, and the now-soggy bread slid down the hatch.

Nesting Needs of Crows and Jays

Nest building reaches an extreme in the homes of magpies. A pair may spend more than a month to construct its nest, and no wonder: It's a huge bowl of coarse sticks, lined with a thick, heavy layer of mud, and finished off with an inner cup of fine plant stems and horsehair.

But that's just the start. Over this bowl, the birds construct a gigantic dome. By the time they're done, the nest can be 3 feet across and 4 to 7 feet deep! Imagine a couple of laundry baskets, one upended on the other, and you have a rough idea.

Many magpie nests are about half that size, which is still on the extreme end of the scale. Why would birds spend so much time fashioning

A shallow basin of water is a popular hangout. If you're accustomed to jays with crests, the smooth head of a pinyon jay can be a surprise.

such a thing? Protection is the first guess. Owls roam where magpies do, and the domed roof keeps them out.

Magpies often use the same nest for more than one year, but other birds are quick to adopt them, too. Owls often shelter in the nests during the daytime. And hawks recycle them, using the magpie's former home to raise their own brood.

It's easy to spot these huge nests, whether they're in shrubs or high in trees. But most jays' nests are much harder to find. Not only are they smaller and usually well-hidden, but the parents also keep their location a well-guarded secret.

For all their whooping it up, jays quickly become closemouthed around the nest. The birds are so silent when approaching or leaving the nest that you'll probably never notice their presence. The young birds get louder as they grow, but even then, the parents rarely make a sound except for very quiet murmurings.

If you live in magpie country, you can try making a mud puddle to attract nest-building birds. But magpies are adept at finding their own mud—or cow manure, which they sometimes substitute. You'll probably have better luck with a brushpile, to provide a selection of sticks for magpies or jays at nesting time.

Little Extras for Crows and Jays

If you ever come across a shop called "The Magpie's Nest," expect to find a jumble of all kinds of odd treasures inside. European magpies, which look very much like our own American magpie, are famed for collecting odds and ends to add to their homes of basic sticks and mud. Bright baubles and shiny things are favorites.

The American members of the Crow and Jay family aren't quite such dedicated collectors, but they do have a certain fondness for shiny things. A pet crow I had years ago eagerly grabbed quarters from my fingers and collected anything else that caught his eye, from bright buttons to safety pins. He spent hours hiding his treasures in nooks and crannies. His most prized possession was one he lifted when I wasn't looking: a small pocket mirror in a plastic frame, which he would arrange so that the mirrored glass caught the light. Unlike robins and cardinals, which will batter themselves silly when they see a "rival" in a mirrored surface during breeding season, my crow was

Moderation? Not for magpies. Need more sticks, need more mud, more sticks, more mud, sticks, mud, until their nest is as big as a laundry basket.

content to tilt his head curiously at the bird in the mirror. Did he recognize it as himself? I never could tell.

Wild crows and jays also have a weakness for flashy stuff. I've watched them collect the metal bits from gun shell casings in the woods. And I got an expensive lesson in bird behavior right on my own deck.

One day, after running errands, I went out to the deck to relax. Unclipping my polished silver earrings, I set them aside on the table, and buried my nose in a book. Big mistake. A Steller's jay saw the flash of sterling, swooped in, grabbed an earring, and flew away.

Now I keep a stash of junk jewelry from thrift shops and garage sales handy. Rhinestones, silver- or gold-colored metal, and shiny metal buttons get the most interest.

Chapter 9

The Swallow Family

FAMILY NAME: Hirundinidae

EASE OF ATTRACTING ★ ★ ★ (moderately easy)

BIRDS IN FAMILY: Swallows · Purple Martins

Meet the Swallow Family

Your yard space doesn't end at the treetops. It goes up, up, up, into the sky. And that's where you'll most often see the Swallow family—on the wing.

How to coax those aeronauts down to Earth? Ah, that's the beauty of bird-by-bird gardening. A few simple tricks will bring them down to eye level, at least once in a while. And then you can admire them as more than sky-high silhouettes.

Look and Listen

Before we get too distracted by family details, let's start by hauling out the best piece of equipment for getting to know swallows.

Nope, not those high-power binoculars or a million-dollar martin house. I'm talking about your favorite chaise lounge. Mine's a relic that I rescued from the recycling center years ago, an aluminum frame with a faded, never-was-fashionable cushion. Its big advantage is that it has wheels, so it's easy to move to wherever I want it.

You'll want to wait for a sunny summer day to try this trick. Put that lounger in place, not under a shady tree, but out in the open part of your yard. Lower the head end to an almost-flat position, climb aboard, and make yourself comfortable.

Now, look up. And keep watching.

Amazing, isn't it?

Day after day, sunrise to sunset, all summer long, the sky is alive with swallows and martins. Circling, swooping, diving, winging back and forth in an ebb and flow as tireless as the tides.

It's easy to forget about what's going on over our heads. Which is why I keep my trusty chaise lounge around for those summer days when nothing sounds more appealing than meditating on the marvelous flight of swallows.

The Swallow family is built for flying. Their long, pointed wings make for fast strokes and agile curves, and their forked tails serve as rudders for super steering. The birds have dark plumage on top, often with a beautiful iridescent sheen of green or blue, and a pale breast and belly.

Up close, you can see that these birds have tiny beaks. Tiny when closed, that is. Swallows and martins have an extra-wide "gape" to their mouths, so they can open wide when they're in hot pursuit of flying insects.

All hold forth with high, twittering notes, and a few species are surprisingly musical. Not to mention loud. My neighbor kept a martin house, and the morning wake-up routine was so loud in my bedroom—50 feet away, with windows closed—that it often had me reaching for a pillow to hold over my head when the birds sounded their 5:00 A.M. reveille.

When you spot a barn swallow or other swallow on the ground, it's probably collecting nest material: dry grass, mud, or feathers.

country. In much of that huge range, swallows remain throughout the entire summer season; in some areas, they only pass through during migration. You'll see swallows in the air, no matter where you live.

The purple martin comes close to that expanse, but it's absent in a swath of the West. The violet-green swallow picks up the slack there, blanketing the western half of the country. In parts of Texas, the cave swallow adds to the mix, and in the tip of Florida, the Bahama swallow adds some local color.

Range of Swallows

Five of the nine species in this family—the northern rough-winged, bank, tree, cliff, and barn swallows—cover the skies across this

Now You See 'em . . .

Swallows eat mainly flying insects, and dinner-on-the-wing is missing in action when the air grows chilly. That's why swallows depart from our skies beginning in late summer. They return in spring, when temperatures are favorable for flying insects.

Tree swallows do stick around in some areas in winter, mostly because they can adapt to eating berries. They hang out along the Atlantic and Gulf Coasts and linger in parts of the Southwest, including Southern California.

Family Habits of Swallows

The marshes along the Atlantic coast, in New Jersey and Delaware, are one of my favorite places to watch birds. I've seen all kinds of wonderful birds and behavior there, but the memory

Why are swallows and martins most plentiful around water? Because that's where the bugs are. Millions of insects, including mosquitoes, begin their life in water, hatching into the air as adults.

that sticks with me most vividly has to do with swallows.

In late summer, swallows begin gathering into groups for the flight to winter headquarters. You'll see them perched on utility wires in ever-growing numbers as smaller groups connect and form bigger congregations that can reach massive proportions.

One year, we were exploring the little-traveled roads of a wildlife refuge in coastal Delaware when we came upon a flock of thousands of tree swallows, sitting right on the sandy road. The birds showed no sign of moving as our car drew up to them. We sat and waited for a while, then got out to see what was going on.

It was a heartbreaking scene. Apparently, a more impatient driver had actually driven right through the flock, crushing a handful of birds in its wake. Swallows mate for life, and the surviving partners were absolutely grief-stricken. Each victim was attended by a mate, who touched it repeatedly with its bill and kept up a pitiful keening. The rest of the flock sat and murmured, like mourners at a funeral.

You won't see such a huge gathering in your backyard, but you may be visited by swallows and martins in number, especially if you live within a mile or so of water. I once tried to count the birds from my chaise lounge, and I reached more than 200 before I gave up trying to sort out the swarm.

At-Home Habitat of Swallows

Swallows and martins are called aerial birds, because they spend so much time in flight. Their "habitat" is the sky, most often. But when it's time to raise a family, these birds seek out more grounded homesites.

The Wild Side

Swallows and martins are most plentiful near water because insects are enormously abundant there. Mayflies, mosquitoes, dragonflies, and other insects live as larvae in water and emerge as winged adults, quickly taking to the air. That's when uncountable numbers of them get snapped up by swallows.

Home-base habitat for family-minded swallows depends more on suitable nest sites than it does on particular plants or natural surroundings. This family likes to live in communities of its own kind. The nests may be plastered side-by-side or spaced out, depending on species. But where's there's one swallow or martin family, there's most likely more.

Homesites near water are always popular, because flying insects are abundant. Rough-winged and bank swallows nest in holes in banks, especially sandy ones, maybe because the soil is easier to scoop out. Cliff swallows mortar their nests to rocks or buildings. For cave swallows, it's natural caverns or their reasonable facsimile of manmade culverts.

Backyard Matchup

Swallows and martins often nest in or on human structures. Barn swallows have the delightful habit of nesting in or on buildings in rural areas. Tree and violet-green swallows and purple martins are beloved bird-box tenants.

Many swallows, including these purple martins, prefer tight-packed communities. But tree and violet-green swallows allow more elbow room between neighbors.

Purple martins are a different subspecies west of the Rockies, and they've been reluctant to use apartment-style birdhouses. The western birds still nest in colonies, but they like more elbow room than the easterners.

Save your money and skip the fancy birdhouse if you live west of the mountains. Your martins will find their own cavities: in old woodpecker holes in cacti or trees, in wooden pilings in rivers or bays, or in bridges or other structures. They may also adopt single-pair nest boxes or gourds.

(continued on page 142)

Simple Sustenance

High-flying swallows on the move will appreciate easy access at this beckoning crop of berries.

It's flying insects that attract swallows to the open air, and you'll have plenty overhead in the summer. To coax swallows down to where you can actually see them, you can plant bayberries (*Myrica pensylvanica,* or, in the South, *M. cerifera*) to lure tree swallows to your yard. Cliff swallows have been reported to sample the berries of eastern redcedar (*Juniperus virginiana*); if swallows don't make use of the berries, cedar waxwings will.

Many backyard birds, including cardinals, jays, native sparrows, juncos, towhees, and thrushes, will appreciate the extra cover this planting provides. In milder winters, bayberries are evergreen; even if they lose their leaves, the redcedars will offer winter shelter. Both kinds of plants grow fast. In only 2 or 3 years, the bayberries should knit together to form one inviting sweep of cover.

If you have a large, open area of lawn, you can put up a birdhouse on a post about 4 feet high at one edge of it, facing the open area, for tree swallows or violet-green swallows who may come winging in. Birdhouses rarely go unused, so even if swallows don't show up, a chickadee, titmouse, or nuthatch may make use of it.

Plant List

1. Eastern redcedar (*Juniperus virginiana*) (3 trees) (Hardiness Zones 3–9)

2. Bayberry (*Myrica pensylvanica*) (3 shrubs: 2 females with berries; 1 male, without berries) (Hardiness Zones 3–6)

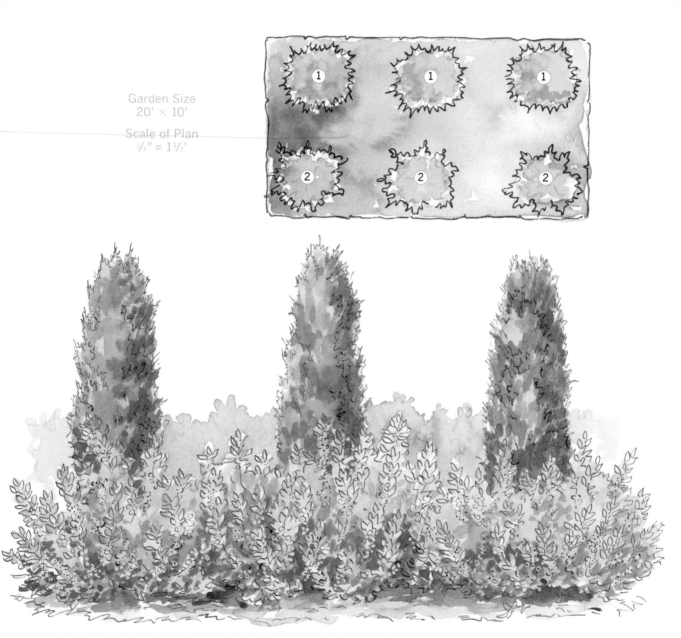

Garden Size
20' × 10'

Scale of Plan
¼" = 1½'

Just two kinds of plants supply inviting cover for birds, plus generous berries for fall and winter feeding. Spaced, columnar redcedars have a formal look; for a more casual feel, you can group them at one end.

Natural Foods for Swallows

Flying insects are the bill of fare for the Swallow family. Nearly all insect food is taken in flight, although purple martins occasionally forage on the ground.

Berries are also eaten, but by only two species of this family.

Main Menu: Insects

Swallows' and martins' bailiwick is insects in the air, especially those high up. Many kinds of flying insects are eagerly devoured by this family, from tiny gnats and midges to large dragonflies, grasshoppers, bees, and wasps.

These birds will also swoop low to catch insects stirred up by, say, a birdwatcher strolling the yard or a farmer mowing hay. They often patrol low over water, too, to catch aquatic insects, including mosquitoes, mayflies, and others, that are rising from the surface for the first—and last—time.

Only two kinds of berries are known to be eaten by swallows. Cliff swallows have been reported to eat the berries of eastern redcedar (*Juniperus virginiana*), though I've never managed to catch them

Fragrant juniper berries (*Juniperus* spp.) may attract cliff swallows passing through your area. If not, waxwings, thrushes, and other birds will dig in.

in the act. But it's bayberries (*Myrica pensylvanica*) that attract the crowds—of tree swallows.

During fall migration and in winter, tree swallows alight to eat bayberries. The bayberry thickets of the Atlantic coast have been a tradi-

One Surefire Plant to Attract Swallows

Bayberry (*Myrica pensylvanica*) is an evergreen or semi-evergreen shrub to small tree that can reach about 10 feet tall. It's known for its aromatic foliage, which has inconspicuous flowers followed by waxy, grayish white berries that thickly stud the stems. The berries make an ideal food for the Swallow family in fall, winter, and spring. This plant, which grows in Zones 3 to 6, comes in both male and female, and you'll need both to get a good crop. Buy your plants at a local nursery, if possible, so that you can pick out females with lots of berries already on the stem, and a much less prolific male to keep them company. In the South, you can also try southern bayberry or wax myrtle (*M. cerifera*), which thrives in Zones 6 to 9. Bayberries will also attract yellow-rumped warblers and may bring in mimic thrushes, thrushes (including bluebirds), flickers, and other woodpeckers.

tional tree swallow gathering place in fall and over winter since before Europeans arrived on these shores.

Backyard Fare

I wouldn't be without bayberries in my yard, and not just because they attract swallows. They're good-looking, trouble-free plants, and they grow fast. In just a single year, my young shrubs reached 3 feet tall and just as wide. By the following year, they'd doubled in size.

Tree swallows act as if bayberries are delicious, but don't be tempted yourself. The waxy berries are horribly bitter and astringent to the human palate, and evoke an instant *"Pttooey!"* response.

Any planting in your yard that attracts flying insects may capture the attention of swallows, as long as there is enough open space for these aerialists to maneuver. The most abundant flying insects in your yard—not counting those dratted mosquitoes—are likely to be butterflies. A flower garden dancing with butterflies, or a vegetable garden that attracts white cabbage butterflies, may entice swallows to fly in at low level to grab a bite of butterfly. Herb gardens also attract a bevy of butterflies, and possibly swallows, too.

Martha's Bayberry Nursery

No, not *that* Martha—we're talking about Martha's Vineyard. This island off of Massachusetts is a prime wintering spot for tree swallows, which gather there in flocks so immense that they look like shifting clouds of smoke.

It's the bayberries that draw the swallows to this pricey chunk of real estate. The glossy bushes form thickets in many areas, thriving in the sand and salt air.

When I explored the island, salivating at the shingled beach "cottages" bigger than any house I've ever lived in, I found several areas in the dunes that were covered with the weirdest stuff. It seemed to be a patchy layer of round, nubbly, blackish seeds, with bits of dirty gray stuff mixed in, and it stretched over many square feet.

It turned out to be the droppings of bayberry-eating tree swallows. The birds settle on the dunes

Early settlers used waxy, aromatic bayberries to make candles.

to eat sand to aid in grinding their food. When I watched a flock lift off into the air, I noticed many of the birds, um, lightened the load as soon as they took wing. The indigestible parts of the bayberries were excreted, including the seeds. A little later, I came across the makings of a new thicket, an area of young bayberry bushes that had apparently sprung up from just such a "nursery" deposited a few years before.

Water gardens as small as a backyard garden pool may also nurture flying insects for swallows. Some insects live as larvae in water, then emerge as winged adults that quickly take to the air.

Mayflies are a possibility in any pool, because the adult female lays her eggs on water wherever she finds it. If you've ever lifted a stone in your pool and noticed an odd creature plastered to the bottom of the rock, with a long, forked hair-thin "tail" protruding from its hind end, you've found a mayfly larva.

Mayflies are called ephemeral insects because they live only a very short time after they emerge from the water. In some species, it may be just a single day, just long enough to mate and lay eggs for the next round.

Water gardens also nurture dragonflies, craneflies, and, quite possibly, mosquitoes. Once they transform into winged creatures, all of these insects become fast food for swallows, as long as there's enough room near your pool for the birds to use the "fly-thru" lane.

Cabbage butterflies are a draw for swallows. Their aerial insect "dances" above the flowers put them in easy reach.

Feeder Foods for Swallows

Swallows don't visit feeders, but martins may accept an offering of mealworms or waxworms.

Water Wishes of Swallows

Swallows and martins drink on the wing, and they need a large expanse of water to do it. Single birds may swoop low and grab a sip in their open beak. Or an entire flock often circles down to the water, dips their beaks, then circles back up, over and over, like a feathered Ferris wheel.

Wait until it's warm to plant birdhouse gourd seeds, then stand back: They can climb 30 feet.

Top To-Dos for
SWALLOWS

1. Plant bayberries for tree swallows.
2. Put up nest boxes for tree swallows and violet-green swallows.
3. Put up a multi-apartment house for purple martins.
4. Grow birdhouse gourds for possible purple martin houses.
5. Offer crushed eggshells for purple martins.

Nesting Needs of Swallows

Here's where you can do some "gardening" for this bird family: Plant a bunch of birdhouses.

Nest boxes are eagerly occupied by tree swallows and violet-green swallows. You can create a small colony by spacing the mounting posts a dozen feet apart. Or you can try a single box, which may get a taker.

You can also try your hand at supplying lodging another way: Plant birdhouse gourd seeds. The gourds have been used for purple martin houses for hundreds of years. You'll find the recommended step-by-step process in books or on the Internet.

Purple martins have a lot of fans, and a whole industry revolves around them. You can find ready-made martin houses with multiple compartments from about $50 on up.

Tree swallows quickly claim a birdhouse, even after a squirrel made some adjustments to the door.

Little Extras for Swallows

Purple martins eagerly peck up crushed eggshells. To kill any potentially harmful salmonella germs, rinse a few eggshells in cold water, then spread them out on a cookie sheet. Bake in a preheated 200°F oven for 10 minutes. Cool, then crumble them with your hands into pieces of about ¼ inch. Scatter the eggshells on your lawn or driveway, or in an open feeder tray, so that martins can flutter down to eat them.

Chapter 10

The Chickadee and Titmouse Family

FAMILY NAME: Paridae

EASE OF ATTRACTING: ★★★★★ (practically guaranteed)

BIRDS IN FAMILY: Chickadees · Titmice · Verdins

Meet the Chickadee and Titmouse Family

Who doesn't love these small, friendly, faithful birds? They're plentiful and polite, never grabby or aggressive. And they have small appetites, so they never become pests.

Add in the entertainment factor of their acrobatics, and no wonder bird lovers proudly wear sweatshirts with the birds' pictures. They feel like friends!

Look and Listen

My husband still remembers the day I called him at work—about 25 years ago—with the big news: Finally, I'd figured out what bird it was that had been driving me crazy with its loud, clear whistle.

Every spring, I had tried to track down the owner of that voice. It was a distinctive call, a repeated "*Pee-ter*!" So easy to imitate that I couldn't resist.

But the only bird I ever saw anywhere nearby was a little gray tufted titmouse, one of my favorite feeder friends.

Couldn't be him, I reasoned, because he was such a small bird and this was such a big, loud whistle.

Meet the Verdins

Chickadees are one of the first birds we learn the name of, and titmice are well known to anyone who keeps a feeder. But not many are familiar with their close cousin, the verdins.

Small, quick, and gray, just like the other members of its family, the verdin lives in the arid brush of the desert Southwest. Both male and female sport a gorgeous, bright yellow head and a snazzy bit of red at the shoulder.

Like its chickadee and titmouse relatives, this bird is an ever-busy insect eater, and it often moves about in small groups. But what it's famed for is its unbelievable nest.

Picture an 8-inch ball made of hundreds to thousands of thorny twigs, tightly interwoven. That's home for a verdin.

In the scrubby desert, where most trees and shrubs are short and have minimal, thin leaves, these things stand out, yes, exactly like a sore thumb.

The colorful verdin is the only member of the Remizidae family.

The birds usually place the nest out near the end of a branch, where they're extra conspicuous but safer from predation. Any predators (and in this area, snakes are plentiful) will have to slither out the thorny branch to reach the nest.

For extra insurance, the bird arranges the sticks around the entrance hole with their thorns pointing out, ready to jab any invader who dares to try for the inner sanctum.

You'll see lots of nests in verdin land. That's partly because they build winter quarters as well as summer places. But it's also because the nests last for years. They're so densely constructed, you couldn't pull one off the branch if you tried (and you won't, because disturbing a bird nest is a federal offense).

You simply can't miss 'em.

So I kept looking for the mystery singer I was sure must be concealed in the treetop.

You may already know the humbling end to this story. Sure enough, one day I actually caught the titmouse in my binoculars just as he opened his beak to whistle.

I'm still convinced that the titmouse planned it that way, clamping his beak shut whenever he saw I was looking, and flitting from branch to branch or tree to tree, just to keep me guessing. Not to mention get a good laugh out of making me climb through brambles and trip over branches while I was trying to get closer. Grrr. Little joker.

But the quest was worth it. Because now I had a new behavior to put with what I already knew about titmice from watching them at the feeder.

Chickadees and titmice are friendly at the feeder and in the yard. Even in their natural habitat of the woods, they're unafraid and often come close to us. But in breeding season, these birds show a more secretive side. They court in privacy, and the male's love songs are performed for her ears only.

One thing you can count on, though: This family isn't the silent type.

Although titmice are often quiet at the feeder,

The tufted titmouse downs dozens of insects in your trees for every sunflower seed it eats at your feeder.

Alert, inquisitive black-capped chickadees and others in this family are social with other birds and with us.

they whistle back and forth and keep in touch with thin, rapid, high-pitched calls when they're roaming about.

And chickadees are real chatterboxes. Most of them say some variation of their own onomatopoetic name in all seasons. And they touch base with each other when foraging by using high-pitched, buzzy calls that sound a lot like titmice (and brown creepers and kinglets—birds this family often pals around with).

But chickadees, too, have a trick up their sleeve, especially as breeding season nears: A pretty two- or three-note whistle, with the last note lower (think "Three Blind Mice," or in shorter versions, "Three Blind"). I'm not naming names, but one birdwatcher I know very well—the same one who spent years trying to pin down a singing titmouse—was fooled for a while by this one, too.

All chickadees and titmice are small, gray birds, many with jaunty black or dark brown trim on their heads. Some show a wash of pale rusty orange, usually along their sides; the well-named chestnut-backed chickadee is mostly rust instead of gray. In cold weather, chickadees can look like little butterballs, with their feathers fluffed up for better insulation.

Range of Chickadees and Titmice

How does that old Joni Mitchell refrain go: "You don't know what you've got 'til it's gone"?

I was so used to seeing titmice everywhere, in my Pennsylvania and Indiana backyards as well as

Chickadees are instantly recognizable as chickadees, even when details of the species are different. This is the chestnut-backed chickadee.

I used to take for granted. Luckily, I still have plenty of chickadees to befriend.

Each of the five species of titmice and the seven kinds of chickadees (that number includes the gray-headed chickadee of Alaska) has its own niche, but there's plenty of overlap. It's common to enjoy the antics of two or three species in your yard.

Now You See 'em . . .

Chickadees and titmice live year-round within their range. They do migrate, but they stick within those borders. So, if you live in an area outside their range, you don't even have a chance of seeing them when they're passing through, as you would with warblers, vireos, and other migrating birds.

All right, I'll stop whining now. The good news is that, because the birds can be seen in all seasons, you'll get to watch every bit of their behavior, including courtship and family life.

"Your" birds will probably relocate in winter, returning to nesting grounds in spring. But others soon move in to fill any gaps. Even though I like to believe I really "know" my individual birds, I can't tell the difference. It's darn hard to distinguish one from the next.

Family Habits of Chickadees and Titmice

Did somebody say party? Chickadees and titmice are social birds. They hang out in small flocks of their own kind or with compatible pals that share their habitat and eating habits. Only

when traveling across the country, that it never dawned on me that they might be totally missing from some areas.

Proving that a birdwatcher is never too old to learn. It wasn't until I put up my feeders here in southwestern Washington a few years ago that I noticed the lack of my perky pals. Chickadees galore, sure. But nary a titmouse.

Flipping open a field guide, I discovered that I'm not the only one who has to live without titmice. Various chickadee species cover just about every part of the country (sorry, little corner where California, Oregon, and Nevada come together). But titmice have never moved into the Pacific Northwest, the tier of northern states, and a big part of the Plains.

Now that they're not here, I miss the titmice

Young conifers like this hemlock hold the promise of plentiful food and cover for chickadees and titmice.

Take a Time-Out

I find birders' journals a constant source of amusement, probably because I'm so hopeless at keeping the kind of obsessive notes that seem to be their norm.

One of my favorites, written in the old-fashioned naturalist style I love, comes courtesy of William Leon Dawson, from a 1909 book called *The Birds of Washington*:

"Chickadee refuses to look down for long upon the world; or, indeed, to look at any one thing from any direction for more than two consecutive twelfths of a second."

Got that stopwatch ready?

during nesting season do they leave the scene behind and focus on the family.

You'll usually see them in motion, foraging through the branches so quickly that it's hard to tell what they're doing along the way. These are real gymnasts, with a great sense of balance, and feet and legs that are built for grasping and getaways.

At-Home Habitat

Birds of this family are naturally at home in woods, but that doesn't mean they're always in the treetops. Often, they drop down to small trees, shrubs, or brush during their never-ending search for food.

The Wild Side

The first thing I like to do when exploring a new patch of woods is to stand still for a while. Usually, it takes just a few minutes before a band of chickadees or titmice swing into sight. Their call notes sound from all sides as the birds move through, and past. Wait a while, and it'll happen again. This family patrols its feeding areas constantly.

Both deciduous woods and conifers attract this family. These birds will include any trees within their range in their forays. In the dry West, where shrubby junipers (*Juniperus* spp.) are often the biggest trees around, the birds make do perfectly well with what grows in their homeland. But don't be fooled by the name: The juniper titmouse frequently forsakes its namesake tree and forages in oak trees or in the dry, open woods within its range.

Backyard Matchup

Since this family is one of the most frequent visitors to feeders, you may think your yard is already prime territory. It very well may be—in winter. But for nesting season and summer, you'll probably want to make a few improvements. Gardening for chickadees and titmice will pay off in fall and winter, too, by tempting your birds to linger instead of flying away after feeder visits.

Backyards are a favorite habitat of many species, so you already have a head start. Any de-

Fiery fall color is reason enough to plant a red maple (*Acer rubrum*). Birds will be more impressed by the tasty buds, seeds, and insects on the tree.

ciduous tree, such as oaks (*Quercus* spp.), maples (*Acer* spp.), sweetgums (*Liquidambar* spp.), tulip tree (*Liriodendron tulipifera*), ashes (*Fraxinus* spp.), and many others will appeal to this tribe of eager eaters. Why, there are so many wonderful native species of maples and oaks alone, that I've often thought about planting a whole side of the yard with a sampler of one of these species.

An older shade tree or conifer is a super foundation that you can enhance with young trees and shrubs, to entice the birds down to eye level. Dogwoods (*Cornus florida, C. pacifica, C. kousa, C. mas*), redbuds (*Cercis canadensis, C. texensis*), and tree-type shadblow (*Amelanchier arborea* and hybrid cultivars) flourish under taller trees, and they're just the right height for you to admire chickadees up close.

These birds find lots of food in conifers, too, so try to find room for a fast-growing spruce (*Picea* spp.), hemlock (*Tsuga* spp.), fir (*Abies* spp.), or pine (*Pinus* spp.). Evergreens such as these also offer the birds shelter during bad weather. In dry gardens, mesquites (*Prosopis* spp.), palo verdes (*Parkinsonia* spp.), and western juniper (*Juniperus occidentalis*) will suit these birds. Nonnative species are welcome, too, as long as they host plenty of insects.

Lots of cover will make this family feel at home, so try a hedge, or plant shrubs among your trees. Flower gardens offer suitable feeding habitat for this family. You can intersperse a few shrubs or trees with flowers to make the area easier for the birds to get to; they'll use these larger plants as stepping-stones when foraging.

(continued on page 156)

Instant Appeal, Future Potential

Spend time with friendly chickadees and titmice in a small shade garden full of attractions.

Here's the start of a shady garden, and it'll look good from the time you plant it. Birches and redbuds are racehorses; they may double in size in a single year. All the plants tolerate sun but will adapt to shade as the trees gain height.

This space of about 10 by 15 feet provides plenty of temptations for the Chickadees and Titmice family: a bounty of insect food, buds, seeds, and in a few years to come, acorns. A birdhouse begs for a happy family, and ferns supply soft lining for the nest. A bench gives you a good view of all the action. Friendly chickadees and titmice, and their displaced relatives, the bushtits, won't be shy about splashing in the birdbath just a few feet away.

In winter, when the leaves are down and the ferns have died back, the delicate tracery of bare branches and seeds will invite repeat visits by chickadees and titmice, while native sparrows, towhees, and mimic thrushes may explore the leaf-covered mulch.

To avoid wasting growing time and money, buy ferns in pots at your local nursery, so you can see what you're getting. Paying a little extra for potted plants is worth it. The fern species in this garden grow fast and furious, and in about 2 years they may reach almost shrub size. Royal ferns do best with generous helpings of water, so the site next to the birdbath is perfect. Every time you dump and refill the birdbath, the fern will get a drink.

Plant List

1. Redbud trees (*Cercis canadensis, C. occidentalis,* or *C. texensis*) (2 trees) (Hardiness Zones 5–9, depending on species)

2. Oak, of whatever kind you like best (I vote for scarlet, *Quercus coccinea*) (1 tree) (Hardiness Zones 4–10, depending on species)

3. Clump birch of any kind (*Betula* spp. and cvs.); buy a plant with more than one trunk (1 tree) (Hardiness Zones 2–9, depending on species or cultivar)

4. Cinnamon ferns (*Osmunda cinnamomea*) (6 plants) (Hardiness Zones 4–8)

5. Royal fern (*Osmunda regalis*) (1 plant) (Hardiness Zones 4–9)

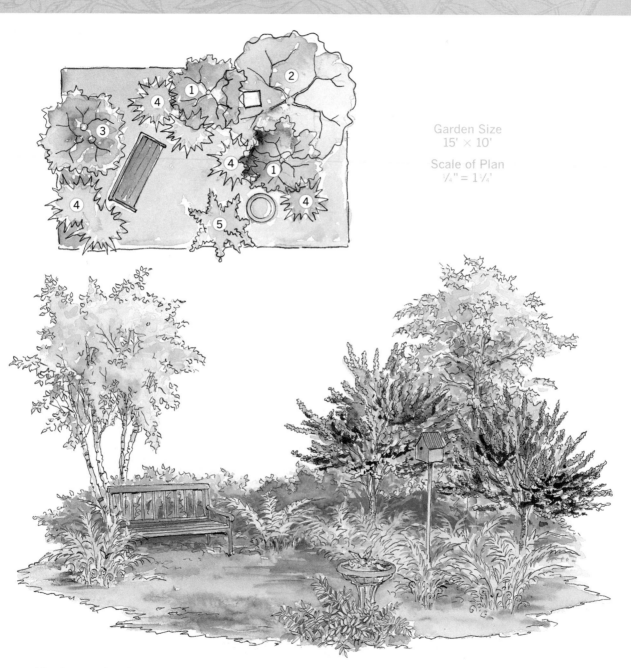

Garden Size
15' × 10'

Scale of Plan
¼" = 1¼'

Here's a garden that needs no fussing after you plant it, an extra benefit as far as birds are concerned. It will look well established even in its first year, thanks to the fast-growing ferns, redbuds, and birch.

Surefire Plants to Attract Chickadees and Titmice

You'll never notice the zillions of insects on the foliage, bark, and flowers of these trees, but they won't escape the sharp eyes and sharp beaks of chickadees and titmice. As the plants mature, their seeds add other temptations. The ferns aren't for bird food—but you may see their fuzz harvested for a soft nest lining.

Plant	Type	Description	Zone
Birch (*Betula* spp.)	Deciduous tree, to about 30 ft	Graceful, multitrunked, with beautiful bark; appealing catkins; yellow fall color; fast-growing	2–9, depending on species or cultivar
Chinquapin (*Castanea pumila*)	Deciduous shrub or small tree, to about 20 ft	Long, coarsely toothed leaves with sprays of greenish flowers followed by small edible chestnutlike chinkapins	5–9
Redbud (*Cercis canadensis, C. occidentalis, C. texensis*)	Small deciduous tree, to about 20 ft	Purplish-pink flowers stud the branches before the heart-shaped leaves appear; thin, flat, pealike seedpods.	*C. canadensis*, 5–9; *C. occidentalis*, 7–9; *C. texensis* (also known as *C. canadensis* var. *texensis*), 6–9
Cinnamon and royal ferns (*Osmunda cinnamomea, O. regalis*)	Perennial, deciduous ferns, 3 to 5 ft	Both have brown-felted stems and lush, beautiful fronds.	Cinnamon fern, 4–8; royal fern, 4–9 Royal fern does best in moist to wet soil; great near a pond or birdbath.
Spruce (*Picea* spp.)	Evergreen conifer, to 100 ft or more	Prickly, short needles; cones	3–8
Oak (*Quercus* spp.)	Stately deciduous or evergreen tree, to 100 ft	Glossy leaves, tassels of flowers, and acorns, with age	4–10, depending on species
Hemlock (*Tsuga* spp.)	Evergreen conifer, to 100 ft; quickly grows to about 20 ft, then slows down	Short, soft needles, small cones	4–9, depending on species

Used for	Comments	Other Birds Attracted
Food	Another top choice for bird gardens, may be short-lived	Vireos, warblers, flycatchers, large finches, small finches, and others; many birds use birches for perching, nesting, and cover, and eat buds, catkins, and seeds
Food	Burrs can be pesky; rake fallen burrs beneath the bush to avoid close encounters	Large finches, jays and crows, woodpeckers, warblers, vireos, orioles, tanagers, wild turkeys and other gallinaceous birds; many other birds
Food	One of the best trees for a bird garden. The plain, unimproved species type is beautiful and bird-approved. 'Forest Pansy', named for its dark leaves, is a newer cultivar that's part of the fad for plants with deep-colored foliage.	Warblers, woodpeckers, vireos, flycatchers, and many other birds
Nesting material	Cinnamon ferns are long-lived. Beautiful from the time you plant them, they need a few years to grow into an impressive clump.	Useful as cover for ground-dwelling birds such as towhees, thrushes, and native sparrows
Food, roosting	Natural shapes are better for birds than contorted or dwarf forms	Small finches, large finches including cardinals, many birds, for roosting; many birds eat buds
Food	Valuable even when young. Try native species, which attract native moths and butterflies as host plants (more bird food!)	Tanagers, orioles, vireos, warblers, woodpeckers, grosbeaks, jays and crows, wild turkeys and other gallinaceous birds
Food	A thing of beauty, even when young, and especially in snow	Large finches, grouse; many birds, for roosting

Natural Foods for Chickadees and Titmice

It's a mixed menu for this family, with insects as the entree and seeds, nuts, fruits, and berries filling the rest of the plate.

Main Menu: Insects and Plant Seeds

Hard to believe, but the little birds we think of as cute, friendly characters are actually the premier caretakers of our country's trees. These common, widespread birds do a fine job of controlling the insects that target trees. Just about any insect they find in the foliage is fair game, from tiny ants and aphids to caterpillars, moths, and beetles.

Even better for our trees, these birds are super-skilled at ferreting out insect eggs. Since an insect may lay dozens to scores to hundreds of eggs, every insect egg that a bird eats has a huge effect on future populations.

This family eats insects at any stage of development. Egg, larva, pupa, adult—it all goes down the hatch with equal alacrity. Winter doesn't mean the end of their insect food; they simply switch to more durable forms, such as cocoons.

When I was a kid, giant silk moths were a lot more common than they are now, and every winter, I'd see dozens of their giant-size cocoons, as big as my thumb. One year, every spicebush (*Lindera benzoin*) in my neighborhood drew extra attention from chickadees. This shrub is a host plant on which the caterpillars of the huge and lovely Prometheus moth feed, and every bush held at least one dangling Prometheus cocoon.

They looked very much like dead leaves, but the chickadees weren't fooled. One by one, the cocoons were raided. Often I watched two chickadees working together, pulling away the thick wall of silk with their tiny, sharp beaks.

The frenetic habits of this family mean that each tree gets a thorough going-over. Watch the birds in your yard, and you'll see they examine just about every possible hiding place for insect treats, including rolled-up leaves, stems, and both the upper side and underside of the leaves.

When seeds of trees and other plants ripen, this family grabs a big share. Ragweed is a favorite. So are the small "beans" in redbud (*Cercis*

Desert plants are well used by desert dwellers: Mesquite tree seeds (*Prosopis* spp.) are ground into flour by Native Americans and devoured by birds.

Bushtits Get Booted

The western birds known as bushtits share a lot of habits with the Chickadee and Titmouse family. Among the smallest of the songbirds, bushtits are friendly gray birds full of nervous energy. Strongly social, they forage through the foliage in lively, chattering groups, and are often at home in the woods and dry lands of the West.

Sorry, bushtits. Although you once were part of this family, you've now been relegated to the Long-Tailed Tit family, or *Aegithalidae*.

The bushtit is the only representative of its family in America; all of the others are Eurasian, except for one species in Java.

Next time you're in China or the Himalayas, take a look and you'll see that the birds in this family are a close match to our own chickadees and titmice. The black-chinned tit, a cute little bird with, yep, a black chin, plus a red cap and a blue back, looks like a chickadee seen in color instead of black-and-white.

The Long-Tailed Tit family, bushtits included, build big, impressive nests that dangle from a branch, somewhat like an oriole nest, with a hood made of spider silk at the top.

A leafy yard will win their favor; so will suet and mealworms at the feeder and a birdbath.

It takes a camera to stop a busy little bushtit.

---

canadensis, *C. occidentalis, C. texensis*) seedpods and on western trees such as mesquite (*Prosopsis* spp.), paloverde (*Cercidium* spp., also known as *Parkinsonia*), and acacia (*Acacia* spp.) The birds also visit small cones, such as those of hemlocks (*Tsuga* spp.) and alders (*Alnus* spp.), as well as larger pinecones. The seeds of pinyon cones (*Pinus edulis*)—the ones we cooking fans know as pine nuts—are a big hit, and no wonder: They're huge and meaty, and high in oil.

Acorns, beechnuts, chinquapins, and other nuts round out the list. Fruit isn't a top favorite, although these birds do indulge in hackberries (*Celtis occidentalis*), mulberries (*Morus* spp. and cvs.), and wild cherries (*Prunus virginiana, P. pensylvanica, P. serotina*).

Backyard Fare

Insects are always welcomed by these birds, and your unsprayed trees, shrubs, and flowers will offer plenty.

The more leaves and branches, the better: That's my rule of thumb when it comes to this family. If your yard is mostly open lawn or flower beds, you can add small trees to multiply the leafy garden of bugs for birds. Don't worry; you won't have to do anything special to encourage insects to move in!

Remember to choose plants that will bear seeds or nuts, too. Small trees, including birch (*Betula* spp.), alder (*Alnus* spp.), and ever-reliable redbud (*Cercis canadensis, C. occidentalis, C. texensis*), are pretty enough for any yard. A group of

Only the mountain chickadee adds a striped twist to the standard "black cap, black bib" of the clan.

redbuds looks even better than a single tree. Invest in an oak for the future; while you're waiting for it to grow old and stately, it'll harbor thousands of insects in the years before it bears acorns.

Titmice and chickadees (and bushtits) are most at home in plants that are about 8 feet tall or better. Although the birds will come down to check out low shrubs, taller varieties get most of their attention. Upright plants seem to be more attractive than mounded shrubs. I rarely see a chickadee in a dwarf or weeping Japanese maple (*Acer palmatum*), no matter how artistically it's shaped. But upright cultivars of Japanese maple are well attended.

The verdins of the Southwest will investigate any plant, so height isn't a concern.

Enticing chickadees and titmice is a great excuse to get to know the chinquapin (*Castanea pumila*). This native chestnut grows from Missouri to New Jersey, south to Texas and Florida. Yet many folks have never even heard of it, and even fewer have tasted its sweet, delicious nuts, which are adored by birds. It grows fast, has large, long glossy leaves, and may become a large shrub or small tree (or you can clip off extra branches to train it into a tree shape, too). You'll want to put this one way back in an out-of-the-way corner, because its nuts are enclosed in ultra-spiny burs. But if you have the room, and no concerns of pets, small children, or bare feet blundering into the burs, it's an interesting possibility.

Seeds of the classic annual sunflower (*Helianthus annus*) are popular with these birds. When sunflower seedlings spring up from seeds dropped by feeder birds, I let them stay. Even a puny flower head will buy a week of entertainment as the little acrobats pluck them out, one by one.

Feeder Foods for Chickadees and Titmice

This family is easy to please. Try any of these foods:

Sunflower seeds
Peanuts and other nuts, coarsely chopped
Suet
Peanut butter and other nut butters
Insect-enriched suet, mealworms, and other insects

Top To-Dos for
CHICKADEES AND TITMICE

1. Plant a short-needled conifer, such as hemlock (*Tsuga* spp.), fir (*Abies* spp.), or spruce (*Picea* spp., not dwarf or contorted forms).

2. Give a redbud tree (*Cercis canadensis, C. occidentalis, C. texensis*) a place of honor, or plant a group of them.

3. Plant a native oak tree (*Quercus* spp.).

4. Plant seeds for annual sunflowers (*Helianthus annuus* 'Russian Giant' or use a handful of seed from your feeder).

5. Provide nesting materials and birdhouses.

6. Install a birdbath with a drip tube.

Water Wishes of Chickadees and Titmice

Did you notice the birdbath in the garden design for this family? Fresh water is a huge draw for these birds. Add an inexpensive drip line to your birdbath, anchored with a rock, and you're guaranteed to get bathing beauties, drawn to the irresistible trickle of fresh water.

Nesting Needs of Chickadees and Titmice

Once your yard has a good amount of small trees and shrubs, and maybe a big tree or two, chickadees and titmice will be willing to consider it as home. These birds nest in cavities—and birdhouses. You won't even need to pull out the ladder; a location about 5 feet from the ground will suit them to a T.

Nest Materials

Who'd ever have thought that ferns were an important source of nesting materials? Not I, until I saw it with my own eyes in Georgia one springtime.

A pair of Carolina chickadees was so interested in a clump of royal ferns (*Osmunda regalis,* one of my favorites, too), that I bent down when they took a break, to see what treasure trove of insects they'd found.

Not bugs at all—they'd been removing tiny bits of the brown fuzz from the stalks. Cinnamon ferns (*Osmunda cinnamomea*), native to eastern North America, are popular in the same way, with the soft downy stuff put to use as a nest lining for the birds.

Besides growing ferns for nest materials, you'll have good luck by putting out a selection of these other nest supplies:

Milkweed fluff
Fur, especially rabbit and raccoon
Wool
Moss
Cotton balls (not synthetic)
Cow hair
Spanish moss

Chapter 11

The Nuthatch Family

FAMILY NAME: Sittidae

EASE OF ATTRACTING: ★★★★★ (practically guaranteed)

BIRDS IN FAMILY: Nuthatches

Meet the Nuthatch Family

Plato's student Aristotle is famed for his musings on philosophy and politics, which he wrote, oh, about a thousand-and-a-half years ago. My son David leans toward philosophy himself, and he's a big fan of Aristotle's works. But I get a huge kick out of knowing that this revered intellectual was also a nature nut.

Like us backyard bird lovers, Aristotle spent hours observing the birds and other creatures around him. I suppose it helped that he had the support of the king, not to mention a retinue of servants to do his bidding. (I can see it now: "Carry my litter to that tree! Faster! No, not that tree, doggone it, *that* tree!")

When he noticed a bird that pecks at the bark of trees, he came up with the name *Sitte,* which you'll notice is the root of this family's name. Nuthatches roam about Greece, too, so it's possible he was describing these birds. Whether or not he was looking at nuthatches, it's pretty neat to know that even ancient philosophers took time out to notice birds.

Look and Listen

These birds look like no other. They're plump but streamlined, with a pointy beak and stubby tail. And those short little legs? All the better for clinging to bark, my dear.

All four species are two-tone: a slate-gray upper side, and, usually, a white breast and belly. The

Our largest nuthatch, the white-breasted is a familiar feeder bird in most parts of the country.

Nuthatches are familiar friends at feeders, visiting daily, especially in winter.

Whenever anyone who's fairly new to bird-watching asks me about an unusual little gray and white bird that showed up at his or her feeder in winter, I always ask, "Does it look like it's wearing a tuxedo?"

The white-breasted nuthatch wears the most formal outfit, and he's the biggest of the bunch, but he's still pretty small among birds. The others are irresistibly cute, like tiny toys.

Range of Nuthatches

You have a good chance of seeing a nuthatch in any backyard in the country. The white-breasted and red-breasted species show up in every state.

While the brown-headed nuthatch sticks to the Southeast, the pygmy nuthatch stays close to areas of the West.

red-breasted nuthatch has to live up to its name, so it's rusty-red below. A brown or back cap is part of the costume for all species. All in all, it's a tidy, dapper outfit.

Focus on Fine Points

I thought I had a pretty good handle on nuthatch calls—a variety of squeaks, nasal notes, and peeping—until I was brought up short by a bird in the Pacific Northwest.

Instead of the customary "Yank! Yank! Yank!" call, this bird was loudly calling "Eeern," with that complaining kitty quality I associate with sapsuckers.

I thought I was tracking down a red-breasted sapsucker yelping from a tree. When I finally found the calling bird, it turned out to be a white-breasted nuthatch.

I was shaken right down to my muddy sneakers. It was as if I'd just seen a robin open its beak and say "Chick-a-dee-dee."

That was a great lesson in subspecies, or races. Taxonomists use these categories to separate birds based on fine points of appearance, behavior, or vocalizations. Most differences are so slight that you can still easily recognize the bird's species.

But when you're "watching" birds by ear, that variation can be a real surprise. Now that I know what the Pacific race of the white-breasted nuthatch sounds like, it makes me wonder what else I've missed.

The brown-headed nuthatch roams the pines of the Southeast; its lookalike, below, sticks to the West.

Smallest of the tribe, the pygmy nuthatch is an inch shorter than a black-capped chickadee, beak to tail tip.

Now You See 'em . . .

The red-breasted is a wintertime treat in the eastern two-thirds of the nation, and a year-round pleasure in the West, in New England, and in the Appalachians. In some winters, red-breasted nuthatches come down from the frigid North in big numbers.

The white-breasted stays around all year in most areas but is absent in the far Southeast and a few other spots. The tiny pygmy and brown-headed nuthatches show up summer and winter within their range.

Family Habits of Nuthatches

Nuthatches move from one tree to the next, alighting high on the trunk. Then, using their strong feet to cling to the bark, they quickly hitch around the trunk, spiraling downward. Often, they travel along the underside of a tree limb in short, jerky hops, to glean insects missed by birds that don't have the ability to cling like a fly.

When you're scouting for insects in bark crevices, keeping your head close to the tree trunk is a great trick for finding treasure.

In his 1885 book, *Birds of the Bush,* Bradford Torrey commented on the peculiar posture of nuthatches:

> *Strange—is it not?—that any bird should find it easiest to do such work while clinging to a perpendicular surface! Yes; but how does it look to a dog, I wonder, that men can walk better on their hind legs than on all fours?*

Nuthatches usually visit the yard or feeders singly or in pairs. But in winter, often more birds will come to seek a good meal at your place.

At-Home Habitat of Nuthatches

Wherever you find trees, you're likely to see a nuthatch. Forests are their usual habitat, but they frequent parks, golf courses, street trees, and backyards, too.

The Wild Side

Just about any kind of good-size tree, deciduous or conifer, will snag the services of the white-breasted nuthatch. You'll often see the red-breasted nuthatch at conifers, but it visits oaks, maples, and other deciduous trees, too. The pygmy and brown-headed species generally stick to conifers, and pines (*Pinus* spp.) in particular.

Trees of significant size, with trunks about 6 inches or more across, are the main targets of these birds. Young trees aren't as appealing, and very young saplings are usually ignored.

Backyard Matchup

Maybe I'm just an eternal optimist, but I've planted trees at every house I've lived in—even the rentals. I may not be around when they achieve a grand stature, but I don't mind.

But who thinks about 50 years into the future when they're making a garden? If we stopped to think how old we'd be when that brand-new oak we just put in the ground reaches old age, I don't think many of us would ever plant a tree at all!

In the meantime, while that tree is growing, turn your energy toward filling the other needs of these birds: food and housing.

(continued on page 168)

The Congenial Creeper

The brown creeper is often seen in the company of nuthatches—when it's seen at all, that is. This tiny brown bird blends right in against the bark, but you may glimpse it when it flies off to begin working on another tree. It will land near the bottom, ready to start the trek upward, probing the bark with its long, curved beak.

The creeper sticks tight to the trunks of trees, tirelessly scouring the bark just as nuthatches do, but with one big difference: Nuthatches go down, creepers go up.

One or two of these birds often join roving bands of chickadees, titmice, kinglets, and nuthatches to forage for food from fall through winter. The brown creeper ranges from coast to coast in winter and is becoming more common at feeders, joining nuthatches at suet and insect foods.

But although the creeper is a tree-hugger like the nuthatches and shares some eating habits, it's in a different family, *Certhiidae*. Next time you visit the British Isles, keep an eye out for this little guy; the exact same species lives there, too.

The brown creeper's long, thin bill is the perfect tool for extracting insects from bark crevices.

Living History

Nut-loving nuthatches are just as pleased with a garden of ancient native American sunflowers.

Other parts of the world, including Aristotle's Greece, can claim their own nuthatches, but sunflowers, one of their favorite foods, are all-American. Their heavy, seed-rich heads were a staple for Native Americans of the West for thousands of years.

Heritage sunflower varieties may not get as much publicity as heirloom tomatoes, but they'll give you a wonderful connection with gardeners from way back. Try the pure white-seeded sunflower of the Tarahumara Indians, the glossy blue-black seeds of the Hopi sunflower, or a handful of other prized varieties, all for about the same price as a packet of ordinary 'Russian Giant' sunflower seed.

This planting adds an 'Autumn Blaze' maple, a modern hybrid that was selected Urban Tree of the Year in 2003 by the Society of Municipal Arborists. It's a beauty that inherits the fast growth of one of its parents, the silver maple. Unlike silver maple, it tops out at about 40 to 50 feet tall. Its flaming orange-red autumn color will light up this garden of antique sunflower varieties. Ornamental grasses add fine texture and grace to the planting, as well as cover for ground-dwelling birds. When the sunflowers are blooming, you may see hummingbirds nectaring at them, or wrens, flycatchers, and many other birds looking for the insects drawn to them. Let the stems stand in winter, and you have a perfect foraging area for finches, native sparrows, juncos, quail, and all sorts of other seed eaters.

You'll need an area about 15 feet long and 6 feet wide. You can easily expand the size to include even more unusual old sunflowers. How about 'Havasupai Striped', found at the bottom of the Grand Canyon?

Plant List

1. 'Autumn Blaze' maple (*Acer* × *freemanii* 'Autumn Blaze') (1 tree) (Hardiness Zones 4–7)

2. 'Sky Racer' molinia grass (*Molinia* subsp. *arundinacea* 'Sky Racer') (2 plants) (Hardiness Zones 5–9)

3. 'Hopi Black Dye' sunflower (*Helianthus annuus* 'Hopi Black Dye') (1 packet of seed)

4. 'Apache Brown Striped' sunflower (*Helianthus annuus* 'Apache Brown Striped') (1 packet of seed)

5. 'Tarahumara White-Seeded' sunflower (*Helianthus annuus* 'Tarahumara White-Seeded') (1 packet of seed)

6. 'Hopi Branched' sunflower (*Helianthus annuus* 'Hopi Branched') (1 packet of seed)

Garden Size
15' × 6'

Scale of Plan
¼" = 1¼'

Nuthatches will find plenty to yammer about in this garden. It's a short flight from seed-rich sun-flowers to the maple, which harbors insects on its bark and branches. In winter, other seed eaters will glean leftovers.

Surefire Plants to Attract Nuthatches

These plants provide insects for nuthatches to seek among the foliage and on their bark. The conifers will supply plenty of tasty seeds, too, after a few years of growth in your yard. All are popular with lots of other birds, too.

Plant	Type of Plant	Description	Zones
Firs (*Abies* spp.) and Douglas fir (*Pseudotsuga menziesii*)	Evergreen conifer trees, to about 100 ft	Short needles and dense branches; multitude of cones with age	3–8, depending on species and cultivar
Maples (*Acer* spp.)	Large deciduous trees, to about 80 ft	Moderately fast-growing; beautiful fall color of yellow, red, or orange	3–9, depending on species or cultivar
Annual sunflower (*Helianthus annuus*)	Annual flowers, 4–8 ft or taller	Classic sunflowers with a single large head are guaranteed to attract birds; other cultivars, with fancier flowers or multiple flowerheads, will also appeal.	All
Pines (*Pinus* spp.)	Evergreen conifer trees, many spp., from about 25–100 ft	Long-needled, relatively open-branched pines produce a bounty of cones.	3–10, depending on species or cultivar
Oaks (*Quercus* spp. and cultivars)	Large deciduous trees, to about 80–100 ft	Stately, slow-growing trees with catkinlike flowers and acorns	4–10, depending on species or cultivar
Hemlocks (*Tsuga* spp.)	Evergreen conifer trees; to 100 ft with age	Short-needled and densely branched, hemlocks are graceful even when young.	4–9, depending on species

Used for	Comments	Other Birds Attracted
Seeds from cones, insects from bark and branches	Appealing to birds even when young, because of dense cover and insect food	Kinglets and bushtits eat insects from foliage; gallinaceous birds eat buds, investigate fallen seeds; many birds use as cover or roost
Insect food from bark	Investigate maples that are native to your area; many serve as host plants for caterpillars of moths and butterflies—a.k.a. "bird food!" Maples cast a dense shade, and their thick foliage and large leaves inhibit rain from getting through to the ground beneath. This "dry shade" is inhospitable to many ornamental plants, but native shrubs, such as spicebush (*Lindera benzoin*) and vine maple (*Acer circinatum*), thrive there.	Vireos, warblers, tanagers, orioles, and other birds visit even young maples, to glean insects from foliage. Large finches eat seeds; waxwings and large finches may eat flowers or leaf buds. Mature trees attract woodpeckers, chickadees and titmice, jays, large finches, and other birds, for insect food or as nest sites. Warblers, orioles, tanagers, and vireos eat insects at the blossoms.
Seeds	A sneaky way to win the loyalty of nuthatches—as long as the seeds hold out!	Large finches (especially cardinals), woodpeckers, jays, small finches, and chickadees and titmice pluck seeds from heads; native sparrows and juncos, doves, gallinaceous birds forage for dropped seeds
Seeds from cones; insects from bark and twigs	Pines look gawky when very young, but they grow fast into beautiful specimens.	Kinglets eat insects from foliage; gallinaceous birds eat buds, investigate fallen seeds; many birds use as nighttime roost
White oaks have tastier acorns than red oaks and are highly popular with birds.	Scout your local nursery and you may find an oak that already has a few acorns on it, for a head start.	Woodpeckers, jays, chickadees and titmice, gallinaceous birds, doves, small finches, and others eagerly eat acorns. Tanagers, orioles, vireos, warblers, and flycatchers eat insects from foliage or at flowers. Tanagers or jays may use as nest site.
Seeds from cones; insects from bark and branches	Quick to bear cones; trees at nursery may already have a few.	Kinglets and bushtits eat insects from foliage; native sparrows, juncos, and towhees seek cover beneath.

Natural Foods
for Nuthatches

Nuthatches have long, sharp, strong beaks. They're built that way to pry insects out of deep bark crevices and to whack open nuts or extract seeds from pinecones.

Insects, nuts, and conifer seeds are the three basics for nuthatches. Naturally, all are found in trees, conveniently close at hand for these tree-dwelling birds.

No matter how well-camouflaged a caterpillar might be, any passing nuthatch is apt to nab it.

Main Menu: Insects, Nuts, and Seeds

Beetles, moths, scale insects, spiders, pine needle spittlebugs, and other insects found in or on the bark are standard fare for nuthatches. Caterpillars and insect eggs are on the list, too.

I once happened to come across a luna moth—a beautiful, long-tailed moth with wings the color of celadon porcelain—laying her eggs on a big old sugar maple. What luck! I could just picture the new brood of lunas, dozens of them, gracefully fluttering about my neighborhood.

Fat chance.

When I went back to the tree the next day, I found I wasn't the only one who'd noticed what was going on. The discarded wings of the luna lay below the tree, and a white-breasted nuthatch was industriously dabbing up the last of the eggs.

Another big menu item? Take a look at the name of these birds. Nuts! White-breasted and red-breasted nuthatches eagerly eat any nut they can get their beak into—acorns, pecans, beechnuts, whatever's ripe for the picking. One of the

most important nuts in a nuthatch's diet isn't a true nut at all, but a seed. The seeds hidden within pinecones and other conifer cones are vital to this family, so much so that a bad year for cones in the North may touch off a southward swell of red-headed nuthatches. Pygmy and brown-headed nuthatches also rely heavily on pine "nuts."

Backyard Fare

Young conifer trees produce cones at an early age, usually just a few years after planting. I make it a habit to scout the Back 40 of my local nursery, to ferret out container-grown trees that already have a few cones on them. Might as well plant a tree that has a solid head start!

If you live in pygmy or brown-headed nuthatch territory, you'll have good luck attracting these birds by planting a pine that's native to your area, such as loblolly (*Pinus taeda*) in the South or lodgepole (*Pinus contorta*) in the West.

Both short- and long-needled conifers appeal to red- and white-breasted nuthatches, so it's a good idea to include a mix of conifers. These far-ranging avian charmers can turn up anywhere.

Oaks (*Quercus* spp.) are an excellent choice, too. Here's another opportunity to try out native species, instead of planting whatever the garden center has on sale. Shop local nurseries and you may turn up some gems. All oaks grow into stately trees, and they're vital to wildlife, including dozens of bird species.

Nuthatches will ferret out other insects in your yard, not only those on trees. You can't miss an outbreak of spittlebugs in your yard—you'll see their globs of white foam on the stems of many kinds of plants. Nuthatches will notice, too. I've often seen a nuthatch make a quick trip from the trees to pluck the soft-bodied insect from its hiding place. Keep watching the bird if you happen to spot this action, and you'll see the nuthatch wipe its beak thoroughly, to get rid of clinging bits of foam.

Caterpillars are nuthatch favorites, too. 'Pil-lars are plentiful in any yard that isn't treated with pesticides. If you want to ensure a good crop of caterpillars, just tuck a few broccoli plants among your flower garden, where you won't be dismayed to see cabbage white butterflies settle on them to lay their eggs. Just remember, that broccoli's not for the table, unless you don't mind an extra helping of protein from the green caterpillars perfectly camouflaged among the stems of the broccoli head.

Thanks to feeders, nuthatches have become big fans of a nontraditional food: sunflower seeds. It's always a delight to watch these agile birds maneuver on the smiling face of a tall sunflower (*Helianthus annuus*). They'll pick out the ripe seeds from around the outer edges and keep coming back for weeks, until those in the very center have filled out.

A Midwest prairie plant stands proudly in my Northwest yard, sprouted from seeds brought across the country—well, gee, I'd love to say by wagon train, but actually it was by Toyota. It's

The original form of our native sunflower (*Helianthus annuus*) is graceful and branching.

Maximilian sunflower (*Helianthus maximilianii*), a perennial species that reaches regal heights of 12 feet or better. The seeds don't look like much, but the little red-breasted nuthatches don't seem to mind. When they're done pulling out seeds from the cones of Douglas fir (*Pseudotsuga menziesii*) in my yard, they zip down to the sunflowers and get to work. A small step for a bird, but I like to think of it as a leap across 1,000 miles of ecosystem.

Feeder Foods for Nuthatches

Just follow the natural menu as a guideline and you'll have no trouble attracting nuthatches. Sunflower seeds, chopped nuts, and suet—which mimics their soft insect food—are perfect as staples. They may sample peanut butter treats or baked goods, too, and they're wild about mealworms and other insect-based foods.

Nuthatches often cache nuts in nooks and crannies of trees or posts, to eat later.

Water Wishes of Nuthatches

A very shallow, rough-bottomed basin is the ideal for these short-legged birds. Once in a great while, a nuthatch will sip from my pedestal bath, but the most popular "water feature" in my yard is a shallow puddle that forms in a slight depression atop a big rock in the shady part of the garden. When the puddle dries up, I refill it with a squirt from the hose. You can try putting a few rocks in your bath, so the birds can choose a water level they like.

Holly berries are a magnet for thrushes, but not for this red-breasted nuthatch. Insects are what he's after.

Nesting Needs of Nuthatches

Now we're talking! Birdhouses are a great tactic when it comes to enticing nuthatches. The members of this family are cavity nesters, and they often quickly adopt a birdhouse that's just their size. Invest in two types: one for the tiny species, and one for the larger white-breasted. That way, you'll avoid territorial battles between small nuthatches and birdhouse-seeking house sparrows. Mount the box on a tree—or the shady side of your house at a height of about 15 feet.

Nest Materials

Help nuthatches line their nests by setting out a supply of cotton tufts or balls (not synthetic), soft feathers, fur, and moss. Nuthatches are quick to take advantage of any bits of dog hair they can find in my yard.

I'd love to find a taker for my dryer lint, but I don't offer it to birds. Ever try to empty the lint screen with wet fingers? The stuff turns into a sticky mass that's hard to get off when it's damp. I sure wouldn't want nestlings to get coated with the stuff. The layer of lint may feel soft and fluffy, but don't be fooled; it's not good for birds.

Chapter 12

The Wren Family

FAMILY NAME: Troglodytidae

EASE OF ATTRACTING: ★★★★ (very easy)

BIRDS IN FAMILY: Wrens

Meet the Wren Family

Sweet, bubbling songs and as friendly as a chickadee: No wonder wrens are beloved backyard birds. Their territories are small, and it's simple to make your yard so welcoming to some species that it becomes the neighborhood of choice.

Look and Listen

With so much going on in spring, I often forget to keep track of which birds are due back from winter vacations. But I love surprises, so it's as good as Christmas morning to be awakened on a fine spring day by the tumbling, liquid trill of a house wren outside my window. Oh boy, the wrens are back!

You'll often hear a wren's loud, musical song long before you spy the singer. This family is full of fabulous soloists, and each species has its trademark song. Trills, gurgles, and whistled phrases are the hallmark, except for the cactus wren, which produces an unmusical series of low, raspy notes. Wrens have a sharp rattling or buzzy call, too, often sounded when the birds are alarmed.

The stereotype "wren" pose, of a jaunty, upright tail on a small brown bird, isn't foolproof. Wrens don't always have their tails raised. And some wrens are as big as a robin! The large western cactus wren and rock wren look more like thrushes at first glance.

Friendly habits, though, are a mark of distinction in this family, at least for some species. The house wren, Carolina wren, Bewick's wren, and cactus wren are most likely to call your backyard home. They're inquisitive birds and often investigate around our houses as well as our gardens.

The tiny winter wren may show up in gardens, or stay in the forest. And the sedge, marsh, rock, and canyon wrens prefer the wilds to our backyards. Just look at their names and you'll see where these guys live.

Range of Wrens

The house wren, known to many old-timers and country folk as "Jenny Wren," can be seen over the entire country. The Carolina wren was once a bird of the Southeast, but its range has expanded and it's now a reliable sight in most of the eastern half of the country. Bewick's wren takes up where the Carolina leaves off, covering the southern half of the western states and a wide swath along the western edge.

Winter wrens can show up just about anywhere, although their traditional range is the eastern half and the northwest part of the country. Cactus wrens, as you've no doubt guessed, stick to the cactusy areas—the Southwest.

Now You See 'em . . .

Wren migration habits depend on the menu of the particular species. The wrens that depend on insects—the smallest species—fly the coop when cold weather approaches, while the larger birds,

The Carolina wren varies its songs so much, it can keep you hopping trying to figure out who's singing. Pin down the ID by listening for its rattling buzz in between.

which switch to berries in winter, generally stay put. The rock wren, however, withdraws from the northern half of the West in fall, maybe because deep snow covers the Rockies.

In the South, the house wren is only a winter treat. Is it the heat or the humidity? The birds aren't saying.

Family Habits of Wrens

You won't have to crane your neck to spot a wren. These birds stick to low levels of brush and plants instead of hanging out in the treetops. You'll often see them on the ground, too.

But you will have to look fast: Wrens are quick. They don't stay in one place for long, except when the male is pouring out song—which he'll also do while on the move.

Wrens often look as if they're crouching down to get a better view. Strong, thin legs and agile feet support their plump bodies. They're built for quickly climbing over rocks and logs or hopping from one perch to another. Their long beaks are perfectly tailored for snatching insects from crevices or cactus thorns, or from dense clumps of grass.

For birds as comfortable around humans as wrens are, they sure are fond of playing hide-and-seek. Partly, it's because they stick to the thick vegetation where insects are plentiful. But often it seems like a game. So of course I play right along, straining my eyes to pick out the quick brown bird. Aha! Gotcha!

At-Home Habitat of Wrens

There's a wren to fill just about every niche of low-level habitat, say, within about 10 feet above ground level. Some specialize in rocky areas, but most are at home anywhere there's low-level vegetation. What kind of vegetation? Practically anything, from cholla cactus to marshy reeds to the ferns and shrubs in the understory of a forest. Only grassy fields or pastures—unless dotted with bushes—hold no appeal for wrens.

The canyon wren makes rocky western cliffs come alive with a cascade of beautiful, whistling song.

Viciously spiny to our clumsy fingers, cholla cactus is just another perching place for wrens of the desert.

Barberry Brunch

Don your leather gloves to gather the berries for this recipe, and wear long sleeves so you don't get scratched! All that work will pay off when Carolina wrens, robins, woodpeckers, catbirds, bluebirds, and other eager eaters come to see what you've cooked up.

1 cup barberries
1½ cups cornmeal
½ cup creamy peanut butter

1. Use a pair of scissors to harvest barberries; they dangle from thin stems that are easy to snip through. Hold a large, lightweight bowl beneath the branch, and let the berries drop in as you clip them off.
2. Add the cornmeal and peanut butter to the bowl of berries. Wearing a pair of disposable plastic gloves, mush everything together until it's thoroughly combined. It'll resemble a crumbly cookie dough. If it doesn't quite hold together and falls apart into fine crumbs, mix in another quarter-cup of peanut butter.
3. Serve small amounts at a time in a tray feeder.

The Wild Side

Wrens patrol just about any kind of vegetation. Specific plants don't seem to matter to wrens; they'll scour anything within their home range, whether it's chaparral, mesquite, or sedges, to name just a few of the native plants in wren country.

When it comes to nesting time, though, wrens tend to stick to their niches. Marsh wrens and sedge wrens, for instance, usually raise their family within the sheltering stems of grassy marsh plants. But when it's time to feed the kids, they'll venture out to search for insects on any low-level plants within their range.

Backyard Matchup

Thank goodness wrens aren't picky! Because they're not dependent on particular plants for habitat, and because they prefer lower levels, they're a perfect fit for our backyards.

You won't need to add trees to your yard for wrens. Instead, think waist-high and lower plants, plus a few larger shrubs. Rocky areas suit wrens, too, because there's bound to be a bounty of spiders among the rocks. You will want to supply cover so that the birds can practice their hide-and-seek habits. A few shrubs, a vegetable patch, and a flower garden will suit them to a tee. In the desert West, cholla cactus (*Opuntia* spp.) is always a safe bet.

I wish we could each have a Jenny wren, but that's not the case. There are too few birds to go around. Wrens have limited territories, and they may decide to stay in that backyard down the block.

(continued on page 180)

Wet Your Whistle, Wrens

Perky, vocal wrens find four seasons of fruit and bountiful bugs, plus a spot to splash.

This looks like a garden of the West, but it would make an equally good planting as far north as Pennsylvania and New York State—which is where I first came across prickly pear (in that case, *Opuntia humifusa*) growing wild. Fruit-eating wrens, such as the Carolina and canyon wrens, will appreciate the juicy berries of the serviceberry and the grapes, and eventually, the red fruit of the prickly pear. Orioles, tanagers, and waxwings may also join in the feast. When the grape and serviceberry bloom, insects will come swarming, and so may insect-eating warblers, vireos, and orioles. The hollyhocks add color plus a bonus of possible caterpillars: They're host plants for painted lady butterflies and other species. The low basin of water is an inviting focal point for birds, too, including desert-dwelling quail.

You can fit this garden into a sunny area about 8 feet square.

Plant List

1. Grapevine (*Vitis* spp. and cvs.; 'Concord' is usually trouble-free; desert grape, *V. girdiana,* thrives in dry gardens) (1 plant) (Hardiness Zones 4–9)

2. Serviceberry (*Amelanchier alnifolia, A. utahensis,* or *A. utahensis* var. *covillei*) (3 plants) (Hardiness Zones 3–9)

3. Prickly pear cactus (*Opuntia* spp.) (1 plant) (*O. compressa,* also known as *O. humifusa,* is hardy in Zones 6–8; other species, Zones 8 or 9–11)

4. Hollyhock (*Alcea rosea*) (1 plant) (Hardiness Zones 2–8)

Garden Size
9' × 8'

Scale of Plan
¼" = 1'

Fruit beckons to wrens and other birds in this garden with desert flair. Some types of prickly pear cactus (*Opuntia* spp.) are amazingly cold hardy, enough to add a Southwestern accent even in the Northeast.

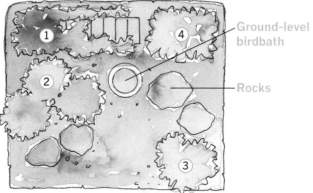

Ground-level birdbath

Rocks

Surefire Plants to Attract Wrens

Wrens are interested in insects, with some occasional delectable fruits or berries. These plants will give you a good mix of temptations in all seasons for the perky birds.

Plant	Type of Plant	Description	Zones
Serviceberry (*Amelanchier* cultivars and hybrids)	Deciduous shrubs or small trees, to about 12 ft	Graceful plants, often multistemmed; intense fall color of red, orange, purple mixed together; abundant small white flowers in spring, followed by blueberry-like fruit	3–9
Broccoli (any cultivar)	Garden vegetable, to about 2–3 ft	The buds of this cabbage-family plant are the "broccoli;" they open into large sprays of small yellow flowers.	Annual
Autumn-blooming clematis (*Clematis terniflora*)	Deciduous vine, to about 15 ft	A vigorous vine that forms a dense, tangled mass of stems and foliage; clouds of small, fragrant white flowers late summer to fall	4–9
Burning bush (*Euonymus alatus, E. fortunei*)	Deciduous shrub, to about 6 ft	Fabulous fall color that lives up to its name; wrens are more interested in small, dangling berries.	5–9
Strawberry (any cultivar)	Low-growing perennial fruit plant, to about 6 in	A pretty plant with glossy leaves and sprays of yummy berries	4–9
Cholla cactus (*Opuntia* spp.)	Bushy or treelike cactus, to about 6 ft	Spiny cacti with showy flowers and waxy fruit	8 or 9–11

Used for	Comments	Other Birds Attracted
Fruit	You can't have too many serviceberries! Plant in hedges or groups; plant tree types in flower beds.	All fruit-eating birds adore the berries: orioles, tanagers, thrushes, mimic thrushes, waxwings, and many others. Warblers and vireos are attracted to insects at flowers.
Insect food from caterpillars and adults of cabbage white butterflies.	Snuggle a few plants into your flower garden for the birds.	Small finches, including native sparrows and juncos, towhees, doves, and others forage for seeds; flycatchers, vireos, cardinals, chickadees and titmice, and other birds also seek the caterpillars and butterflies attracted to the plants.
Cover, roosting, nesting	Fast-growing and trouble-free, autumn clematis is useful to wrens in all seasons; in winter, the thick stems provide shelter.	Brown thrasher, mockingbird, and other mimic thrushes use as cover or for nesting.
Cover, food from fruit, insect food from flowers and foliage	Use in a group or in a hedge to provide cover and a safety corridor.	Mimic thrushes also eat berries. Many birds use for cover. Robins may select as nest site.
Juicy red berries are irresistible to wrens.	Strawberries make a pretty ground cover in sunny spots.	Thrushes, mimic thrushes, towhees, and many other birds are attracted to the fruit. Native sparrows may nest among the plants.
Nesting, cover; food from fruit	An excellent plant for desert gardens; beloved by western wrens	Mimic thrushes and gallinaceous birds may also eat fruit.

Natural Foods for Wrens

A long, pointy beak spells *insect eater,* and that's the main diet of this family. Wrens may also sample soft-bodied critters, such as snails and lizards.

Berries and fruits are reliable foods for many wrens, especially in winter, when insects are few and far between.

Main Menu: Insects, with Sides of Fruits and Lizards

Another thing I'm always forgetting about when springtime rolls around is something that's a lot less pleasant than the wren's song: ticks. It's always a surprise—and not a good one!—to find that first tick of the year crawling on my own skin. If you're not fond of ticks, either, you'll definitely approve of wren eating habits. Ticks are a specialty.

Most insects in the wren's repertoire are the

A heavy speckled and streaked throat and breast are the clues to a cactus wren's identity. This bird helps out by singing from a perch on its namesake plant.

I Spy Spiders!

My back porch wall in Indiana was a favorite homesite for mud-dauber wasps. They weren't a threat to people on the porch; they just wanted a wall upon which to plaster their interesting nursery, a series of mud tubes that looks a lot like a primitive pipe flute.

The wasps laid eggs within the tubes, then stuffed each cylinder with as many spiders as they could cram in and sealed the end. It sounds horrid, but those spiders were a living larder for the wasp larvae.

The Carolina and house wrens in my yard had their own opinion about the practice. "Yum, spiders!" was the prevailing sentiment. Often while I was sitting on the porch, a wren would fly to the eave, flutter to the wasp nest, and get a solid grip on the tubes. Then it would quickly stab an opening with its beak and extract the spiders.

I did have to rearrange my porch furniture after such a maneuver caused spiders to drop into a guest's lemonade. But "Look out below!" was a small price to pay for the front-row seat.

Mud-daubers aren't alone in this habit; many wasps stock their nurseries with paralyzed spiders. And wrens are always on the lookout for such bounty.

creepy-crawly kind. This family downs bushels of beetles, millipedes, sow bugs, stinkbugs, grasshoppers, and other lower-level insects. Caterpillars are hugely popular with wrens. So are lizards, snails, and tree frogs.

On the fruity side of the menu, some wrens are fond of small berries that they can eat in a single gulp. Elderberries and wild strawberries are favorites. Redcedar (*Juniperus virginiana*), bayberries (*Myrica pensylvanica*), and, in the West, cascara berries (*Rhamnus purshiana*) fill the bill. Wrens also peck at larger soft fruits, including mulberries (*Morus* spp.), wild apples (*Malus* spp.), wild grapes (*Vitis* spp.), and cactus fruits (*Opuntia* spp.).

Backyard Fare

Your usual garden plants will suit wrens just fine from spring through early fall, when they're crawling with insects. The birds will forage in your flower beds, cruise your tomato cages, and otherwise help themselves.

A layer of dead-leaf mulch is perfect, too, because it will hold zillions of spiders, beetles, millipedes, snails, and other tasty bites. Let leaves lie where they fall under shrubs and trees, instead of raking them up, to improve the food value of your yard.

Carolina and cactus wrens are the backyard berry eaters. Tempt them with a grapevine (*Vitis* spp. and cultivars), prickly pear fruits (*Opuntia* spp.), serviceberry shrubs and trees (*Amelanchier* spp. and hybrids), and, if you have room, a mulberry tree (*Morus* spp.). A hedge of barberry

At Your Service

A freeway motel where I once pulled in to spend the night provided some excellent snacks—for me and the birds. Easily visible from my room was a simple planting of serviceberry trees (*Amelanchier arborea*), surrounded by mulch. The branches were dotted with ripe fruit, which tastes a lot like blueberries, so I made a note to stroll over to pick a handful later.

Then I saw that I wasn't the only one who'd noticed the crop. Cedar waxwings, robins, and Carolina wrens were already busy in the branches, greedily downing the berries. I splashed some water on my face to freshen up after a long day on the road, then I hurried outside to join them. Only the robins flew off across the parking lot; the wrens and waxwings simply moved over, letting me share the feast.

Want to soften the look of a new privacy fence in a hurry? Plant elderberry, which will reach 5 feet tall and wide by its first summer. Wrens love its tiny berries.

(*Berberis* spp.) and burning bush (*Euonymus alatus, E. fortunei*) is just the ticket for winter berry eaters. Squeeze a few blueberry or elderberry bushes in, too, or try strawberries as a groundcover, to boost the fruity possibilities.

Don't forget that butterfly garden, and try to include some host plants for caterpillars. Mallows (*Malva* spp., *Alcea* spp.) are favored as host plants by several butterflies, so I always plant plenty of them, including a row of old-fashioned hollyhocks (*Alcea rosea*) along the fence.

Speaking of caterpillars, if your yard is overrun by gypsy moth caterpillars, tent caterpillars, or the latest plague of winter moth caterpillars, you can count on wrens to gobble up their share of the horde.

Feeder Foods for Wrens

Carolina and cactus wrens are the main customers, but Bewick's wrens are learning to make use of feeders, too. You'll have good luck with suet, mealworms and other insect foods, fruit, and baked goods. Peanut butter treats and millet are also sought by Carolina wrens, especially in winter.

Water Wishes of Wrens

Wrens love a good splashing bath. They'll use a pedestal birdbath, or you can try a ground-level setup, especially one with a dripper to lure them in.

Nesting Needs for Wrens

Some wrens are cavity nesters, and you know what that means—it's birdhouse time! Putting up a birdhouse is the quickest way to get a house wren or Bewick's wren to call your yard home, and it may attract a Carolina wren, too. Wrens are famed for choosing their own cavities, too; they've been known to nest in everything from scarecrow pockets to mailboxes to a pail hanging on a peg. They'll sneak in a broken window or beneath a door, too, to nest inside a shed. For years, a Carolina wren nested in the drawer of an old table on our back porch.

The grayer-bellied Bewick's wren takes over where the similar Carolina wren leaves off, covering much of the West.

Nesting Plants

Carolina and Bewick's wrens often make use of a dense vine as a nest site. I've hosted Carolina wren families in honeysuckle (*Lonicera japonica*), small-flowered clematis (*Clematis montana, C. alpina, C. virginiana*), and dense grapevines (*Vitis* spp.). They're likely to appeal to the similar Bewick's wren, too.

In desert gardens, cactus wrens may choose one of your cholla cactuses (*Opuntia* spp.), yuccas (*Yucca* spp.), or a catclaw acacia (*Acacia greggii*) as a homesite.

Nest Materials

Why is it that the smallest birds often make the biggest nests? Extra protection is one guess.

A wren's nest is big and messy—a large conglomeration of twigs, dead blades of grass, leaves, and anything else that's handy. To get the wrens' attention, try casting soft feathers under shrubs, where they can collect them.

Are you lucky enough to host a pair of house wrens in your backyard? These little songsters blanket the country, but there just aren't enough nesting pairs to fill a birdhouse in every backyard.

Chapter 13

The Kinglet Family

FAMILY NAME: Regulidae

EASE OF ATTRACTING: ★★★★ (very easy)

BIRDS IN FAMILY: Kinglets

Meet the Kinglet Family

Easy birds to overlook, kinglets share the job of caring for the trees with chickadees, titmice, and other small, active birds that flutter about the branches.

Look and Listen

Two species of kinglets represent this family: the golden-crowned and the ruby-crowned. Don't go looking for any eye-catching tiara on these birds. In fact, it's downright hard to see the tiny patches of colored head feathers that give them their names.

What you *will* notice are pairs or small groups of tiny, plump, greenish gray birds, hovering in the air near the tips of branches and moving quickly among the foliage. They often forage in the company of like-minded families, forming a sort of feathered vacuum cleaner squadron as they move through an area.

Kinglets are just as hyperactive as their frequent companions, the chickadees. But they have a trademark habit of hovering to pluck their insect prey, often at the tips of branches.

Look close at a kinglet and you'll notice distinct light bars on the wings. The red-crowned has an eye ring that gives it a wide-eyed look, while the golden-crowned sports a striped effect above its eye.

That colored head patch is hard to spot in real life, because a ruby-crowned kinglet is always in motion.

These tiny birds have very different voices. The golden-crowned's song is as small as itself: a high, thin chatter of *si-si-si* calls that's very similar to the soft voices of the chickadees, titmice, and brown creepers it hangs around with.

The ruby-crowned's song is so loud, you'll be looking for a much bigger bird. It's a beautiful, clearly whistled effort, very musical. But ruby-crowned kinglets don't perform the same song over and over; they vary the phrases and notes. Luckily, these birds are so active that their presence is easy to detect. When in doubt over a small, loudly singing bird, take a guess at ruby-crowned—you might be right.

Range of Kinglets

The "Kinglet family" is a bit of a misnomer by scientific custom, but it's right on target for backyard birds. Kinglets actually belong to the larger Old World Warbler family, which also includes gnatcatchers and a few other birds you're unlikely to see in your backyard. Who thinks, *Ah! An Old World warbler!* when they see a kinglet? Not you or I, I'd bet.

You can see kinglets all across the country, in various seasons.

Now You See 'em . . .

The golden-crowned kinglet spends its winters across a huge part of the country, from the Atlantic coast to the Pacific. But when nesting season comes, this bird retreats to the cool forests, usually in the mountains. Only in the northern tier of a few states is the golden-crowned kinglet a temporary treat, during migration.

The ruby-crowned kinglet, on the other hand, is seen mostly as a migrant in much of the country. In winter, it's at home in the southern and southwestern states and along the Pacific. If you want to find a ruby-crowned kinglet on its nest, you'll have to trek the Rockies, Sierras, or Cascade Mountains, or explore near the Great Lakes and northern New England.

Family Habits of Kinglets

Peripatetic. Perpetual motion. And any other word you can think of that means quick, fast, frantic: That's a kinglet in action. It's mighty hard to get binoculars focused on these birds. All the more reason to invite them into your backyard and multiply the opportunities of getting to know them.

Feathered Flyswatters

In an article in an 1884 issue of a long-defunct periodical called *Ornithologist and Oologist*, A. H. Wood recounted an experience with golden-crowned kinglets. I'm not sure I'd have wanted to be at that dinner, but I'll bet all of the guests were pleased in the end by the presence of feathered flyswatters:

> One morning we found our boat invaded by eight or ten of these birds . . . [T]hey found their way into the cabin, no doubt attracted by the large number of flies, and at dinner time they caused no little amusement and some annoyance by perching on the heads of the passengers and on the various dishes that covered the table. I caught flies, which they would readily take from my hand with a quick flutter.

By the way, that boat was on Michigan waters, so the "flies" may well have been blackflies, a notorious springtime pest of the North.

Golden-crowned kinglets are superb insect catchers.

Add *flutter* to that list, too, because the typical feeding behavior of kinglets is hovering at foliage or twigs to grab a bite.

Kinglets move through trees and tall shrubs, often in gregarious groups. And *move* is the operative word; you won't catch these guys sitting still. They have a lot of territory to cover.

These little birds, especially the golden-crowned species, are surprisingly and delightfully tame, even more so than chickadees. They show absolutely no fear of people, which makes it a cinch to walk up and watch what they're doing, or snap a quick photo—or feed them from your hand. Some folks have even managed to gently touch or stroke the birds. In the snowy season, they can become so much like pets that they'll follow you about the yard or even land on your head or shoulder.

At-Home Habitat of Kinglets

Conifer forests are a big part of kinglet habitat. But these birds also patrol deciduous trees and hedgerows or shrubs.

In migration, the birds may show up anywhere, including a backyard without a conifer in sight. Grabbing a quick bite is vital when the birds are on the long journey, so they refuel anywhere they can. Any place that has trees or bushes will serve the purpose.

The Wild Side

Whenever you're in a conifer forest, look for kinglets in the branches; conifers are a favorite hangout. Deciduous trees of all sorts also benefit from their attention to insects, including oaks, maples, birches, and any others that hold the potential for a meal.

Backyard Matchup

Plant conifers. That's one of the best ways to attract kinglets, whether they're staying to nest or just passing through.

I like to experiment with conifers that are native to my area, because they're guaranteed to host the insects in this area, too. Ornamental species may not attract as many aphids, budworms, or other goodies. Dozens of excellent, beautiful conifers are native to almost every corner of the country. You can try pinyon pines in the Southwest, Sitka spruce in the Northwest, black spruce or balsam fir in the North, white pines and hemlocks in the East, and so on. Most local nurseries stock a good selection of "nonimproved" native conifers, and any of them are ideal for kinglets and their fans.

Deciduous trees of all sorts are popular, too. I notice that the kinglets sweep through any tree in my yard, whether it's tall, middling, or sapling-size. Shrubs get "vacuumed" as well. If you're unsure what kind of trees will attract a good number of bugs for bird food, try honey locust (*Gleditsia triacanthos*), willows (*Salix* spp.), hawthorns (*Crataegus* spp.), maples (*Acer* spp.), or birches (*Betula* spp.). In the backyard, kinglets visit another kind of "habitat": flower gardens

Leave those ripening balsam fir cones to the chickadees and other birds—it's insects that draw kinglets to conifers, not seeds. Start with an "unimproved" native conifer for best bug appeal.

and flowering trees. Any plant that draws a myriad of insects is apt to make a kinglet's hit list. Each spring, I see kinglets at flowering crabs (*Malus* cultivars) and fruit trees, drawn to the insects that buzz about the blossoms.

(continued on page 192)

Fit for a King

Always in motion, tiny kinglets will soon take inventory of the insect potential in this leafy retreat.

Or a whole bunch of kinglets! These tiny birds will find plenty to grab their attention in this garden, even when the trees are young. They'll forage for insects in the foliage of the hemlock, maple, and fast-growing sumac and elder. Kinglets may sample a few bites of elderberries or sumac berries, too. And if a twig breaks when the sap is running in the maple, watch for kinglets to take a sip of the mildly sweet stuff.

Other birds will also make use of this planting, which offers abundant cover, as well as roosting sites and perches. Bushtits and chickadees and titmice are likely to examine the foliage and flowers for insects, too. Large finches may nip off some of the maple buds or flowers. Fruit-eating tanagers, thrushes, orioles, mimic thrushes, waxwings, and others appreciate elderberries, and bluebirds and other thrushes are fans of sumac for winter food.

In fall, this garden is a real stand-out, when the sumac flames red, the sugar maple goes to orange and gold, and the elderberry leaves turn warm yellow—all contrasted with the deep green hemlock. If hemlocks in your area are beset by wooly adelgid, try a fir (*Abies* spp.) instead, or any other dense conifer that catches your eye. Expect the young maple to be slow to take off, but look for the elderberry and sumacs to zoom to nearly full size in just a single growing season.

You'll need an area about 20 feet long and 8 feet wide to put in this planting. As the trees grow, it will eventually expand to about 30 feet long and 15 feet wide.

Plant List

1. Hemlock (*Tsuga* spp.) (1 tree) (Hardiness Zones 4–9)

2. Winged sumac (*Rhus coppalina*) (3 trees) (Hardiness Zones 5–9)

3. Elderberry (*Sambucus* spp. and cultivars) (1 shrub) (Hardiness Zones 3–9)

4. Sugar maple (*Acer saccharum*) (1 tree) (Hardiness Zones 4–8)

Garden Size
20' × 8'

Scale of Plan
¼" = 1½'

This garden offers glorious fall foliage, but its appeal—for birds or for you—doesn't end there. In winter, the candelabra form of the sumacs and the conifer keeps things looking good.

It's not the beauty of the blossoms that draws kinglets to flowering trees and shrubs: It's the swarms of tiny insects at those flowers. These selections of plants offer multitudes of blossoms—and that means multitudes of bugs. Short-needled conifers provide even more insect possibilities; feel free to substitute other species, if you prefer.

Plant	Type of Plant	Description	Zones
Balsam fir (*Abies balsamea*)	Evergreen conifer tree, to about 50 ft	Classic conical "Christmas tree," with short needles that are strongly fragrant	3–6
Birches (*Betula* spp. and cultivars)	Small deciduous tree; most to about 25 ft	Delicate trees with small leaves and open branches; catkin flowers in spring followed by small "cones;" golden fall color	2–9
Hawthorns (*Crataegus* spp. and cultivars)	Small, deciduous trees; most to about 20 ft	These small trees are covered in a cloud of small white blossoms, followed by prolific red berries. Branches have thorns.	3–9
Flowering crabapple (*Malus* spp. and cultivars)	Small deciduous trees, to about 25 ft	Many cvs., usually with pink, reddish pink, or white flowers, followed by abundant small "apples"	2–9 (most, 5–8)
Elderberry (*Sambucus* spp. and cultivars)	Deciduous shrubs, most to about 8 ft; blue elder (*S. caerulea*) to about 15 ft	Fast-growing, with multiple stems and tropical-looking foliage; Large clusters of fragrant, creamy white blossoms followed by huge sprays of small, juicy berries	3–9
Hemlocks (*Tsuga* spp.)	Evergreen conifer tree; to 100 ft with age	Short-needled and densely branched, hemlocks are graceful trees even when very young; quick to bear cones.	4–9

Used For	Comments	Other Birds Attracted
Insects from foliage	Best in cooler areas; in warm climates (Zone 7 and higher), substitute any fir recommended by your local nursery, such as silver fir (*A. alba*).	Nuthatches, chickadees, and titmice eat insects and seeds from cones. Cardinals, small finches, jays, and other birds use as cover or for nest sites.
Insect food from catkins and foliage	Fast-growing and pretty right from the start. "Clump" birches—those with more than one main trunk—are the most graceful, and they give more bird benefits in the same amount of space as a single-trunked specimen.	Vireos, warblers, orioles, and many other birds scour birches for insect food. Chickadees and titmice may visit for cones.
Insects at flowers	Select a site away from children's play areas, due to thorny branches. Explore the wide variety of native species.	Thrushes, waxwings, mimic thrushes, and other birds eat the berries. Orioles, vireos, tanagers, warblers, and flycatchers may visit flowers for insects. Possible nest site for robins, cardinals, and other birds.
Insects from flowers	Many crabapple cvs. have lost appeal to birds when it comes to their fruit, but the flowers and foliage attract swarms of small insects.	Vireos, tanagers, orioles, and warblers also visit the flowers in search of insects.
Insects from flowers	Cut back hard in late winter to reinvigorate older plants.	Wrens, thrushes, mimic thrushes, orioles, and many other birds are attracted to the fruit. Warblers, vireos, orioles, and flycatchers come for insects at the flowers.
Insects from foliage	Excellent choice in groups or in a hedge; provides dense cover	Nuthatches, chickadees, and titmice eat seeds from cones; native sparrows, juncos, and towhees seek cover beneath. Many birds seek shelter in hemlocks in bad weather.

Mmm, aphids! Agile, sharp-eyed kinglets are adept at picking off soft-bodied aphids from a rosebud.

Natural Foods for Kinglets

The tiny beak of kinglets shows that these are insect eaters. Insects of the trees, both flying and sedentary types, are their specialty. They also sample small berries and may swallow a few seeds.

Main Menu: Insects

Kinglets do a great job of protecting conifers from insect pests. Spruce budworm moths, whether adult moth or caterpillar, are a top menu item. So are aphids. Beetles, scale insects, ants, butterflies and moths and their caterpillars, and a huge helping of insect eggs round out the list.

Elderberries attract kinglets to their flower clusters, thanks to the insects that await there. I've seen them eat the fruit of elderberries (*Sambucus* spp.), poison ivy and poison oak, and of native shrubby dogwoods, too. They also nibble the berries of winged sumac (*Rhus copallina*) and eastern redcedar (*Juniperus virginiana*).

Backyard Fare

Insects are the top attraction for kinglets, so avoid using pesticides, and they'll find plenty to eat among your trees and bushes.

When Opportunity Knocks

Kinglet feeding habits borrow from other bird families, when the opportunity arises.

If you have sapsuckers in your neighborhood, keep an eye on the feeding holes they've drilled. Kinglets often sip sap when the "owner" is away. They also take tiny sips from sap "icicles" created when a maple branch is broken in late winter, and they have been known to share the bounty at a tap when it's maple-sugaring season.

That taste for sweets is also what draws these tiny birds to nectar feeders. The habit seems to be on the rise with kinglets across the country, and more and more folks are spotting kinglets at their hummingbird or oriole feeders.

Kinglets also engage in "flycatching" behavior, the typical pattern of, you guessed it, the Flycatcher family. When small flying insects are filling the air, these tiny birds often sally forth from a perch to nab a mouthful.

You can plant a flowering crabapple or hawthorn (*Crataegus* spp. and cultivars) to draw in kinglets in spring, when insects are swarming at the blossoms. Later in the year, try elderberries of any kind (*Sambucus* spp.) to catch the eye of fall migrants. I won't be planting poison ivy anytime soon, but I do like to include silky dogwood (*Cornus amomum*) and gray dogwood (*Cornus racemosa*), two multistemmed shrubby types, to provide another choice of berries.

If you're considering a new shade tree, try a sugar maple (*Acer saccharum*), guaranteed to please kinglets with its free-flowing sap. Snap a twig in late winter to early spring, when days are crisp and sunny and nights are still *b-r-r-r,* to make the flow accessible.

Feeder Foods for Kinglets

Mealworms and other insect foods are the key to a kinglet's heart at the feeder. They may also sample suet and other soft foods, including peanut butter mixes and fruits. Don't be surprised if these birds take turns sipping from your nectar feeders, too.

Water Wishes of Kinglets

Here's your reason to invest in a faux-rock birdbath. Formed in a series of shallow pools, these baths may include a dripper that makes sure every bird within range hears the siren song of trickling water. During migration, this kind of a birdbath is a real draw for kinglets.

Nesting Needs of Kinglets

Kinglets build nests in evergreen forests, rarely in a backyard.

Nest Materials

If you live within their nesting range, they may help themselves to nest materials. An assortment of soft feathers and moss will suit their needs.

Chapter 14

The Thrush Family

FAMILY NAME: Turdidae

EASE OF ATTRACTING: ★★★★★ (practically guaranteed)

BIRDS IN FAMILY: Bluebirds · Robins · Thrushes · Veeries

Meet the Thrush Family

I guarantee you already know one of the members of this family: the American robin. And it's a pretty safe bet that you also are familiar with bluebirds. Even if you've never seen a bluebird in your backyard, this beloved bird has such high appeal that its image graces everything from calendars to kitchen towels to sweatshirts to limited-edition collectors' plates.

The other members of the family aren't as well known these days as they were 100 years ago, when folks lived closer to the land. But by planning a yard that includes their favorite plants, you have a good chance of getting to know all of the special birds of this family that visit your area.

Look and Listen

Start by listening, because the Thrush family includes the most talented songbirds in the land. Their songs are long and musical, with passages that are often described as flutelike.

The voice of a thrush "steals upon the sense of an appreciative listener like the quiet beauty of a sunset," noted Montague Chamberlain in 1882.

Speaking of sunsets, dim light is when thrushes sing the most. You'll hear them in early morning, on rainy days, and at twilight. They're among the earliest and latest singers in the daily symphony.

One of these fabled singers is probably performing right in your own backyard every day in spring and early summer. The American robin is so common that most of us don't give it a second thought. But its song is beautiful, and it's one of the main components of the dawn chorus in our backyards. Next time you spy a robin in a tree, listen for its song, and you'll have a whole new appreciation for these worm pullers.

Members of the Thrush family are the quintessential passerines, or perching birds, that shaped the way most of us would draw a generic bird. They're medium to fairly large in size, with relatively long tails, somewhat plump bodies, rounded heads, and legs and feet built for perching. The hermit thrush has a habit of raising and lowering its tail or flicking its wings—a habit that's sometimes shown by other family members, too.

Most thrushes are brown, with pale, freckled breasts and bellies. The American robin and its much less common cousins, the rufous-backed and clay-colored robins, are orangish rather than white below. The varied thrush looks a lot like a robin, but its back is steel gray rather than brown and it adds a dramatic dark necklace. Townsend's solitaire is a gray bird.

Bluebirds, though, live up to their name: All are blue, with the western and eastern bluebirds also sporting orange breasts and sides.

Interesting, it's the dowdiest thrushes—the look-alike brown species, such as the hermit thrush and veery, and the gray Townsend's solitaire—that sing the best. The beautiful bluebirds sing only short snatches of low, soft, sweet whistled notes.

Birders like to argue over which of the thrushes is the best singer. Three species are perennially listed at the top. Some give the prize to the wood

This male American robin has a darker head and brighter belly than the female. When you notice a paler, muted robin, you're looking at a female.

Bluebirds often hunt from a prominent mid-height perch, from which they flutter down after insects. Even a rock may serve as a vantage point.

Let a Virginia creeper (*Parthenocissus quinquefolia*) scramble up a trellis or over a log to catch the eye of a berry-loving hermit thrush in fall. .

No mistaking this bird—it's the varied thrush, a western species that wanders as far east as the Atlantic coast.

thrush; others nominate the hermit thrush; and a third fan club roots for the veery. But other thrushes have their boosters, too. Townsend's solitaire earns support in the West, where its clear, glorious song rings out. I'm sure the other members of this 15-species family have their supporters, too.

Me? I get goosebumps when I hear the rich, fluting song of a wood thrush, and I wait every evening for the poignant, ethereal lilting of the hermit thrush. But I still have to vote for the American robin as the best singer in the family. Common, sure, but any bird that sings with such sweetness, and so untiringly, wins a special place in my heart.

Range of Thrushes

The American robin, hermit thrush, and Swainson's thrush show up across the entire country. Townsend's solitaire, mountain and western bluebirds, and the varied thrush are limited to the West; all of the other species appear in the East, with the veery sneaking into some western states, too. If you're in the Southwest or southern Texas, you may spot a rufous-backed or clay-colored robin.

Now You See 'em . . .

Another reason to appreciate the American robin? It lives year-round across nearly all of the country, except for the northern tier. The varied thrush, too, is an all-year bird in some areas of its range. Bluebirds and the hermit thrush may live year-round in your area, or they may migrate. All

Wood thrushes may turn up under shrubbery or at berries in any backyard along their migration route.

many birds that are shown in "year-round" ranges on field guide maps, robins move around.

As your robins move out in fall, others move in. Your robins may winter a few hundred miles southward, while birds from a few hundred miles northward come into your area for winter.

In spring, when robins turn from winter habitat to nesting grounds, and when those that left for winter head back north, your lawn will be full of the birds whose movements announce "It's spring!"

Family Habits of Thrushes

Flocks in winter, pairs in summer. That's the general rule for thrushes.

Once the babies leave the nest, members of this family often pal around in small family groups. In fall, the families gather together, forming loose flocks for winter.

Bluebirds, especially, are seldom seen all by their lonesomes: Usually you'll see a small bunch of the birds together, even after the youngsters are full-grown. Seems like the kids just like to stay close to Mom and Dad.

the other thrushes are spring and summer birds; they leave the country in fall.

So why is the return of the robins such a sign of spring? Partly because robins, like many other members of this family, live in different habitats depending on the season. But also because robins migrate within their "year-round" range. Like

Birds in the Bushes

"You want to see robins in winter?" an old-timer in eastern Pennsylvania once asked me. "Just go up on the mountain and kick 'em out of the bushes."

I was young and dumb then, and I thought he was pulling my leg. It took me a few years to take his advice and see for myself. Turned out that country wisdom was right again.

And "kick 'em out of the bushes" was pretty close to the truth. I didn't see any robins until I parked along the narrow, graveled mountain road and explored the brushy edges. Sure enough, I flushed out a whole bunch of robins.

But they weren't acting like the robins that hopped about on my lawn. They were skulking in the bushes and foraging for food on the ground, well beneath the branches. They were behaving like . . . thrushes!

At-Home Habitat of Thrushes

Cover is vital to most members of this family. Any area with shrubs, brush, or scattered trees, including fields and woods' edges, may host some of these birds.

All thrushes spend a large part of their time on the ground, usually near the cover of sheltering shrubs or other vegetation. But they also come out into full view to forage for their favorite foods.

If you can grow azaleas or rhododendrons, you can succeed with blueberries. Read their tags to choose the right varieties for cross-pollination.

The Wild Side

The brown thrushes—the veery and the birds whose names include the word *thrush*—are the most secretive members of this family. They skulk about in thickets, forests, and other areas with plenty of cover. Generally, they prefer large, unbroken areas of such habitat, where they can range about freely, although they also visit backyards. Townsend's solitaire and the varied thrush mostly stick to coniferous forests, while the other thrushes live in deciduous or mixed woods.

Bluebirds aren't such skulkers. They often perch in the open, frequenting fields, pastures, cemeteries, and golf courses, as well as brush and woods' edges.

You'll often see the American robin out in the open on lawns, at least in spring and summer. In winter, this bird returns to its more secretive side, and like other thrushes, it retreats to shrubby thickets and brush.

Backyard Matchup

Cover is the key word for thrushes. Hedges, groups of shrubs, trees underplanted with shrubs, and other gardens that offer dense, low-level cover are what make them feel at home. Even the more outgoing American robin and bluebirds appreciate the cover of leafy shrubs and small trees, although they will also visit an open yard.

This family is particular about its eating habits, but not about the plants used as cover. Any shrub with dense foliage and stiff, twiggy branches—needed to support these larger, perching birds—is likely to be well received. Old reliable shrubs, such as forsythia (*Forsythia × intermedia*), lilacs

Holly-Jolly Suet

Holly berries seem to need a cold treatment before birds really relish them. This recipe lets you collect the berries when they ripen, then freeze them until their palatability improves. It's a real hit with robins and other thrushes, and catbirds and mockingbirds are likely to try a taste, too.

1 cup holly berries, removed from branch (Wearing gloves, clip the branch, then use scissors to snip off the berries into a bowl.)
1 commercially made suet block, any kind

1. Pour the berries into a resealable plastic freezer bag. Freeze overnight, then set out to thaw in the bag, on the counter. Repeat two or three times. When the berries have had a few cycles of freezing and thawing, go on to the next step.

2. Unwrap the suet block, break into chunks, and place them in a microwave-safe bowl. Zap for 60 seconds, then check; if most of the suet is melted, go on to the next step. If not, zap it for another 30 seconds.

3. When most of the suet is melted, pour the holly berries into the bowl. Place the bowl in the fridge, to thicken up the melted fat.

4. Check the suet in half an hour; it should be white and semisoft (if it's still runny, return it to the fridge).

5. Using a spoon, stir the suet and berries until they're well combined.

6. Scrape the cooled, semisoft mixture onto a cookie sheet, making a layer about $\frac{1}{2}$ inch thick. Freeze overnight, until solid.

7. Remove the suet from the tray with a spatula; it will break into pieces.

8. Slide the pieces into resealable plastic freezer bags, keeping the suet only one layer thick so the pieces don't stick together into a thick, solid mass. Store the bags in the freezer until you're ready to serve.

Larger birds like suet just as much as our acrobatic small friends, the chickadees and nuthatches. But they'll have trouble eating it from most suet feeders, because they prefer to perch rather than cling. Give them free access to your holly-jolly suet by placing it in a tray feeder, where they can perch and peck.

(*Syringa* spp. and cultivars), and rose-of-Sharon (*Hibiscus syriacus*), will get plenty of use. In fact, lilacs are a favorite spot for robins' nests.

Since space is always at a premium in my yard, I concentrate on food plants, such as blueberries and other berry bushes. Besides attracting the Thrush family to their fruits and berries, they also serve as cover. You'll find plenty of possibilities in the next section.

Your gardening habits can definitely affect your yard's appeal to this family. Wintering thrushes prefer privacy, so a hedge or other area that doesn't get a lot of fussing from you is ideal.

(continued on page 204)

Thrill Your Thrushes

Bring in migrating thrushes with all the best berries, nestled among flaming fall foliage.

A feast of berries, coupled with cover, makes this planting a success in all seasons. The berries and fruit ripen over a period of months, and they will nourish thrushes from early summer through winter. Tanagers, warblers, orioles, wrens, and other birds that savor fruit may also visit. In spring, the abundant pear blossoms and dogwood flowers may attract vireos, flycatchers, orioles, and warblers.

Winterberries and blueberries require at least two plants for the necessary pollination of the flowers, which leads to bountiful berries. You'll need a male winterberry to service the females. And you'll need at least two *kinds* of blueberries to get berries; read the labels to make sure you get the right partners.

The spicebushes (*Lindera benzoin*) will quickly send up new shoots to expand their clump and grow together into a small thicket. In fall, this garden takes on extra flash, when the foliage turns to shades of red with golden accents. Dogwood and Callery pear turn deep red, and blueberry foliage burns an intense red; spicebush and winterberry add yellow to the show.

This garden will need an area about 10 by 20 feet; as the trees mature, it will gradually expand to about 10 by 30 feet.

Plant List

1. Callery pear (*Pyrus calleryana* 'Aristocrat' or 'Red Spire'; *not* 'Bradford') (1 tree) (Hardiness Zones 5–8)

2. Flowering dogwood (*Cornus florida*) (1 tree) (Hardiness Zones 5–8)

3. Winterberry (*Ilex verticillata,* species or 'Winter Red') (3 bushes) (Hardiness Zones 5–8)

4. Blueberries (*Vaccinium* cvs., any suited to your area) (4 bushes) (Hardiness Zones 2–10)

5. Spicebush (*Lindera benzoin*) (4 bushes, which will form one thicket) (Hardiness Zones 5–9)

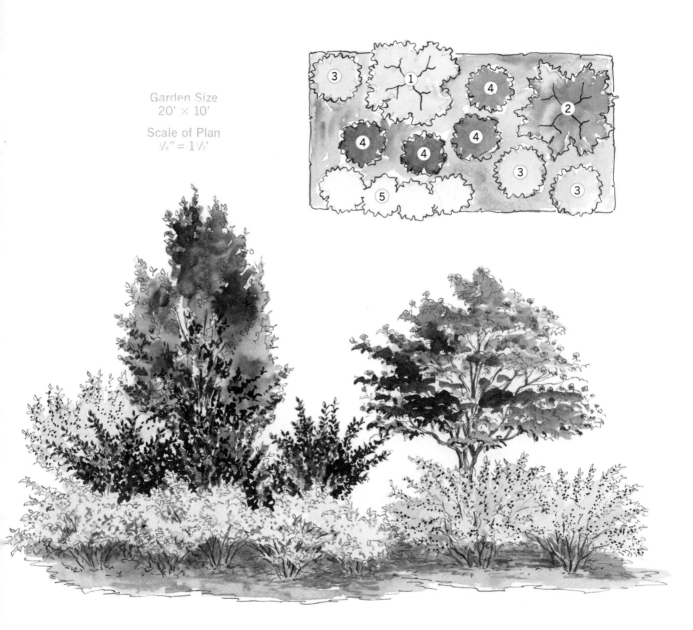

Garden Size
20' × 10'

Scale of Plan
¼" = 1½'

A standout in fall, this berry-heavy garden is beautiful in spring, too, when it's in bloom. Thrushes will feel at home here when the berries beckon, so be sure to plant this garden where you can watch the arrivals.

Surefire Plants to Attract the Thrush Family

What's guaranteed to bring thrushes to your yard? Bite-size berries. Here's a menu that will bring in berry-loving thrushes—and that's every species of this family—from early summer through winter. Try some of these trees and shrubs in your yard, and you're sure to see robins, and possibly hermit thrushes, gray-cheeked thrushes, varied thrushes, or (shhh, don't jinx it!) maybe a bluebird.

Plant	Type of Plant	Description	Zones
Silky dogwood (*Cornus amomum*)	Deciduous shrub, to about 8–10 ft	Forms a thicket or large clump as new shoots emerge around the parent plant. White flowers followed by clusters of metallic steel-gray berries	4–8
Flowering dogwood (*Cornus florida*)	Small deciduous tree, to about 20 ft	Showy, large white or pink flowers mature into tight clusters of elongated red berries.	5–8
Gray dogwood (*Cornus racemosa*)	Deciduous shrub, to about 15 ft	Forms a thicket or large clump as new shoots emerge around the parent plant. White flowers followed by clusters of white berries on bright red stems	4–8
Winterberry (*Ilex verticillata*, species form, not cultivars)	Deciduous shrub or small tree, to about 10 ft	Forms a clump or thicket as new shoots emerge around the parent plant. Small white flowers followed by brilliant red berries closely studding the stems	5–8
Sumac (Staghorn sumac, *Rhus typhina*; shining sumac, *R. copallina*)	Large deciduous shrubs or small trees	Striking plants with tropical-looking foliage; spires of tiny flowers followed by tight clusters of reddish berries. Vivid red fall color	*R. typhina*, 3–9; *R. copallina*, 5–9
Elderberry (*Sambucus* spp. and cvs.)	Deciduous shrubs, most to about 8 ft; blue elder (*S. caerulea*) to about 15 ft	Fast-growing. Large clusters of fragrant, creamy white blossoms followed by huge sprays of small, juicy berries	3–9

Used for	Comments	Other Birds Attracted
Berries	Great choice in a hedge or group	Warblers, vireos, orioles, and other birds visit flowers for insects. Wrens, native sparrows, and other finches eat berries. Excellent cover for many birds
Berries	Unfortunately susceptible to dogwood blight, a disease that can be fatal. I'd still take my chances anyway; dogwood is just too good of a draw for my favorite birds. Kousa dogwood (*C. kousa*) is not nearly the magnet its cousin is.	Tanagers, mimic thrushes, waxwings, and other birds eat the berries. Warblers, vireos, orioles, and others may seek insects at flowers.
Berries	Perfect in a hedge or along a fence	Warblers, vireos, orioles, and other birds visit flowers for insects. Wrens, native sparrows, and other finches eat berries. Excellent cover for many birds
Berries	Recent cultivars seem to have lost bird appeal; the berries remain on the branches without being eaten. Play it safe and stick to the species or the older and bird-approved cultivar 'Winter Red'. You'll need both male and female plants; read the catalog or label.	Waxwings and other birds may eat the berries, but bluebirds are the prize with this bush. They're often the first birds on the scene when the berries are ripe for plucking.
Berries	Berries often go uneaten until winter. To encourage a thicket, cut back plants in late winter; new shoots will spring up from the roots.	Warblers, vireos, flycatchers, orioles, and others seek insects at flowers. Mimic thrushes may also eat berries.
Berries	Cut back hard in late winter to reinvigorate.	Wrens, mimic thrushes, older plants. orioles, and many other birds are attracted to the fruit. Warblers, vireos, orioles, and flycatchers come for insects at the flowers.

Natural Foods for Thrushes

The familiar long, pointed beak of the robin is shared by all members of this family. It's built for eating insects and other soft foods, and it's the perfect size for gulping down berries or pecking at fruits.

Main Menu: Insects and Fruits

Anything on the ground is pretty much fair game for the Thrush family. The menu starts with the usual beetles, grasshoppers, crickets, ants, sowbugs, and spiders—the creepy-crawlies you'd expect to see at ground level. Cicadas and cater-

Mushy, withered, frostbitten rose hips seem to be more desirable to birds than fresh, hard ones. Often the fruit isn't sampled until winter.

pillars are also prized food items, and bluebirds have perfected the art of snatching butterflies on the wing.

Then, the diet takes a turn toward the slimy. Slugs, snails, salamanders, and earthworms are favored by many members of this family.

Flying insects are also nabbed when available. Bluebirds are best at this, but other thrushes also snatch their share. In Maine, the olive-backed race of the Swainson's thrush was once called the "mosquito thrush," thanks to its propensity for catching those pesky critters.

Fruits are the other mainstay of the Thrush family. All species eat a huge quantity of fruits and berries, wherever they can find it. In fall and winter, fruit is vital to thrushes. Those robins I "kicked" out of the bushes in winter were thriving on frost-shriveled wild grapes, wild crabapples, mountain ash (*Sorbus americana*) berries, and wild rose hips, even when the snow was deep on the ground.

Some of our least-favorite plants, including poison ivy, poison oak, deadly nightshade, and multiflora rose, are spread far and wide, courtesy of the Thrush family. Like other birds that feed on these fruits, thrushes swallow the berries whole, later depositing the undigested seed where it may sprout into a new plant.

Sumacs (*Rhus* spp.), barberries (*Berberis* spp.), elderberries (*Sambucus* spp.), and wild cherries (*Prunus serotina* and other spp.) also get a big assist from the fruit-eating, seed-spreading members of this family.

Some of our rarest plants also draw the attention of the Thrush family. Forest-dwelling species of these birds dine on the berries of ginseng (*Panax quinquefolius*) and its much larger relative, American spikenard (*Aralia racemosa*).

Spikenard was described in 1940 as "becoming extinct" in southern Indiana, so I was thrilled when I discovered a vigorous bush of this beautiful plant thriving in the woods there, 60 years later.

Feeling about as proud as the first man on the moon, I walked closer to the spikenard to get a better look at it. So much for planting that flag of discovery—gray-cheeked thrushes had found the spikenard long before me. Three of the birds were perched on the bush, contentedly working their way through the berries.

That same day, I came across another hard-to-find plant that always gives me a thrill: ginseng. Gray-cheeked thrushes were at work there, too, gobbling up the red berries. Ginseng has charming berries that look exactly like small puffed hearts when they're plucked from the plant, but I don't think thrushes stop to admire the aesthetics of what they're eating.

American spikenard (*Aralia racemosa*) is a beautiful plant for the collector's garden, and it's just about impossible to find for sale. But why spicebush (*Lindera benzoin*) isn't in every nursery is a mystery to me. The bare branches of this multistemmed all-American shrub are as graceful as any fancy nursery plant. Every bit of the plant smells wonderful when you rub it between your fingers—it's as sharply aromatic as wintergreen. In early spring, before the leaves appear, the branches are studded with small yellow flowers that mature into gleaming, bright red berries in fall. You won't get to admire them very long, though, because thrushes clean them off as soon

American spicebush (*Lindera benzoin*) is practically guaranteed to draw in thrushes. Smash and sniff a berry: smells like tangerine!

as they appear. Whenever I want a long, lingering look at the more elusive thrushes, such as the gray-cheeked or hermit, I sit and wait by a spicebush that's loaded with berries. I've never been disappointed!

I quickly learned to check pokeweed (*Phytolacca americana*) in fall, too, because the berries of these fantastic fuchsia-stemmed plants never fail to attract bluebirds, veeries, and other migrating thrushes.

In Costa Rica, where the veery and other thrushes winter, the similar berries of *jaboncilla* (*Phytolacca rivinoides*) attract our thrushes on their winter vacation. Instead of being joined at the feast by waxwings, tanagers, and mimic thrushes, as the birds here often are, they keep company with toucans, manakins, and honeycreepers while they dine on the exotic "pokeweed."

The vines of wild grapes (*Vitis* spp.) and Virginia creeper (*Parthenocissus quinquefolia*) supply good Thrush family food, too.

Most members of this family usually stay at low to mid-levels, but they'll fly into the treetops to feast on mulberries (*Morus* spp.) and hackberries (*Celtis occidentalis*). Smaller fruiting trees, including dogwoods (*Cornus florida, C. amomum,* and other spp.), sour gum (*Nyssa sylvatica*), sassafras (*Sassafras albidum*), and serviceberries (*Amelanchier* spp.), are on their hit list, too.

Backyard Fare

Depend on fruits and berries to tempt this family to your yard. Fruit-bearing shrubs and trees will lure them in with foods that are harder to come by in the wild than, say, slugs. Plus, they'll supply the cover many of these birds crave.

Before we get to the backyard, though, let's stroll down a city street. Many towns plant tolerant, fast-growing Callery pear trees (*Pyrus calleryana*) along the streets. They're beautiful, with fragrant, profuse white blossoms, glossy leaves, and deep red fall color. But it's the plentiful small fruits that attract members of the Thrush family during fall migration.

Callery pear makes a great small tree for the backyard, too. Try 'Aristocrat' or 'Red Spire.' Avoid the cultivar 'Bradford,' which many cities are removing from public property due to its propensity for suddenly splitting apart after a decade or so of growth.

Bluebirds and other thrushes may be enough of a reason to risk planting a flowering dogwood

Cornelian cherry (*Cornus mas*) blooms extra early, weeks before forsythia. But its berries wait until late summer to ripen—perfect for migrating thrushes.

(*Cornus florida*), a traditional beauty that's sadly susceptible to a fatal blight. If you prefer not to take a chance, try shrubby native dogwoods, which also tempt this family. Cornelian cherry (*Cornus mas*), gray dogwood (*C. racemosa*), and silky dogwood (*C. amomum*) eventually grow into thickets, offering excellent cover and ground foraging, besides their bounty of berries.

And how about a dogwood that's 6 inches tall? Meet bunchberry (*Cornus canadensis*), a beautiful wildflower of woodsy places. Bunchberry looks like somebody made a nosegay of a single dogwood flower: Each plant has a collar of green leaves topped with one white blossom. The flower matures into a cluster of red berries, very similar to those of a dogwood tree. The plants spread to form colonies, so they're ideal for covering ground in shady parts of your garden.

Evergreen hollies (*Ilex* spp.) often attract

members of the Thrush family, especially in winter. A deciduous holly, winterberry (*Ilex verticillata,* species and 'Winter Red'), is irresistible to bluebirds. Other thrushes appreciate the thickly clustered red berries, too.

But beware: Many recent winterberry cultivars seem to have lost their bird appeal. The native species may not have as many berries as some of the cultivars, but the natives are guaranteed to attract birds. Meanwhile, some of the most beautifully berried cultivars go uneaten. When I find winterberry at nurseries, I watch to see whether birds have any interest in it. If robins are eating the berries, that's a good sign.

Try a mulberry tree (*Morus* spp. and cultivars), or, if the potential mess of all that juicy fruit isn't appealing, add a sweet or pie cherry (*Prunus* cultivars) to your plantings. Or take a tip from the wild menu of this family and add spice bush (*Lindera benzoin*), serviceberry (*Amelanchier* spp. and cultivars), sumac (*Rhus typhina* and other spp.), and sour gum, or tupelo, (*Nyssa sylvatica*), a lovely small tree.

The effect of a single tupelo (*Nyssa sylvatica*) is incredible in fall, when the tree turns a showstopping red. But it's even better when a half-dozen trees stand shoulder to shoulder, as they did in a yard I visited years ago, in Georgia. It was early autumn, and the graceful, drooping branches of the trees were in full fall glory.

"Come under," the gardener beckoned me. From underneath, the brilliant red leaves, backlit by the sun, were as luminous as stained glass. It was magical—until the spell was broken when we were pelted with something from above.

The tupelos were full of thrushes who were gorging on the small blue berries and knocking an occasional fruit onto our heads. I spotted hermit thrushes flicking their tails, and I caught a flash of the cinnamon back of a veery. Robins and a few bluebirds were dining on the tupelo berries, too. Among "people fruit" shrubs, blueberries and huckleberries (*Vaccinium* cultivars) have prime appeal. Blackberries and raspberries (*Rubus* cvs.) draw attention, too. Elderberries (*Sambucus* spp. and cultivars) deserve a spot, as well; try them as part of a mixed hedge.

For extra fruit appeal, I'm all in favor of growing vines. You can squeeze them in just about anywhere. I may not have room for 12 new trees, but I can sure tuck a dozen prefab metal trellises, tuteurs, and bamboo tepees into the yard. Not to mention the fence that keeps my dogs in—while serving as one gigantic trellis.

Grapes are my top candidate, once I discovered I don't need to be a pruning wizard to get a great crop. I simply plant a bareroot vine, tie it in place when it needs it, and stand back. In late winter, after it's served up fruit for thrushes, orioles, wrens, and other grape lovers, I hack it back with pruners until it's just a few main stems with stubs of branches. Seems to be the perfect approach for bird grapes! By the way, don't toss those clippings: Pile them in a discreet area, and you can have the fun of watching thrushes, cardinals, and other birds sorting through them for nest materials next spring.

Much of the natural food for this family is found on the ground. To ensure a bounty of beetles, snails, and other tidbits, you'll want to put a layer of chopped leaf mulch around new plantings and let fall leaves stay in place. Decomposing leaves attract top-notch thrush food.

If you learn to live with slugs and snails, instead of using slug-killer products, your thrushes will have more to eat. The depredations of slugs in my garden drive me crazy (I don't even bother with hostas anymore), but I tolerate them because those slimy slugs are a top draw for beautiful varied thrushes. Wait 'til you see a thrush dining on slugs: Just as you'd expect, there's an awful lot of beak wiping between bites. A varied thrush I watched one morning spent a solid 5 minutes trying to get the goo off by swiping its beak against rocks.

Snails are a big part of the diet for the wood thrush, or they used to be. The scourge of acid rain has caused a decrease in snail numbers, be-

Southern Accent

Most American native shrubs and small trees get short shrift in nurseries and gardens, yet they're tops for birds. In some areas, the tide seems to be turning, with more natives showing up in garden centers.

In the Southeast and Florida, I've seen thrushes feasting on three plants that are well worth inviting into your garden: yaupon (*Ilex vomitoria*), Carolina cherry laurel (*Prunus caroliniana*), and wax myrtle (*Myrica cerifera*). These adaptable, easy-care shrubs or small trees are gaining popularity and are turning up in more garden centers.

Yaupon or yaupon holly was known to native Americans for the purgative effect described in its botanical name. This evergreen shrub or small tree reaches about 20 feet tall and forms a dense clump. Its bright red berries darken as they mature, and birds are drawn to them in late winter.

Carolina cherry laurel can eventually grow to 20 feet or more, but it often forms a shrubby clump, and it is easily pruned to keep at a lower height. Fuzzy, fragrant white flowers show off against the dense evergreen leaves and are followed by blue-black berries that are eagerly eaten by many birds.

Southern bayberry or wax myrtle is the southern version of bayberry (*Myrica pensylvanica*). Usually evergreen, it sends up shoots to form a dense thicket. Small, waxy, pale blue berries crowd the stems.

Yet another good reason to explore the varieties of your native shrubs and trees: Carolina cherry laurel has sweet-smelling flowers, bird-beloved berries, and thrives without fuss.

All three of these natives are fast-growing, trouble-free, and just the ticket for berry-eating birds in the Southeast and Florida. Thrushes, mimic thrushes, warblers, gallinaceous birds, and many others seek them out. Plant them as a hedge or in a group, and the vigorous plants will quickly knit together, providing abundant cover and food for birds and other wildlife.

cause it softens or dissolves the material of their shells. Some experts theorize that the decline in wood thrush populations could be related, as this food source becomes harder to find.

Feeder Foods for Thrushes

Well, now, this is the kind of news a feeder keeper loves to hear: Of all the members of the Thrush family, bluebirds are easiest to bring in!

Mealworms and waxworms are the way to go. Now that these delectables are widely available, you'll find that it's easy to supply bluebirds and other thrushes with these five-star favorites.

Bluebirds also adore a mix of peanut butter and cornmeal, or a mix of peanut butter, cornmeal, and suet. Many other fat-based foods will also satisfy their tastes, but these are the place to start. You can make your own or use commercial products. Once bluebirds discover your feeder, it's a lot of fun to experiment with recipes for them. I've found them to be a grateful group for just about anything I put together, as long as it's heavy on suet, peanut butter, vegetable shortening, or other fats, and of a soft, crumbly consistency.

Varied thrushes also visit feeders, usually in winter. At my feeders, they prefer millet to other foods. Robins appreciate a handout during snowstorms and ice storms, when they'll eagerly eat bread, chick scratch, apple halves, and other soft foods.

All members of the family may eat mealworms and other insect foods or sample fresh or dried fruits at the feeder. But except for blue-birds and the varied thrush, they're usually not feeder regulars.

Water Wishes of Thrushes

Moving water is the trick to attracting the Thrush family to your birdbath. Although they usually discover a basin of still water on their own, you'll have faster results if you can make your water trickle, gurgle, or splash.

Small, solar-powered water pumps are becoming more affordable, so you may want to invest in one for your birdbath. I use a simple model that powers a small, gentle fountain, but only when the sun is shining on the solar cell to which the pump is connected. When the clouds come, the spray instantly shuts off.

You can also try a drip tube, which you secure to your birdbath and connect to your hose. Attach a timer, if you like, so that the bath doesn't overflow constantly.

Nesting Needs of Thrushes

Bluebirds are cavity nesters: They make their nests in natural holes in trees or fence posts, or in birdhouses. All other members of the family nest in trees or shrubs, without benefit of a cavity. The American robin may also use a hanging basket, window ledge, or other protruding support to hold its bulky nest; you can help by nailing a nest shelf to a porch or other sheltered area.

Tons of information and advice have been written about bluebird houses and house tending. Most of it boils down to: "How do you keep out house sparrows?"

Quick answer: You can't.

Until the day when someone invents a sparrow–proof birdhouse, you'll probably be a lot less frustrated if you stick to planting for and feeding bluebirds, instead of housing them. Buy a bluebird box and mount it out in the country, away from human habitation, if you want to help increase the suitable real estate. House sparrows only hang out around humans, and country bluebirds are spared the competition.

Nesting Plants

Except for bluebirds, members of this family nest in a variety of trees and shrubs, mostly in the wild, but sometimes in yards with dense cover that are near their wild haunts.

Robins, however, often select a site in a dooryard shrub. Lilacs and maples are popular, but many other plants also serve the purpose.

Nest Materials

Bluebirds may accept feathers for their nests. Robins are fond of pieces of white string. Cut the string into lengths about 8 inches long, to prevent entanglements.

Robins also often collect old fishing line to use in their nests, a habit that can result in an unfortunate accident when a bird gets snarled in the line. I've seen too many robins (and orioles) meet with a sad fate due to fishing line. When I come across a snarl of fishing line on the riverbank or

Cheap and easy: A clay saucer makes a perfect low-level birdbath when thrushes pass through in spring.

Like all thrushes, bluebirds love fruit. But they also visit flowering trees like this redbud (*Cercis* sp.) for insects.

1. Plant a hedge or a group of berry bushes to supply cover and food.
2. Add native shrubs or small trees that bear fruit or berries.
3. Consider a collection of dogwoods of all kinds: trees (*Cornus florida, C. pacifica,* and other spp.), shrubs (*C. racemosa, C. amomum, C. mas,* and others), and bunchberry (*C. canadensis*).
4. Learn to tolerate slugs and snails; avoid using chemicals to kill them.
5. Let fall leaves nestle under shrubs and trees; they'll nurture thrush-favored insects and other foods.
6. Invest in a small fountain or drip tube for your birdbath.

dangling in trees or bushes, I collect the stuff (watch for hooks, I've learned the hard way), and shove it in my pocket to take home and dispose of. Birds have enough problems without getting snared when they're making a nest.

Little Extras for Thrushes

Cavity-nesting bluebirds often return to a natural cavity or birdhouse to take shelter on cold nights or in snowy weather. Groups often roost together. You can put up a roosting box to provide shelter in your own yard: It looks like an open-bottomed birdhouse, with perches inside for birds to congregate and huddle together. Although house sparrows are quick to take over a bluebird house, they usually don't bother making a claim for a roosting box.

Robins use a lot of mud in their nests. You can help them out by devoting a small patch of your yard to a mud puddle. Remove any vegetation, scoop out the soil to make a depression, then simply run the hose to make mud. Refresh when it begins to dry out.

Chapter 15

The Mimic Thrush Family

FAMILY NAME: Turdidae

EASE OF ATTRACTING: ★★★★ (very easy)

BIRDS IN FAMILY: Northern Mockingbirds · Gray Catbirds · Thrashers

---

Meet the Mimic Thrush Family

The mimic thrushes are great confidence boosters for us birdwatchers. They're big birds, so they're easy to spot when they're out and about. They sing a lot, so they're easy to hear. And they don't look much like any other birds, so identification is usually a cinch.

You might guess from the name of this family that they're all a bunch of copycats. That's true mainly for the mockingbird, which holds forth like an unstoppable karaoke singer with phrases borrowed from other birds' songs.

Look and Listen

The voices of mimic thrushes may be what first grabs your attention, but take a look at the other end, too. A long tail is a big giveaway to the ID of many members of this family. All mimic thrushes are large, slender birds, robin-size or better, and many have noticeably long tails.

Meanwhile, back at the head end, mimic thrushes carry some of the weirdest looking beaks in birdland. They're long and pointy, and in some species they're exaggeratedly long and strongly curved, like a Turkish scimitar.

All mimic thrushes are either brown or gray, or a mix of both. The catbird is soft medium gray all over, with the discreet accents of a black head patch and chestnut feathers under its tail. The mock-

About the only time you'll get a good look at the outrageous bill of the California thrasher is when the bird is perched and singing; otherwise, it hides in brush.

Once a bird of romantic Southern nights, the mockingbird throws its weight around in the North, too.

ingbird is flashier: gray with a paler underside and big white wing and tail patches that are a real *wow* when it flies.

Some thrashers, including Crissal, LeConte's, and sage, lean toward the gray side of coloration, but most thrashers are brownish. The, ahem, brown thrasher, the most widespread species, is a beautiful warm cinnamon with a streaked white chest and belly. The long-billed thrasher is similar but darker. Many western thrashers, including Bendire's, California, and curve-billed, are pale brownish gray, with a warm, faintly orangish wash of a color that birders call "buff" on their underparts.

The catbird lives up to its name by mewing like dear Kitty, but it's the mockingbird that wins the prize when it comes to imitation. Of course, if the mockingbird is perched on your rooftop and holding forth at 3:00 A.M., you may be more inclined to wish for a slingshot than another go-round. That's another trait of many mimic thrushes: They sometimes sing at night.

The fabulous warbled songs of mimic thrushes are made up of run-on phrases, often repeated in pairs. That repetition of phrases is one of the easiest ways to peg a mimic thrush, long before you get a glimpse of the bird.

Range of Mimic Thrushes

Only one part of the country loses out when it comes to mimic thrushes: the rainy corner called the Pacific Northwest. Just about every other area has at least one species of this entertaining family.

By far the most common is the officially named

northern mockingbird, which isn't "northern" at all. It covers the country from coast to coast—*except* for the northern tier of states and a swath of the California mountains.

The brown thrasher ranges over the eastern two-thirds of the country, and it often strays outside its official range to delight residents of western states. The other thrashers are strictly birds of the West. Only the sage thrasher, a bird that looks more like a thrush than a thrasher, stretches its wings to range over all of the western states; the others generally stick to the dry Southwest.

Page through a field guide and you'll see that there's quite a bunch of mimic thrushes that lives in the arid Southwest. Now look closer, and you'll notice variations in the length and curve of those long bills. That array of beaks allows the many species to coexist, because their diets are just dif-

ferent enough not to outcompete each other, even when they live in the same habitat. The long, sickle-shaped bill of LeConte's thrasher, for example, can access insects that the shorter-beaked Bendire's thrasher can't get at.

Now You See 'em . . .

In most areas of their wide range, mockingbirds are easy to spot year-round. They nest and winter over the same wide area. But the mocker you see in summer may not be the same one you see in winter; individual birds may take short jumps to spend the seasons in different areas. If the one that's been singing on your roof is gone for several weeks, then shows up at your winter feeding station, it might not be the same bird.

The sage thrasher of the West has become a species of concern because it has declined in areas where its sagebrush habitat has dwindled.

The brown thrasher nests all over its wide range, but in winter it retreats to the South and Southeast, although an occasional hardy soul may stay put in northerly regions. Some experts think that could be because of our feeding stations, which can sustain a brown thrasher even in a cold, snowy winter. Same for catbirds, which seem to be a bit cold-hardier.

Most of the western thrasher species stick around year-round. The individuals you see in summer may be replaced by relocating birds in winter, or they may simply stay in the same place. Those that do migrate to a definite winter range are the Bendire's and sage thrashers, which head down near the Mexico line when cold winds howl across their summer homelands.

The word about feeders seems to be spreading among gray catbirds. Until yours finds the suet and mealworms, keep your catbird content with berries.

Family Habits of Mimic Thrushes

Mimic thrushes may be ear-catching singers, but they're not always such show-offs when it comes to hanging out in the open. These are birds of the bush rather than of open spaces. They're generally skulkers. But they often perch atop a bush, tree, or cactus to sing.

When mimic thrushes do come out of hiding, they're easy to spot. They have an erect, alert look, and many species have light-colored eyes that add to the wide-eyed effect. You'll often see them hopping or running over the ground, often with tail cocked up, instead of flying.

Tics of the tail are a quick giveaway, too. These birds twitch, wag, and swing their tails around like nervous nellies. Some folks think that's how thrashers got the name "thrasher"—because of the tail thrashing—but others believe the name comes from the birds' habit of swinging their beaks back and forth as they shuffle through leaf litter to find insects.

Mimic thrushes eat a diet that's heavy on insects, and most of them are nabbed on the ground, under or very near a bush. But mimic thrushes are also fond of fruit. When the crop is ready, they're quick to alight on a tree, shrub, or strawberry patch to pluck their share from the branches or stems.

When nesting time arrives, mimic thrushes go into total cloak-and-dagger routine, becoming even more sneaky. You'll rarely find a nest except by accident, because the parents are so secretive when raising their young. Yet, these birds often nest in a welcoming backyard. If you happen to blunder too near a nest, you'll hear harsh alarm notes from the parents. If you ignore that early warning, a pugnacious mockingbird may follow through on the threat and dive-bomb your head.

When it comes to feeder behavior, the mimic thrushes are well behaved, feeding calmly among other birds—with one glaring exception. Any guesses who needs anger management? Yep, it's the mockingbird, who can quickly become an absolute tyrant. If a mocker claims your feeder as its own, the bird will vigorously drive off any other poor feathered souls that wander nearby in hopes of getting a bite to eat.

At-Home Habitat of the Mimic Thrushes

Think "thicket" for this family's habitat. In the wild and at home, the best place to look for mimic thrushes is in or near shrubs and dense brush along roadsides, at forest edges, and in shrub-dotted grasslands or deserts. Thorny thickets are even better from a mimic thrush's point of view.

The Wild Side

Nearly all species of the mimic thrush family, except for the show-off mockingbird, spend most of their time among dense, multistemmed "thickety" shrubbery. A couple of the desert species, Bendire's and Le Conte's, can be spotted in grasslands and more open areas, possibly because shrubbery is hard to come by in the drylands they frequent. But for the others, the denser the brush, the better. In the West, "brush" includes sages (*Artemisia* spp.) and cactuses, especially the ultra-prickly cholla cactus (*Opuntia* spp.).

All mimic thrushes may move into an appealing backyard with lots of shrubs. You'll see them even at little islands of greenery in 50-acre parking lots. But city mimic thrushes still show a preference for shrubby habitat. The mockingbird that lived at my local fast-food joint could often be seen skulking in the dense firethorn bushes (*Pyracantha* cultivars) used in the landscaping.

Thornbushes are great from the mimic thrush viewpoint. Brambles, wild roses, and other stickery brush are favored hangouts for all of these birds. Cactus and mesquite, among others, satisfy the thorny side of dryland mimic thrushes.

Backyard Matchup

To make mimic thrushes happy, go dark and deep. Dense shrubs and vigorous tangles of vines are the way to win these birds' attention.

Choose multistemmed plants with thick, twiggy growth, such as burning bush (*Euonymus*

A thicket of sagebrush (*Artemisia tridentata*) is the ticket for privacy-seeking thrashers in the West.

alatus) or red-twig dogwood (*Cornus sericea*), and plant them in groups or let them send up suckers, so they resemble a wild thicket. Be sure to include some thorny subjects among your collection, too. A patch of blackberries, raspberries, or other brambles is perfect for mimic thrushes, and it may be quickly claimed by a pair of nesting birds. Large, mounding shrub roses help make your yard prime real estate, too.

In the West, depend on native shrubs and small trees to create the kind of habitat favored by mimic thrushes. You can plant sagebrushes (*Artemisia tridentata* and other spp.) and mesquites (*Prosopis* spp.); these natives are favored choices. Yuccas (*Yucca* spp.) and cholla cactuses (*Opuntia* spp.) are top picks, too, and easy in a dry garden. But don't be surprised if the birds adopt nonnative plants instead. Many garden shrubs used in low-water western gardens are just as good as the natives at mimic thrush appeal.

Consider planting a thick, unclipped hedge as an inducement for these privacy-loving birds, too. Mixed plants offer a variety of insect food and berries. And remember to "think thicket"—look for shrubs with many main branches supporting a multitude of dense, short side branches.

Stay away from the pruners, so your plants grow into naturally dense specimens. Dead stems hidden within the plant are fine for mimic thrushes; they just add to the dark, deep ambiance. Clip off branches that interfere with walkways or dead branches that offend your eye. And remember to plant stickery shrubs and trees well out of the way of passersby. Barberry branches against a bare leg, or a branch of thorny mesquite in your hair, are no fun.

Common, cheap, and quick to fill out, burning bush (*Euonymus alatus*) has the twiggy growth favored by mockingbirds and catbirds, and berries to boot.

Vines will do just fine, too, so squeeze them in wherever you can find a bit of vertical space. Again, it's dark and deep that you're after. Annual morning glories (*Ipomoea* spp.) won't do the trick, but multibranching honeysuckles (*Lonicera* spp. and cultivars) or grapevines (*Vitis* spp. and cultivars) will. Don't bother with large-flowered clematis, either; their growth isn't thick enough to give a mimic thrush the cover it craves. Instead, try autumn clematis (*Clematis terniflora*) or smaller-flowered clematis (*C. montana*).

Even in cold winters, mimic thrushes are just as likely to be spotted in a thicket of twiggy shrubs as in an evergreen. I often wonder whether the criteria for making a mimic thrush feel at home is that, while it's hard for us to see in, it's easy for the bird to see out.

(continued on page 222)

A Private Dining Room

Give mockingbirds, catbirds, and thrashers the cover they crave and the berries they seek.

A hedge is an old-fashioned idea that's worth embracing, thanks to its major bird appeal. Unlike modern privacy fences, hedges provide birds with food and cover and give them a safe path to travel along your yard. This one is chock-full of fabulous fruits and berries for our friends, the mimic thrushes. Maintaining a bird hedge is simple: Just plant it, mulch it, and forget it. The plants will quickly knit together to form a solid sweep of dense branches about 20 feet long overall—just the kind of hangout many mimic thrushes favor. In succeeding years, fallen leaves will form a natural mulch that's loaded with yummy bugs for thrashers and other mimic thrushes.

From early summer through winter, a steady banquet of berries will boost the allure. Thorny twigs add even more appeal, and they may convince a mimic thrush to build its nest here.

Plant List

1. 'Heritage' everbearing red raspberry (3 bushes) (Hardiness Zones 3–8)

2. Rugosa rose, any color (*Rosa rugosa*), or other hardy shrub rose (2 bushes) (Hardiness Zones 5–9)

3. Hawthorn (*Crataegus* spp. and cultivars) (1 tree) (Hardiness Zones 3–8)

4. Common privet (*Ligustrum* spp.) (3 shrubs) (Hardiness Zones 4–9)

Garden Size
20' × 5'

Scale of Plan
¼" = 1'

Hedges are hot spots for birdwatching, because that long strip of cover, with a mix of food sources, attracts so many kinds of birds. Mimic thrushes may even use the thorny plants in this hedge for nesting.

Surefire Plants to Attract Mimic Thrushes

Just about any kind of fruit or berry will eventually be investigated by mimic thrushes. But some are simply irresistible. Here are a half-dozen guaranteed to please.

Plant	Type of Plant	Description	Zones
Barberries (*Berberis* spp. and cultivars)	Shrub	Small to medium size, with ultra-thorny stems, small, neat leaves, and dangling red, oval berries decorating the stems	3–9
Bayberries (*Myrica pensylvanica, M. californica, M. cerifera*)	Evergreen shrub to small, multi-stemmed tree	Large shrub to small tree, with aromatic foliage and upright, multistemmed habit. Sprouts suckers from roots to form a larger clump	*M. pensylvanica*, 3–6; *M. californica*, 7–9; *M. cerifera*, 6–9
Currants (*Ribes* spp. and cultivars)	Shrubs	Small to medium size extremely thorny shrubs with dangling clusters of flowers in yellow, white, or pink to red shades, followed by chains of beautiful, translucent berries	2–10
Shrub roses (*Rosa* spp.)	Shrub	Large, mounding or arching shrubs, usually deciduous, although the leaves may be held into winter. Colorful, fragrant flowers, thorny stems	2–9; most, 5–9
Red raspberries ('Heritage' and other cultivars)	Shrub	Deciduous, multistemmed; sprouts suckers. Long, arching branches with thorns; clusters of delicious red fruit in early summer and again in fall on everbearing varieties	3–8

Used for	Comments	Other Birds Attracted
Cover, food from insects on foliage and flowers, food from fruit	Mimic thrushes don't mind what color the foliage of your barberries is, so why not try the cultivars with unusual chartreuse or moody, dark red leaves. These prickly shrubs help deter cats and kid traffic when you plant them as a hedge.	Thrushes, wrens, woodpeckers
Food from fruit	Waxy white bayberries attract mimic thrushes from winter through early spring, when most berry bushes have already been stripped of their bounty. You'll need a male and a female plant to get a good crop of fruit.	Woodpeckers, swallows, thrushes, wrens, small finches, warblers
Food from fruit and insects on foliage and flowers, cover	Explore currants native to your area; they are prized by your local mimic thrushes, and they make attractive garden plants. The native golden currants (*Ribes aureum*, a western native, and *R. odoratum* from the Midwest) adapt well to other areas, too. Some states regulate the planting of currants because they can harbor white pine blister rust. Reputable nurseries won't sell currants in areas where they're restricted.	Thrushes, woodpeckers
Cover, nesting, or food from insects or rose hips	Yellow 'Father Hugo' and pink 'Dr. Van Fleet' are easy to grow without resorting to a chemical arsenal. Rugosa roses (*R. rugosa*cultivars) are more upright in growth, but they too have lots of thorny suckering stems.	Thrushes, wrens, crows, and jays; warblers and vireos may eat insects from flowers
Cover, nesting site, food from insects or rose hips	Plant away from human traffic, and let it go wild. Let the interior grow dense and thorny.	Thrushes, woodpeckers

Natural Foods
for Mimic Thrushes

One glance at the beak of a mimic thrush, and you can see that it's quite an eating tool. Variations in length and curve among the species reflect the types of natural foods found in their home range, just as the bills of Darwin's finches did on those deserted islands.

These big beaks mean business. Mimic thrushes use them as hoes, to search through leaf litter on the ground; as shovels, to dig deep for earthworms and other delicacies; as hackers, to whack foods into smaller pieces; as snatchers, to make a quick grab for a scurrying beetle or a lightning-fast lizard; as tweezers, to grasp leaves or litter and flick it aside; and even sometimes as hammers, to split and pry apart the occasional acorn. Those serious-business beaks of some western species are also perfect for finagling in between spines to pluck cactus fruit.

It's mostly a half-and-half menu for mimic thrushes: half insects, half fruits and berries.

Main Menu: Insects, Berries, and Fruits

Most of the insect half of the mimic thrushes' diet is eaten when insects are at their peak, in late spring through early fall; the fruits and berries fill in the diet mainly during fall, winter, and early spring. A few other foods make the list, too, including snails, earthworms, lizards, and snakes. The brown thrasher and other species may eat seeds during the fall and winter or at feeders, or they may sample acorns and other nuts.

Naturally, most of the insects and related

Multiflora Madness

Mimic thrushes shoulder a big part of the blame for spreading the pesty wild rose called multiflora (*Rosa multiflora*). Distributed decades ago by the USDA to landowners in rural areas to encourage wildlife, this nonnative rose has gone way beyond its boundaries and now dots any stretch of open space where it can find a roothold. The bushes are super fast growing and can cover an unused pasture in just 3 or 4 years. They're pretty, with multitudes of tiny white blossoms, followed by armloads of tiny red rose hips. Mimic thrushes find the hips irresistible, and the seeds that pass through their digestive tracts undamaged soon sprout into more multifloras. If you want to find a thrasher or mockingbird in winter, just check any multiflora with remaining hips. Sooner or later, it probably will draw the bird you're seeking. Multiflora is on the noxious species list in many states; for an equally bountiful crop of bite-size hips, try *Rosa maximowicziana*, a Manchurian native that supposedly is better behaved.

Abundant, tiny hips attract birds to multiflora roses.

Birds, people, and animals relish prickly pear fruits (*Opuntia* spp.). The juice can stain feathers or face.

menu item in the desert Southwest—it's amazing to watch one of these birds deftly maneuver through the spines to get the goods.

Backyard Fare

Fruit is foremost, since this family does a fine job of finding insects on its own. Once you start looking around your yard, you'll see dozens of places where you can shoehorn in a fruiting plant. Need a groundcover for a sunny spot? Make it strawberries. Looking for greenery to soften your house? How about blueberry bushes, or a trellised grapevine?

Shrubs with fruits or berries are just as pretty as other garden plants, and you'll get the great big bonus of a healthy crop to tempt tanagers and mimic thrushes. True thrushes, including bluebirds and robins, love fruit and berries, too, and so do many other birds. Choosing plants with an edible bonus is a real winner of an idea.

Start by planting some of the fruits *you* love best. Mimic thrushes are extremely fond of many of the same fruits we are. They eagerly gulp down grapes, strawberries, blueberries, raspberries, elderberries, Juneberries, figs, mulberries, and cherries. In the depths of winter, any apples still hanging on a tree are fair game.

If you still have room, consider squeezing in a few ornamentals. The berries of dogwood (*Cornus florida*), bayberries (*Myrica pensylvanica* and *M. californica*), burning bush (*Euonymus alatus*) and other euonymus species, and Oregon grapes (*Mahonia* spp.) are popular with these birds.

foods are found on the ground or in the shrubs—where mimic thrushes spend most of their time. The "mostly insects" part of their menu includes such goodies as beetles, ants, grasshoppers, tent caterpillars, centipedes, spiders, bees, wasps, and sow bugs.

Just about any fruit or berry is fair game, and that covers a lot of ground. Native shrubs and trees that produce fruit, such as wild cherries, chokecherries, serviceberries (*Amelanchier* spp.), hackberry (*Celtis occidentalis*), redcedars (*Juniperus* spp.), and wild roses, are just a few of the wild plants that nourish mimic thrushes—and they're perfect for a garden, by the way. In the West, mahonias (*Mahonia* spp.) and native currants (*Ribes* spp.) are always a hit. Cactus fruits (*Opuntia* and other spp.) are a popular

For thorny fruiting plants, which mimic thrushes may consider for nesting or cover as well as the crop, try hawthorn trees (*Crataegus* spp. and cultivars), barberry bushes (*Berberis* spp.), cholla cactus (*Opuntia* spp.) in the Southwest, and anything else that looks too evil to touch.

You can be as fussy as you like about selecting plants, but mimic thrushes like eating down-home style as much as they do upscale. Ultra-common plants such as privets (*Ligustrum* spp.), bush honeysuckles (*Lonicera* spp.), and autumn olives (*Eleagnus* spp.) will get plenty of takers. These can be pesty plants because birds are so fond of the berries that they drop the seeds everywhere. I let a few of them grow, moving them to better locations if needed. In just a few years, their fruit attracts birds to continue the cycle. In some areas, these plants are on "noxious species" lists because they spread rapidly by seeds dropped by birds and infiltrate farmlands, roadsides, and woods' edges. Planting them is discouraged or outright banned in some places. It's a good idea to check with your local extension office before planting.

If you plan smart, you can keep mimic thrushes coming back for more from the time the very first berries ripen, well into winter.

When you're selecting "people fruits," look for early-season, midseason, and late-season varieties, to stagger the crop of, say, blueberries, over a 2-month period instead of just 2 weeks. Fruits labeled "everbearing" are a great choice, too. Be sure to choose apples that stay on the branches instead of dropping to the ground, so the birds can forage for leftovers. Ask your nursery person or read catalogs carefully to find this info.

Grape holly (*Mahonia* sp.) tastes nothing like grapes, but thrashers give it thumbs up. Good cover, too.

A dramatic bird, the brown thrasher is hard to overlook, especially when it's "thrashing" through leaves.

Ornamentals with berries are trickier to plan, because we ourselves don't generally pay much attention to when they're ripe or how long they last. That's why I like to include a good selection of native berries and fruits in my yard: Planting a bunch boosts my chances of getting the timing right. Many natives ripen their crop from late summer into early fall, when songbird traffic is at its peak, because they depend on birds to do the work of spreading the species.

The insects that mimic thrushes enjoy will appear in your yard naturally. But you can do a few things to nurture them. Of course you'll avoid using pesticides and herbicides that will kill them.

Letting fallen leaves stay in place is another good way to make sure there are plenty of ground-dwelling bugs. One of my favorite tricks is to pile the leafy clippings or dead flowers from other plants under shrubs. There they can compost in place and invite insects, earthworms, and other critters to their decomposing depths.

Feeder Foods for Mimic Thrushes

Except for the mockingbird, mimic thrushes take some patience to lure to a feeder.

But as bird feeding grows in popularity, mimic thrushes are getting accustomed to associating a feeder with food. A brown thrasher used to be a rare sight at a feeder. Now, it's an everyday delight for many feeder keepers.

Offer suet and other fat-based foods, such as peanut butter mixes, treats made with solid vegetable shortening, or bacon grease recipes. Insect-enriched suet, mealworms, and other insect foods are always a hit. Thrashers, mockingbirds, and other mimics love fruity, fat-based treats, too, and in winter, they'll eat millet and chopped nuts.

Water Wishes of Mimic Thrushes

A birdbath is one of the best places to admire mimic thrushes up close. These big songbirds

Mulch for Mimics

Retire the rake, and mimic thrushes will be much happier in your yard. Leaves and plant debris are rich with insects, snails, earthworms, and other critters. They'll eventually turn the stuff back into soil.

When I was a kid, I used to look under my mom's hedge of forsythia bushes for brown thrashers and catbirds scratching around. That's where many of the leaves that fell from our oak tree would settle into drifts, snuggling under the weeping branches of the bushes.

One day, I got curious and investigated to see what the birds were finding. When I scraped away some of the dead leaves, I discovered a whole cache of "curl-up bugs," or sowbugs—the odd, gray, segmented not-quite-insects that roll up into perfect balls when disturbed. Beetles, too, scurried away from the exposure, and earthworms quickly recoiled into their burrows. No wonder it was thrasher heaven.

From a bug-eyed perspective, the combination of darkness, moisture, and warmth from decomposition under a deep layer of dead leaves makes an ideal home. If you don't like the look of whole wind-blown leaves, chop them with your lawnmower and pile them under and around your shrubs. They're the absolute best mulch for mimic thrush needs.

love to sip and splash with abandon. The classic pedestal birdbath, with a wide, shallow concrete basin, gets a solid vote of approval from mimic thrushes. That rough bottom offers stability when they're splashing, and the usual water depth of about 2 inches is ideal. That's the simplest solution, and an inexpensive one.

Nesting Needs of Mimic Thrushes

Mimic thrushes make big, messy nests. None use nest boxes. Another reason not to rake: Thrashers will search beneath bushes to collect dead twigs for their nest.

Mimic thrushes often turn to thorny trees and shrubs, such as this palo verde, to shelter their nests.

Hip, Hip, Hooray!

Here's a quick fix that will add fruit to your feeder for the Mimic Thrush family. Catbirds, mockingbirds, and thrashers all eagerly eat rose hips in the wild and appreciate suet at the feeder. This combo meal will suit their tastes. Thrushes and wrens may also sample your fruity suet.

I make this treat in winter, after cold weather has softened the rose hips and improved their taste. Wear leather garden gloves and long sleeves to guard against thorns when you harvest the hips. Snip off the hips with a pair of garden pruners, or, if the stems are thin, use a pair of scissors for a closer cut. If the hips are small and in clusters, clip off the whole cluster, then separate hips from stems in the kitchen, with scissors.

About 1 cup rose hips, any kind
1 commercially packaged suet block, any kind

1. Pour the rose hips into a blender or food processor, and chop into small pieces, about 1/4 inch in diameter.
2. Unwrap the suet and place in a bowl. Add the chopped rose hips.
3. Use the back of a wooden spoon to mash the hips into the suet. Continue until the rose hips are evenly distributed throughout the suet.
4. Pack the mixture into the corner of an open tray feeder, or use a wire suet cage. You can also form it into balls and serve in a homemade or store-bought "nut feeder," a cylinder of wire mesh. Just poke a few dowels through the feeder and suet balls, so perching birds can get a bite.

Top To-Dos for
MIMIC THRUSHES

1. Plant thicket-forming shrubs, especially thorny ones, in groups.
2. Plant a hedge.
3. Grow a grapevine up a trellis or on an arbor, and let it become rampant rather than keeping it neatly pruned.
4. Plant berry bushes or fruit trees to suit your taste: Mimic thrushes will also enjoy them.
5. Let fallen leaves remain under shrubs so that there's a good supply of insects.
6. Keep a birdbath freshly filled.

Nesting Plants

Each species of this family has its own special favorites for nest sites, but the overriding principle is the same: dense growth. Wild or backyard nest sites are equally appealing, as long as privacy is assured.

Your best bet is to plant an inviting thicket of large, thorny shrubs or small thorny trees for them to use as a homesite. Nests are usually placed low, but they may also be built in a small tree, such as a paloverde (*Cercidium* spp.) or a young honey locust.

In backyards, nesting brown thrashers are partial to privet (*Ligustrum* spp.), lilac (*Syringa* spp. and hybrids), deutzia (*Deutzia* spp. and cultivars), and forsythia (*Forsythia* spp. and hybrids). Sometimes they nest at ground level, especially in brushpiles.

Western thrashers use western plants, including mesquites (*Prosopsis* spp.), currants (*Ribes* spp.), sagebrushes (*Artemisia* spp.), and paloverdes (*Cercidium* spp.). Prickly pears (*Opuntia* spp.), cholla cactuses (*Opuntia* spp.), and yuccas (*Yucca* spp.) are also in high demand as real estate.

Nest Materials

I once watched a brown thrasher painstakingly gather fluff from fallen catkins of cottonwood trees and carry them off, no doubt to line its nest.

Offer clean, unspun sheep's wool from a craft store; just snag tufts of it onto twigs and let the birds discover it. Mimic thrushes were big fans of the golden retriever we used to have, because he shed his soft blond undercoat just in time for nesting, leaving bits of it all over the yard.

Little Extras for Mimic Thrushes

Mimic thrushes often visit brushpiles to search for insects amid the branches. The pile keeps them comfortably hidden from view, just like a twiggy thicket.

To make your own brushpile, pile the clippings from pruning or cleanup in a discreet area of your yard. Add larger branches that drop during storms; they'll help create openings for the birds to move about within the pile. I've sometimes surprised my neighbors by asking for their fallen branches after a storm, when my own collection is scanty.

Chapter 16

The Waxwing Family

FAMILY NAME: Bombycillidae

EASE OF ATTRACTING: ★★★★★ (practically guaranteed)

BIRDS IN FAMILY: Waxwings

Meet the Waxwing Family

Only two species are in this family, the cedar waxwing and the Bohemian waxwing. And only one of the two, the cedar waxwing, is wide-ranging. But this family is well worth planning a garden around. They're not interested in feeders, so most backyard bird appreciators never get a chance to admire them. But they'll flock—in literal flocks—to fruit.

Look and Listen

When red rooms became all the rage in home decorating, I often felt like I was way out of step. Whenever I tried to imagine myself living in a red room, I realized I could only take the color in small doses.

Thank goodness I can look at cedar waxwings to confirm my sense of style. That dab of red wax on the wings is the perfect accent against their quiet color scheme of taupe with touches of gold. At least to my eye. Add a bold black mask and a yellow tail tip, and who could resist?

Range of Waxwings

The cedar waxwing ranges over every last bit of the country. The larger, plumper Bohemian waxwing is seen mainly in the northern states, but a bird of this species may hook up with a cedar waxwing flock and appear far outside its usual range. In some years, Bohemians leave the North in large numbers, and huge flocks—hundreds of birds!—may be spotted.

Now You See 'em . . .

Cedar waxwings live year-round in the northern third of the country. In winter, they cover every state. Bohemian waxwings are winter birds only; they nest in the extreme north in Canada and Alaska. In winter, they regularly appear in New England, the Great Lakes region, and in the West as far south as northern Colorado.

Keep cedar waxwings coming back to your yard by planting shrubs and trees with berries that ripen at different times of year, or hold their fruit into winter.

Why the Wax?

That red daub of wax that tips several of the shorter, outer wing feathers of waxwings is still a mystery.

Contemporary ornithologists suggest that the wax tips may play a part in mate selection. But I have my doubts about that one, since these birds mate for life, and presenting food seems to be the main part of courtship.

I still haven't heard a better explanation than the one that American naturalist Alexander Wilson proposed in 1892, in the old journal *American Ornithology*:

> *Six or seven, and sometimes the whole nine, secondary feathers of the wings are ornamented at the tips with small red oblong appendages, resembling red sealing-wax; these appear to be a prolongation of the shafts, and to be intended for preserving the ends, and consequently the vanes, of the quills, from being broken and worn away by the almost continual fluttering of the bird among thick branches of the cedar. The feathers of those birds which are without these appendages are uniformly found ragged on the edges, but smooth and perfect in those on whom the marks are full and numerous.*

Waxwings are easy to identify because they're unique. They wear a distinctive crest on the head, and they often perch on isolated branches, where their silhouette is unmistakable. Plus, they hang around in small flocks, from a dozen birds to more than 20, so they're hard to miss when they settle to feed. Seen through binoculars or up close, they're absolute beauties, in an understated way. The two species are very similar; look for a white patch on the Bohemian's wings to tell them apart from the cedar waxwings.

Their voices are just as easy to remember. These are talkative birds, and they keep up a constant stream of high, thin, wheezy notes when they're feeding or flying. Just hiss "*sreee, sreee, sreee, sreee*" until your tongue is tied in knots, and you've got it. The call sounds a lot like a sound sometimes made by our friend the robin, but listen for the repetition.

Family Habits of Waxwings

Ah, now here's an enviable way of life. Waxwings nest very late in the season, unlike many songbirds, which immediately get busy raising families in spring. The rest of the time, waxwings pal around in flocks, moving from one eating place to another.

Wanderlust is bred into the bones of these birds. Their daily flights cover many miles. Mostly, it's a matter of opportunity: When food beckons, waxwings pause to scarf it up — then it's on the go again.

These calm birds often spend a lot of time perched. Partly that's because of their eating habits, which include flying insects. Perching is part of the "flycatching" style of feeding, and this family does a lot of it.

They're also delightfully tame birds. You'll find that it's easy to approach a feeding group without raising the alarm.

One of the most endearing habits of waxwings is their game of "pass the berry." Several birds on the same branch will take turns passing a cherry or other bite of fruit from one to another, until, at no signal I've ever been able to discern, one of the players will suddenly eat it. No problem — another round soon begins.

Passing little gifts is part of courtship, too. If your mate occasionally presents you with, um, unusual gifts (did somebody say "frying pan"?), you'll appreciate this waxwing routine. I've seen a cedar waxwing present its mate with a tiny bit of flower petal, and her accept it as if it were the most beautiful bouquet of roses in the world. Often the female will pass the present back to the male, who receives it with equal appreciation.

Try a white mulberry instead of one with red or purple fruit, and you'll avoid staining paved surfaces or tracking stains into the house.

Watch for waxwings to play a few rounds of the charming game, "Pass the berry." It's often played during courtship, or among young birds.

They'll continue the ritual through several back-and-forths.

At-Home Habitat of Waxwings

A scattering of trees is the usual habitat of waxwings. Those trees may be along the edge of an open woods, dotted across a field, or in your backyard.

The Wild Side

Waxwings are nomads, with no particular home base except at nesting season. If "home" is where the nest is, then look to trees big and small to see cedar waxwings. Cedar waxwings nest in open woods, in old fields, along water, and in backyards—wherever a tree suits their fancy.

Whenever the birds aren't nesting—every season but for a couple of weeks in summer, that is—you'll find waxwings wherever the food is. The flocks fly around, scouting for berries and fruits. It doesn't matter whether the bush or tree is in the wild or in a mall parking lot.

Backyard Matchup

Waxwings are one of the easiest birds to attract to your yard. That's because the flock spends so much of its time patrolling, on the lookout for fruits or berries or other feeding possibilities.

Beautiful waxwings may be easy to coax into your yard, but getting them to stick around for long is another story. They're loyal only as long as the food holds out. When the berries are gone, the waxwings are, too. That's why you'll want to plant more than one of their favorites—to extend the waxwing season!

As for habitat, you can easily make waxwings feel at home by planting small trees and shrubs. Stick to those that supply fruits or berries to get the most waxwing appeal out of your plants. You'll find recommendations in the next section of this chapter.

(continued on page 236)

Cedar Birds

Deciduous trees are the best for waxwings, with one outstanding exception: the eastern redcedar (*Juniperus virginiana*), from which the cedar waxwing gets its name. These upright, super-prickly evergreens produce abundant bluish berries, which are eagerly wolfed down by waxwings as well as by 45 or so other species of birds.

A hundred years ago, when American gardeners were just getting started, waxwings were highly dependent upon the cedar berries to get them through the winter—so dependent, in fact, that the birds were famed for concentrating by the thousands in regions where the cedar grew.

Now that there are more people and more gardens across America, waxwings have increased in numbers and in range. It's directly due to human actions, and gardening has played a big role because it allowed waxwings more food choices. From 1965 to 1979, the population of cedar waxwings doubled; today, the birds are going strong.

Red Hots Right Here

Elegant gluttons, cedar and bohemian waxwings will make a beeline for red berries.

Nothing catches a waxwing's eye like red fruit and berries, and this garden has plenty. This is a good 20-foot-long planting along a fence, where the overflow crowd of waxwings can perch between bites. Expect to see waxwings daily until the goodies run out. But with the staggered ripening times of the fruits and berries in this design, the next crop will soon be coming along—and the waxwings will be back.

If you're thinking about sharing the cherries in this garden with waxwings, you'd better be quick. It's hard to beat these birds to the punch, because waxwings are superb at getting the timing right. As soon as cherries show any patches of red, they're on the ball, nipping off the ripe parts of the fruit as if to check whether they're ready to eat. Antibird netting is your best recourse if you expect to get more than a taste for yourself.

The roaming waxwings in your neighborhood are likely to discover this garden the first year you plant it, thanks to that tempting red. The birds will return daily until every bite is gone. And once waxwings discover a food source, they'll come back year after year to the same plant, just like hummingbirds hover at the place where you usually hang their feeder.

Plant List

1. Sweet cherry (any cultivar) (1 tree) (Hardiness Zones 5–8)

2. Red elderberry (*Sambucus* spp.) (4 bushes) (Hardiness Zones 4–9, depending on species)

3. Hawthorn (*Crataegus* spp. and cultivars) (1 tree) (Hardiness Zones 3–8)

4. Mountain ash (*Sorbus aucuparia, Sorbus* × *Crateagus* 'Ivan's Belle,' or other cultivars) (1 tree) (Hardiness Zones 3–9)

Garden Size
20' × 6'

Scale of Plan
¼" = 1½'

This planting is perfect along a wood privacy fence; it'll cover about 20 to 25 feet of length and extend about 6 feet from the fence. Plant the trees about 6 to 8 feet apart and place the elderberries about 4 feet in front of them.

Surefire Plants to Attract Waxwings

Catch the eye of scouting flocks of waxwings with many months' worth of bright fruits and berries that will make your yard a destination from early summer into winter. Red and orange berries will get their attention in a hurry, but they won't overlook blues and purples, either.

Plant	Type of Plant	Description	Zones
Serviceberries (*Amelanchier* cultivars and hybrids)	Deciduous shrubs or small trees, to about 12 ft	Graceful plants, often multi-stemmed; intense fall color of red, orange, purple mixed together; abundant small white flowers in spring, followed by blueberry-like fruit	4–9
Hawthorns (*Crataegus* spp. and cultivars)	Small, deciduous trees; most to about 20 ft	These small trees are covered in a cloud of small white blossoms, followed by prolific red berries. Branches have thorns.	3–8
Sour or pie cherries (*Prunus* cultivars, such as 'Montmorency')	Small to medium-size deciduous tree; dwarf cultivars to about 12 ft; nondwarf to about 30 ft	Fast-growing; often produce white flowers and tart, juicy red fruit the first year after planting	3–9
Sweet cherries (*Prunus* cultivars, such as 'Bing' or 'Stella')	Small to medium-size deciduous tree; dwarf cultivars to about 12 ft; nondwarf to about 30 ft	Fast-growing; often produce white flowers and sweet red fruit the first year after planting	5–8
Red elderberries (Pacific red elder, *Sambucus callicarpa*; eastern red elder, *S. pubens*)	Deciduous shrub, to about 8 ft	Fast-growing and vigorous, with multiple stems and tropical-looking foliage. Clusters of fragrant, creamy blossoms followed by huge sprays of small, juicy berries	*S. callicarpa*, 6–9; *S. pubens*, 4–9
Mountain ashes (*Sorbus* spp. and cultivars)	Small deciduous tree, to about 20 ft	Open-branched tree with fronds of leaflets; clusters of creamy flowers followed by heads of profuse small berries in orange, pink, red, or salmon	3–9

Used for	Comments	Other Birds Attracted
Fruit	You can't have too many serviceberries! Plant in hedges or groups; also plant tree-types in flower beds.	All fruit-eating birds adore the berries: orioles, tanagers, thrushes, mimic thrushes, wrens, some fly-catchers and many others. Warblers, vireos attracted to insects at flowers.
Berries; insects at flowers	Select a site away from children's play areas, due to thorny branches. Explore the wide variety of native species.	Thrushes, waxwings, mimic thrushes, and other birds eat berries. Orioles vireos, tanagers, warblers, and fly-catchers visit flowers for insects. Possible nest site for robins, cardinals.
Fruit	Huge crops of juicy cherries, excellent for pies or eating fresh, if the birds save a few for you. Very fast-growing. Tuck a dwarf cultivar into a flower bed.	Thrushes, mimic thrushes, orioles, and many other birds eat the fruit; vireos, orioles, warblers are attracted to insects at flowers.
Fruit	Choose a cultivar suited to your area and your own taste—you may get a few cherries for yourself if the birds don't beat you to them. Many cultivars need another cultivar as a pollinator; read the catalog or label.	Thrushes, mimic thrushes, orioles, and many other birds eat the fruit; vireos, orioles, warblers are attracted to insects at flowers. Hummingbirds may nest in young trees.
Fruit; insects at flowers	Top-notch bird plant; grows to large-shrub size in a single year. Avoid gold-leaved or other fancy cultivars; they aren't as appealing to birds. Cut back hard in late winter to reinvigorate older plants.	Wrens, thrushes, mimic thrushes, ori-oles, and many other birds are at-tracted to the fruit. Warblers, vireos, orioles, kinglets, and flycatchers come for insects at the flowers.
Fruit; insects at flowers	Fast-growing and quick to produce fruit. Tolerant of streetside conditions. Spotlight by planting as a specimen.	Thrushes, mimic thrushes, tanagers, orioles, some flycatchers, and gallin-aceous birds eat fruit; vireos, warb-lers, flycatchers, tanagers, orioles are attracted to insects at flowers.

Natural Foods for Waxwings

You've already gotten the idea: Waxwings are fruit eaters.

This family is the only North American bird family that lives mostly on fruits and berries.

Insects play a secondary role, but waxwings do flycatch for them, or pick them from foliage. The birds also sip sap when they can get it.

The most intriguing food of waxwings is flowers. Pollen is packed with protein, and that's likely the attraction.

Main Menu: Fruits and Berries

Imagine all the many kinds of fruits and berries you could find across the country. No wonder waxwings don't seem to have any problem finding something to eat.

Wild cherries (*Prunus* spp.), mulberries (*Morus* spp.), fruits in orchards, rose hips (*Rosa* spp.), and the berries of mountain ashes (*Sorbus* spp.) are just a few of their specialties.

The flowers of ash trees (*Fraxinus* spp.) are often visited by waxwings, which eat the bundles of brownish yellow "blossoms," complete with pollen. The birds may also eat buds of deciduous trees, especially maples.

Backyard Fare

Whenever I hear the hissy calls of waxwings, I wonder, "What's ripe?" Waxwings follow the food, and I often pick up new ideas for planting in my own garden just by keeping an eye on the birds.

My latest find is red-tipped photinia (*Photinia* × *fraserii*), a landscaping shrub that's ubiq-

Few birds can resist a juicy caterpillar. Although fruit is the entree on a waxwing's plate, insects are a frequent side dish.

Pollen is packed with protein. Tree flowers, like these ash blossoms, are a favorite food of waxwings in spring, before any fruits are ripe.

uitous here in the Northwest. There are lots of other shrubs I like better so I haven't planted it in my yard—yet.

The other day, I heard a flock of waxwings overhead when I stepped out of my car at my favorite pizza shop (Vinnie's, in Ridgefield, Washington, because I too follow the food, and real New York-style pizza is a rare thing in these parts).

The birds alighted on the red-tipped photinia bushes along the parking lot and began gobbling the pinkish berries. By the time I came out with my pizza, they'd already stripped one bush and were on to the next.

The list of waxwing-favored fruits and berries is a long one. The list of proven winners begins with cherries of any kind (*Prunus* spp.), especially the same kind of sweet or pie cherries we like to eat. They didn't earn the nickname "cherry birds" for nothing. The little devils, oops, I mean the beautiful birds, will gulp down the cherries even before they're fully ripe.

Other top-notch plant choices are hawthorns (*Craetegus* spp. and cultivars), mountain ashes (*Sorbus* spp. and cultivars), elderberries, espe-

Cedar waxwings were called "cherry birds" because they are absolute fools for the fruit.

cially red elder (*Sambucus racemosa*), and serviceberries (*Amelanchier* spp. and hybrids), among others. Trees and shrubs are equally tempting; the birds will flutter to any plant with tasty fruit.

The heavy crop of orange berries of firethorn, or pyracantha (*Pyracantha* spp. and cultivars), is a long-time waxwing target. But beware: Some newer cultivars have been specially bred to taste bad so that they retain berries for ornament. Per-

The Tattletale Tail

Take a really close look at the tail tips of the next cedar waxwings you come across. In the early 1960s, an unusual trend developed: Many birds showed orange tips instead of yellow.

What caused the change? Chalk it up to an introduced honeysuckle (*Lonicera morrowii*), Morrow's honeysuckle, which had gone wild by the 1960s in many areas of the East and Midwest. If the bird happens to be growing a new tail feather at the time it dines on berries of this honeysuckle, pigments in the red berries can affect the feather's color.

This shrub is so common along roadsides, in fields, and anywhere else it can get a start that in some regions it's classified as a noxious weed. It has small white to yellow flowers, and its branches are absolutely loaded with prolific red berries. They ripen right about the time that waxwings are molting—and growing tail feathers that may be tipped with tattletale orange.

Old-fashioned privet is a good hedge plant. But let it grow naturally so that it knits together into a wall of good bird cover and produces flowers and berries.

sonally, I'd much rather see waxwings decorating the bush for a few weeks than a whole winter's worth of berries.

In the West, you'll find waxwings happily dining on the fruit of date palms (*Phoenix dactylifera*), toyons (*Heteromeles arbutifolia*), and pepper trees (*Schinus mole, S. terebinthifolius*). On my one and only stay in Los Angeles, I was more thrilled to encounter a flock of waxwings moving through the pepper trees along the boulevard than I would've been to run into Robert Redford.

I've noticed that the berries of old-fashioned privets (*Ligustrum* spp.), tough plants that fell out of favor for hedges once arborvitae appeared on the scene, are a big draw for waxwings, too.

If you're the patient sort, plant a juniper. It may take years to get a good crop of berries, but in the meantime, the plants will supply cover for other birds. Eastern redcedar (*Juniperus virginiana*) is a perennial favorite, and junipers of other areas also attract waxwings. In the West, you can try *J. scopulorum, J. osteosperma, J. deppeana,* and others. In the South, look for *J. silicicola* (*J. virginiana* var. *silicola*).

If you have room for a shade tree, consider planting an ash (*Fraxinus* spp.). It's fascinating to watch waxwings devour the flower buds, releasing little puffs of pollen as they do so.

Feeder Foods for Waxwings

Cedar waxwings haven't come to my feeders yet, nor to anyone else's I know about. If they visit yours, please share your secret! I had high hopes

Tipsy Birds

I'm not sure who first had the bright idea of planting bird-attracting bushes in the middle of a busy freeway, but you'll notice them everywhere you travel.

Birds take a big risk getting to the bushes. And drunk birds have an even slimmer chance of surviving. As fruit freezes and thaws, it softens and ferments, producing alcohol. And birds that eat the fermented fruit quickly turn into the neighborhood drunks. Pyracantha is one of the most notorious for fermented fruit. It was once commonly planted in the median strips of California highways, to (yes, it's crazy) attract birds.

The combination of cars and fermented fruit was deadly to so many cedar waxwings and other birds that the state's department of transportation (CDOT) stepped in. The bushes were removed, and, we hope, replaced with something more "bird friendly"—in this situation, I'd vote for solid macadam.

in mealworms, but so far they haven't shown any interest. Bohemian waxwings, though, do show up at feeders in their winter range. Raisins, chopped prunes, and other dried fruits tickle their fancy. Fresh apple halves are a hit, too, even after they freeze in the feeder.

Water Wishes of Waxwings

Waxwings are enthusiastic bathers. In my yard, they visit low-level baths much more often than my pedestal basin, perhaps because they're used to bathing in puddles and at the edges of creeks. I've also seen the birds fluttering under the dripping edge of a fast-melting snowbank.

Add a device that drips, sprays, or mists for extra temptation. A naturalistic, multibasin, low-level birdbath is just the ticket for these birds because they often come to the water in flocks. And get the camera ready: It's quite a spectacle to see a dozen waxwings fluttering and splashing all at once.

Nesting Needs of Waxwings

Supply nest materials, and you may convince a waxwing that your yard is the best place to nest.

Nest Materials

Putting out nesting materials isn't a new idea. Fortysome years ago, my mom did it for orioles, and way back in 1920, Mary Benson related her experience in a magazine called *Bird-Lore*:

> [I] began putting out string, as usual hanging it upon a clothes line on the back porch. Within half an hour the Waxwings spied it and began carrying it to the apple tree. They made no efforts to collect twigs or any other nesting material . . . My supply of twine threatening to become exhausted, I began tearing old [white] cloth into strips about one-half an inch wide and from five to twelve inches in length. This, the birds liked even better; and they at once redoubled their efforts. How fast they worked, and what yards of cloth they used. . . .
> We called [the nest] "The Waxwing's Rag Bag."

If your own ragbag is looking a little slim, you can also set out tufts of natural sheep's wool (available at craft stores) and moss. But white cotton twine or yarn is by far the most desirable material. Keep the pieces less than 6 inches long to prevent dangerous entanglements.

Chapter 17

The Warbler Family

FAMILY NAME: Parulidae
EASE OF ATTRACTING: ★★★ (moderately easy)
BIRDS IN FAMILY: Warblers

Meet the Warbler Family

Our sporadic Roth family reunions are quite the gathering, thanks to big families and lots of cousins. But warblers would give our big bunch a run for the money: This extra-large collection of relatives includes more than a dozen genera and an incredible number of species—more than 50. Only the Finch family outnumbers the Warbler in terms of species.

Considering that the Nuthatch family includes a resounding four, count 'em, four, species, you can see why warblers get so much attention from birdwatchers. Keeping track of how many of them you've seen—in a lifetime, or in a year—can become habit-forming.

More insects than you'd ever want to count occupy every niche in nature, and trees and bushes are loaded with them. Warblers to the rescue! These tiny birds are on the go from sunup 'til sundown, gobbling every bug that they can find in the foliage.

Look and Listen

Sorting out warblers is a challenge, to put it mildly. What I usually say is more like, "These warblers are driving me crazy!"

Every spring and fall, waves of these migrating songbirds, a dozen to scores at a time, pass through backyards and wild places. At first glance, most of them look a lot alike. They're tiny yellowish-green birds, and they rarely sit still.

If you do manage to get your binoculars focused on warblers, you'll see that these birds are beautiful. Each species has distinct markings, some subtle, some so bright that it's hard to miss them.

I'd been watching warblers for years without appreciating their colors and patterns. That's because I didn't own a pair of binoculars until I was in my twenties.

Each spring, the giant oak tree beside our family home served as a "path" for warblers moving north. The birds would stream across a bit of open space in a loose flock, then alight on an outstretched limb and move on through. For days, usually around mid-April, waves of these tiny birds kept coming through.

More than 50 species of warblers, or wood warblers as they're also called, migrate through or make their home in this country. These birds have been declining fast in the last few decades, but

The yellow warbler lives up to its name, head to tail, but many other warblers also are decorated with yellow feathers.

there are still enough warblers around to make anybody's day, especially if you catch a wave.

As for that name *warbler*—don't you believe it. Only a few are musical virtuosos. Most hold forth with high-pitched trills or buzzy songs.

The Witchity Bird

I like common yellowthroats for a couple of big reasons: They're quick to adopt a yard as their home, and they have a voice that's unmistakable.

Like all warblers, yellowthroats sing a lot, all day long. That gives you plenty of opportunity for tracking one down.

Just listen for a loud "*Witchy-witchity-witchity*" ringing out from a hidden spot in the garden, and you've got him pegged. Lots of birdwatchers nickname this little guy the "witchity bird." The female yellowthroat doesn't sing the *witchity* song. But like the male, she has a distinctive buzzy, low *chip* call that you'll hear if you get too close to her chosen territory.

Look for the male common yellowthroat within a few feet of the ground.

The yellow-rumped warbler often shows up at bayberry bushes, a favorite food in winter.

They often get lost in the background among the more noticeable songsters of spring, such as thrushes or wrens.

Range of Warblers

Only a handful of species—the Nashville warbler, the yellow warbler, the yellow-rumped warbler, and the American redstart—can be seen practically anywhere across the country.

The vast majority of this big family is found only in the eastern half to two-thirds of the United States. A few species, just enough to make life interesting, live in the West, Northwest, or Southwest.

Now You See 'em . . .

Every spring, when I was a kid, there'd come a day in April when my mom would return from a stroll around the yard and announce, "The yellow birds are here!"

We'd sit together on the front steps and strain our eyes to see the flow of motion in the oak next to our house. Its leaves were still small, but dangling catkin flowers decorated every twig, and that's what drew the warblers. Even with bare eyes, we could tell they were picking bugs from the flowers.

Our family had never even heard of field guides, so guessing what these birds might be was part of the occasion.

"I don't think they're goldfinches," my mom would say. "Goldfinches don't act like that."

"And goldfinches would be brighter yellow," I'd add.

"Maybe they're all lady goldfinches," she'd suggest.

But both of us knew we were looking at something unique. "Yellow birds," we'd pronounce, as if naming a new species.

The stream of birds would continue for an hour or more, new arrivals replacing those that continued northward. Then there'd be a lull; then another flock would arrive. The flight really was in waves, just as birders describe it.

Later, when I'd become the proud owner of a pair of heavy, cheap binoculars, my mom loved to take a close look at her yellow birds. She couldn't believe how different they looked up close, through the lenses—why, some were even orange, and others had beautiful rusty trim; and while some had streaky breasts, others were as plain as Quakers.

Unless your yard is huge and natural, or right next to a large area of wild habitat, you'll find that only a few warblers choose to share your backyard other than during migration. Their habits are just too specific. That's why habitat protection is so vital to this family; they simply don't adapt like, say, blackbirds.

Any species whose migration path includes your region may show up in your backyard in spring or fall, when the birds are on the move.

But these are the species you have the best chance of attracting as regular visitors, or even as nesters:

Orange-crowned warbler: During nesting season (summer) in the West; during winter, in the South and southeastern Atlantic coast

Yellow warbler: Nesting season (summer) in all but the South and areas of the Southwest

Yellow-rumped warblers, myrtle race, and Audubon's race: Nesting season (summer) in the West and Southwest; winter, in much of the southern half of the country and the Atlantic and Pacific coasts

Palm warbler: Winter, in the Deep South

Pine warbler: Nesting season (summer) in the Northeast and Appalachians; year-round in the South and Southeast

Black-and-white warbler: Nesting season (summer) in much of the eastern half of the

Dangling oak catkins attract tiny insects—fast food for hungry warblers during spring migration.

country; winter, in Florida and occasionally across the country

Townsend's warbler: Winter, far West; year-round, Northwest

Common yellowthroat: Nesting season (summer) across all of the country except for areas of Texas and California; winter, along a wide strip of much of the Gulf, Atlantic, and Pacific coasts

Plan a Do-Nothing Day

"Do nothing" as far as physical labor, that is. You'll be watching warblers, which can be as exhausting as digging the garden, even though you won't be lifting anything heavier than binoculars. The spring migration is a sight to behold, but it's easy to miss unless you take some time to observe.

April to early May is prime time in most areas. Call your local chapter of the Audubon Society, or ask a nearby nature center, and they'll gladly help you pinpoint the date.

I look for a location where there's a hedgerow or scattering of trees that funnels the birds past me, rather than a big woods, where they're more likely to be spread out. Golf courses, tree-dotted pastures, or your own backyard can be great. Just park yourself in a comfy spot and wait to experience the wave.

Family Habits of Warblers

Warblers have a lot of nervous energy. They're quick, active birds, constantly on the move. Only the Kinglet family beats them in the perpetual motion department. Their occasional pauses, often when they break into song, are your best bet for zeroing in on a bird.

Fluttering and flycatching are trademark behaviors of many warblers. Like kinglets, bushtits, and other small insect eaters, they often flutter before a branch tip or leaf to home in on insects. Some species, including the northern parulas and the black-and-white warblers, also cling to tree bark, as nuthatches do.

The palm warbler nests way up near the Arctic. It gets its name from its wintering grounds in the South, where it seeks insects among the palms.

At-Home Habitat of Warblers

Staying hidden seems to be high on the agenda for warblers, but it's not because they're particularly shy. It's simply that their food is among the foliage.

"I wonder why we don't see them in the yard," my mom would often muse when we watched our little yellow birds. "There's so many, you'd think they'd be all over the place."

It's disappointing, all right, but the answer is simple: Most warblers nest in the woods, not in our yards. Each species has a distinct habitat preference, and they can be mighty picky.

Some live in dark rhododendron thickets, others in sun-dappled willows on a riverbank. Some stick to swamps, others to the banks of clear, rushing streams. Some spend their time high in the tops of hundred-foot conifers; others head for sunny pastures dotted with shrubs.

Kirtland's warbler lives in stands of young jack pine (*Pinus banksiana*). Forget trying to attract it by planting jack pines—Kirtland's warbler only nests in stands of pine more than 80 acres in size. It's so specific that you can actually take a guided tour to its home grounds in Michigan, the only place where this habitat occurs.

Being so particular has turned out to be a losing strategy for warblers. Many species are declining in numbers, as their habitat is lost both on nesting grounds and in wintering areas. And there's even more bad news: Warblers are one of the top targets of cowbirds, that parasitic species that lays its eggs in other birds' nests. As warbler habitat gets carved up by development or road building, cowbirds can more easily reach nests that were once safe deep in the wilds.

If you want to keep track of how the birds are doing or learn more about warbler ecology and conservation, a good place to start is the Audubon Society watch list, http://audubon2.org/webapp/watchlist/viewWatchlist.jsp.

Backyard Matchup

The few warbler species with backyard potential prefer a natural habitat that's brushy or woodsy, but they're not too particular about just which plants are in it. That's why they're likely to come to your yard! Because our targeted warblers are more adaptable than their cousins, it's pretty easy to make them feel at home.

Cover is the watchword here. If a small, greenish yellow bird could easily stay out of sight in your yard, you're on the right track. Low, thick growth about 5 to 8 feet tall will make them feel at home.

The other big trick to attracting these warblers is to give them some privacy. Plan an area that you won't be fiddling with, and they're more likely to come to call.

Hedges or closely planted groups of deciduous shrubs are great for warblers. I usually mix in a few small trees, such as flowering crabs (*Malus* spp. and cultivars), willows (*Salix* spp.), and wild cherries (*Prunus* spp.), and some clumps of native prairie grasses, such as switchgrass (*Panicum virgatum*), big bluestem (*Andropogon gerardii*) or Indian grass (*Sorghastrum nutans*), just to make it seem more like a natural brushy hedgerow.

An established bed of tall, tough perennials is perfect for the common yellowthroat—I've had them make themselves at home in a naturalistic

The male American redstart shows off its dashing colored patches by fanning out its wings and tail.

patch of goldenrods (*Solidago* spp.) and bee balms (*Monarda* spp. and hybrids). And in another area, they set up housekeeping among sheltering clumps of tall Shasta daisies (*Leucanthemum superbum*) and red swamp mallow (*Sphaeralcea coccinea*). Perennial sunflowers (*Helianthus maximilianii, H. angustifolia,* and others), which can be too aggressive in a tidy garden, are ideal for creating welcoming habitat for warblers.

That doesn't mean that these plants have some special magnetism for warblers. It's not the particular plants but the amount of cover they provide that counts. I'm sure my good luck has more to do with me staying out of those areas than with the types of plants.

(continued on page 250)

Privacy, Please

Common yellowthroats may move in if you stay out of this patch of low-care perennials.

With so many kinds of warblers traveling over such a wide migration route, you're likely to see some of these lively, colorful birds in your yard in spring, even without planting anything special. That's because, although they fly long-distance at night, they also move constantly during the day, vacuuming up insects from trees and shrubs as they travel.

After migration, though, only a handful of warbler species is likely to call your backyard home. To entice these warblers to linger in your yard, you'll need to give them plenty of privacy. This garden includes hardy plants that can take care of themselves, so you won't need to be fiddling around among them. They'll quickly grow to fill the area, interweaving their stems or standing shoulder to shoulder, to crowd out weeds—another way to keep human interference at a minimum.

This small garden fits perfectly into a corner; it will be about 6 feet long and about 4 to 5 feet deep. Wait until early spring to cut back the perennials, and you'll have good habitat for foraging sparrows, juncos, and towhees in winter. Goldfinches will also approve of the coneflower seeds, and the many butterflies and other insects this garden attracts may interest flycatchers, vireos, and other insect fans.

Plant List

1. Hibiscus or rose mallow (*Hibiscus moscheutos*) (3 shrubs) (Hardiness Zones 5–10)

2. 'Heavy Metal' switchgrass (*Panicum virgatum* 'Heavy Metal') (1 plant) (Hardiness Zones 5–9)

3. 'Fireworks' goldenrod (*Solidago rugosa* 'Fireworks') (3 plants) (Hardiness Zones 5–9)

4. Shasta daisy (*Leucanthemum superbum*) (4 plants) (Hardiness Zones 5–8)

5. Purple coneflower (*Echinacea purpurea*) (3 plants) (Hardiness Zones 3–9)

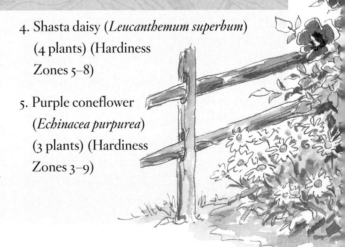

A garden that provides low-level cover and lots of insects may attract a dashing, black-masked common yellowthroat looking for a meal—or a place to call home. Keep your distance, so the birds don't feel threatened.

Garden Size
6' × 4'

Scale of Plan
⅝" = 1'

Surefire Plants to Attract Warblers

Warblers on spring migration are attracted by flowering plants that bloom in spring, such as flowering crabapples (*Malus* cvs.), because the blossoms attract insects. But the plants below will help you attract warblers, such as the captivating common yellowthroat, that stick around in your yard.

Plant	Type of Plant	Description	Zones
Redtwig dogwoods (*Cornus alba* spp. and cultivars)	Deciduous shrub, to about 8 ft	Multistemmed shrub with open branches; clusters of white flowers followed by white to bluish berries	2–8
Hibiscus or rose mallow (*Hibiscus moscheutos* spp. and cultivars, such as 'Lady Baltimore', 'Lord Baltimore', and the Disco Belle Series)	Multistemmed shrubby perennials, to about 5 ft	Knockout flowers the size of a salad plate, in pink, white, reddish pink; super fast growth	5–10
Bayberry (*Myrica pensylvanica*)	Evergreen shrub, to about 15 ft	Dense branches of small glossy leaves; barely noticeable flowers but striking whitish berries thickly studding the stems	3–6
Red raspberries (*Rubus* spp.)	Deciduous shrub, to about 6 ft	Quickly grows into a large clump or thicket of arching, prickly canes that hold clusters of sweet red berries	3–8
Pussy willows (*Salix discolor* spp. and cultivars; *S. gracistyla*; *not* weeping pussy willow, *Salix caprea* 'Kilmarnock' or 'Pendula')	Deciduous shrub or small tree, to about 10 ft	Super fast growing, with erect branches hugged by silvery catkins in early spring	2–9
Goldenrods (*Solidago* spp. and cultivars, such as 'Fireworks')	Perennial flower, to about 4 ft	Clump-forming perennials with masses of small golden flowers	5–9

Used for	Comments	Other Birds Attracted
Insects at flowers; some warblers eat berries; excellent for cover	Great fast-growing, wide-spreading plant for cover or hedges. Variegated cultivars just as appealing to birds	Mimic thrushes, thrushes, waxwings, and other birds may eat berries. Used for cover by many birds; may be used as nest site by native sparrows
The common yellowthroat may forage for insects or build its nest low among the thick stems.	Plant in an undisturbed part of your flower garden, along with other tall, easy-care perennials, such as goldenrod and Shasta daisies, to attract the common yellow-throat.	Vireos and orioles may glean insects from foliage.
Yellow-rumped warblers attracted to berries in winter	You'll need both a male pollinator and a female for fruit; shop for a plant that already has berries at your nursery, as well as a sparsely fruited male plant, to make sure you get one of each.	Waxwings, thrushes, and other birds may eat fruit; many birds use the multistemmed shrubs for cover, for shelter in bad weather, or as travel corridors.
Fruit eaten by some warblers; insects from foliage and flowers. Also used as cover	The hardiest or most cold tolerant of the brambles, this is a good plant for a wild corner or hedge in your yard. Try a cultivar, such as 'Heritage.' Let it grow unpruned to provide nesting sites.	Fruit is sought by thrushes, mimic thrushes, wrens, orioles, tanagers, and other birds. Mimic thrushes may nest in dense canes.
Warblers seek insects at catkins or use fluff for nesting material. Yellow warbler may use as nest site.	The world of pussy willows is fun to explore; many native species of willow, such as Hooker's willow (S. hookeriana), produce beautiful catkins, too.	Vireos, orioles, and others may visit for insects; chickadees and titmice may collect fluff from catkins.
Insects from flowers and foliage; cover; possible nest site by common yellowthroat	Spreads fast by roots; may also seed itself. Plant in a mixed hedge with hibiscus and other tough perennials, where its bushy habits are appreciated by privacy-seeking common yellowthroats.	Attracts butterflies and other insects appreciated by mimic thrushes, flycatchers, vireos, wrens, and other birds. Stems used by mountain blue-birds and others as nest material.

Spiders are predators, but they become prey themselves when warblers are around.

Natural Foods for Warblers

The short, slender, pointed bill shared by all warblers shows that these birds are insect eaters.

Nearly all warblers eat a diet of 100 percent insects. A few also eat berries or sip sap.

Main Menu: Insects

During spring migration, warblers may move through any leafy plants, searching for snacks along their way. They're also drawn to trees and shrubs with flowers that attract small insects. During nesting season, each species gleans the insects from the habitat in which it lives. Caterpillars (the "worms" from which the worm-eating warbler gets its name) are always a hot item. Craneflies, mayflies, beetles, and other insects, as well as spiders, round out the menu.

When wild grapes (*Vitis* spp.) and mulberries (*Morus* spp.) ripen, some larger species of warblers, including the yellow-breasted chat and the ovenbird, join in the fruity feast.

Virginia creeper berries (*Parthenocissus quin-*quefolia) are also eaten by a few species. I've seen my favorite species, the beautiful bay-breasted warbler, feasting on a vine that covered a fence at one of the charming "Painted Lady" Victorian houses in Cape May, New Jersey, a hot spot for fall warbler watching.

In fall and winter, the myrtle warbler seeks out berries to augment the insects. Visit the Atlantic Coast where bayberries (*Myrica pensylvanica*) are thick, and you're bound to see them.

Backyard Fare

Clusters of tiny flowers are most appealing to small insects and thus to warblers. I've become a big fan of elderberries and Indian plum (*Oemleria cerasiformis*), for just that reason, but there are hundreds of other good plants. You can try spireas (*Spiraea* spp.), viburnums (*Viburnum* spp.), dogwoods (*Cornus* spp.), flowering crabs (*Malus* spp.), hawthorns (*Craetaegus* spp.), and many others. Any of them may entice migrating warblers to a place where you can actually watch them.

Other than insects, a selection of small fruits may help bring warblers to your backyard, especially during fall migration. Take a hint from their wild habits and tuck in a grapevine (*Vitis* spp.) or add a mulberry tree (*Morus* spp.), if you like.

Waxy white bayberries (*Myrica pensylvanica*; in the South, try *M. cerifera*) are irresistible to myrtle warblers. And palm warblers passing through to winter grounds in the South are fond of them, too.

I've also had good luck attracting warblers to

the fruit of serviceberry trees and bushes (*Amelanchier* spp.). Insects at the small white flowers also attract warblers in the spring.

American redstarts have been seen eating the seeds of magnolia trees (*Magnolia,* unreported spp.) in the South. But since these birds are heavily insectivorous, it's not worth planting a magnolia just for them. If you like magnolias, though, why, by all means add one to your yard! Even if a warbler never samples the seeds, these birds may still investigate the foliage or flowers for insect food.

Feeder Foods for Warblers

I was stunned the first time I saw a myrtle warbler at my suet feeder: I thought there was no way I'd ever get the Holy Grail of bird families to my bird feeder.

Since then, I've noticed what seems to be a developing trend of warblers visiting feeders in fall and winter. Suet is a prime draw, and the birds also adore mealworms and other insect foods.

Cape May warblers, orange-crowned warblers, and some others sip sap in the wild, and now that they've figured out what's in our nectar feeders, they're showing up as customers there, too.

Water Wishes of Warblers

The sound of water is a big attraction for warblers during spring and fall migration. My new secret weapon is a small solar-powered fountain. At about $50, it's expensive, but it draws in some wonderful birds. The gentle fountain sprays only a few

Watch for migrating warblers feasting on insects at spring-blooming trees. Flowering crabapple or dwarf fruit trees can fit into almost any yard.

You probably won't even know a yellow warbler nest is in your yard until the leaves come down in fall, revealing the silky cup.

inches into the air. I keep it in a deeper than usual basin, so that the recirculating pump doesn't run dry when wind blows the spray out of the bath. A few flat rocks in the bowl, around the deeper pump, allow birds to bathe in shallow water.

Nesting Needs of Warblers

Warblers nest from ground level to the tallest treetops. Only a few species are likely to consider your yard, and they'll build their homes in your existing shrubs, trees, or flower garden.

Nest Materials

The yellow warbler may accept an offering of cotton tufts or balls (no synthetics), or small tufts of natural wool, fur, or moss. The common

yellowthroat may scout your compost pile or your garden to select long, dead blades of grass to use in its bulky nest.

Little Extras for Warblers

Many bird books refer to warblers as "secretive," but in most cases, I don't think of them as shy at all. They're simply hard to see. Some species are as friendly as chickadees, and many are so tame that you can stand just a few feet away from them.

Yellow warblers are among the tamest warblers, and they're one of the few species that visits backyards. Once I got over my squeamishness about handling mealworms, I found that these treats are a great way to get a warbler eating out of your hand. Their fondness for caterpillars may be why they quickly recognize the roasted larvae as a treat.

Chapter 18

The Tanager Family

FAMILY NAME: Thraupidae

EASE OF ATTRACTING: ★★★ (moderately easy)

BIRDS IN FAMILY: Tanagers

Meet the Tanager Family

Tanagers are medium-size, colorful birds of the forest treetops. Brilliant as any parrot, and just as exotic, the members of this family look like they belong in a steaming jungle. And they do—for parts of their lives. These migrants spend their nesting season with us, then travel to the tropics to spend the winter.

Even their name is exotic in origin. *Tanager* comes from the Tupi Indian word *tangaras.* Never heard of Tupi Indians? They live near the mouth of the Amazon, in the area where some tanagers spend the winter.

Look and Listen

A close friend who often walked the eastern woods with me was simply baffled when I went into throes of delight over a scarlet tanager singing from a spring-green oak one perfect May morning.

"Sure, it's a pretty song," he said, "but I can't find the bird."

"Right on that branch," I said, pointing and practically quivering with excitement. "Just to the right, at the very top of the tree."

The bird was in full view, its vivid red body shining like a spotlight against the green backdrop of oak leaves. Simply beautiful.

What a treat for bird lovers—the male scarlet tanager is becoming an occasional customer at bird feeders in spring.

"Where?" he asked again, and I tried harder to pinpoint the location.

"Just look for the red," I said, finally. "You can't miss it."

Finally, while my friend was still squinting at the branch, the tanager moved down a few feet to another perch.

"Oh, now I see it," said my pal. "But it's not bright at all. Just sort of grayish."

That's when we discovered that he was color-blind. Red against green became gray to his eyes. No wonder he'd had such a hard time spotting the cardinal flowers (*Lobelia cardinalis*) along the woodsy creeks. And what a pity he couldn't see the breathtaking effect of a springtime tanager.

When these birds return from their winter haunts, they're in fresh breeding plumage, and they're absolutely stunning against that tender green of new leaves.

Males in this family are the showboats, with spectacular red or yellow and red plumage. Two of the four species, the western and scarlet tanager, have sharply contrasting black wings and

Doubled Danger

Neotropical migrants is a phrase you'll often hear when birders are talking. It simply means migrating birds of the New World tropics. We're part of the New World, but we're not in the tropics: That'd be Central and South America, where these birds spend the winter.

And why will you hear this phrase so often? Because neotropical migrants are the species that are most at risk. They're vulnerable to negative influences at both ends of their journey—here in North America, and in the tropics of Central and South America. Combine the destruction of habitat and the spraying of pesticides and herbicides, multiply by two, and you can see why so many folks are concerned about these birds.

Sure, your own backyard is just one tiny piece of the puzzle. But if you do whatever you can to nurture neotropical migrants, you help boost the chances of the species' survival.

tails. The females are dressed in subtle green so that they're harder to see on the nest.

After breeding season, the males shed their bright plumage and grow new feathers in the same olive green as their mates. Often in late summer or fall, you'll see tanagers with blotchy feathers, some colored, some green, before the changeover is complete.

Tanagers are talented singers. Their whistled songs are long and lyrical, something like a robin's, and their voices carry from the treetops.

Range of Tanagers

There are only four species in this family, but they live in or travel over a wide stretch of the country. So you may spy a tanager wherever you live.

The western and scarlet tanagers, our black-winged friends, are the most widespread. The eastern half of the country belongs to the scarlet species, while the western tanager shows up all over the western half—and often strays into the eastern side, too.

In the Southeast and eastern Plains states, as well as in the Southwest, the all-red summer tanager joins the group. And in the Southwest, the hepatic tanager, a softer red, roams the mountain forests.

Now You See 'em . . .

If you live smack-dab in the middle of a large woods, you may see tanagers all summer long. But for most of us, these forest birds are a tem-

Like all female tanagers, this hepatic tanager wears greenish yellow. Males, too, are drab except in breeding season.

porary treat, showing up in our backyards only during spring and fall migration.

Those special occasions are worth waiting for—and planning a garden around. In late May, 1920, after a sudden heavy snowfall, Ira Gabrielson and Stanley Gordon, the authors of the 1940 book *Birds of Oregon,* were exploring together in the sagebrush desert of Harney County, Oregon.

Suddenly they encountered a "multitude" of migrating western tanagers forced to a halt by the snow. The men wrote, "It was curious to walk through the sagebrush and see the topmost stalks flame-tipped with the brilliant red, yellow, and black of these birds."

The western tanager looks like a living flame, but it's surprisingly hard to see in its western forest haunts. In winter, it often shows up in backyards.

birds, except in fall, when an attractive source of berries may draw a crowd of hungry travelers.

You'd think that birds this brightly colored would stand out like spotlights. Sometimes they do, when they're perched out in the open. But usually they're tricky to see because they forage within the cover of trees, or in some cases, shrubs. And they move slowly. You'll often see these birds in a crouched position, with head lowered, as if they're trying to sneak up on something.

At-Home Habitat of Tanagers

Woods are the watchword for this family. But *woods* is a relative term, depending on the region of the country in which you live.

Family Habits of Tanagers

Talk about family values—tanagers often remain in pairs all year, unlike other birds that go their separate ways as soon as the kids are on their own.

Usually you'll see just one or a pair of the

The Wild Side

Scarlet and summer tanagers rummage around in the mixed deciduous forests of their eastern, midwestern, and southeastern homelands, where oaks (*Quercus* spp.), maples (*Acer* spp.), hickories (*Carya* spp.), and tulip trees (*Liriodendron tulip-*

Elegant Escapees

Florida is famed for its own fabulous birds—plus a number of escaped exotic birds that have set up housekeeping in the wild. A few manage to establish a thriving population, but most eventually peter out.

The blue-gray tanager, a beautiful sky-blue bird of southern Mexico and southward, is one of the caged species that managed to slip out the door in Florida, sometime in the early 1960s. For at least a dozen years, the species managed to hang on in the wild, even producing some young. But as of 2005, the blue-gray tanager appears to be on the loose no more. At least until the next time somebody lets the cage door open.

ifera) are plentiful, often with a few hemlocks (*Tsuga canadensis*) or white pines (*Pinus strobes*) mixed in. In the Southwest, "woods" are often a stand of cottonwood trees (*Populus deltoids*) along water, or patches of scrubby oaks (*Quercus* spp.) and junipers (*Juniperus* spp.) in the cool mountains. And that's where you'll find hepatic and summer tanagers.

Western tanagers have a lot of woods to pick from, and you may come upon them in the moist, mossy conifer forests of the Northwest (including Douglas fir, *Pseudotsuga menziesii*, and other conifers); the dry ponderosa pine (*Pinus ponderosa*) woodlands east of the mountains; the coastal woodlands; or those famous stands of aspens (*Populus* spp.) that turn to pure gold in fall.

Backyard Matchup

Whew. I don't seem to have the energy today to plant a forest of 50-foot trees in my backyard, so I'm happy that going to such measures isn't required to round up a tanager.

A neighborhood dotted with trees is welcomed by these birds, especially the scarlet tanager. And if you live in surroundings like that, all you need is a single big tree in your own yard to attract tanagers, and possibly even a nesting pair. Any tree native to your area is a good choice.

Native trees are a lot easier to find at nurseries than native shrubs or wildflowers. They make excellent shade trees or conifer specimens, so you're likely to find a good selection at your local nursery. Just ask the staff for help, if you're not sure what kind of big trees those are in the natural woods around you.

Look to native trees for top tanager appeal. In the dry West, tanagers visit pinyon pine (*Pinus edulis*), a slow grower that reaches only 40 feet tall.

Think about how your neighborhood looks from the air, when you figure your chances of attracting tanagers. Many older neighborhoods look surprisingly like a forest when viewed from above, and that may encourage migrating tanagers to drop down and take a break.

If your area is woodsy enough, you may be graced with a resident pair of tanagers. A backyard mix of shrubs and trees can be enough to entice a pair of birds to count your yard as part of its nesting territory.

In fall, you won't even have to go that far—they'll eagerly investigate a good berry plant, even if it's the only thing in your yard!

(continued on page 262)

Summer Plenty

Tops for tanagers, mulberry and cherry trees bear bushels of irresistible bite-size fruit.

The spotlight is on fruit in this garden for tanagers. As the cherries and mulberries ripen, any tanagers in the neighborhood are likely to be drawn in, along with orioles, waxwings, thrushes, and other fruit lovers. The cherries and mulberry will bear a few fruits the first year you plant them, and they only get better with age.

A mulberry? Aren't those messy pest trees? Not to birds, and not to bird lovers, with a bit of foresight. If you don't live on acres in the country, start by investigating cultivated varieties, where you'll find mulberries with nonstaining white fruit, trees with delectable 3-inch-long fruit, and trees that mature at 30 feet instead of double that height. To prevent stepping in fruit, underplant the tree with groundcover. A bed of fast-growing groundcover liriope (*Liriope muscari* cultivars) below the trees will hide any dropped fruit and add extra cover for low-level birds. You can choose your favorite liriope cultivar from a wide range of foliage effects: All quickly knit into a thick mat of turf, with small spikes of flowers, usually blue, followed by dark berries that appeal to bluebirds.

You'll need an area about 18 feet long and 6 feet wide. Eventually, the mulberry will reach about 35 feet tall, but you can easily prune it back to keep it smaller. Of course you'll want a chaise longue nearby, so you can watch the fabulous birds this low-care garden brings in.

Plant List

1. Red mulberry (*Morus rubra*) (1 young tree) (Hardiness Zones 5–9)

2. Sour or pie cherry (*Prunus* cultivar, such as 'Montmorency') (2 trees) (Hardiness Zones 5–9)

3. Liriope (*Liriope muscari* cultivars) (12 to 15 young plants, all the same kind or mixed kinds) (Hardiness Zones 6–10)

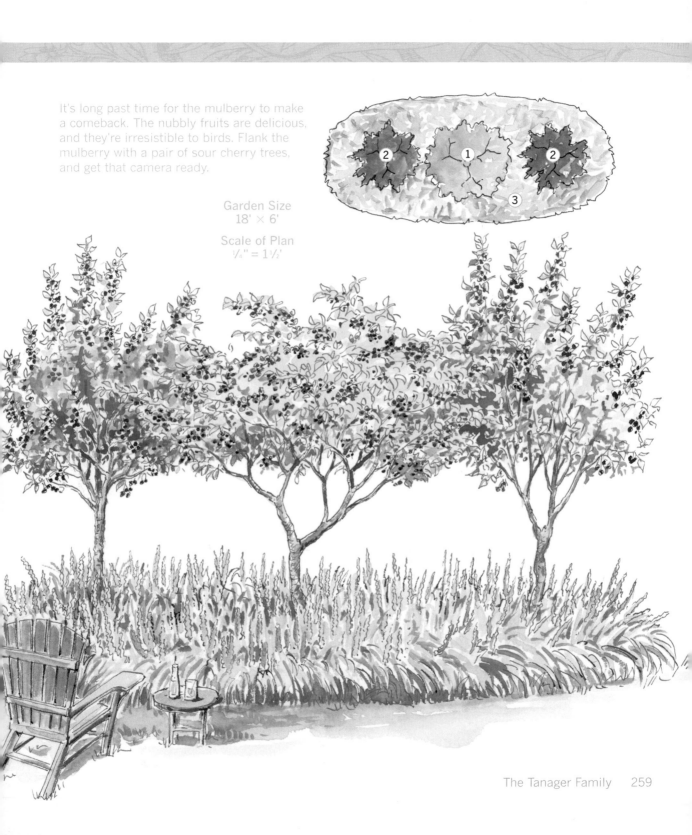

It's long past time for the mulberry to make a comeback. The nubbly fruits are delicious, and they're irresistible to birds. Flank the mulberry with a pair of sour cherry trees, and get that camera ready.

Garden Size
18' × 6'

Scale of Plan
¼" = 1½'

These plants supply the fruit, berries, and insects that tanagers depend on. They also create good habitat and possible homesites for these beautiful songbirds.

Plant	Type of Plant	Description	Zones
Flowering dogwood (*Cornus florida*)	Small deciduous tree, to about 20 ft	Showy, large white or pink flowers mature into tight clusters of elongated red berries.	5–8
Figs (*Ficus* spp. and cultivars)	Small to medium-size tree, deciduous to evergreen, to about 15 ft	Lush, large leaves are beautiful in the garden, and fruit is delicious.	8–11; 'Brown Turkey', 7–11
Mulberry 'Illinois Everbearing' (*Morus alba* × *M. rubra*)	Small to medium-size deciduous tree, to about 30 ft	Greenish flowers followed by multitudes of juicy, red to purple fruits, as soon as the first year after planting	5–9
Ponderosa pine (*Pinus ponderosa*)	Evergreen conifer, to about 100 ft	Long-needled and open branches, with large cones as tree matures	5–8
Sweet cherries (*Prunus* cultivars, such as 'Bing' or 'Stella')	Small to medium-size deciduous tree; dwarf cultivars to about 12 ft; nondwarf to about 25 ft	Fast-growing; often produces white flowers and sweet red fruit the first year after planting	5–9
Oaks (*Quercus* spp. and cultivars)	Large deciduous trees, to about 80-100 ft	Stately, slow-growing trees with catkinlike flowers and acorns	3–10

Used for	Comments	Other Birds Attracted
Berries	Susceptible to dogwood blight, a disease that can be fatal, but well worth taking a chance on. Buy a vigorous tree with flower buds already set (they look like round gray buttons) for berries the first year.	Thrushes, mimic thrushes, waxwings, and other birds eat the berries. Warblers, vireos, orioles, and others may seek insects at flowers.
Fruit	Grows rapidly. Some cultivars are suited to areas as cold as Chicago ('Chicago King'), where they freeze to the ground in winter and come roaring back in spring. Wild and cultivated figs are a hit with western spp. of tanagers.	Waxwings, orioles, and other fruit eaters may sample the figs. Leafy plants provide cover.
Berries; insects from foliage and flowers	A true bird magnet for all fruit-eating birds, but can be messy. Surround with ground-cover to prevent staining pavement or stepping in fallen fruit. Prune to keep at a height of about 15–20 ft, for a better view of the birds	Orioles, flycatchers, thrushes, mimic thrushes, wrens, waxwings, and many other birds eat fruit. Vireos, warblers, flycatchers seek insects at flowers and foliage.
Nesting by western tanager spp.; insect food from foliage	A good choice for tanager lovers in the West	Kinglets, nuthatches, chickadees, and titmice seek insect food among foliage and on bark; nuthatches, chickadees, titmice, and others eat seed from cones.
Fruit	Choose a cultivar suited to your area and your own taste—you may get a few cherries for yourself if the birds don't beat you to them. Many cultivars need another cultivar as a pollinator; read the catalog or label to select one.	Thrushes, mimic thrushes, orioles, and many other birds eat the fruit; vireos, orioles, warblers attracted to insects at flowers. Hummingbirds may nest in young trees.
Insect food from flowers and foliage; possible nest site	Scout your local nursery and you may find an oak that already has a few acorns on it, for a head start. White oaks have tastier acorns than red oaks and are highly popular with birds.	Woodpeckers, jays, chickadees, titmice, gallinaceous birds, doves, small finches including juncos, and many other birds eagerly eat acorns. Orioles, vireos, warblers, and flycatchers eat insects from foliage or at flowers. Jays may use as nest site.

Natural Foods for Tanagers

Tanagers have long but stout beaks, and they're dual-purpose tools. A tanager uses its beak primarily to eat insects, especially large-bodied ones such as grasshoppers and cicadas. But it works just fine on fruits, too.

Insects are the bulk of this family's diet in spring and summer. Before and during migration, berries and fruits are the big items.

Main Menu: Insects and Fruits

After my own terrifying and painful encounter with a nest of yellowjackets, I've become an even bigger fan of tanagers. And not because of their beauty: because of their eating habits. Wasps and bees are right at the top of the list for summer tanagers.

"Flycatching" behavior is part of this family's bag of tricks. The summer tanager depends mainly on this method of hunting. It sallies forth from a perch, snatches a bee or wasp on the wing, then returns to wait until the next one passes by. The hepatic tanager also flycatches on occasion, but you're more likely to see it stealthily moving through the foliage, intent on finding insects.

The scarlet tanager is a skulker, too. It reminds me of a lion stalking antelopes—or the neighbor's darned cat trying to sneak up on a bird in my yard. Head lowered, the scarlet tanager sneaks through the trees, alert for leaf beetles, cicadas, caterpillars, or other insects in its path. This gorgeous bird also combs shrubs for insects, and it sometimes forages right on the ground.

Tanagers are one of the best allies we have against gypsy moths. The hordes of hairy caterpillars are a savory treat to these birds. Grasshoppers and crickets are favored, too. And

Blast from the Past

Talk about how times have changed. Today, we're keeping our fingers crossed for a tanager; a hundred years ago, shotguns were in vogue.

In a 1903 issue of the *Condor*, the journal of the Cooper Ornithological Society—one of the largest ornithological societies in the world today, but only 10 years old at the time—W. Otto Emerson submitted this report:

One of the most wonderful occurrences of the movements of birds in the season of migration, which ever came under my notice, took place at Haywards [California] during May, 1896, when countless numbers of Piranga ludoviciana, or Louisiana tanagers [the bird we know today as the western tanager], began to make their appearance between May 12 and 14.

So far, so good. But the tanagers, unfortunately, settled in a cherry orchard. That's when the mood changed.

Two men were kept busy shooting them as fast as they came into the trees. . . . The tanagers at first seemed to take no notice of the gun reports, simply flying to other parts of the orchard. . . . [D]ozens of the birds were lying about. For the first two weeks the birds were mostly males, but later on the greater numbers were composed of females and young of the year.

Mulberry trees fell out of favor as yards got smaller and life got neater. Plant one, or learn to recognize it wild: Tanagers are huge fans of the ripe fruit.

big, buzzy cicadas are no problem to get down the hatch.

Can we go back to those bees and wasps for a minute? Maybe I'm so enamored of tanagers because I can trust them to devour yellowjackets, but the skills of these birds, especially my pal, the summer tanager, deserve a closer look.

After catching a bee or wasp in flight and returning to its perch, the tanager beats it against the branch to kill it, then deftly rubs the body on the bark—to remove the stinger!

And when the tanager takes on a wasp's nest, it first dispatches the adults, one by one, before it rips open the nest and gobbles up the larvae. You go, birds!

In late summer, tanagers begin bulking up for their long flight south. That's when you'll see them gobbling berries by the bushel. Those juicy treats sure help pack on the pounds, er, ounces.

In the wild, you may spy tanagers gathered at any of their favorite berries and fruits in late summer and fall. Wild cherries (*Prunus* spp.), orchard cherries (*Prunus* cultivars), dogwoods (*Cornus florida*), blackberries and raspberries (*Rubus* spp.), mulberries (*Morus* spp.), elderberries (*Sambucus* spp.), and hawthorns (*Crataegus* spp.) are among their favorites—perhaps because they ripen when the birds are moving through.

Backyard Fare

Doggone that dogwood blight. This disfiguring, often fatal fungal disease threatens many wild and backyard dogwood trees (*Cornus florida*), and it moves fast. One day, you'll notice a wilted branch; before you know it, the whole tree is affected.

There's no cure for dogwood blight, although you may stave it off by removing an infected branch as soon as you see it. And resistant varieties are still years away, I'm guessing.

So what's a tanager lover to do? Dogwood berries are the number one, five-star, satisfaction-guaranteed food for fall tanagers. Each of those big white blossoms matures to a cluster of tempting berries. They're simply tops for tanagers. And they attract bluebirds—well, let's not get into that now.

If you have a dogwood, treasure it. If you don't have one, it's worth risking it and buying a tree from a reputable nursery. (Discount garden centers helped spread the blight because of their large volume of sales, which inadvertently included infected plants).

Second best are cherries (*Prunus* spp., such as 'Bing' or 'Rainier') and mulberries (*Morus* spp.).

Come to think of it, a backyard orchard—which can be dwarf trees in containers, or fruit trees in your flower beds—is a great way to garner a group of tanagers. Any fruits that we enjoy are just as favored by this family. You can try apples (*Malus* cultivars), peaches (*Prunus* cultivars), nectarines (*Prunus* cultivars), plums (*Prunus* cultivars), figs (*Ficus* cultivars), or anything else that suits your taste. Don't forget the blueberries (*Vaccinium* cultivars), too.

Oranges (*Citrus sinensis*) and other citrus fruit may attract the birds, too. They may also pay a visit to your veggie patch, in search of tomato hornworms.

Round out the fruity menu with the same foods tanagers eat in the wild: elderberries (*Sambucus* spp. and cultivars), and late-season varieties of blackberries and raspberries (*Rubus* spp.).

Hawthorns (*Crataegus* spp. and cultivars), especially native species, are small trees that are immensely tempting to tanagers. Nurseries usually stock only a very few hawthorns, and often they're nonnative trees.

I find that unbelievable, because there are more than 180 species—yep, that's not a typo—of hawthorns native to just about every part of North America. What a lot of interesting trees to get to know!

You can meet Great Smoky Mountain hawthorn (*Crataegus penita*), Grand Rapids hawthorn (*C. ambitiosa*), Berks County hawthorn (*C. bona*), Dallas hawthorn (*C. dallasiana*), Kansas hawthorn (*C. coccinioides*), and Caughuawaga hawthorn (*C. suborbiculata*), just for starters.

Or maybe your interest is tweaked by prairie hawthorn (*C. pratensis*), pineland hawthorn (*C. pinetorum*), redclay hawthorn (*C. impar,* a.k.a. *C. inanis*), or buffalo hawthorn (*C. xanthophylla*).

Tanagers may lend a hand, or a beak, rather, to hornworm control in your tomato patch. The giant caterpillars go a long way toward filling a nestling's belly.

Perhaps you'd rather go for beauty: shining-branch hawthorn (*C. corusca*), beautiful hawthorn (*C. pulcherrima*), or elegant hawthorn (*C. poliophylla*).

Doesn't it make sense to grow fascinating trees that have a real connection to your region, instead of planting "one-size-fits-all" types? You'll find sources for native trees, including hawthorns, in the Resources section near the back of this book. Or maybe you can inspire a locally owned nursery to help you in the hunt. With so many to meet, collecting bird-attracting hawthorns could be a new hobby.

Feeder Foods for Tanagers

Tanagers often show up at feeders, especially during spring migration. At the feeder, they're delightfully tame.

1. Plant a native species of oak (*Quercus* spp.) if you don't have a large deciduous tree in your backyard. Even better, plant a small grove of oaks, to provide more insect food.
2. Plant a flowering dogwood (*Cornus florida*), and keep your fingers crossed that it stays blight-free.
3. Be the first in your neighborhood to bring back the red mulberry (*Morus rubra*) to the place of honor it deserves. Sure, it's messy. But nothing beats it for attracting fruit-eating birds.
4. Plant a sweet cherry (*Prunus* cultivar, such as 'Bing', 'Stella', or other cultivars).
5. Keep a birdbath brimming with fresh water. Add a drip tube for extra temptation.

Fruit is the first course, and fresh is preferred. Try grapes, cut-up pears and apples, bananas, and halved oranges. On the dry side, offer raisins, currants, dates, and figs.

Mealworms, crickets, and other insect foods are popular, too. And oddly enough, tanagers contentedly eat seeds at the feeder. Millet seems to be the favorite.

Consider at least a few of the hundreds, yes, hundreds, of native hawthorn species for your tanager garden.

Water Wishes of Tanagers

If you ever needed evidence to make you glad that you keep a birdbath, how about a flaming red tanager splashing with abandon?

Tanagers are quick to settle at a birdbath of any sort. A pedestal type will serve, but a naturalistic multibasin style, set low to the ground, and with a dripper or small solar fountain—well, that's pure heaven.

Nesting Needs of Tanagers

Tanagers build their nests in trees of various species, including large dogwoods (*Cornus florida*), pines (*Pinus* spp.), aspens (*Populus* spp.), sycamores (*Platanus occidentalis*), oaks (*Quercus* spp.), and others. If they select yours, hallelujah! If not, there's always next year.

Chapter 19

The Large Finch Family

FAMILY NAMES: Cardinalidae; Emberizidae; Fringillidae
EASE OF ATTRACTING: ★★★★★ (practically guaranteed)
BIRDS IN FAMILY: Northern Cardinal · Pyrrhuloxia · Grosbeaks · Crossbills

Meet the Large Finch "Family"

Ay-yi-yi. The Finch family is a mess, as far as backyard birders are concerned. Even taxonomists can't seem to stop arguing over who belongs where.

Not so long ago, all of the birds commonly called "finches" were lumped together into one family, Fringillidae. It was a massive group, with 83 species, and it included everything from grosbeaks to goldfinches and sparrows.

A second family, Emberizidae, was created as a place for sparrows and their close kin, juncos and towhees. Hallelujah! A sorting that made sense.

Then the family Cardinalidae was thrown into the mix, subtracting even more birds from the family Fringillidae. It includes the cardinal, most grosbeaks but not all, and the buntings, plus a few extras.

Nowadays, all that's left in Fringillidae are mostly birds of the North: rosy finches, redpolls, crossbills, siskins—plus goldfinches and the evening grosbeak.

That's the current standing, according to the American Ornithologists' Union. I'm sure it makes sense by taxonomic standards. But for backyard purposes, it's easiest to think of the Finch family in terms of birds' size: large finches, such as cardinals, crossbills, and grosbeaks, and small finches, such as buntings, goldfinches, siskins, and sparrows.

That's why you'll find the "Large Finch family" and the "Small Finch family" in this book. Both corral species from all three families—Cardinalidae, Fringillidae, and Emberizidae.

Scientifically speaking, they're a mishmash. But to backyard enthusiasts, the groupings make sense.

Look and Listen

Large finches add a welcome splash of color in our yards and at our feeder. They come in red, yellow, orange, and even blue, and they often show off flashy white or black markings, too.

You'll notice their splashy colors first. But you won't be able to overlook those schnozzes, either. The birds in this group sport big, conical beaks that would look comical if these weren't our favorite friends. (Check out the next cardinal or grosbeak you see, from a head-on view—pretty silly!)

Crossbills have a unique twist to their bills: the top and bottom halves overlap like crossed fingers.

Now that I'm thinking about all the attributes of these birds, I realize how bare our yards would be without them. Nearly all of these birds are great singers. No matter how often I've heard a cardinal whistling *"What cheer-cheer-cheer,"* I never get tired of it.

Too bad for me, because there are no cardinals in my part of the country. The friendly black-headed grosbeak makes a fine backyard substitute, though, in my neck of the woods. These vivid orange-and-black birds are terrific songsters, too, and they even warble while they fly.

Only the evening grosbeak and the crossbills, which you may remember were relegated by taxonomists to a different family, lack a lyrical song. Instead, their vocalizations are jerky or chirring.

Large finches, large bills: Super cracking power is built into a cardinal's bill. It's strong enough to open tree seeds that we'd need a hammer for.

A strong beak, with a twist. Like a pair of bypass pruners, the crossbill's beak can scissor through the scales of pinecones to reach the seeds.

Range of Large Finches

Most of these birds range across large areas of the country. The cardinal is in the eastern half and along the southwest border, where it's joined by the pyrrhuloxia. The blue grosbeak covers the southern two-thirds of the nation, and the pine and evening grosbeaks are mostly in the northern areas and the high mountains.

Other grosbeaks seem to split down the Plains, with some species sticking to the eastern side, and one species, the black-headed, to the west. Crossbills can show up anywhere in the country, though only the red crossbill regularly nests anywhere south of the northern tier.

Now You See 'em . . .

The cardinal and pyrrhuloxia are year-round birds, but many others in this bunch are migrants. Black-headed, rose-breasted, and blue grosbeaks leave the country in fall. Not to worry: They'll return in spring.

You may have noticed birders getting excited at the sighting of a pine grosbeak or crossbill. That's because it could be an indicator of an "irruption"—a massive movement of birds of the Far North, sweeping southward when food in their homeland is scanty. A sudden influx of evening grosbeaks, pine grosbeaks, and crossbills is a real treat for backyard birdwatchers.

Family Habits of Large Finches

Most of the time, large finches stay at middle to high heights, foraging in large shrubs or trees or in dense stands of tall weeds.

In southern Arizona, New Mexico, and Texas, the pyrrhuloxia overlaps with the similar cardinal.

Ever notice shoes squeaking in a basketball game? That sounds like the call note of the rose-breasted grosbeak.

You'll get a crop of cones from white pine just a few years after planting. Fast-growing conifers are valuable for cover and insects, even before they bear cones.

The blue grosbeak and pine grosbeak frequently forsake the trees and shrubs to forage on the ground. You'll often spot a large finch singing from a perch, often at the very tip of a tree. The concert can last for minutes at a time.

These birds are strong fliers, so you'll frequently see them on the wing as they move from one place to another.

In winter, many of these birds congregate in small groups, usually of a single species. If the large northern finches—evening grosbeak, pine grosbeak, or crossbills—show up in your yard, you'll find that they're among the tamest birds around. They seem to have little or no fear of us, maybe because people are scarce in the mountains or northern regions where they spend most of their time.

At-Home Habitat of Large Finches

You'll find large finches in forests and thickets in the wild.

The Wild Side

Crossbills, which rely on conifer cones for much of their food, are partial to conifer forests. In fact, they use strictly conifers for nesting, although they frequently visit deciduous trees.

Most other species don't show much preference; they forage and nest in deciduous trees as well as evergreens. The gorgeous rose-breasted grosbeak, though, sticks mainly to deciduous trees.

In the wild, these birds are found in the native trees of their area. That's a long list, including oaks, maples, willows, sweet gums, birches, alders, cottonwoods, poplars, and many others, plus all kinds of conifers: spruce, fir, pine, juniper, and larch.

Backyard Matchup

Backyard maples (*Acer* spp.), poplars (*Populus* spp.), birches (*Betula* spp.) and any other tree you might name will make suitable habitat for large finches in the backyard. So will lilacs (*Syringa* spp.), roses (*Rosa* spp.), and many other shrubs.

These birds will use just about any tree or shrub in our yards for cover and insect food— and, darn it, they'll be just as accepting of whatever trees and shrubs are in our neighbors' yards.

That's why I put my energy into food plants. Berries and seeds are what give our yards the "Wow!" factor when it comes to large finches.

(continued on page 274)

Wet 'n' Wild

Seduce bath-loving cardinals and grosbeaks with the gentle sound of trickling water.

Right from the start, this planting will attract cardinals, grosbeaks, and other large finches: These birds are particularly fond of taking a good bath. The low-level basin draws them in with the sound of water. Young trees supply perching places out of harm's way, for primping those wet feathers. In a few years, the birds will be visiting the trees for their tempting seeds. But even when young, these trees offer tasty buds and insects. Bush honeysuckles add another layer of cover and food. They grow surprisingly quickly to a substantial size, making the garden look established right from the start.

This plan shows Morrow's honeysuckle (*Lonicera morrowii*), a species that's highly appealing to birds, including crossbills and waxwings. So is Tatarian honeysuckle (*L. tatarica*). Both species are considered invasive in some areas. Check with your USDA extension agent, listed in the blue pages of the phone book, to find out whether these plants are discouraged in your area. If so, you can easily substitute any of the many other fast-growing bush honeysuckles that have been introduced from other countries. Or try a native, such as twinberry (*L. involucrata*), a western species that thrives in Zones 6 to 8.

Plant List

1. Red maple (*Acer rubrum*) (1 tree) (Hardiness Zones 3–9)

2. Bush honeysuckles (*Lonicera* spp. and cultivars, such as *L. morrowii*) (3 shrubs) (Hardiness Zones 3–9)

3. White ash (*Fraxinus americanus*) (1 tree) (Hardiness Zones 6–9; farther north, try the similar green ash, *F. pensylvanica,* hardy in Zones 4–9)

Garden Size
20' × 10'

Scale of Plan
⅛" = 1'

Naturalistic ground-level
birdbath with drip tube

"One generation plants the tree; another gets the shade," says a Chinese proverb. But birds profit from the trees you plant right from the beginning, finding food and cover in them as part of a multi-level habitat.

These plants supply the hearty seeds that are sought by these strong-billed birds. They also provide tender buds for eating, plus plenty of insects, while providing naturalistic habitat.

Plant	Type of Plant	Description	Zones
Boxelder (*Acer negundo*)	Deciduous tree, to about 50 ft	Fast growing and often short-lived. Fancy cultivars with variegated leaves, such as 'Flamingo', are easier to find, but the plain green species is more attractive to birds.	5–8
Alder (*Alnus* spp.)	Deciduous trees, to about 70 ft	Beautifully shaped when young; they eventually lose lower branches and are crowned with a mass of foliage. Often form open thickets	3–8
Birches (*Betula* spp. and cultivars)	Small deciduous trees, most to about 25 ft	Delicate trees with small leaves and open branches; catkin flowers in spring followed by small "cones"	2–9
Ashes (*Fraxinus* spp. and cultivars)	Deciduous trees, to about 80 ft	Moderately fast-growing trees with inconspicuous flowers followed by hanging clusters of seeds that look something like a bunch of itty-bitty flat bananas	4–10
Tulip tree (*Liriodendron tulipifera*)	Large deciduous tree, to 80 ft	Dignified and stalwart, a tulip tree has a perfectly straight, tall trunk. The leaves are shaped like a child's tulip drawing; fragrant, gorgeous large flowers also resemble tulips. Clusters of narrow seedpods, resembling cones, eventually shatter and flutter to the ground in late winter.	5–9
Bush honeysuckles (*Lonicera morrowii, L. maackii, L. korolkowii,* and others)	Large deciduous shrubs, to about 15 ft	Among the earliest shrubs to sport new greenery in early spring. Small tubular flowers, usually white to to yellow or pinkish, are followed by prolific juicy red berries.	3–9

Used for	Comments	Other Birds Attracted
Seeds	Boxelders sprout like weeds, thanks to birds and the wind spreading their winged, maplelike seeds. Good in mixed hedges.	Vireos, tanagers, orioles, and other insect eaters scour the foliage for insects.
Seeds, buds	These trees are racehorses: they can grow to 4 ft tall in a single year—from seed!—and to 12 ft the following year.	Vireos, warblers, orioles, tanagers, and other birds scour foliage and flowers for insects.
Insect food from catkins and foliage	Fast-growing and pretty right from the start. "Clump" birches—those with more than one main trunk—are the most graceful, and they give more bird benefits than the specimen.	Vireos, warblers, orioles, and many other birds scour birches for insect food. Chickadees and titmice may visit for cones.
Seeds	Ashes are trouble-free trees that don't attract a lot of human attention, because they're not particularly showy. They won't go unnoticed by birds, though.	Ash buds and flowers are a prized food for waxwings as well as large finches. Vireos, warblers, orioles, and tanagers scour foliage and flowers for insects; nuthatches and creepers forage on the bark.
Seeds	A superb native tree for attracting many birds. Orioles, tanagers, and others may use it as nest site.	Warblers, vireos, tanagers, orioles, and others glean insects from foliage and flowers. Nuthatches, chickadees, and titmice patrol for insects in bark and twigs. Gallinaceous birds eat seeds that fall to the ground.
Berries	Many bush honeysuckles are considered invasive, because birds have spread their seeds everywhere. Still, they're one of the prime plants for birds, including the beautiful pine grosbeak, which feasts upon the berries during its irregular winter vacations.	Tanagers, waxwings, small finches, and many other birds eat the berries. Vireos, warblers, orioles, and others search for insects at the flowers. Hummingbirds seek nectar at flowers. Thrushes, small finches, and other birds may select as a nest site.

Natural Foods
for Large Finches

All you need is one quick glance at the business end of a large finch to see that those beaks are heavy-duty eating machines. You'd expect these birds to take on the biggest, toughest seeds—tree seeds—and many of them do.

But now take a closer look at how a large finch's bill is made. Those sharp edges also function as strong shears, better than a pair of classy Felco pruners when it comes to neatly nipping off the buds of trees.

Large finches can also be surprisingly adroit at eating small or soft foods. They use the point of their beak to snap up insects, and many species open wide for fruits and berries.

Maple tree flowers are packed with pollen, a protein source for grosbeaks and other large finches that nip off the blooms.

Main Menu: Buds, Insects, Seeds, and Fruits

Speaking of pruners, those big beaks remove a lot of potential growth from trees. Tree buds are one of their most beloved foods.

What kind of trees? Maples, elms, ashes, alders, and all sorts of deciduous trees are—sorry, can't resist—nipped in the bud.

Crossbills are notorious for nipping off the buds of spruces. That's not a problem in the North Woods. But if the birds visit your yard in winter, it may leave you wondering why your backyard spruces fail to produce those "candles" of soft new greenery. Don't get too mad at the crossbills, though; they also eat spruce budworms, which are a far more serious problem for your trees.

Crispy critters are a major item in the diet of large finches. They eat long-horned beetles, bark beetles, Japanese beetles, May beetles, and lots of other beetles, plus wasps and big, plump cicadas.

Plenty of soft-bodied sorts go down the hatch, too, including butterflies and moths (both adults and caterpillars), plus cutworms, squash bugs, and weevils, to name a few.

Ever try to crack a cherry pit in your teeth? Just the idea gives me a new respect for the power that's exerted by the beak of a large finch. Tree seeds are another big item for these birds. Cherry stones (*Prunus* spp.), winged maple "samaras" (*Acer* spp.), and the seeds of boxelders (*Acer negundo*), catalpas (*Catalpa* spp.), ashes (*Fraxinus* spp.), birches (*Betula* spp.), alders (*Alnus* spp.), willows (*Salix* spp.), tulip trees (*Liriodendron tulipifera*), mesquites (*Prosopis* spp.), and others fill the bill, so to speak. Conifer seeds are popular, too, especially with those dexterous crossbills.

Large finches are wild about weed seeds, too. In winter, flocks of cardinals often feed among the stalks of a thick stand of giant ragweed.

Fruit isn't a top draw for some large finches. But cardinals often sample grapes (*Vitis* spp.), and the "gray cardinal," better known as pyrrhuloxia, often takes a bite from the bright red fruits of desert Christmas cactus (*Opuntia leptocaulis*).

The black-headed and pine grosbeaks are the fruit gluttons in this group. They'll chow down on blackberries, raspberries, elderberries, cherries, and—pucker up!—mistletoe berries. Red-fruited bush honeysuckles (*Lonicera* spp., especially *L. morrowii*) are another favorite, and they may also eat barberries.

Backyard Fare

Ever hear of the "potato-bug bird"? That's an old name for the rose-breasted grosbeak, which was once a much-appreciated friend of the farmer. When striped potato bugs attacked a planting, these big finches were usually hot on their heels.

If potato beetles or squash bugs invade your vegetable garden, look for large finches picking them off the plants. Nothing like letting the birds do the work.

You won't have to go out of your way to supply insects for large finches, though you'll want trees and shrubs to provide the cover these birds prefer.

Focus on seeds instead, with a side order of fruits, and you may literally have these calm, friendly birds eating out of your hand.

In the desert Southwest, you can plant desert Christmas cactus to catch the eye of a pyrrhuloxia. For black-headed grosbeaks, try "people fruits," including strawberries, raspberries, and cherries. There's always room to squeeze in a grapevine on a trellis, too. Any cultivar will do the trick. If large finches fail to eat the fruit, you'll draw lots of other eager eaters.

If you have no seed-producing trees, now's the time to plant. Large finches will sample their tasty buds and nip off their flowers while the trees grow big enough to produce seeds.

Even though their bills can do heavy-duty work, large finches are also partial to soft, juicy fruit. Try a grapevine of any variety, and see what visits.

The black-headed grosbeak, a western species, is famed as a stray. Occasional birds have shown up from Maine to Florida, and every state in between.

Fill in the gap with flowers. Sunflower seed is superb for these birds at the feeder, but they're usually not interested in harvesting their own. Instead, try an oddity among bird-attracting plants: flowers of the *Impatiens* genus. That includes our shade-garden favorite, impatiens (*Impatiens walleriana*), as well as garden balsam (*I. balsamina*). I've often spotted large finches, especially rose-breasted grosbeaks and cardinals, sampling their seeds.

If the interesting orange wildflower called jewelweed or touch-me-not (*Impatiens capensis*) grows near you, bring home a few seeds and start your own patch. I like to plant it beside a birdbath, where these moisture-loving annuals can get an extra drink every time I refill the basin.

You will no doubt notice how tricky it is to collect the seeds of jewelweed. Any movement is apt to set off the spring-loaded seedpods. Closing your hand around the ripe pod is the only way to do it, and even then you'll have to be careful not to jostle the plant. Garden impatiens works the same way. That's why it's amazing to watch large finches at work in a patch of impatiens. Eating the seeds requires deft beak work.

Feeder Foods for Large Finches

Sunflowers. That's the guaranteed draw for large finches of any kind at the feeder. They'll quickly work their way through a tray of striped or black-oil sunflower seed, then look around for more.

Of course, they'd snatch up pine nuts, too. But at the prices I've seen for pine nuts, I'd rather save them for myself and stick to sunflowers.

I also happen to know that black-headed grosbeaks—at least those in western campgrounds—are very fond of crumbled Wheat Thins®. My son David remembers only dimly the fantastic rock spires of Chiricahua National Monument in Arizona, which we visited when he was 7. But he vividly recalls the black-headed grosbeaks gently taking crackers from his hand at our nearby campsite.

Water Wishes of Large Finches

A brimming birdbath is one of the best ways to bring large finches to your yard. The simple pedestal type works fine, or if you like, you can invest in a naturalistic ground-level model.

These big birds appreciate a mister or fountain spray, too.

In my neighborhood, the black-headed grosbeaks instantly forsake my yard and feeder when they hear the *Fffttt! Fffttt! Spissssh* of the neighbor's irrigation system kicking in. Each bird positions itself beside an emitting head, then absolutely wallows in the spray. When the irrigation shuts off after its allotted few minutes, the birds look around as if to say, "What happened?"

Nesting Needs of Large Finches

Large finches nest in trees or shrubs of various kinds. They may even accept a helping hand with materials.

Nesting Plants

A mix of trees and shrubs in your yard boost your chances of hosting a nest of large finches, if you live within their breeding range.

The cardinal often claims a climbing rose or shrub rose as a nest site, but it's equally at home in lilacs (*Syringa* spp.), mock orange (*Philadelphus* spp.), and other common backyard shrubs.

Nest Materials

Cardinals and some other large finches often weave a few pieces of paper into their nests. Here's your chance to enlist your kids: They love to help tear sheets of paper into strips. It's a satisfying job because it doesn't require much skill. Just start at a short edge of a sheet of paper, and

Break out the sunflower seeds, the evening grosbeaks have come to call! For most of us, this female and others of her kind are only temporary visitors—good news for the birdseed budget.

tear up (or down). It will rip easily into a fairly straight strip. Make the strips about an inch wide and about 8 inches long, then offer them on the ground or draped over a bush.

Large finches may also come for feathers, fur, or horsehair. You can put these into an empty tray feeder or on your lawn for easy access.

Little Extras for Large Finches

Bird lovers often worry over whether to feed salted nuts to birds. If large finches ate nuts—

which they don't (except for pine "nuts")—we wouldn't have to fret. These birds are salt fiends.

Salt is an excellent plant killer, though, so be sure to keep it away from vegetation and soil. For an eye-pleasing permanent setup, install a square of inexpensive concrete paving blocks at least 4 feet square, and set up your "salt lick" there. Visit a feed store or horse supply store to buy an inexpensive salt block. Salt blocks come in various sizes and weights, and some are pinkish rather than white, because they have added nutrients. I use the plain-Jane variety, mainly because it's cheaper.

Or you can try the quick temporary arrangement that I use from fall through early spring, when large finches are at their peak in my yard. You'll need a waterproof container with a rim; I use a lid from a plastic storage tub. Cover the container with an inch or so of gravel, so that the rim is still exposed, then set the salt block in the center.

For an even easier setup, and no worries about affecting plants, simply sprinkle a few tablespoons of coarse rock salt, such as that sold for making ice cream, in a large clay saucer, and set it on the ground at your feeding station.

Chapter 20

The Small Finch Family

FAMILY NAMES: Cardinalidae; Emberizidae; Fringillidae
EASE OF ATTRACTING: ★★★★★ (practically guaranteed)
BIRDS IN FAMILY: Sparrows · Finches · Buntings
Juncos · Siskins · Redpolls · Towhees

Meet the Small Finch Family

Scientifically speaking, this group of birds isn't a family at all. It's a collection of species that I drew from three separate finch families, Cardinalidae, Emberizidae, and Fringillidae.

But, hey, there's method to my madness: The birds share a similar shape and almost identical eating habits. So the same tricks will work to attract all of them (or as many as you're within the range of) to your inviting backyard.

For more on finch taxonomy, turn to Chapter 19, the Large Finch family.

Or set aside the science for now, and simply get started making your yard inviting to the small finches.

These little birds are some of the best friends a backyard bird lover could ever dream of. It

For most of us, the perky little chipping sparrow is a spring and summer friend that may build its home in a tree or shrub not far from our own front door.

takes very little coaxing to bring them to your yard—in fact, many of them are probably already there.

Look and Listen

See a little brown bird scratching about on the ground? There's a good chance it's a native sparrow, one of the biggest groups in the Small Finch collection. "Little brown birds" are the bane of many a birdwatching trip. But they're a real pleasure in your backyard, because you'll have plenty of time to appreciate the fine points that set apart each of the 30-plus species of sparrows. Don't worry; you won't see all of them at your place!

Siskins are brown, too. Towhees? Brown. Redpolls are brown with a streaky white belly and a splash of red on head and breast. And rosy finches are brownish gray with hints of lovely rose-red.

Juncos switch to a gray color scheme, with a white breast and belly.

Buntings, though, are birds of a different color. How about sapphire blue; lazuli blue; red and purple; or parrot-colored red, green, and blue? At least the males display all these colors. The females are, guess what, brown. Or, in the case of the brilliant painted bunting, greenish.

As for the little birds with the word *finch* in their names—the house finch, purple finch, Cassin's finch, and goldfinch—their females are, um, brown (except for the olive female goldfinch). But the males are standouts, with rich strawberry red, raspberry red, or sunshine yellow feathers.

The classy white-throated sparrow, a winter resident or migration visitor, scratches for seeds on the ground under shrubs or other cover.

Most small finches are brown, but not this male indigo bunting. Dandelion seeds are its favorite.

Purple finches and other birds named "finch" spend more time in trees than most native sparrows, which usually forage on or near the ground.

Keep an eye out for that snazzy black face: Harris's sparrow is famed for straying as far as both coasts.

Most small finches have lovely, musical voices, and they sing frequently. Even the females are known to break into song, sometimes when they're sitting on the nest.

Range of Small Finches

With so many species in this group, you're guaranteed to see some small finches wherever you live.

The house finch, dark-eyed junco, pine siskin, and savannah sparrow range from sea to shining sea, and the American goldfinch covers all but the spine of the Rockies and Cascades. The many other species are found in less expansive ranges, but a lot of them cover huge regions of the country, too.

Now You See 'em . . .

House finches and towhees are year-round birds, as are a few sparrow species. But most of the small finches migrate, so they may be summer residents for some of us, winter treats for others, or year-round delights when winter birds move in to replace migrants that went bye-bye.

I often don't notice the exact day when my winter finches leave, though after a day or two, it will dawn on me that I haven't seen a junco in a while.

But I sure sit up and take notice when these birds arrive in spring. Small finches aren't usually loners—where you see one pine siskin, you'll probably see a dozen. Sparrows migrate in mixed flocks, and it's not uncommon to stumble across scores of the birds in your backyard on a March or September morning. Juncos, too, usually arrive in fall in a bunch. And part of the pleasure of a bird-friendly yard is watching goldfinches gather in ever-increasing numbers in late spring.

Some winters, an "irruption" of small finches takes place, as species of the Far North fly south when food is scarce. Then, even gardeners outside the usual range may see redpolls, rosy finches, pine siskins, or other northern species.

Family Habits of Small Finches

Small finches are little sprightly birds. They move fast, but not nearly at the hyper speed of kinglets or warblers.

Most species live within 15 feet or so of ground level, although the birds with the word *finch* in their name typically frequent trees.

Many small finches, including native sparrows, juncos, and towhees, spend the bulk of their time right on the ground, foraging in leaves or fields.

At-Home Habitat of Small Finches

Some of this group are at home in forests, but most frequent more open areas. And some live in fields where there's nary a bush in sight.

Whatever their usual habits, all small finches are drawn to low levels when there's tempting food for the taking.

Unless you look closely for that cap and bib, you may miss the common redpolls feeding alongside other finches in your yard or at your feeder.

Birds that live in grass or brush, like this grasshopper sparrow, are streaky brown to blend right in.

Male buntings are the gems among finches. This lazuli bunting is a nesting bird in the West.

Every birdwatcher soon knows the slate-colored junco, a common sight in winter from coast to coast.

The Wild Side

Small finches are prime prey for hawks and other predators, which may be why they have such a predilection for cover. You'll rarely see them out in the open, unless there's a sheltering tree, shrub, or tussock of grass to hop to in a hurry.

With so many species, these birds cover just about every niche of low-level habitat. Most aren't dependent on particular plants; it's the overall effect that makes them feel at home.

Backyard Matchup

A big percentage of the birds in your yard from fall through early spring are going to be small finches. There are simply more individuals in this family. For every cardinal you see in December, for example, you might host 10 or 20 juncos; for every wren or oriole that shows up in May, you may count 50 or 100 goldfinches at your feeder.

Since your yard is going to be popular with small finches, it makes sense to give them some space to spread out.

Cover is vital for putting small finches at ease. Since the birds aren't picky about what kinds of plants provide that cover, it makes sense to focus on food plants. You'll find plenty of mouthwatering suggestions in the section that follows.

Small finches are a great reason to let some of your flowers stand, even after frost makes them drop their leaves and the plants get bleached and brittle. These birds can usually find something worth investigating there, even in the depths of winter. And the thicket of plant stems will give them that all-important cover.

(continued on page 288)

Wildflower Meadow

Seeds a-plenty are the temptation for juncos, white-throated sparrows, and a host of other small finches.

It may look like a pretty wildflower garden, but this little garden is a powerful finch attraction. Seeds, seeds, and more seeds, plus plenty of cover, will make finches feel at home, while satisfying their cravingseeds for their favorite foods. The millet and mustard add fine texture to the rest of the flowers. Let the patch stand through fall and winter so that birds can peck up every last bite.

You'll need an area about 6 feet square for this garden, but you can expand it for even more appeal. It looks great on a hillside because of the large swatches of color. Any dropped seeds overlooked by the birds will start a new generation the following spring. And best of all, the colorful flowers and natural look will help disguise any weeds that sneak in—whose seeds finches will also welcome.

All of these annual flowers are simple to grow from seed. Cosmos, however, can take its time coming into bloom, so if you want faster flowers, buy started plants already in bud or bloom at a garden center. You'll find millet seed at a whole foods market or in the natural foods aisle of your grocery store. Or you can plant a few handfuls of birdseed millet.

Plant List

1. Calliopsis (*Coreopsis tinctoria*) (1 or 2 packets of seed)

2. Blue bachelor's buttons (*Centaurea cyanus*, blue cultivar) (2 packets)

3. Yellow mustard (*Brassica* spp. and cultivars) (1 packet)

4. Sensation Series cosmos (*Cosmos bipinnatus*, Sensation Series) (2 packets)

5. Annual lupine 'Arroyo' (1 packet or 12 plants) (*Lupinus succulentus* 'Arroyo')

6. 'Autumn Beauty' or other color-mix sunflower (*Helianthus annuus* 'Autumn Beauty') (1 packet)

7. White proso millet (scatter throughout the calliopsis, bachelor's buttons, and cosmos) (about ¼ pound)

Garden Size
6' × 6'

Scale of Plan
$\frac{3}{8}" = 1'$

Once you start gardening for birds, you might start looking at flowers as seeds in the making. This seedy garden, er, flower bed, will sustain native sparrows and other small finches all winter.

Surefire Plants to Attract Small Finches

Your small finches will harvest a banquet of their favorite small seeds from these plants, which provide cover while the birds dine. Plenty of seeds will drop to the ground, so your finches will be foraging through fall and winter.

Plant	Type of Plant	Description	Zones
Mustards (*Brassica* spp.; one of the best is rapeseed or canola, *Brassica nappus*)	Plants to about 3 ft	Mustards have four-petaled flowers shaped like a cross; they produce tons of small yellow blossoms, which mature into pods filled with small round seeds.	Annual
Sensation Series cosmos (*Cosmos bipinnatus* Sensation Series)	Flowers to about 3–4 ft	Feathery-leaved cosmos produce abundant pink to red or white flowers.	Annual
Purple coneflower (*Echinacea purpurea*)	Perennial flower, to about 3 ft	Purple coneflower is a relative newcomer to American gardens, coming onto the scene back in the 1970s. It became an instant favorite, thanks to its easy-care habits and its abundant purple daisies.	3–9
Annual sunflower (*Helianthus annuus*)	Flowers 4–8 ft or taller	Classic sunflowers with a single large head are guaranteed to attract birds; other cultivars with fancier flowers or multiple flower heads will also appeal.	Annual
Lettuces (*Lactuca* spp. and cultivars)	Plants to about 5 ft	Leafy lettuce becomes a bird plant when it produces a flowering stem crowned with small daisies that mature to fuzzy seeds, like mini-dandelions.	Annual
Zinnia (*Zinnia elegans* cultivars)	Flowers to about 4 ft	Big, bright flowers in bold or pastel colors top these easy-to-grow plants.	Annual

Used for	Comments	Other Birds Attracted
Seeds	Wild mustards of many species grow across America; they're a common garden weed. Check a field guide or take a guess, and let a few of these pretty plants stay in your garden.	Gallinaceous birds, doves, and blackbirds also eat seeds. Flycatchers, orioles, thrushes, mimic thrushes, and jays will enjoy the butterflies drawn to the plants; many birds will enjoy the caterpillars and other insects for which the plants provide a home.
Seeds	Goldfinches begin eating seeds while other flowers on the plant are still in full bloom.	Warblers may forage for insects during fall migration. Gallinaceous birds, doves, and blackbirds will glean fallen seeds from the ground all winter.
Seeds	Large plants make good cover; let them stand in winter.	Gallinaceous birds, doves, and blackbirds will glean fallen seeds from the ground all winter.
Seeds	Plant giant sunflowers close together (about 4 in. apart) and their stems will help support each other as they get top-heavy and prone to toppling. Or grow shorter cultivars.	Large finches, especially cardinals, plus nuthatches, woodpeckers, jays, chickadees, and titmice pluck seeds from heads; native sparrows and juncos, doves, gallinaceous birds forage for dropped seeds.
Seeds	Look for bargain seeds (often 10 for a dollar) and stock up. Any variety of garden lettuce is a temptation once it goes to seed. Plant thickly, in a patch or row, where you'll have a good view of your visitors.	House sparrows and small finches may nibble the green leaves.
Seeds	Zinnia leaves may get straggly and mildewed in late summer, so plant them near the back of your bed, where other plants can hide their foliage. Large plants make good cover; let them stand in winter.	Gallinaceous birds, doves, and blackbirds will glean fallen seeds from the ground all winter. Hummingbirds sip nectar at the flowers. Attract butterfly-eating vireos, flycatchers, large finches, jays, and other birds.

Natural Foods
for Small Finches

Take a gander at that conical beak: For a bird this small, that tool promises quite a bit of strength. Seed cracking is the name of the game for small finches.

While other birds concern themselves with insects, small finches focus on seeds. A side of six-leggeds is welcome, though, especially during nesting season.

Main Menu: Weed Seeds

Okay, gardeners, let's all join in a great big cheer for small finches. These little guys are huge consumers of weed seeds—and each one they eat means that another dandelion-, ragweed-, pigweed-, or chickweed-to-be bites the dust. Not to mention all the hundreds or thousands of progeny that would've been produced by the plant that sprouted from that single seed.

These lightweight birds are built for clinging to plant stems, even when they bow under their weight. Siskins, buntings, redpolls, and "-finches" usually feed in this manner.

Other small finches prefer vacuum cleaner duties. Sparrows, juncos, and towhees forage busily on the ground below plants, picking up any seeds that dropped. It's a great system, and it cleans up a myriad of seeds that would otherwise sprout.

Small finches win the prize when it comes to eating weed seeds. These eager eaters devour zillions of weed seeds each year.

Grass seeds are another small finch favorite, and goodness knows, my own garden has plenty

A bird of the tundra, the gray-crowned rosy finch hops about on open ground when it spends its winters in the western quadrant of our country.

Weed? No, indeed! Chicory adds sophisticated bitterness to our salads, and small finches eat its seeds.

The eastern towhee with shining black wings and back is not nearly as gaudy as the spotted towhee that replaces it about halfway across the United States.

The sunny yellow clusters of goldenrod mature into a great number of small seeds to sustain small finches.

to spare. Cheatgrass, with its habit of burrowing its seeds into my socks and sneakers, is my nemesis here, but I also have crabgrass, orchard grass, and lots of other seedy types I'd be happy to see less of. Bet you do, too.

Most of the plants we think of as weeds came to America from other countries, hidden in the fleece of a sheep, the tread of a boot, the track of a tire, or mixed with desirable seed.

I often wondered what finches ate before these imported weeds were so widespread. Then I visited the Midwest for the first time and found sunflowers (*Helianthus annuus,* the multibranched, small-headed species form) stretching along every roadside. These native plants fill wild spaces across the Plains to the foot of the Rockies. Well, that took care of part of my question.

Small finches also eat the seeds of native asters (*Aster* spp.), goldenrods (*Solidago* spp.), vetches (*Vicia* spp.), lupines (*Lupinus* spp.), smartweeds (*Polygonum* spp.), and a whole field guide's worth of other native wildflowers.

The advent of weeds hasn't changed that be-

Golden-crowned sparrows and other small finches seek out mature lupines (*Lupinus* spp.) to crack open their dry pods and nibble their seeds.

havior. But the onward push of civilization has made many of these native wildflowers scarcer than they once were. Weed seeds fill the gap.

Backyard Fare

What was I just saying about weeds? Was I pointing out that they're terrific plants for luring small finches to your garden? Well, they are, and if your yard is fairly big, you may want to consider letting weeds take over a little corner. Of course, if your weeding talents are anything like mine, there are bound to be plenty of weeds

hiding here and there around the yard. If anyone looks askance at that tall pigweed in your garden bed, just tell them you're saving it for the finches. Great face-saver!

Let's set aside the idea of a garden given over to weeds, though, because you'll discover hundreds of other plants that suit the tastes of small finches. And most of them are fabulous flowers.

Annual flowers are the top pick for small finches because they produce so many seeds. But some perennials offer a bounty of good seeds, too.

Among the annuals, 'Sensation' cosmos (*Cosmos bipinnatus*) is my top pick, but maybe that's because I like its pretty pink flowers myself. Zinnias (*Zinnia* spp. and cultivars) of any kind produce plenty of bird-attracting seeds, too, as do calliopsis daisies (*Coreopsis tinctoria*), marigolds (*Tagetes* cultivars), and annual asters (*Callistephus chinensis*).

In the perennial garden, look to lupines. The fat spikes of lupine flowers (*Lupinus* spp. and cultivars) are eye-catching in any garden, but they bloom for only a few weeks. Then the flowers slowly ripen into plump pea pods. That's what yellow-crowned sparrows and other small finches are waiting for. They'll tug at the dry, brown pods until they snap, then pick out the plump seeds within.

Purple coneflower (*Echinacea purpurea*) gets as much attention for its herbal effects as it does in the flower garden. But it's the insect-attracting flowers and the bounty of seeds that catch the attention of backyard birds. The beautiful, big purple daisy flowers are always dancing with insect attendants, including butterflies of every color and size. In fall, when the seeds ripen, a bird can pull apart the seed head and enjoy an all-you-

You can tell spring is coming by listening for the sparrows that winter in your yard to start to sing. The golden-crowned has a sweet, whistled song.

Big, plump, and unusually tame, the fox sparrow may stop on migration or spend winter in your yard.

can-eat meal. And, in winter, the dropped seeds will sustain a multitude of munchers, including juncos, sparrows, and towhees.

All coneflower species (*Echinacea* spp.) are likely to lure in small finches; so are annual and perennial sunflowers (*Helianthus* spp.). Many plants in the large Daisy family (Compositae) produce seeds approved by finches.

Even after almost 50 years of watching small finches, the birds still surprise me. My latest discovery was annual forget-me-not (*Myosotis* spp.) as a bird plant: When the plants were looking so ratty I was ready to pull them out, the patch was swarmed by a mixed flock of American and lesser goldfinches, all of them busily picking out the small, fuzzy seeds.

When you see small finches feeding on a plant's seeds in your yard, it's easy to add it to your list of favorites. But it's hard to tell exactly what ground-feeding birds are pecking up. If your flower garden is full of foraging sparrows and juncos in winter, your plant choices are perfect.

I like to scatter handfuls of finch seed mix in my flower beds, too, wherever I can find a scrap of open space. Usually those mixes include red and white proso millet, German millet, annual canary grass (not to be confused with the horribly invasive perennial canary grass, an unrelated species), and rapeseed, a mustard. The grasses and mustard add airiness to the bed—and a full-service buffet for small finches when they ripen.

In the veggie garden, allow any plant in the mustard family to flower and go to seed. Small finches will appreciate the bonus of turnip seed, radish seed, and broccoli seed in fall and winter.

Your flower garden will be even more delightful with American goldfinches in it, seeking seeds.

A song sparrow in every backyard—not an unlikely goal with this common and charming bird.

Garden peas are relished by some finches, after they've dried on the vine. Lettuce is an irresistible treat, too, once its stems are topped with sprays of tiny parachute seeds.

Feeder Foods for Small Finches

This one's a no-brainer: Seeds are the secret to successfully attracting small finches to your feeder. Nyjer seed is favored by "-finches" and redpolls. All small finches enjoy millet, and a surprising number of species manage to crack black oil sunflower seeds.

Water Wishes of Small Finches

Make a birdbath part of your plan for a finch-friendly yard. Some species will take to a pedestal-type birdbath, but all of them are more at ease in a low-level bath tucked near cover. I love to watch birds playing in the water, so I've added a naturalistic ground-level bath, with a series of shallow pools, so there's room for more birds. A dripper tube will ensure that your bath doesn't escape notice.

And how about a plant that helps finches satisfy their thirst? The fleshy, juicy leaves of live-forever sedum, such as *Sedum spectabile* 'Autumn Joy', are almost liquid refreshment for some finches. I thought I had insect problems when I first noticed V-shaped notches along the edges of my sedum's leaves; they turned out to be from house finches who had helped themselves to a cooling treat on a hot summer day.

Nesting Needs
of Small Finches

The result of planting for small finch food is so satisfying, you may consider a nest just icing on the cake.

If you live within the range of a particular species, you have a chance of hosting a nest in your yard. Keep in mind that generous cover is the key word, no matter whether the species nests in trees or on the ground.

Nesting Plants

Many native sparrows make their nests right on the ground, tucked among sheltering plants. Groundcovers, including pachysandra (*Pachysandra* spp.) or strawberries (*Fragaris* spp. and cultivars), allow such birds to snuggle a nest among their stems. Or the birds may select

Where's a bird to quench its thirst? At the birdbath, sure, an ideal pedestal style for small finches. But perhaps also by nipping a succulent leaf of the plant in the foreground, *Sedum spectabile*.

Cosmos Cuisine

Mix up a batch of this custom seed mix, and you'll win the heart of every goldfinch in the neighborhood! Start in late summer, when cosmos seed heads are ripe for the picking.

2 parts black-oil sunflower seeds
1 part nyjer seed
1 part 'Sensation' cosmos seeds (*Cosmos bipinnatus* 'Sensation')

1. In late summer through fall, collect cosmos seed heads. Look for seed heads in which you can see visible brown or black seeds. Clip them into a paper grocery sack, using scissors. Roll the bag loosely at the top, and set them aside in a dry place.

2. When you're ready to make the mix, cover your work surface with newspaper. Take one seed head from the bag and, holding it over the newspaper, roll it lightly between your thumb and finger so that the seeds drop out. Repeat until you have a handful of seeds.

3. Combine the cosmos seeds with the black oil sunflower and nyjer seeds.

4. Pour the mix into a tray feeder and watch goldfinches flock to it.

Top To-Dos for
SMALL FINCHES

1. Look around your yard as if you were a bird that's nothing but a snack to cats and hawks. Plant cover—shrubs, hedges, flower beds—accordingly. Let flower beds stand all winter instead of cutting them down to the ground in fall.

2. Sow fast-growing zinnia, sunflower, cosmos, and marigold seeds in any sunny niche.

3. Start a birdseed garden by sowing finch seed mix, packaged for bird feeding.

4. Let lettuce plants go to seed in your vegetable garden.

5. Cultivate toleration of some of the weeds you find least annoying; small finches love 'em all.

6. Provide a clean, nonslip, shallow birdbath.

Pine siskins may show up just about anywhere in winter, and they'll be bringing their friends. Listen for their buzzy voices when the flock gathers in a tree.

your flower or vegetable garden, or an inviting shrub to make its new nest.

Little Extras for Small Finches

Minerals are a big attraction for small finches, and sodium chloride or calcium chloride—salt—is at the top of the list. Set out a salt block, and you'll see small finches visiting it daily.

Salt is just what the doctor ordered for small finches, but it can create a dead zone in your yard. Place a salt block on a waterproof container with a rim about 4 inches high, so that it doesn't leach into the soil or into nearby plants when rain arrives. Or dole out rock salt, sold for ice cream making, a small handful at a time in a clay saucer.

Chapter 21

The Blackbird and Oriole Family

FAMILY NAME: Icteridae

EASE OF ATTRACTING: ★★★★★ (practically guaranteed)

BIRDS IN FAMILY: Blackbirds · Grackles · Orioles · Meadowlarks · Bobolinks

---

Meet the Blackbird and Oriole Family

Oh, I'm sorry—you've already met? But of course. Blackbirds are backyard birds with a capital B, and you won't have to do anything at all to attract them. Grackles, cowbirds, and other blackbirds are already very much at home at your place—perhaps a little too much. Most bird lovers would rather see fewer blackbirds than bring more to their backyard.

Meadowlarks and bobolinks are the grassland relatives of the ubiquitous blackbirds. If you live near open fields, you may see meadowlarks at your feeder. But when they're done eating, they'll quickly return to those wide-open spaces.

Birders often call this the "Blackbird family,"

Unless your yard adjoins open fields, you're not likely to see a meadowlark in your backyard. But nearby birds may pay a visit during snow or ice storms.

but I added orioles to the family name because it's hard to think of orioles as blackbirds, due to their vivid color. Only the red-winged and yellow-headed blackbirds look like they're related to orioles in any way.

I'm waiting for the day when taxonomists realize they made a mistake, and give orioles their own family. Although they're shaped much like other blackbirds and have similar beaks, their habits seem very different.

Or maybe that's just because we pay more attention to these bright-colored beauties.

Orioles live in trees and are usually found in open woods. Same deal with the rusty blackbird, which frequents wooded swamps.

Orioles depend on insects and fruits. So do blackbirds, although all of them will also eat seeds, and grackles add meat to the menu.

Hmm. Looks like orioles are a good fit with this family after all.

In this chapter, we'll focus on attracting orioles, since blackbirds will be around whether you want them or not.

Blackbirds, such as grackles, red-winged blackbirds, and Brewer's blackbirds, often behave more like big sparrows than they do like orioles, because their diet and eating habits are more adaptable than orioles'. No matter where they live in the wild, blackbirds have no qualms about spending most of their time on the ground, and they seek out open areas rather than treetops much of the time. If blackbirds are your passion, a garden and feeder filled with millet, corn, and other seeds will make them loyal customers in your yard; you can follow the food plant suggestions in Chapter 23 to offer natural foods. But if

Red-winged blackbirds often stop at feeders while on migration, or if their nesting territory is nearby. They'll also scout out corn or grain in your garden.

Female orioles, like this Bullock's, aren't nearly as flashy as their vivid mates. All the better for keeping the nest and nestlings safe.

it's orioles you prefer, read on for more tricks for attracting them.

Look and Listen

Oh, wow! Did you see that flash of orange? It has to be an oriole!

Orioles are our only big orange birds. In fact, there's only one other orange bird in America: the Blackburnian warbler, a tiny guy that isn't often seen.

These flamboyant birds have fabulous—am I running out of superlatives yet?—orange or yellow feathers, contrasted with a dramatic black hood and back, and flashy black-and-white wings. Females are greenish, with hints of orange or yellow.

Orioles are outstanding in more ways than one.

Not only are they drop-dead gorgeous, but they also have the grace to come out into the open frequently, so we can admire them. True standouts.

Orioles are strong fliers, so you'll often see them on the wing as they move from tree to tree.

Their musical songs are loud and sweet and last long enough that you can track down the singing bird with binoculars, if you like. The reddish-brown orchard oriole isn't as vivid as its cousins, but it has the best voice of the bunch.

All in all, it's quite a package. For a "blackbird."

Range of Orioles

No backyard is bereft of the possibility of orioles. These birds make sure that every one of us has the possibility of oohing and aahing.

Worth the trip! A target for vacationing birdwatchers in the Southwest, the hooded oriole nests in fan palms, backyards, or Joshua Tree National Park.

The closely related Baltimore and Bullock's orioles, once classed as a single species, divvy up the country. The Baltimore, as you'd expect, covers the eastern three-fifths or so, ranging well into the Plains. Bullock's, which has a black cap and throat instead of a full hood, overlaps the Baltimore, picking up in the Plains and carrying onward to the Pacific.

The orchard oriole is at home from the Plains to the Atlantic and Gulf. Western birders, take heart: It often shows up outside its typical range. The Southwest and western states that lie east of the Rockies are home to the yellow-and-black Scott's oriole. The hooded oriole, an orange bird, is limited to the Southwest. Speaking of the hooded oriole, will somebody please explain this bird's name to me? It's the only oriole that *lacks* a hood!

Now You See 'em . . .

Orioles are migrants: here today, gone, well, around September, in most areas. They can be found nesting anywhere in their range, north of Mexico.

Only the Baltimore is a tease: It migrates through the Southeast and Gulf Coast, but it doesn't stop to raise a family until it's in the northern part of those states. On the other hand, it does winter in Florida and along the southeastern Atlantic coast, so I suppose we'll call it even.

Family Habits of Orioles

When they're not stopping to sing or to work on their fantastic hanging nests, orioles are busy gleaning insects from the foliage.

You'll usually see only one or a pair of orioles at a time because, unlike blackbirds, they don't hang around in flocks.

Unfortunately, the personality of these birds isn't as pretty as their plumage. The male can be absolutely vicious in driving away others of its kind from its selected territory.

Elms and Orioles

American elm (*Ulmus americana*), a huge, graceful, wide-spreading tree with small leaves and fine branches, is as beautiful in winter as it is in summer.

A century ago, the fast-growing tree was commonly planted along roads and streets, to keep passersby shaded and cool. That shade was a favorite destination for picnics, and most towns had elms in the village square.

That widely flared shape is easy to recognize, and you'll see American elm trees in many old postcards and paintings.

But finding the real thing will be a challenge.

In the 1920s, Dutch elm disease came to America. By the 1940s, the fatal disease had devastated American elms so that today, finding a healthy tree is hard to do.

When I moved to the Midwest in the early 1990s, I was stunned to find many more elms than I'd ever seen before—and they were looking healthy. By the time I left, a decade later, I'd watched most of the elms in my small town become stricken and die, one by one. Only a very few survivors still stood.The death of the American elm is a tragedy to tree lovers—and that

Graceful American elms still thrive in some towns.

includes orioles. Orioles had to make a big adjustment when Dutch elm disease swept across America, because elms were one of their top sources of insect food and a favored nest site.

If an American elm still survives near you, scan the tree in winter, and chances are you'll spot an oriole nest hanging from one of the outermost branches. Check it in summer and you may see the birds themselves.

Luckily, orioles weren't dependent on elms alone. When the trees began to die out, the birds switched to sycamores (*Platanus occidentalis*), tulip poplars (*Liriodendron tulipfera*), and other species.

This isn't always smart. I've noticed that one dead oriole on the road today will often be two dead orioles tomorrow. Those orange feathers, even when they're flattened, must trigger such a rage in the attacking bird that it becomes oblivious to oncoming traffic.

At-Home Habitat of Orioles

Orioles are birds of the trees. But they're not birds of the woods. Most species prefer open woods, suburbia, city parks, or backyards.

The Wild Side

These birds freely move between trees and shrubs, and they often fly across open spaces. But you'll rarely see them on the ground, unless they're fetching pieces of string you've put out— or fighting ferociously with a trespassing male.

You won't usually find orioles in conifers or evergreens either. Except for Scott's oriole, they stick to deciduous trees and shrubs.

Backyard Matchup

Planting your yard with trees and shrubs of different heights suits the style of these birds. They'll use small trees or tall shrubs beneath major shade trees as a ladder to get back and forth. Species that spend more time at low levels, such as Scott's oriole or Audubon's oriole, will be just as comfortable as those that like the trees.

Any deciduous tree may be used by orioles. Native trees of your area are always a sure bet. In the East, that might be a 60-foot tulip tree (*Liriodendron tulipifera*); in the Southwest, a 10-foot mesquite (*Prosopis* spp.).

Scott's oriole has a penchant for nesting in yuccas (*Yucca* spp.), but it may also use sycamores (*Platanus occidentalis*), oaks (*Quercus* spp.), or junipers (*Juniperus* spp.).

If you don't have tall trees in your yard, no problem. Orioles fly fairly long distances to reach food, as well as traveling on migration, and the fruit and berry plants you provide will bring them in. *(continued on page 304)*

Scott's oriole often sips nectar at desert agave (*Agave deserti*) or eucalyptus, and it craves prickly pear fruits. Its nest is usually in yucca.

Purple Glory

Sweet grapes and fat-bodied butterflies will appeal to oriole families in summer.

Even if you don't wear a red hat to sit in this garden, you'll still enjoy the shades of purple. And just wait until a flash of orange or yellow shows up—an oriole zeroing in on the fruit and insects the plants attract. The small sitting area offers the perfect vantage point for appreciating orioles at the plants and at the bath, as well as any flycatchers, tanagers, waxwings, or other birds that may arrive. Expect to see plenty of butterflies dancing over the flowers, too. Purple flowers have big appeal for these nectar seekers. Last but not least, this garden will smell wonderful from spring, when the grape blooms, through fall, thanks to the honey-sweet alyssum.

You'll need a sunny area about 8 feet wide and 12 feet long for this plan. Buy young plants, already in bud or bloom, of the verbena and alyssum: They'll grow fast once they're in the ground, and they'll soon blanket a big area with flowers that keep going into fall. 'Homestead Purple' verbena can be finicky as far as surviving over winter, but it grows so fast that it's worth planting just for a single summer; one young plant can grow to as much as 3 to 5 feet across in a single season! You can buy bare-root grapevines packaged in plastic bags early in spring for just a few dollars; they grow like wildfire and may even bear a few bunches of grapes the very same year you plant them. Don't worry about fancy pruning for the grapevine; just cut it back whenever it needs it, to keep it within bounds.

Plant List

1. Grapevine (*Vitis* spp. and cultivars, any kind) (2 plants) (Hardiness Zones 4–10)

2. Butterfly bush (*Buddleia davidii,* any cultivar) (2 plants) (Hardiness Zones 6–9)

3. 'Homestead Purple' verbena (*Verbena canadensis* 'Homestead Purple') (3 plants) (Hardiness Zones 6–10)

4. Lavender sweet alyssum (*Lobularia maritime,* lavender cultivar) (12 plants) (annual; all hardiness zones)

Garden Size
12' × 8'

Scale of Plan
¼" = ¾'

Grapes ripen late in the summer to early fall, right about the time that oriole families are leaving the nest or beginning their migration. That extra traffic means more potential customers for your fruity arbor.

Surefire Plants to Attract Orioles

The flowers and fruits of these plants are like a siren song to orioles. The birds will find plenty of insects among the blossoms and foliage, too.

Plant	Type of Plant	Description	Zones
Agaves (*Agave* spp. and cultivars)	Perennial succulents, to about 6 ft	A rosette of long, fleshy, usually spiny leaves is accented with stems of tubular blossoms—which in some species may top 20 ft tall!	9–11
Orange (*Citrus sinensis* cultivars, such as 'Washington')	Medium-size evergreen tree, about 20–40 ft	Sublimely fragrant flowers are a hallmark of citrus; the white blossoms are followed by delectable orange fruit.	9–10
Eucalyptus (*Eucalyptus* spp. and cultivars, especially red-flowered types such as *E. filicifolia*)	Evergreen trees and shrubs that vary widely in habit, depending on species	Clusters of fuzzy blossoms contain abundant nectar.	8–10; most, zones 9–10
White mulberry (*Morus alba*)	Large deciduous tree, to 50 ft or more	Fast-growing and quick to produce a prolific crop of white, soft berries—which don't stain like other mulberries!	4–8
Chokecherry (*Prunus virginiana*, including cultivars such as 'Schubert' or 'Canada Red')	Small deciduous tree, to about 20 ft	Dangling chains of fuzzy, creamy flowers mature to purplish fruits, bitterly astringent to our taste but manna to birds.	3–8
Grapes (*Vitis* spp. and cultivars)	Deciduous vines, to about 20 ft	Fast-growing vines with large leaves and abundant clusters of fruit	4–10

Used for	Comments	Other Birds Attracted
Nectar from flowers	A terrific choice in desert areas of the Southwest and California	Hummingbirds also sip nectar at flowers.
Fruit; insects at flowers; cover	Orioles often winter in citrus groves, or in a backyard with an orange tree.	Some finches and other birds also sample oranges. The leafy evergreen trees make good cover. Warblers, vireos, and other birds may visit flowers for insects.
Nectar; insects at flowers	Eucalyptus burns hot in western wildfires; do not plant near buildings.	Hummingbirds may also visit for nectar or insects. Vireos, warblers, tanagers, and other birds may also glean insects.
Fruit; insects from flowers and foliage	Keep mulberries at a lower height, if you like, by pruning in late winter. Excellent in a mixed hedge	Tanagers, flycatchers, vireos, warblers, and many other birds are attracted to the fruit and to insects on the flowers and foliage.
Fruit; insects at flowers and foliage	Fast-growing and quick to bear fruit. Wild chokecherry trees are so abundant that the fruit (with plenty of sugar added!) was once popular for homemade jelly.	Tanagers, thrushes, mimic thrushes, flycatchers, vireos, wrens, warblers, and many other birds are attracted to the feast of insects at the flowers and to the fruit.
Fruit; insects at flowers	Fast-growing cover and a crop of fruit the first year after planting	Wrens, tanagers, large finches, mimic thrushes, thrushes, and many other birds covet the fruit. Peeling bark and dead stems are used for nest materials by many birds.

Natural Foods for Orioles

Orioles share a similar beak, whether they're birds of the desert or birds of the forest. It's long and tapering, with a sharp tip—just the tool for eating insects and other soft foods.

Insects and fruits are the mainstays of orioles' diets. Orioles are one of the few types of birds that frequently visits flowers—not only for insects but also for nectar.

Main Menu: Insects, Fruits, and Nectar

Butterflies, caterpillars, beetles, and ants, plus a varied menu of other insects, are the big insect items in an oriole's diet. The birds scour the foliage and sometimes forage on the ground to find these goodies.

Mulberries (*Morus* spp.) and wild cherries

Serviceberries (*Amelanchier* spp.) are showstoppers in fall, with flaming red foliage. But it's the summer berries that stop orioles in their tracks.

(*Prunus* spp.) are irresistible to orioles. The birds also love serviceberries or Juneberries (*Amelanchier* spp.), wild grapes (*Vitis* spp.), and wild blackberries (*Rubus* spp.).

Here in the Pacific Northwest, where introduced Himalayan blackberries (*Rubus discolor*) smother whole acres of ground, Bullock's orioles do their best to make a dent in the crop.

The abundant berries of hackberry trees (*Celtis occidentalis*) are a temptation, too. They ripen about the time orioles begin to move southward, and they make great snacks along the road.

Backyard Fare

If you have enough room for it, planting a mulberry tree (*Morus* spp. and cultivars) will pay off handsomely in orioles. The trees can be messy, though, so you may prefer to stick to less troublesome plants.

Orioles give a big thumbs-up to many of the fruits we also find most delectable. Strawberries, cherries, apricots, raspberries, grapes, figs, peaches—*mmmm,* the oriole menu makes me hungry. Citrus growers aren't fond of orioles, because the birds adore oranges. That may be a problem if you're growing for Tropicana, but on a backyard scale, it's fun to share the wealth. If your climate is conducive to growing citrus, give it a try.

Flower gardens are another great secret of oriole attraction. Western and Southwestern birds seem to visit flowers for nectar more often than eastern species. But all orioles will fly through or alight in a flower garden if it's brimming with butterflies.

Purple flowers with many small blossoms attract clouds of butterflies. Try to find some space for a butterfly bush (*Buddleia davidii*), a fast-growing shrub that offers lots of perching places for orioles, plus dozens of delectable small and large butterflies. Add purple coneflower (*Echinacea purpurea*), too, if you don't already have it.

And explore the wonderful world of verbenas, especially those with purple flowers. These are tough plants that thrive in dry summers. Some are annuals; others are perennials. All have similar, long-blooming flowers, with clusters of tiny blossoms.

My top favorite is the perennial rough-foliaged *Verbena rigida,* which some gardeners don't plant

The stout stalks of red-hot poker (*Kniphofia* cv.) provide a perch for a nectar-seeking hooded oriole.

Live and Learn

When I was a kid, I used to spend summer afternoons lying under our two venerable red mulberry trees (*Morus rubra*). Well, not under them—lying on squishy, staining berries wasn't too appealing—but nearby. Those mulberries were a hot spot for birdwatching, because every fruit-eating bird in the neighborhood came to get its share. A half-dozen Baltimore orioles were usually on the scene; with their territorial nesting-season battles over, they could concentrate on filling their bellies.

My older sisters weren't as fond of watching the birds, and as teenagers they were far too cool to lie on the ground in their snazzy madras shorts. But they did enjoy the other aspect of the mulberry tree hot spot: hunting for feathers.

In late summer, when mulberries ripen, birds have begun to exchange their breeding plumage for a more serviceable outfit for the long trip south. My sisters and I found handfuls of golden flicker feathers, chestnut brown thrasher feathers, faded red cardinal feathers, elegant taupe mourning dove feathers, and striped blue jay feathers under those mulberry trees. Plus an assortment of mostly brown or black feathers that we usually didn't bother picking up. Nearly all of our finds were the long, pointed wing feathers, the "primaries" that birds shed first.

For years, I looked for orange flight feathers from a Baltimore oriole. But it was a wild goose chase.

But we never found any bright orange oriole feathers. My sisters weren't bothered by the lack, but I used to puzzle over it. I could see the orioles in the trees—where were their feathers?

It wasn't until I grew up that I realized why long orange wing feathers weren't in my fist. Orioles, duh, have black wings.

because it spreads fast by roots and may also seed itself. My opinion? You can't have too much!

I also like 'Homestead Purple' verbena (*Verbena canadensis* 'Homestead Purple'), a better-mannered, ground-hugging perennial. For variety, I let tall, bare-stemmed *Verbena bonariensis* seed itself wherever it wants in my butterfly-happy garden. And I always find room for those small pots of annual verbena I can't resist bringing home.

The eucalyptus trees in the West are far from native, but they've gone wild in many areas as well as being common in landscaping. Originally from Australia, these shaggy-barked trees have the distinctive aroma of Vicks VapoRub. Hordes of insects visit their flowers, and numbers of orioles do, too, because they are full of nectar. If you have eucalyptus in your yard, take a look with binoculars, and maybe you'll see traces of sweet stuff on the birds' beaks.

In Southwestern gardens, you can plant aloes (*Aloe* spp. and cultivars) and agaves (*Agave* spp. and cultivars) for orioles. The flowering stems that arise from the clumps of spiky leaves bear tubular flowers rich in nectar, and orioles are pleased to sample them. I've also seen the birds getting nectar from red-hot poker flowers (*Kniphofia* spp. and cultivars), but so far, not in my own yard.

Feeder Foods for Orioles

Mealworms and other insect foods, fresh or dried fruits, and accessible suet may win you an oriole at the feeder.

But you're probably more likely to attract orioles with feeders just for them. Nectar feeders,

The word is spreading among orioles about feeders, so give them a try. Here, a Scott's oriole finds a comfortable position for nectar sipping.

holders for grape jelly (or other flavors), and orange feeders are becoming more popular with orioles, as the feeders become more popular with those who feed birds.

As for the rest of the Blackbird and Oriole family—the blackbirds, grackles, meadowlarks, and bobolinks—they'll eat just about any seeds you serve them. Cracked corn, millet, baked goods, and generic birdseed mix will feed the masses.

Water Wishes of Orioles

Keep that birdbath filled to the brim for these water-loving birds. They're likely to take a bath even more often than you do. Make sure your bath has a nonslip bottom, or add a large flat rock for a better grip.

A small fountain, drip tube, or mister makes the experience even better for these birds, and it may attract migrants who aren't familiar with your yard.

Nesting Needs of Orioles

Rock-a-bye baby, in the treetops: Oriole nests are beautiful creations: hanging pouches made from plant fibers and finished with an extra-soft lining. When the wind blows, the cradle will rock.

Nest Materials

Orioles will choose their own trees in which to build their nests. But they'll gladly accept your help in supplying raw materials. Offer white string or twine in lengths about 6 inches long; white linen or cotton yarn; cotton tufts or balls (not synthetic); natural wool; and any other fibrous materials you can think of.

How would you like to weave a sock using only a beak and claws? The Baltimore oriole and others are masters at the art—and grateful for raw materials.

The Hummingbird Family

Meet the Hummingbird Family

I can see it now, the life of a taxonomist in the early days of categorizing birds: Weeks, years, a lifetime even, of painstaking observation and examination, not to mention plenty of good arguments over which bird goes into what family. Should juncos go with cardinals? Orioles with tanagers?

With so many headaches over the fine points, the taxonomists probably wished they'd become plumbers. I can also easily imagine their relief when they got to the Hummingbird family. Finally—an easy one! Nothing else comes close to these itty-bitty birds, with bills so long they look like lethal instruments, and wings so fast they're just a blur.

Look and Listen

Incredible flying skills, tiny size, adorable miniature feet, and speed that would beat a Ferrari, ounce for ounce—welcome to the world of hummingbirds.

Oh, and let's not forget jaw-dropping beauty. One good look at a hummer's throat feathers flashing in the sun, and you'll want more, more, more of these fantastic little birds.

Sixteen species of hummingbirds are found in North America. Central and South America have even more of these gems. In fact, the only place you'll find hummingbirds is in the Americas. Europe and the other continents don't have any to call their own.

All share the same outrageous shape and style. And all have iridescent feathers that practically ignite in the sun.

The throat of male birds is nearly always brilliantly colored, when the light is right. Depending on the species, it may glow orange, pink, purple, blue, ruby red, or magenta.

Hummingbirds make squeaky, chittery noises that sound more like mice than birds. Their wings make noises, too, and in gardens that host multitudes of hummingbirds, the loud humming sounds like an industrial machine.

Ever heard a child make fighter jet noises? That vrooming noise is something like the sound of hummingbirds when they engage in the steep, deep dives and loop-de-loops that are part of the courtship routine. I've gotten pretty good at imitating the rufous hummingbirds in my yard: I pretend I'm a jet airplane, and go "v–v–v–veerrr!"

Range of Hummingbirds

The Southwest gets the lion's share of hummingbirds. But there are enough to go around. Wherever you live, there's at least one species of hummingbird that will make your yard more interesting.

The ruby-throated hummer is the only species in the eastern half of the country.

In the West, the calliope, broad-tailed, black-chinned, rufous, and Anna's heat things up.

In the Southwest, all of the western species may be seen—plus 10 other kinds! It's enough to make us hummingbird-poor people think about planning a trip to one of those guest ranches for birders that have cropped up in Southwest hot spots.

Bright as a new penny, the rufous hummingbird of the West seems to have wanderlust. It's been turning up more frequently in every state in the country.

Another reason to take a second look at any hummer—like other species, Costa's strays far outside its limited Southwest range, as far north as Canada.

Most hummingbirds are migrants. But in a few lucky areas of the West, and at the very tip of Florida, hummingbirds are part of the scene year-round.

As nectar feeders gained popularity during the last couple of decades, hummingbirds began to change their habits. Winter and summer ranges are shifting for many species, with the birds expanding into new territory where sugar water awaits.

Family Habits of Hummingbirds

Pull your eyes away from those bright feathers the next time a hummingbird visits your feeder, and take a gander at those feet instead. Even though a hummingbird seems to be on the go all day long, it's actually taking quite a few breaks. They actually spend more time perched than in the air.

It can be tricky to spot a hummingbird when it's sitting still, but it gets a lot easier with practice. Look for that unmistakable silhouette, because the birds seek exposed perches, probably so that there's no interference from branches or foliage when they take off again.

Once you see a hummer on a perch, it's likely to show up there again. I can count—let me see, one, two, three . . . nine regular perches in my yard, or at least in the part that gets the most attention from hummers.

At-Home Habitat of Hummingbirds

Hummingbirds live in a variety of habitats, with each species having its particular niche. Generally speaking, the birds are usually found in or

The long spurs of a columbine guarantee a waiting drop of nectar for this pair of ruby-throated hummingbirds.

Hummers buzz about azaleas, whether they're in soft pastel colors like this Exbury type or zesty brights.

near woods and in areas with shrubby vegetation.

The Wild Side

Hummingbirds follow the food. Wherever there's an inviting supply of nectar flowers, the birds will be buzzing.

In the eastern part of the country, the ruby-throated hummingbird is found anywhere there are trees, shrubs, and food plants. Vigorous trumpet vine (*Campsis radicans*) and thick stands of spotted touch-me-not (*Impatiens capensis*) are hot spots when the flowers are in bloom.

The canyons and river edges of the West are favored by many hummers. Others, such as the magenta-throated Lucifer hummer, are often seen near the agave (*Agave* spp.) or ocotillo (*Fouquieria splendens*) plants of their desert home.

Even hummers that are often found in woods may show up in cities or towns, too. Many cities in California have planted exotic trees from foreign lands along their streets, and some of these are tailor-made for hummingbirds.

I'll never forget watching my first Anna's hummingbird feeding at a silk tree or mimosa (*Albizzia julibrissin*) on a Santa Monica street corner. Inline skaters whizzed by, a parade of every fashion of the last 50 years strolled along, Porsches and Bentleys rolled down the boulevard—and right in the thick of this "wilderness" was a hummingbird, oblivious to it all.

Many western hummingbirds move higher after nesting season is over. They leave the canyons and lowlands behind and relocate in the mountains. Flowers bloom later at higher alti-

Hummers take frequent breaks on favorite perches, so look for that little silhouette on exposed twigs or the very tips of shrubs in your yard.

tudes. So, once again, they're simply following the food supply.

Backyard Matchup

The usual mix of backyard shrubs and trees provides abundant perching places for hummingbirds and, with any luck, possibly a nest site.

All hummingbirds include backyards as part of their "wild" habitat—if there's plenty of excellent nectar flowers or a feeder to lure them in.

(continued on page 316)

Hummingbird Haven

Sweeten the deal for hummingbirds with nectar-rich shrubs perfect for perching.

Here's a hot spot for hummingbirds that will catch their eye from spring through late summer, thanks to all the nectar flowers. But other birds will keep it humming, too, as they use the plants for cover and possibly for nesting. You may see song sparrows, robins, cardinals, thrashers, or catbirds sneaking into this shrubby haven. In winter, the dwarf spruce will provide a nighttime roost for juncos and sparrows. In summer. it's another attraction for hummingbirds, which may collect spider silk from its branches.

You'll need an area about 10 feet wide by 6 feet deep, in sun to part shade, to plant this garden. As the shrubs grow, it will eventually reach about 15 feet long. You can plant this garden along your house or garage, as a foundation planting, or try it along a fence or to mark a boundary line of your yard. Wherever you put it, you'll want to make sure there's a window or sitting area nearby so that you can enjoy the hummingbirds that come to it.

Plant List

1. Evergreen azaleas, any color (*Rhododendron* cultivars) (3 plants) (Hardiness Zones 5–9)

2. Exbury-type azalea, pink or pale yellow (*Rhododendron* cultivars, Exbury Hybrids group, also called Knapp Hill–Exbury Hybrids) (1 plant) (Hardiness Zones 5–9)

3. Purple-leaved weigela 'Minuet' (*Weigela florida* 'Minuet') (1 plant) (Hardiness Zones 4–8)

4. Globe-shaped dwarf blue spruce 'Globosa' (*Picea pungens* 'Globosa') (1 tree) (Hardiness Zones 3–8)

5. Coral bells (*Heuchera* × *brizoides* cultivars, red-flowered; 'Firefly' is a good one) (6 plants) (Hardiness Zones 4–8)

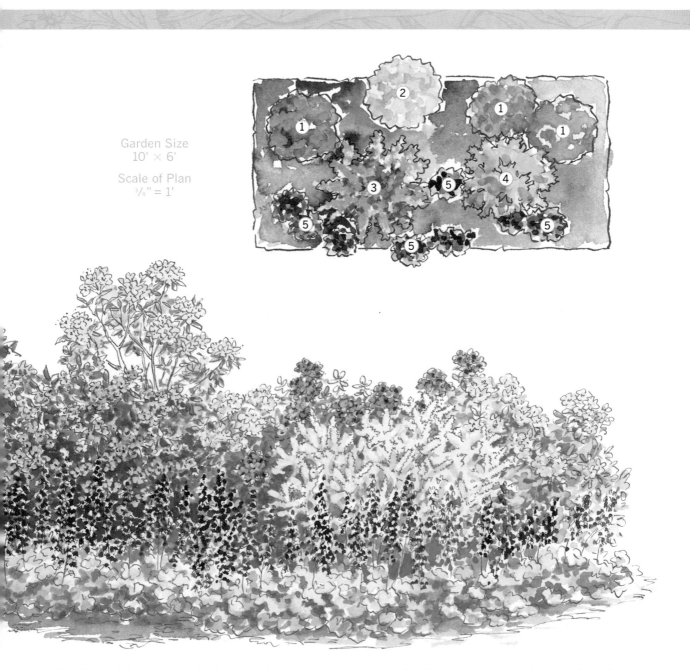

Garden Size
10' × 6'

Scale of Plan
³/₈" = 1'

Besides adding nectar, shrubs provide better cover for other birds than a hummingbird garden of flowers alone. While hummers are buzzing at the bushes, robins or mimic thrushes may be building nests within.

Surefire Plants to Attract Hummingbirds

It's all about the sweet stuff for hummingbirds. These plants will give your hummers a long-blooming garden full of good nectar sources, with small insects to snack on, too. Also, turn to page 319 for a regional listing of more flowers that bring in hummers!

Plant	Type of Plant	Description	Zones
Columbines (*Aquilegia* spp. and cultivars)	Perennial flowers, about 1–3 ft tall	A dainty plant with unusual blossoms with long spurs extending backward; often gray-green foliage	3–9
Crocosmia (*Crocosmia* cultivars)	Perennial, to about 5 ft	Forms a clump of sword-shaped leaves from which emerge dramatic arching stems of brilliant flowers, in red, orange, or yellow	6–9
Red-flowering honeysuckle (*Lonicera sempervirens*; *L.* × *brownie*)	Vine, to about 15 ft	Fast-growing vines with clusters of vivid tubular flowers from early summer into fall.	4–9
Bee balm, red cultivars (*Monarda didyma* 'Gardenview Scarlet' and other red cultivars)	Perennial, to about 3 ft	Fragrant foliage crowned with unusual whorled flowers, each made up of many individual "florets" with a dab of nectar	4–9
Cape fuchsia (*Phygelius capensis*)	Shrub, to about 3–4 ft	Bushy and branching; bears spikes of many dangling tubular blossoms in red, orange, pinkish, yellow, or yellow-green	8–9
Red zinnias (*Zinnia elegans*, red cultivars)	Height varies, depending on cultivar, from 1–3 ft	Drop-dead simple to grow from seed, these easy plants bloom fast and furious. Snip off dead flowers to keep 'em coming.	Annual

Used for	Comments	Other Birds Attracted
Nectar of paving, in steps,	Columbines self-sow, popping up in cracks and anywhere else they can get a grip.	Larger columbines, such as golden columbine (*A. chrysantha*), form good-sized clumps that contribute to low-level cover for native sparrows and thrushes.
Nectar	Start from inexpensive bulbs, or buy potted plants. Multiplies fast. In Zone 6, mulch in winter with 3 in. of chopped leaves.	The clumps are too thick to provide cover within the plant, but useful to native sparrows, juncos, and doves to increase the general sheltering aspect of the garden.
Nectar	There's always room for another vine! Try these on a trellis, tuteur, or teepee.	Carolina wrens appreciate the mid-level cover.
Nectar	Hummingbirds will visit all colors of bee balm, but the red ones are best for grabbing their attention. Plant spreads rapidly by roots, but it's easy to pull out if it gets out of bounds. "Pinch" the plants when they're about a foot tall by removing the tip and first pair of leaves on each stem, to multiply the number of flowers.	Good cover for small finches and other low-level birds
Nectar	Terrific long-blooming plant; slowly expands its size by sending up suckers.	Good cover for many native sparrows, juncos, and other low-level birds. Orioles may sip nectar.
Nectar; small insects; spiders	Leaves may get mildew; plant catmint (*Nepeta* × *faassenii*) or another flower in front to disguise the problem.	Zinnia seeds are a favorite of small finches, including native sparrows, pine siskins, goldfinches, and juncos. Tall varieties create excellent cover for low-level birds. Flycatchers, orioles, jays, and other birds may visit to collect butterflies or other insects drawn to the flowers.

Natural Foods for Hummingbirds

Nectar is number one. And lots of folks believe it's the one and only.

But surprise, surprise, there actually *is* a number two: insects. And even a number three: spiders.

Main Menu: Nectar

Nectar is nothing more than a bribe. Flowers produce the stuff to lure insects, including but-

No need to spend big bucks for hummingbird plants. A 4-inch pot of fiery red salvia from any garden center will do the trick for about $2.

terflies, and hummingbirds to their flowers. The nectar is stored at the bottom of the flower so that the visitor brushes against the pollen to reach it. In exchange for that sip of nectar, the flower is pollinated by the visitor.

"Hummingbird flowers" are those that are mostly inaccessible to other pollinators, so that hummers are assured of a reward when they visit them. The shape of the flower determines who gets the goods: Daisies, for instance, are visited by every Tom, Dick, and Harry, but trumpet vine (*Campsis radicans*) is reserved for hummingbirds.

Hummingbirds also eat insects. Tiny ones, granted, but bugs nonetheless. It's hard to see exactly what's going on when a hummingbird visits a flower, but if you spend enough time watching the birds with binoculars, you may see them dab up an insect instead of dining on nectar.

Spiders get picked off, too. Sometimes the hummer nabs both the insects in a small spider's web and the spider itself.

Backyard Fare

Hundreds, even thousands, of plants are visited by nectar-seeking hummingbirds. You'll have lots to experiment with!

Start with red-orange, red, and orange flowers; most of them are fashioned to fit a hummingbird's feeding habits. The color alone advertises that they're appropriate, and you can take it as a guarantee: Any flower of these colors will be visited by hummingbirds. And they'll try their best to get nectar out of it.

You can spot a hummer-preferred flower arrangement at a glance: a stem of tubular flowers with plenty of flying room around it, like this penstemon's.

chart on page 319 to fill your yard in any part of the country. But even that chart is incomplete, so have fun branching out and discovering what best fits your gardening taste—and your hummingbirds'.

Hummingbird gardening could fill a book—and it has. I'm partial to my own labor of love, *Attracting Butterflies and Hummingbirds to Your Backyard.* But I already want to add more to it!

Feeder Foods for Hummingbirds

Fill a nectar feeder with a solution of four parts water to one part sugar. Boil or microwave the water so that the sugar dissolves quickly. Make sure that the nectar has cooled before you fill your feeder.

Water Wishes of Hummingbirds

Spending about $20 for a mister will bring you a three-ring circus of hummingbirds. They can't resist the fine spray. Add a timer so you can set the routine: Showers at 4:00 P.M. or whenever suits you best. Hummingbirds will soon learn when to arrive, rubber ducky in hand.

Hummers were the first on the scene when I set up a small solar fountain (about $50) in my pedestal birdbath. They love it, and they frequently zip in and out of the spray, bathing on the fly. The fountain sprays only on sunny days, and that has the birds puzzled.

Then add tubular flowers, those with a flaring rim above a long tube that attaches to the stem: penstemons (*Penstemon* spp. and cultivars), red-hot poker (*Kniphofia uvaria* and cultivars), salvias (*Salvia* spp. and cultivars), bee balms (*Monarda* spp. and cultivars), lobelias (*Lobelia* spp. and cultivars).

Mint family plants (you can recognize them by their square stems) have tubular flowers as well. It doesn't matter if the blossoms are tiny; hummingbirds find them. They nectar at basil, lavender, spearmint, peppermint, catmint, and many others.

You'll find enough recommendations in the

(continued on page 322)

Flowers for Hummingbirds

Orange to red flowers are guaranteed to grab the attention of hummingbirds, because they stand out like a beacon, advertising their nectar. But lots of other blossoms also hold a bounty of sweet stuff. Choose flowers that suit a hummingbird beak: The nectar at the base of a tubular or trumpet-shaped blossom is easily accessible to hummingbirds.

Here's a sampling of hummingbird-favored plants that grow well in various regions of the country, and a quick guide to the hummingbird species you're likely to see in those places.

The more you watch these busy little birds in your garden, the more kinds of flowers you'll add to your list of hummingbird favorites. Basil, a hummingbird flower? Definitely, if you let a few stems produce blossoms instead of harvesting the plant for pesto.

NORTHEAST

Hummingbirds: ruby-throated

Annuals
Spider flower (*Cleome hasslerana*)
Coleus (*Coleus* cultivars)
Foxgloves (*Digitalis* spp. and cultivars)
Garden balsam (*Impatiens balsamina*)
Impatiens (*Impatiens walleriana,* especially red and orange cultivars)
Nicotianas (*Nicotiana* cvs.)
Scarlet sage (*Salvia splendens*)
Nasturtium (*Tropaeolum majus;* red and orange cultivars are best)
Zinnia (*Zinnia elegans,* tall cultivars, especially red or orange)

Vines
Cypress vine (*Ipomoea quamoclit*)
Scarlet runner bean (*Phaseolus coccinea*)

Perennials
Columbines (*Aquilegia* spp. and cultivars, including *A.canadensis*)
Milkweeds, including butterflyweed (*Asclepias* spp.)
Delphinium (*Delphinium* cultivars)
Coral bells (*Heuchera* cultivars)
Red-hot pokers (*Kniphofia* spp. and cultivars)
Cardinal flower (*Lobelia cardinalis*)
Maltese cross (*Lychnis chalcedonica*)

Bee balms (*Monarda* spp. and cultivars)
Salvias (*Salvia,* any spp. or cv.)

Shrubs
Butterfly bush (*Buddleia davidii*)
Flowering quinces (*Chaenomeles* cultivars)
Azaleas (*Rhododendron* spp.)
Lilacs (*Syringa* spp. and cultivars)
Weigela (*Weigela florida*)

Small Trees
Red buckeye (*Aesculus pavia*)
Silk tree or mimosa (*Albizia julibrissin*)

MIDWEST

Hummingbirds: ruby-throated, possibly rufous

Annuals
Hollyhocks (*Alcea* spp.)
Spider flower (*Cleome hasslerana*)
Coleus (*Coleus* cultivars)
Sweet William (*Dianthus barbatus*)
Sunflower (*Helianthus annuus*)
Flowering tobaccos (*Nicotiana* spp. and cultivars)
Basil (*Ocimum basilicum*)
Scarlet sage (*Salvia splendens*)
Tithonia or Mexican sunflower (*Tithonia rotundifolia*)
Zinnia (*Zinnia elegans,* tall cultivars, especially red or orange)

Vines
Cross vine (*Bignonia capreolata*)
Trumpet vine (*Campsis radicans*)
Scarlet honeysuckle (*Lonicera sempervirens*)

Perennials
Columbines (*Aquilegia* spp. and cultivars)
Milkweeds, including butterflyweed (*Asclepias* spp.)
Coral bells (*Heuchera* cultivars)
Red-hot pokers (*Kniphofia* spp. and cultivars)
Maltese cross (*Lychnis chalcedonica*)
Bee balms (*Monarda* spp. and cultivars)
Salvias (*Salvia*, any spp. or cv.)
Fire pink (*Silene virginica*)

Shrubs
Butterfly bush (*Buddleia davidii*)
Flowering quince (*Chaenomeles* cultivars)
Azaleas (*Rhododendron* spp.)

Small Trees
Red buckeye (*Aesculus pavia*)
Rose of Sharon (*Hibiscus syriacus*)

SOUTHEAST
Hummingbirds: ruby-throated, possibly rufous

Annuals
Coleus (*Coleus* cultivars)
Sweet William (*Dianthus barbatus*)
Foxglove (*Digitalis purpurea*)
Flowering tobacco (*Nicotiana alata*)
Plectranthus (*Plectranthus* cultivars)
Texas sage (*Salvia coccinea*)
Scarlet sage (*Salvia splendens*)

Vines
Cross vine (*Bignonia capreolata*)
Trumpet vine (*Campsis radicans*)
Red morning glory (*Ipomoea coccinea*)
Cypress vine (*Ipomoea quamoclit*)
Trumpet honeysuckle (*Lonicera sempervirens*)

Perennials
Turtlehead (*Chelone gabra*)
Standing cypress (*Ipomopsis rubra*) (biennial)
Red-hot poker (*Kniphofia* spp. and cultivars)
Lantanas (*Lantana* spp. and cultivars)
Bee balms (*Monarda* spp. and cultivars)
Salvias (*Salvia*, any spp. or cv.)
Fire pink (*Silene virginica*)
Indian pink (*Spigelia marilandica*)

Shrubs
Flowering quince (*Chaenomeles* cultivars)
Hibiscus (*Hibiscus* spp. and cvs.)
Azalea (*Rhododendron* spp.)

Small Trees
Red buckeye (*Aesculus pavia*)
Silk tree or mimosa (*Albizia julibrissin*)
Rose of Sharon (*Hibiscus syriacus*)

GULF COAST, FLORIDA, AND SOUTHERN TEXAS
Hummingbirds: black-chinned, buff-bellied, ruby-throated, rufous

Annuals
Garden balsam (*Impatiens balsamina*)
Impatiens (Impatiens cultivars, especially red or orange)
Annual phlox (*Phlox drummondii*)
Scarlet sage (*Salvia splendens*)

Vines
Trumpet vine (*Campsis radicans*)
Blood-red trumpet vine (*Distictis buccinata*)
Carolina jasmine (*Gelsemium sempervirens*)
Red morning glory (*Ipomoea coccinea*)
Scarlet honeysuckle (*Lonicera sempervirens*)

(continued)

Perennials

Milkweeds (*Asclepias* spp.), including blood milkweed (*Asclepias curvassica*)

Cannas (*Canna* cultivars)

Coleus (*Coleus* cultivars)

Mexican cigar plant (*Cuphea micropetala*)

Hibiscus (*Hibiscus* spp. and cultivars, especially scarlet hibiscus, *H. coccineus*)

Standing cypress (*Ipomopsis rubra*) (biennial)

Shrimp plant (*Justica brandegeana*)

Lantanas (*Lantana* spp. and cultivars)

Plectranthus (*Plectranthus* cultivars)

Firecracker bush (*Russelia equisetiformis*)

Salvias (*Salvia*, any spp. or cv.)

Texas sage (*Salvia coccinea*)

Bromeliads (*Tillandsia* spp. and cultivars, *Guzmania* spp. and cultivars)

Shrubs

Flame flower (*Anisacanthus wrightii*)

Bottlebrush (*Callistemon* spp. and cultivars)

Coral bean (*Erythrina herbacea*)

Scarlet bush (*Hamela patens*)

Turk's cap (*Malvaviscus drummondii*)

Small Trees

Citrus (*Citrus* cvs)

Coral trees (*Erythrina* spp. and cultivars)

WESTERN MOUNTAIN STATES

Hummingbirds: black-chinned, broad-tailed, calliope, rufous

Annuals

Tiny trumpet (*Collomia linearis*)

Scarlet sage (*Salvia splendens*)

Nasturtium (*Tropaeolum majus*)

Vines

Red morning glory (*Ipomoea coccinea*)

Orange honeysuckle (*Lonicera ciliosa*)

Scarlet honeysuckle (*Lonicera sempervirens*)

Perennials

Columbines (*Aquilegia* spp. and cultivars)

Scarlet gilia (*Ipomopsis aggregate*)

Maltese cross (*Lychnis chalcedonica*)

Scarlet monkeyflower (*Mimulus cardinalis*)

Penstemons (*Penstemon* spp. and cultivars)

Salvias (*Salvia*, any spp. or cv.)

Shrubs

Twinberry (*Lonicera involucrate*)

Red-flowering currant (*Ribes sanguineum*)

Blueberries, huckleberries (*Vaccinium* spp.)

SOUTHWEST

Hummingbirds: Allen's, Anna's, black-chinned, blue-throated, broad-billed, broad-tailed, calliope, Costa's, magnificent, rufous

Annuals

Flowering tobacco (*Nicotiana alata*)

Texas sage (*Salvia coccinea*)

Scarlet sage (*Salvia splendens*)

Vines

Snapdragon vine (*Asarina antirrhiniflora*)

Glory flower (*Eccremocarpus scaber*)

Red morning glory (*Ipomoea coccinea*)

Perennials

Bouvardia (*Bowardia temifolia*)

Penstemons (*Penstemon barbatus, P. centranthifolius, P. eatonii, P. pinifolius*, and other spp. and cultivars)

Salvias (*Salvia greggii, S. lemmonii*, and other spp. and cultivars)

Mexican pink (*Silene laciniata*)

Scarlet hedge nettle, scarlet betony (*Stachys coccinea*)

Shrubs
Desert honeysuckle (*Anisacanthus thurberi*)
Bush monkeyflowers (*Diplacus* spp.)
Pineapple guava (*Feijoa sellowiana*)
Ocotillo (*Fouquieria splendens*)
Texas ranger (*Leucophyllum candidum*)
Yellow trumpetflower (*Tecoma stans*)

Small Trees
Acacias (*Acacia* spp. and cultivars)
Bird-of-paradise shrubs (*Caesalpinia pulcher-rima* and other spp.)
Desert willow (*Chilopsis linearis*)
Coral trees (*Erythrina coralloides* and other spp. and cultivars)

CENTRAL AND SOUTHERN CALIFORNIA

Hummingbirds: Allen's, Anna's, black-chinned, calliope, Costa's, rufous

Annuals
Texas sage (*Salvia coccinea*)
Scarlet sage (*Salvia splendens*)

Vines
Blood-red trumpet vine (*Distictis buccinata*)
Flame vine (*Pyrostegia venusta*)

Perennials
Aloe vera (*Aloe perryi*)
Fuchsia (*Fuchsia* cultivars)
Scarlet monkeyflower (*Mimulus cardinalis*)
Penstemons (*Penstemon* spp. and cultivars)
Rosemarys (*Rosmarinus* spp. and cultivars)
Salvias (*Salvia* spp. and cultivars)

Shrubs
Crimson bottlebrush (*Callistemon citrinus*)
Lemon bottlebrush (*C. citrinus*)
Lantana (*Lantana* spp. and cultivars)

Bird-of-paradises (*Strelitzia* spp. and cultivars)
Cape honeysuckle (*Tecomaria capensis*)

Small Trees
Acacias (*Acacia* spp. and cultivars)
Coral tree (*Erythrina coralloides* and other spp. and cultivars)
Eucalyptus (*Eucalyptus* cultivars)

PACIFIC NORTHWEST

Hummingbirds: Anna's, black-chinned, calliope, rufous

Annuals
Nasturtium (*Tropaeolum majus*)
Zinnias (*Zinnia* spp. and cultivars, especially red and orange)

Vines
Orange honeysuckle (*Lonicera ciliosa*)
Scarlet runner bean (*Phaseolus coccinea*)

Perennials
Columbine (*Aquilegia formosa* and other *A.* spp. and cultivars)
Bearberry (*Arctostaphylos uva-ursi*)
Western bleeding heart (*Dicentra formosa*)
Foxgloves (*Digitalis* spp. and cultivars)
Red-hot poker (*Kniphofia uvaria*)
Lavender (*Lavandula* cultivars)
Columbia lily (*Lilium columbianum*)
Catmints (*Nepeta* spp. and cultivars)
Penstemons (*Penstemon* spp. and cultivars)
Cape fuchsias (*Phygelius* spp. and cultivars)
Salvias (*Salvia* spp. and cultivars)

Shrubs
Shrub fuchsia (*Fuchsia magellanica*)
Twinberry (*Lonicera involucrata*)
Red-flowering currant (*Ribes sanguineum*)

When an Anna's hummingbird arrived the other day and found no spray, it settled for bathing—in the basin! This was a new one for me, and maybe for the bird, too.

With wings ablur, he hovered close enough to dip his belly in the water, then threw his head up and back to toss water onto his back. The performance lasted 5 solid minutes, all in "hover" gear.

Nesting Needs of Hummingbirds

This family will choose its own homesite, and you'll probably never know where it is. The nest is so tiny—picture a Ping-Pong ball sliced in half—and so perfectly camouflaged as a bump on a branch that it escapes our eyes, even when the nestlings have hatched.

Some bird supply stores and catalogs sell crescent-shaped metal hooks designed to appeal to nesting hummingbirds. They're pretty and inexpensive, and if they tempt a nest builder, that's terrific.

Little Extras for Hummingbirds

Ever try to brush a spiderweb out of your hair? Those strands are as sticky as glue. And stronger than steel, so scientists tell us. Lightweight, ultrastrong, and sticky—that adds up to a super building material, if you have the patience to collect enough of it.

I haven't figured out how to put it to use yet, but hummingbirds sure have. They use the stuff to make their nests. The microscopic "branches"

Hummingbirds can splash water over their bodies by hovering at the edge or just above the water in a birdbath. But a fountain or mister makes it easier.

The longer you watch a hummer, the more colors you'll see. A male Anna's can look pink, purple, or even golden, depending on how light strikes its throat.

of the lichens they use in the building process catch firmly in the silk, creating a super-light-weight but super-strong support.

Make a circle with your thumb and forefinger, and you'll have a rough idea of the size of a hummingbird home. Itty-bitty indeed.

Still, it still takes yards and yards of spider silk to build that little cup. So, at nesting time in summer, female hummers work dawn to dusk gathering silk. They collect webs as well as the big prize: the patch of dense silk, almost cocoonlike, that some spiders use to cover their eggs.

It's easy to find small spiderwebs once you start looking. They're all over the place, on the deck rail, in your rhodies, even on your car's side-view mirrors. Your hummers may pluck that strong silk from any location.

Chapter 23

The Gallinaceous Birds Family

EASE OF ATTRACTING: ★★★★ (very easy)
FAMILY NAMES: Odontophoridae; Phasianidae
BIRDS IN FAMILY: Quails · Northern Bobwhites · Grouse
Wild Turkeys · Ring-Necked Pheasants

Meet the Gallinaceous Birds Family

"Gallinaceous birds" is a mouthful, but it's easier than saying "Birds that resemble domestic fowl," which is what it means.

Just like those domestic fowl, these birds are good for eating, so they're sometimes called upland game birds, too.

Whatever the moniker, the species in this group are familiar friends. The group includes members of two families. Our enchanting quail and bobwhite are grouped in the family Odontophoridae, while the larger grouse, the even larger pheasant, and the gigantic wild turkey are perched in Phasianidae. (The families of Gallinaceous Birds are another group that keeps getting shuffled by taxonomists.)

This chapter focuses on birds that come to backyards, so you won't find prairie chickens or ptarmigans. Those species need wide-open, wild spaces. All gallinaceous birds have big ranges, but quail and others of the family are more likely to adopt a tempting backyard as part of their daily rounds. If a ptarmigan does show up in your tundra-themed backyard, it's definitely a day to remember.

Look and Listen

These birds are fowl-like, for sure. They have luscious, plump bodies (is it just me, or are you in the mood for a turkey sandwich, too?), strong legs, and long toes, and they live mostly on the ground. Just like chickens, they often perch in trees to roost for the night.

Clucking, gobbling, and crowing are the usual voices of gallinaceous birds. On spring mornings, when he's looking for love or looking for a fight, a ring-necked pheasant can slice right through all those warbling songbirds when he lets loose with his war cry.

Quail can also let loose with a raucous outburst, and they can cluck with the best of 'em. But they also make low, moaning calls, often from hidden spots in grass or brush, that make you wonder who in the world is sounding so sad. The closely related northern bobwhite is famed for whistling its own name.

Range of Gallinaceous Birds

The wild turkey is the most widespread of the gallinaceous birds, although he's had his ups and downs. In recent years, this giant bird has been staging a comeback, and the flocks are spreading. Except for a few areas of the West, turkeys call every state home.

The bobwhite scurries across the eastern three-fifths of the country, except for the northern states. Quail are western birds, with various species covering most areas from Texas to the Pacific.

Hunting interests imported the ring-necked

Where you see one California quail, you'll soon see more! Plant a strip of milo at the back of a flower bed to keep them busy all fall and winter.

The wild turkey made a strong comeback after it was reintroduced in areas from which it had vanished.

pheasant, a Eurasian bird, to America. It may show up just about anywhere, but the most solid populations are in the Midwest, the Plains, and parts of the East and West. Speaking of imports, various other exotic species, such as the chukhar, the gray partridge, and the Japanese green pheasant, have found footholds thanks to hunting enthusiasts.

Grouse are the "chickens" of the North Woods and mountains. They live in forests within their range.

Now You See 'em . . .

Look for these birds year-round. They live summer and winter within the same range. Short jaunts within the range often occur as the birds

Spruce grouse were called "fool hens" by early hunters because they're so unusually tame.

Anyone See Wile E. Coyote?

That cartoon roadrunner comes from a very real clan that lives in the lower West. Many folks think of roadrunners as birds of the desert, probably thanks to that Saturday morning TV brainwashing. But, with a range that extends almost as far as the Mississippi River and north to Oklahoma, they're actually able to scratch out a living in grassland just as well as in desert.

Roadrunners look like skinny, long-tailed chickens. But they're not part of the Gallinaceous Birds family. Instead, taxonomists group them with the cuckoos in a family called Cuculidae. Cuckoos are secretive birds of the forest treetops, and the only noticeable trait they share with roadrunners are their low-pitched *cooo-cooo-cooo* calls.

Roadrunners often visit backyards within their range. Their natural diet is heavy on lizards and snakes, bolstered by grasshoppers and other insects, prickly pear fruits (*Oputia* spp.), and seeds. They're great to watch in action, when they live up to their name and hot-foot it down the road.

The oddball roadrunner is an icon of the Southwest.

relocate for a seasonal vacation in a more hospitable place.

Family Habits of Gallinaceous Birds

Think of chickens, and you'll have the behavior of many of these birds pegged. Most species hang out in flocks, they cluck, and they peck-peck-peck when feeding, often doing some vigorous scratching to stir up more food.

For quail, turkeys, and pheasants, the rule is one male to a whole batch of females. Pheasant males are notorious for vicious battles in the spring, which may end with one combatant seriously injured—those clawed feet are nothing to mess with. Turkeys get tough, too, when their harem is at stake.

Grouse are generally solitary birds, instead of gathering in flocks. But like the others in this family, they engage in dramatic shows during courtship. They dance and "drum" with their wings or make booming noises with inflatable throat pouches.

Most Gallinaceous birds spend the vast majority of time on the ground and only roost in trees, but grouse have a special fondness for trees, one of their biggest sources of food. You may see them on the ground or in the branches, nibbling at buds or settling to roost.

Gallinaceous birds don't exactly look like athletes, but don't be fooled. They can go from zero to 60 in a heartbeat. These birds may not be long-distance aerialists, but they're speed demons in the short stretch.

The crowing of male pheasants is a sign of spring. Listen for a very loud, harsh, two-syllable noise, more of a hacking cough than a cock-a-doodle-do.

Most of my encounters with grouse and turkeys have been of the heart-stopping variety: I'll be meandering along, minding my own business, when a bird suddenly rockets up from under my feet. Whew! It always takes a minute for my heart to stop pounding. Quail are fond of causing the same sort of reaction, which I suppose comes in handy when you're a popular food item for predators, including the two-legged kind. By the time your pursuer has gathered her wits, you're long gone.

At-Home Habitat of Gallinaceous Birds

Adaptation is the name of the game with gallinaceous birds. They live in grasslands, in deserts, and in dark conifer forests.

The Wild Side

Grouse are mainly forest birds. In winter, they usually stick to conifer forests of spruce (*Picea*

You'd think a covey of bobwhites would be easy to notice in your backyard, but these birds often go undetected as they travel through cover.

spp.) and fir (*Abies* spp.); in summer, they may relocate to deciduous woods. The sage grouse, found in sagebrush country, is pickier in its habits. It depends heavily on sage (*Artemesia tridendata* and other native *Artemesia* spp.) for food and cover and doesn't usually visit backyards.

Turkeys roam the woods, but they also scout out grassy areas nearby. Quail and pheasants prefer open areas dotted with occasional shrubs and small trees. It always startles me to see a pheasant head suddenly pop up out of a meadow, like a periscope. And I can't tell you how often I've scanned shrubby areas in the drylands to make sure I'm not missing anything, then started to turn away just as a squadron of quail scurry out of the brush.

Backyard Matchup

These birds depend more on their legs than on their wings, so you'll want to be sure to plant a corridor of cover that they can follow to get from place to place.

You can use shrubs of any kind to make a hedge.

But it's more fun to create a "hedge" of grasses and flowers, with a shrub or three thrown in along the way. Start with tall, tough native grasses, such as switchgrass (*Panicum virgatum*), Indian grass (*Sorghastrum nutans*), or big bluestem (*Andropogon gerardii*). Then add some equally tough flowers. The rugged perennial wildflowers of the prairie, including compassplants and cup plants (*Silphium* spp.), coneflowers (*Echinacea* spp.), perennial sunflowers (*Helianthus maximilianii* and other spp.), are excellent for this purpose.

Since any shrub will serve as cover, I like to contrast the airy grasses with the dark red foliage of smokebush (*Cotinus coggygria* 'Royal Purple'), a tall shrub I happen to adore myself. You can choose your own favorites.

If you live within grouse country, your yard probably already includes some of the trees that attract them. Spruces (*Picea* spp.), firs (*Abies* spp.), and hemlocks (*Tsuga* spp.), plus poplars (*Populus* spp.), alders (*Alnus* spp.), birches (*Betula* spp.), willows (*Salix* spp.), and apples (*Malus* spp.), will get their attention. But don't stop there. As you'll see in the food section of this chapter, grouse also graze on tons of flowers and shrubs.

Great cover, good food: the blue spruce (*Picea pungens*).

Bah, Says Ben

When the infant United States was selecting a symbol, Ben Franklin championed the rattlesnake. But he's gone down in history as a fan of the wild turkey because of a letter he wrote to his daughter in 1784, after the eagle was voted in.

More than a bit peeved that his rattlesnake had lost, Franklin complained that not only was the eagle of poor moral character, but the drawing they'd chosen looked more like a turkey:

> *For my own part, I wish the Bald Eagle had not been chosen the Representative of our Country. He is a Bird of bad moral Character. He does not get his Living honestly. You may have seen him perched on some dead Tree near the River, where, too lazy to fish for himself, he watches the Labour of the Fishing Hawk; and when that diligent Bird has at length taken a Fish, and is bearing it to his Nest for the Support of his Mate and young Ones, the Bald Eagle pursues him and takes it from him. . . .*

> *I am on this account not displeased that the Figure [drawing] is not known as a Bald Eagle, but looks more like a Turkey. For in Truth the Turkey is in Comparison a much more respectable Bird, and withal a true original Native of America . . . He is besides, though a little vain & silly, a Bird of Courage, and would not hesitate to attack a Grenadier of the British Guards who should presume to invade his Farm Yard with a red Coat on.*

(continued on page 334)

Harvest Home

Grow fast cover and feed a flock of gallinaceous birds with these great grains.

Trees flaming with color. Frost on cool mornings. Time to gather the pumpkins for the final harvest, and start thinking about that Thanksgiving turkey. No, not the bird on the table—the one in your yard. This planting reaches its prime for gallinaceous birds in fall, drawing them in from nearby wild lands to enjoy their own share of the harvest. It's feast time, with this garden of great seeds. You can expect other dinner guests, too: cardinals, nuthatches, chickadees, woodpeckers, native sparrows, juncos, doves, jays, and many other seed eaters will join the crowd at this well-stocked table.

This garden is a long one, about 15 feet long and 5 feet wide. It functions as a corridor so that foraging birds can safely move through its protective cover. You can expand it even farther, if you like, to make a hedge along part of your yard. And not only is this garden chock-full of seeds, but it's a beauty, too, rich in autumnal colors from the time the sunflowers and amaranth begin to bloom in summer.

Plant List

1. Indian corn (annual; *Zea mays*, various cvs.) (4 packets; scatter the seeds for a more casual look, rather than planting in rows)

2. Brown-seeded sunflower (annual; *Helianthus annuus* 'Apache Brown Striped') (4 packets)

3. Red-leaved amaranth, such as 'Hopi Red Dye' (annual; *Amaranthus cruentus* × *A. powelli* 'Hopi Red Dye') (2 packets)

4. Buckwheat (annual; *Fagopyrum esculentum*) (¼ pound)

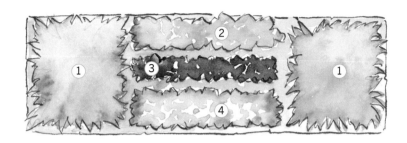

Garden Size
15' × 5'

Scale of Plan
¼" = 1'

This planting is pretty enough for a hedge, but packed with practicality for quail and other gallinaceous birds. The sunflowers and corn will stretch to 6 feet high or better, creating privacy for you—and a beckoning strip of cover for ground-hugging birds. Plus, it's packed with seeds that will keep gallinaceous birds as well as all kinds of native sparrows, juncos, and doves making return trips right through winter.

Surefire Plants to Attract Gallinaceous Birds

This planting is pretty enough for a hedge, but packed with practicality for quail and other gallinaceous birds. The sunflowers and corn will stretch to 6 feet high or better, creating privacy for you—and a beckoning strip of cover for ground-hugging birds. Plus, it's packed with seeds that will keep gallinaceous birds as well as all kinds of native sparrows, juncos, and doves making return trips right through winter.

Plant	Type of Plant	Description	Zones
Buckwheat (*Fagopyrum* spp.)	To about 3 ft, but sprawling	Heart-shaped leaves and a cloud of small creamy blossoms yield to hard seeds.	Annual
Mesquites (*Prosopis* spp. and cultivars)	Small trees and shrubs that vary widely in habit, depending on species	One characteristic shared by all mesquites: They're thorny! Airy foliage, fragrant pea-shaped flowers, followed by pealike pods	10–11
Millet (proso millet, *Panicummiliaceum* spp. *miliaceum*; foxtail millet, *Setaria italica*)	To about 3 ft	Grassy millet has jam-packed heads of tiny seeds; very attractive in a casual garden or with wildflowers.	Annual
Milo (*Sorghum bicolor*)	To about 5 ft	Milo looks a lot like a scrubby corn plant, but it's topped with a spray of flowering stems that turn to small seeds.	Annual
Spruces, any North American species (*Picea* spp.)	Large evergreen conifers, about 70–100 ft	Classic conical "Christmas tree," with aromatic foliage and short, stiff needles. Bears abundant cones with age	2–9
White oaks (*Quercus alba*, *Q. bicolor*, and other spp.)	Large deciduous trees, to about 100 ft	White oaks hang onto their dead leaves into winter, unlike red oaks, which shed them in fall.	5–9

Used for	Comments	Other Birds Attracted
Seeds	Buckwheat makes a good-looking edging along a flower bed; the blossoms attract butterflies.	Vireos, flycatchers, large finches, and jays may visit to catch butterflies.
Seeds	Plant far from passersby or children's play areas.	Large finches and small finches may eat seeds. Orioles, tanagers, hummingbirds, and others are drawn to the flowers and the insects they attract.
Seeds	Let the plants stand all winter; provides cover to foraging birds.	Small finches adore millet.
Seeds	Provides cover for travel corridors. Nice accent at the back of a flower bed.	Small finches, large finches, doves, and other seed eaters may visit all winter to glean dropped seeds.
Buds, roosting	Spruces are a favorite for plant breeders, and many contorted, dwarf, or unusually colored cultivars exist. Stick to natives of your region for best appeal to birds.	Roosting and cover for many birds. The fad for blue spruces as front yard trees, which began back in the 1950s, directly contributed to the spread of house finches across the country; the trees are favored nest sites for these birds.
Acorns	White oak acorns are sweet enough for you to nibble, though "sweet" is a relative term here: They still are astringent, but not as unbearably so as red oak acorns. Nut crops may be irregular, with a prolific year followed by one or more moderate or lean years.	Woodpeckers, jays, chickadees, titmice, doves, juncos, and many other birds eagerly eat acorns. Tanagers, orioles, vireos, warblers, and flycatchers eat insects from foliage or at flowers. Tanagers or jays may use as nest site.

Natural Foods
for Gallinaceous Birds

Turn a flock of chickens loose in your yard, and what will they eat? Just about anything. Seeds, leaves, leaf buds, flower buds, flowers, insects— it's all fair game.

Toss in some tender twigs, and that's pretty much the menu for gallinaceous birds, too.

Main Menu: Seeds, Vegetation, Fruits, and Berries

These fowl eat a huge variety of food in the wild. Much of it is vegetation: Tree buds, tender leaves, conifer tips, young twigs, spruce flowers, sagebrush, fern fronds and fiddleheads, and hundreds of other items go down the hatch.

Magnified way bigger than life-size here, the tiny flowers of chickweed start blooming in winter. Their seeds are a hit with many birds, including quail.

Seeds are another top draw, from tiny grass seeds and weed seeds to acorns, mesquite pods, and other tree seeds.

Many species gladly eat fruits and berries of all kinds when they come across them, such as cranberries (*Viburnum* spp.), persimmons (*Diospyros americana*), blueberries and huckleberries (*Vaccinium* spp.), snowberries (*Symphoricarpus albus*), and wild rose hips (*Rosa* spp.).

In the Southwest, cactus fruits draw a crowd. Quail peck at the juicy fruit of chollas (*Opuntia* spp.) and prickly pears (*Opuntia* spp.), and they even manage to get to the red fruits that crown barrel cactuses (*Ferocactus* spp.).

Insects aren't an important part of the diet for most of these species. But chicks eat various kinds, and adult birds may snack on grasshoppers, crickets, ants, and beetles.

Backyard Fare

You'll have the best chance of attracting these birds if you tempt them with treats they can't find in the wild. Game managers grow plantations of these foods to bolster the birds' population, and their trick also works on a small scale.

Set your sight on seeds. Legumes, including garden peas and beans as well as lupines and other ornamentals, are highly popular. Grains are good, too, and they look pretty in a garden. Try sowing wheat among your flowers, or sprinkle a handful of millet in an open niche. Amaranths (*Amaranthus* spp.) and cockscombs (*Celosia* spp.) supply a myriad of small seeds that are super for these birds.

Buckwheats (*Fagopyrum* spp. and cultivars)

are another proven winner. The fast-growing plants form excellent cover, as well as serving up supper. Remember that corridor planting you're considering? Edge it with buckwheat, and it'll be even more tempting—plus the birds will be in better view.

And, finally, we have birds that appreciate milo! Milo seeds are those dull reddish seeds

The Demise of Mast

Long before Europeans came to America, wild turkeys were roasting on the spit. These birds were once so abundant, numbering in the millions, that I can imagine long-ago Native Americans taking a break from chipping flint to say, "Not turkey *again*."

The main reason the birds were so plentiful? An unbelievable bounty of acorns, nuts, and other tree seeds that covered forest floors in a layer that might reach ankle deep.

Imagine, for a minute, what the country looked like before white settlers arrived.

An unbelievably vast forest stretched from the Mississippi to the Atlantic coast. It was such a huge woods that "forest buffalo" roamed among the trees, just as their cousins once did in western grasslands.

You can still visit the salt licks in Indiana, Kentucky, and other states where the buffalo roamed, and you can almost imagine that you can still see their well-worn trails, which were known as "traces," and which Native Americans used as roadways. Their name lingers on, too: The Cub Scout troop to which my son belonged was part of the Buffalo Trace Council.

Acorns lie thickly beneath oaks in a good mast year.

This was the great eastern hardwood forest, an immense expanse of oaks, maples, beeches, chestnuts, ash, and other deciduous trees.

It's inconceivable now.

And the rate at which it disappeared is even more mind-boggling.

By the 1850s, much of the forest was gone. Cleared for homesites and farms, chopped down by the acre for timber, the vast forest disappeared, state by state.

As settlers cleared the forest, turkeys took a beating. By the early 1800s, turkeys were rare in Massachusetts. A few birds managed to hold out until 1851, when the last known native turkey in the state was shot on the appropriately named Mount Tom. (The birds that now thrive in Massachusetts and across the country were nearly all re-introduced, descendants of the last survivors.)

With the demise of the forests went the "mast"—the layer of acorns, beech seeds, hickory nuts, American chestnuts, American elm seeds, and other tree seeds that were prime food for gallinaceous birds. Millions of now-extinct passenger pigeons also lived in the forest and feasted on the mast.

Oaks and nut trees usually don't bear a bumper crop every year. But when it's an exceptional mast year, wild turkeys, as well as many songbirds and other wildlife, are in hog heaven. If you happen to notice a thick layer of acorns beneath an oak in your yard, keep your eyes open for turkeys and their kin.

you'll find all too often in bags of birdseed mix—the ones that get kicked to the ground or pile up in the corners of the feeder. Feeder birds don't bother with them, because there are so many better seeds to sample. But gallinaceous birds are big fans of milo, and it's an easy plant to grow. Just sow a handful of those scorned feeder seeds.

For the fruity tastes of fowl, rely on shrub roses to supply rose hips. I like to explore native species, which usually aren't as showy but definitely are healthier than finicky tea roses I keep killing. You'll find plenty of native species to pick from. A few of my favorites are Wood's rose (*Rosa woodsii*), Nootka rose (*R. nutkana*), Carolina or pasture rose (*R. Carolina*), and Virginia rose (*R. virginiana*). Birds of all sorts will welcome them.

Rugosa roses (*Rosa rugosa*) are easy to grow, too, and they supply abundant hips. If you have a greener thumb than I do when it comes to roses, you can plant any shrub rose that has small to medium-size (why am I blushing?) hips.

Feeder Foods for Gallinaceous Birds

Set up a low tray feeder full of millet, cracked corn, milo, and other grains for these ground-level birds.

Water Wishes of Gallinaceous Birds

When that wild turkey of yours tries to perch on your pedestal birdbath, the whole thing's going

Seed for buckwheat is sold as a cover crop to turn under, but you'll want to let the seeds mature.

Rose hips make good winter bird food. Try roses native to your area, which birds already know and like.

to come down with a crash. Daintier quail, though, will be regulars at the bath, with no ill effects for your statuary.

A safer approach is to set out low basins of water. These birds are sippers, not splashers. They'll perch on the rim or stand on the ground and fill their beaks, then tilt their heads skyward to let the water run down their throats.

Nesting Needs of Gallinaceous Birds

Quail or bobwhite may tuck a nest into one of your garden beds, but most of these birds don't nest in backyards—unless yours happens to be 10 acres. For most of us, these birds are visitors rather than nesters. If your yard offers tempting food, they'll soon be bringing their babies.

Offer a reliable source of water, and quail in your area will appear like magic. These are mountain quail.

PART 3

Birds across America

WHEN WILL RUBY-THROATED HUMMINGBIRDS SHOW UP IN NEW HARMONY, INDIANA? April 15, give or take a day.

When will ruby-throated hummingbirds show up in southwestern Washington state? Uh, I'm not holding my breath. We don't have ruby-throats here. But we do have rufous hummingbirds, which arrive on March 17 in my backyard. Or March 16 or 18—but hey, it's close enough.

Developed over eons of time, bird travel patterns are so predictable that, today, we know exactly which birds will show up in which part of the country—and when. Almost to the day.

In this section, you'll learn why some birds are around all year and why others come and go with the seasons. You'll find out when you can expect to see the highest numbers of birds. And you'll uncover tips for planting your yard so that it's full of temptations when populations are at their peak.

You'll also discover how the natural features of a particular region are connected to the birds that live there, and which birds you can expect to see in each region. And you'll learn how to take advantage of the climate and habitat in your own backyard.

You'll find plenty to ponder in this section, since bird migration and ranges are subjects that have barely been scratched, scientifically speaking. Although we have come a long way from the days when folks thought swallows spent the winter under the mud in swamps, we still have a lot to learn. In some cases, bird patterns are a mystery: Why are Anna's hummingbirds in my yard all year, but rufous hummers say goodbye in fall? I'm still trying to figure it out.

Chapter 24

Seasonal Specialties

I was helping my mother in the garden one long-ago summer—so long ago that hummingbird nectar feeders hadn't been invented yet—when I noticed that the usual background hum and buzz around the flower beds was missing.

"Uh-oh," I said, "the hummingbirds have disappeared!"

I'd never noticed the ebbs and flows of hummingbirds before, but my mom, who spent most of every day in the yard, sure had.

"They must be doing something else right now. Maybe working on a nest. Maybe sitting on eggs or babies," she told me.

"But why don't they come to eat?" I wanted to know.

"They do. But it might be only one mother bird, so she's easy to miss."

"No," I argued, "I think they're gone. We used to have so many. And look—there's not a one now."

"You'll see her later, before it gets dark. She always comes for supper. I think she must need one last meal to get through the night."

As usual, my mom was right. When I headed for the big patch of bee balm (*Monarda didyma*) after finishing my own supper, I heard that familiar hum long before I saw the bird zipping around the flowers.

The first steep drop in hummingbird numbers happens when the spring migrants disperse, each to its own nesting territory. And when nesting begins, you'll notice another decline in your hummingbirds, because now the females spend more time babysitting than they do hanging out in the garden.

Once the babies fledge, or leave the nest, the birds will be back in abundance. The parent bird now brings the young to your flower beds and feeders, and more than one family may spend the entire day in your garden.

Several weeks later, the tide will once again peak as incoming fall migrants swell the ranks. Just as in spring, the fall hummers will gather in a welcoming garden in growing numbers, eventually departing as they continue their migration journey.

◀ *In spring, ruby-throated hummingbirds seem to be everywhere; in early summer, they "disappear."*

As my mom found out by paying attention to what her birds were doing, the "disappearance" of hummingbirds in early summer has no sinister reason behind it.

It's simply a matter of the birds' natural habits.

By understanding how birds ebb and flow with the seasons, you can plan your garden to match those peaks.

Seasonal Habits

When will you see the most birds in your yard? That depends on the seasonal habits of each species.

At nesting time, as my mother taught me, all birds make themselves scarce, retreating to well-defined breeding territories. If your yard is within a breeding territory, even if the nest itself is elsewhere, you'll see the parents during nesting season.

The peak times of population also depend on the birds' seasonal movements. The tables you'll find throughout this section show how numbers swell and decline for just one species. Multiply the effect by the dozen or more species you may see in your yard, and it's easy to see why, in some seasons, your yard is simply brimming with birds.

As you learn the seasonal rhythms of birds, you'll discover how much fun it is to anticipate spring migration or to watch for families with fledglings to return to your yard.

Many birds are year-round friends, but lots of other species come and go with the seasons. For nearly all birds, the availability of food is the reason they stay put—or say goodbye.

You'll see more hummingbirds in spring and in fall than at other times of the year.

Scott's orioles often attach their nests below the crown of a yucca and use yucca fibers for the cradle.

But it's not quite as simple as supplying food to keep your hummingbirds, orioles, or other favorites around year-round. These patterns of migration or relocation have been established over thousands of years. While the habits of certain birds seem to be changing as a direct effect of bird-friendly yards and feeders, most birds still move on when their internal time clocks say it's time to go.

Hey—There's Nothing to Eat!

The diet of birds has a huge influence over whether they migrate or not. As you've seen, seeds, insects, and a side order of fruits and berries are the main foods of birds. Only a very few birds switch to different foods in winter; most simply leave if their natural food will soon become scarce.

Insect Eaters Say Sayonara

Flying insects are the first to go when the calendar turns toward fall, and so are the birds that eat a mostly insect menu. Insects are cold-blooded, so the temperature around them determines their activity levels. That's why, for most of us, mosquitoes are a summertime plague, and the height of butterfly beauty comes during those warm, lazy, iced-tea days.

By fall, many insects are nearing the end of their lives, or they have laid eggs or produced larvae that will wait until next year to hatch. And when nights start to get nippy, insects dwindle fast.

By then, most of the birds that eat mainly in-

Monarchs are generally safe from birds, thanks to toxins in their bodies. But other butterflies drawn to your flower garden are fair game.

sects are already gone. Swallows, which eat a diet of almost entirely insects, are the first to go. Orioles, tanagers, and other birds that depend heavily on insect food but also eat berries and fruits follow a little later.

In springtime, the process works in reverse. As warming temperatures spread northward, insects become active, and the birds that rely on them soon follow.

Nectar Noshers Follow the Flowers

Although orioles, kinglets, and other birds may have an occasional sip of nectar, it's the mainstay for hummingbirds, which rely on nectar to fuel their hyperactive habits. Since nectar is found only at flowers (and feeders, but that's another

Cold-Snap Care

Birds that rely heavily on insects quickly fall on hard times when an unexpected cold snap occurs in spring. And since spring can be pretty persnickety in many parts of the country, it makes sense to be ready when your friends need you.

Insect feeder foods, such as mealworms, and other foods that mimic insects, such as suet and peanut butter mixes, are an ideal handout when insects are scarce—and they can easily save a bird from starving. Since many insect-loving birds aren't accustomed to feeders, you'll want to make sure your treats are highly visible. If snow is on the ground, you can scatter them over an area that you've packed down or shoveled. Or you can put them in a tray-type feeder that has no roof. You may also want to add a low feeder of this kind, which is ideal for thrushes and other birds that usually forage near the ground for insects.

You'll also want to make sure that the food is accessible to these birds, which usually aren't as acrobatic as other feeder friends, and which often lack a heavy-duty beak. Crumble or finely chop the suet and other high-fat mixes, so that it's in bite-size pieces instead of in a solid block.

---

story), their migration patterns are timed to the blooming season.

Hummingbirds arrive when the first hummingbird flowers bloom. If you don't already have early blooming hummingbird flowers in your yard, you can add them to supply those welcome-back refreshments. Native flowers are perfectly timed to hummingbirds, but many nonnatives will also do the trick. Here are some early bloomers to try:

Red buckeye (*Aesculus pavia*)
Columbines (*Aquilegia* spp., especially native *A. canadensis*)
Bearberry, or kinnikinnick (*Arctostaphylos uva-ursi*)
Redbud (*Cercis canadensis*)
Flowering quince (*Chaenomeles* cultivars)
Azaleas (*Rhododendron* spp.)
Red-flowering currant (*Ribes sanguineum*)

Early-blooming flowering quince bursts into color just in time to welcome hummingbirds in spring.

Seed Eaters Stick Around

Seeds are most plentiful in fall and winter. So birds that eat mainly seeds have no need to leave in winter, as far as food is concerned. Their main food is readily available in fall and winter, even in areas where snow lies deep. These birds often bolster their seed-heavy diet with winter berries or fruit that still hang on the trees. They also extract insect food from bark crevices, plant stems, and other hiding places in fall and winter. So they're all set.

No lean times for seed eaters—as long as they can get to the food. A yard full of seed-bearing plants, from trees to the flower garden, will bring in hordes of native sparrows and other seed eaters in fall and winter. If snow or ice buries the natural supply, you can offer seeds at the feeder.

A Chilling Effect

Those who live in regions with ice-cold winters know that it doesn't take long to get acclimated to even extreme cold. After a few weeks of below-zero temperatures, you don't feel nearly as bone-chilled when you're out and about. And a high of 20°F can feel like a heat wave.

But if I were to spend a winter in Chicago or Maine now, when I'm not accustomed to it, I'm sure it would feel like the Arctic.

Birds work the same way. Some species are

Native sparrows consider a bunch of dead flower stems as a garden for them, full of seeds and cover.

well-adjusted to the winter extremes in their home range.

But, sadly, birds can and do freeze to death. Extreme cold can kill birds just as surely as a lack of food—and that's another good reason to pack up and leave an area for the winter.

Feeder Influence?

As hummingbird feeders sprout across the land, hummingbirds seem to be changing their long-established patterns of movement. Various hummer species seem to be expanding their range, with western species showing up in the East and vice versa.

This "change" could be due to more birdwatchers; previously, the birds might have been overlooked. But it seems more like a definite trend. How much of an effect feeders have on this movement is open for debate; global warming may be influencing it, or it may just be one of those mysteries.

What is known for sure is that the tiny orange-and-copper rufous hummingbird, formerly a western species, is now spotted regularly all the way to the Atlantic seaboard. And it often winters in the Southeast and Deep South. Others seem to be following its lead. At this rate, it's beginning to look like Louisiana may eventually rival Arizona as the hot spot for hummingbird watching!

Cold-hardiness in birds—the minimum temperature a bird can withstand—varies according to species, as well as by factors such as age, weight, and diet. Tree sparrows, for instance, are famed for their ability to thrive in frigid conditions that other sparrows can't tolerate.

What can we do to help vulnerable birds in times of cold? We can provide roosting boxes, for starters, along with plenty of evergreens that offer sheltered sites in wintry weather. Make sure you have plants with winter berries in your yard, such as staghorn sumac (*Rhus typhina*). And keep those feeders filled to the brim with high-fat foods. Mealworms, chopped nuts, suet and peanut butter mixes, and other soft, high-fat foods can help carry these vulnerable birds through a cold spell.

Suspended Animation

When temperatures sink, some hummingbird species have the remarkable ability to enter a state called torpor, in which their body processes slow down to the bare minimum. They look dazed or even half-dead, and they don't respond to things going on around them.

Usually, this state of torpidity occurs at night, but it can also occur in daytime cold weather, probably as a way to conserve energy.

Gorgeous pink-headed Anna's hummingbirds spend the winter in this area, and my five winter regulars were taken by surprise as much as I was when an unusual cold snap moved in here a few winters ago. Rain soon turned to freezing rain, then more than a foot of snow, then another 3

Records of banded eastern bluebirds show that many birds die in February, March, and April, when weather is a major stressor. High-fat food can help.

inches of solid ice. Roads were impassable, even by Humvees. Temperatures plummeted to 17°F, then 15°, then 11°.

And I had hummingbirds?

For 3 days, all I did was replace fast-freezing hummingbird feeders—about every 10 minutes.

My husband was trapped in town, at a hotel within walking—make that sliding—distance of his workplace. So it was my son David, home on Christmas break from college, and I who shared the task of thawing and replacing the feeders as they froze.

It takes only 6 minutes for the feeding ports of a full tube feeder to freeze at about 15°F, I can now reliably report. And less than 15 minutes for the entire thing to freeze.

It was all we could do to thaw the feeders quickly enough to make sure the hummers always had one to drink from. The birds were so desperately single-minded that they settled on each fresh feeder as soon as we stepped outside the door—while it was still in our hands.

In between feedings, they'd perch on an illuminated bulb of our Christmas lights to gain a bit of warmth.

We thought about bringing the birds inside, but I was worried that they'd break their necks against a wall or window once they emerged from what seemed to be their semi-torpid state. So we kept up the nectar effort, and the hummingbirds remained until after dark. Finally they made a short flight to the dense branches of the fir, just a few feet away.

I thought for sure the night would kill them. But I set my alarm for 6:00 A.M., just in case. Sunrise wasn't until about 8:00 A.M., but I wanted to be ready should anybody need an early breakfast.

After hacking ice on my way out of the frozen-in-place door, I stepped into the predawn darkness—and was greeted by three Anna's hummingbirds, who practically fell onto the feeder I held in my hands. The other two hummers showed up a few minutes later. Imagine hummingbirds flying in slow motion—that's how they moved.

I roused David from his warm and comfy slumber. "The hummingbirds are up already," I called through his door.

Another all-day effort, with no respite. And yet another, before the weather broke. But every single one of those five hummingbirds made it, thanks to the nectar brigade and the Christmas lights.

Year-Round Pleasures

Many of our most reliable visitors at the feeder are also our most loyal year-round birds.

"Year-round" is not exactly what it says: It's the species that is present year-round, not the particular birds.

Take the blue jay, for instance, a bird that's easy to spot summer or winter in much of its range. It's a year-round species. But the blue jays you see in summer are probably not the same blue jays you see in winter.

That "year-round" designation, which you'll find on the range maps in field guides, just means that the species is present in your area year-round. Individual birds, often in small family groups, generally travel within that year-round range.

At best, you'll see only a few white-breasted nuthatches in your yard, but they'll visit year-round.

Since it's just about impossible to tell one blue jay from another, we're pretty much unaware of the changing cast of characters.

Sometimes, though, a bird has a characteristic that sets it apart from the crowd. For years, I had a "special" blue jay in Indiana. He did the best imitation of a red-tailed hawk scream I've ever heard, and I'm sure he snickered every time he made me look up and scan the sky for the "hawk."

But he was only a spring and summer friend. In fall, he took off for parts unknown. I always figured with vocal talent like that, he was probably headed to Nashville to try his luck.

And for a few years, a robin with a noticeable white patch of feathers visited my yard—but only in fall and winter. Maybe he was your summer friend?

Year-Round Birds with Wide Ranges

These birds are present year-round in large areas of their range. Keep in mind that it's the species that you may see year-round, not the individual birds, which may relocate to other areas. Check the range maps in a field guide to see whether your area is part of the year-round territory for these birds:

Woodpeckers
Flickers
Jays
Crows
Magpies
Titmice
Chickadees
Nuthatches
Wrens, except house wren, winter wren,
    marsh wren, sedge wren
Thrashers, except sage thrasher
Mockingbird

Cardinal
Pyrrhuloxia
Towhees
Song sparrow
Field sparrow
Meadowlarks
Red-winged blackbird
Grackles
House finch
American goldfinch
Doves

The Rising Tide

You'll notice the movements of these "year-round" birds just as you do with true migrants, as the numbers swell with the seasons.

A few flickers stick around in my area all winter, but I always look forward to the day in March when suddenly that loud "Whick-a! Whick-a! Whick-a!" is ringing out all over the place. When I take a look, sure enough, there'll be a dozen or two big, loud flickers foraging in my yard and all over the neighborhood. They only stay a day or at most a few days, then they're off again. In fall, the same thing happens, but the flickers are mostly silent then.

Flickers and jays both travel during the day, unlike many other songbird migrants, which fly under cover of darkness. When I first began visiting Hawk Mountain, a mountain lookout in eastern Pennsylvania that offers a spectacular view of migrating hawks that follow the ridgeline, the occasional group of blue jays flying past was only a curiosity. That was a long time ago, and nowadays the official hawk counters keep track of the jays (and hummingbirds and monarch butterflies!) as well as the hawks. There's always something new to learn about nature.

Seasonal Changes

Year-round birds often move to happier hunting grounds for fall and winter. Cold weather makes it more important to find a home base where there's plenty to eat, to keep those body temperatures stoked. And appropriate cover is vital during winter, too, both to keep the birds safe

One of the best reasons to put up a feeder: a crowd of cardinals on a snowy day. When bad weather threatens, birds go for the easiest pickings.

from the elements and to shield them from hawks, which are often more focused on birds in winter.

That's one of the reasons bird feeders boom during late fall through winter. You'll notice an increase in birds in your new, improved yard, too, thanks to the food and cover that your plantings continue to provide.

In some cases, birds move from high elevations to lower lands in winter, where they're away from the brunt of the worst weather and where food is more plentiful. Other birds, including robins, retreat from "civilized" lives in our own neighborhoods and move into wilder areas, where food and shelter are abundant.

Many year-round birds band together in small, loose flocks for winter. The downy woodpecker that seems to be such a solitary soul in

The number of each species of bird in your yard will rise and fall with the seasons. Migration is always a high point. The population in other seasons depends on the birds' nesting range and wintering range.

YEAR-ROUND

Year-round bird species are present year-round, but their numbers will vary. You'll see more after the young leave the nest, and the highest number in winter and during migration.

	No Birds	A Few Birds	Several Birds	Several to Many Birds
Spring				▓ (to Several to Many Birds)
Nesting		▓ (to A Few Birds)		
Post-Nesting			▓ (to Several Birds)	
Fall				▓ (to Several to Many Birds)
Winter				▓ (to Several to Many Birds)

NESTING RANGE

If you live within the nesting area of a migrant species, but not within its winter range, you'll see the highest numbers during spring and fall migration, and after the young leave the nest. In winter? You'll see none.

	No Birds	A Few Birds	Several Birds	Several to Many Birds
Spring				▓ (to Several to Many Birds)
Nesting		▓ (to A Few Birds)		
Post-Nesting			▓ (to Several Birds)	
Fall				▓ (to Several to Many Birds)
Winter	▓ (No Birds)			

MIGRANT BIRD

Species that don't nest or winter in your area, but only pass through, reach their highest numbers during spring and fall migration. They're a temporary delight to look forward to.

	No Birds	A Few Birds	Several Birds	Several to Many Birds
Spring				▓ (to Several to Many Birds)
Nesting	▓ (No Birds)			
Post-Nesting	▓ (No Birds)			
Fall				▓ (to Several to Many Birds)
Winter	▓ (No Birds)			

WINTER RANGE

If you live within the winter range of a migrant species, but not within its nesting range, you'll see the highest numbers during spring and fall migration, and in winter. During nesting season, the birds are elsewhere.

	No Birds	A Few Birds	Several Birds	Several to Many Birds
Spring				▓ (to Several to Many Birds)
Nesting	▓ (No Birds)			
Post-Nesting	▓ (No Birds)			
Fall				▓ (to Several to Many Birds)
Winter				▓ (to Several to Many Birds)

spring and summer joins up with a mixed band of chickadees, kinglets, nuthatches, and other foragers on the trees; robins and cardinals pal around with their own kind.

Following my bird-by-bird gardening suggestions pays off in all seasons. When I lived in year-round cardinal territory, I enjoyed watching a flock of 15 or more of these birds at my feeder and in my yard every day in winter. They'd fill up at the feeder, then shelter in the shrubs and trees or search for other edibles still on the stems.

An acquaintance who provided only a well-stocked feeder had a different experience. Cardinals deserted her yard in winter, sometimes coming to the feeder but always quickly departing. Where did they go? she wondered.

Her yard provided very little cover and nothing to eat besides sunflower seeds. But just down the road was a creek, with thick stands of giant ragweed along its banks and dense mounds of wild roses and other shrubs. That's where "her" cardinals were spending the winter—in an area that supplied shelter as well as a variety of natural food.

Nesting season brings a natural decrease in the numbers of year-round birds you see. During this time, your yard will usually host only a pair or a few birds of each species, instead of the crowds you see in fall and winter and during spring migration.

Once the young are on their own in summer, you'll probably see an increase in bird life once again, as your fruits and berries draw them in. Feeders aren't nearly as enticing in summer, when insects and fruits are free for the taking. That's why gardening bird by bird will bring gratifying results.

Because of these seasonal movements and seasonal habitat preferences, these birds will visit your yard in varying numbers.

Expect to see the highest numbers of year-round birds during spring and fall migration, just as with true migrants. You'll also host plenty during winter, if your yard offers food and cover. During nesting season, when they pair off and stake out breeding territories, you'll see the lowest numbers of these birds. But on any day of the year, you may see these birds if you live within their year-round range.

Fair-Weather Friends

In most regions, migrants are only a seasonal treat. Most of these birds are present only in spring and summer and completely absent in wintertime.

We get to enjoy them during their breeding season, from the time they arrive in spring until the time they depart in early fall. They fly away to spend fall and winter in a warmer place, generally Central or South America. Some species are year-round birds, especially in the extreme Deep South and along the seacoast, where the weather is usually milder than inland. The cast of individual characters may change with the seasons, but the species can be seen year-round.

Migrants depend heavily on insects. Flying insects vanish first, and so do the swallows that depend on them. As other insects become harder to find, vireos, orioles, and other birds that scour the foliage for their insect food depart as well. Nectar, too, disappears when the frost is on the pumpkin, so hummingbirds say goodbye in fall as well.

Planning to spend the winter holidays in sunny South America? Watch the sky for wintering purple martins, which leave North America in fall.

The question I've always wondered about is, Why do the birds leave their tropical or subtropical homes to begin with? Why not stay put in Costa Rica, say, and dine on insects and fruits year-round instead of coming to Minnesota to raise a family? I mean, Minnesota's great—but is it worth a hazardous twice-a-year trip? If I were a scarlet tanager, I'd probably say, "Hey, come on, guys, let's stay home this year, plenty to do around the house, and besides, my wings are kind of tired."

Whatever the reason these birds head north, I'm glad they do. Spring just wouldn't be the same without the thrill of spotting the first oriole or the first tanager, or waking to a yard full of singing vireos or house wrens. Not to mention seeing the first swallows cutting through the air.

Migrants are as welcome as spring itself. And once you begin gardening for your favorites, you'll notice more of them in your yard, both on stopovers in spring and fall and also during the nesting season.

Seasonal Shifts

You'll see the largest number of these birds during migration, but you may also see them during the nesting season.

Migrants

These birds are spring to summer friends for most of us. In fall, they leave for wintering grounds, usually in Mexico, Central America, and South America, where their main foods of insects and fruit are abundant year-round.

Orioles
Flycatchers
Phoebes, except black phoebe
Vireos
Swallows
Yellow-headed blackbirds
Purple martins
Wrens, including house wren, winter wren, marsh wren, sedge wren

Waxwings
Warblers
Tanagers
Buntings
Grosbeaks
Most native sparrows
Hummingbirds

The first birds of a species to arrive in spring are the males. You'll see vivid male orioles and tanagers days before you catch sight of the duller-colored females. And the first hummers that show up in your yard are guaranteed to be gorgeous males. After a few days to a week or so later, the females of the species come on the scene.

Year-round birds that travel relatively short distances follow the same pattern as the migrants that move for thousands of miles. Male red-winged blackbirds, with their nifty vermilion shoulder patches, are the first to arrive in spring. Their streaky brown lady friends follow along a bit later.

Male red-winged blackbirds migrate before females.

The spring travel season runs from about March through May in most areas, with each species having its own timetable.

The return trip takes place between late August and September, for many species.

During fall migration, a tempting yard will also draw in big numbers of many of these birds. Most of them won't look like the colorful birds you saw in spring; they'll be wearing muted winter plumage. I've noticed that fall migrants tend to hang around longer on their rest stops in fall than they do in spring.

In spring, the birds seem to be more focused on getting to their destination in a hurry. Those rising hormones cause the birds to make a beeline for their nesting grounds, with occasional stops to rest and refuel.

As the birds claim nesting territories, they spread out. If your yard happens to be within their territory, the parents are likely to become regular visitors to your place, searching for insects, fruits, or other goodies among your plants—or maybe even selecting one of your shrubs, trees, or a birdhouse as a homesite.

As with year round birds, once the young birds leave the nest, it's likely that their parents will introduce them to the wonders of your yard. Here's where your well-planted yard really brings rewards: Foliage and flowers harbor a myriad of insects, and the new family will eagerly seek them out. Plus, the cover of your shrubs and other plants will help keep the birds safe until the youngsters become better skilled at flying.

Winter Friends

For some migrants, such as pine grosbeaks and rosy finches, our country is their winter vacationland; they raise their families far to the north. While these birds have large winter ranges in the United States, they nest in more northerly

Coffee Time—for Tanagers

Mmmm, nothing like a good cup of coffee. Especially when your morning habit helps keep songbirds alive and well.

Next time you sip a cup of coffee on a May morning, look around for a tanager in your trees. That bird may have spent the winter in the same place where your coffee beans were grown.

Tanagers and more than 100 other bird species are finding refuge in shaded coffee plantations in Mexico and Central America. And with tropical forests disappearing at an alarming rate, those shade coffee farms are absolutely vital.

To help make sure that scarlet tanagers, summer tanagers, and other favorites have a winter home, you can support the birds by buying shade-grown organic coffee. Look for the "Bird-Friendly" seal from the Smithsonian Migratory Bird Council on the package of coffee. This certification program awards its seal of approval to coffee growers who practice "rustic shade" growing, which includes a diversity of trees among the coffee plants—and a diversity of birds. It's the next best thing to a natural forest.

Many scarlet tanagers winter on coffee plantations.

Coffee is an adaptable plant that thrives in sun, shade, or partial shade. The Smithsonian's seal is based on stringent criteria. It's awarded to farms that plant coffee beneath existing trees, resulting in the most diverse habitat.

Other organizations also certify coffee as shade-grown, according to looser criteria. In some cases, most of the natural trees are cleared, leaving more room for coffee. Only an occasional bare-trunked tree sticks up above the small coffee trees—not nearly as good for birds or for biodiversity.

You can buy Bird-Friendly coffee by mail, if your local coffee shop doesn't stock it. A part of the price goes to support migratory bird research and programs run by the Smithsonian. (Check out this Web site nationalzoo.si.edu/ConservationandScience/MigratoryBirds/Coffee/Bird_Friendly for a source, or write to Smithsonian Migratory Bird Center, National Zoological Park, Washington, DC 20008.)

areas or in the mountains. In summer, they don't usually seek out backyards, remaining in wilder areas to raise their families.

During spring and fall migration, though, as they move to their northerly or mountainous nesting territories, they may show up in a welcoming yard along the route. And in winter, when they head "south" to our parts, they often become regulars in backyards within their wintering range.

These birds may be winter friends, depending on where you live: Cassin's finch, crossbill (year-round in some areas), evening grosbeak, fox sparrow, golden-crowned sparrow, Harris's sparrow, hermit thrush, junco (year-round in some areas), kinglet (year-round in some areas), pine grosbeak, pine siskin (year-round in some areas), purple finch, redpoll, rosy finch, sage thrasher, tree sparrow, vesper sparrow, white-crowned sparrow, white-throated sparrow, wren.

Whether it's winter residents, year-round friends, or summer delights, birds will come calling to your yard. As you saw in Part 2 of this book, the bird family chapters, I've given you a multitude of suggestions for growing plant foods that are timed to the peak seasons of birds. As you spend more time watching the birds in your own yard, you'll discover for yourself whether you need to fine-tune your plantings—more summer berries? more winter seeds?—so that your yard is ready and welcoming when the birds arrive.

When winter comes, western bird-watchers look for huge roving flocks of rosy finches visiting from the tundra. The flocks settle at ground level to forage.

Regional Delights

Years ago, a friend gave me a big, beautiful chunk of purple fluorite crystals. A little card from the shop, tucked in with the rock, noted, "Fluorite helps you separate reality from illusion." I love the rock, but the supposed power it holds? Good thing I don't believe in crystal therapy because some of my illusions are pretty dear to my heart.

A weed-free garden, where slugs never eat my just-sprouted lilies down to nubs. Knees that slide and glide into joint instead of ratcheting along with a cranky thunk. A dog that comes when I call, even when there's a cat just begging to be chased. And, of course, a yard here in the Pacific Northwest that's filled with all my favorite birds—the cardinals and wood thrushes of my childhood home in Pennsylvania; the meadowlarks I lived with in the Midwest, with their melancholy music; the Blackburnian warblers of my favorite hemlock-filled Appalachian trails; the adorable quail of the Desert Southwest; oh, and maybe a few of those purple gallinules I fell in love with in Florida.

Looking at that wish list in the harsh light of reality, I know I'll probably never see any of those birds in this neighborhood. But it doesn't hurt to dream. Meanwhile, I plant and plan for my real yard. The one that's beset by slugs and weeds and errant dogs, and filled with birds that an Easterner or Midwesterner can only dream about—

The flat fields of the Midwest are home to many meadowlarks, which may show up in nearby backyards when snow is deep and food is scarce.

Plain Janes

Sure, we all want a yard full of orioles, tanagers, and bluebirds. But getting to know a flock of sparrows can be just as rewarding as a flash of bright feathers.

Sometimes it's nice to get a reminder that plain Janes can be just as endearing as the beauty queens. When I lived in the tiny hamlet of Trexler, in eastern Pennsylvania, I delighted in scouting out wood ducks on the nearby Ontelaunee Creek, and climbing the trail at Hawk Mountain a few miles away to thrill to the sight of thousands of migrating hawks. I explored the neighboring Pine Swamp to find wood warblers and tiny, toylike saw-whet owls, and I pushed my way through tangles of underbrush to listen to fluting thrushes and gobbling wild turkeys.

Two houses up, my neighbor Katie Trexler, a descendant of the family for whom the village was named, had a narrower view of the world of birds. Her days of scrambling along forest trails or slopping through mucky wetlands were long gone. But

Song sparrows are common but charming.

she was still enthralled by birds—the house sparrows that thronged her small backyard.

For years, she'd been feeding the birds that many people call pests. She had spent so much time watching her friends, as she called them, that she knew many of them as individuals. And she loved every one of them. Did she feel deprived? Never. She felt lucky.

Another sparrow appreciator was Margaret Morse Nice, who studied the ultracommon song sparrows in her neighborhood as exhaustively as intrepid researchers do with exotic species. More than 70 years after it first hit print, her two-volume *Studies in the Life History of the Song Sparrow* is still a classic, well regarded by scientists and a pleasure to read for anyone who's passionate about sparrows.

Just goes to show that all birds are interesting. Even if the grass does appear to be greener on the other side of that fence, *your* backyard birds are special treasures.

neon-bright Anna's hummingbirds, charming flocks of busy little bushtits, elegant Steller's jays (I know *elegant* sounds like an odd word to describe a boisterous jay, but the Steller's is the class act of the family: sleek navy blue, with a dramatic black crest).

I still dream of snagging the first red bird that crosses the Cascade Mountains into my cardinal-free corner of the Northwest. But until he shows up, I find plenty of delights in everyday reality.

No matter where you live, interesting birds will be pleased to share the space with you. But while you're considering the rational possibilities, don't forget to dream. One of the best things about a bird-friendly yard is that you're bound to get surprises!

Regional Highlights

Every part of the country has plenty of birds worth bragging about. Since so many species

Choosing and Using a Field Guide

A field guide is an invaluable resource for anyone who loves to watch birds. These books can be intimidating at first glance—how will you ever find a single bird among all those pages? Take heart: You can pretty much skip the first half of the book, where gulls, ducks, and other birds that aren't typically "backyard birds" are usually grouped.

In the second half of the book, you'll find the birds you're looking for: the woodpeckers, the hummingbirds we all adore, and the perching birds or passerines, which include the vast majority of backyard birds. In nearly all field guides, the birds are grouped by families; only the vinyl-covered Audubon pictorial field guides are organized by the color of the birds rather than the family.

Choosing a field guide is a matter of personal preference. Experienced birdwatchers, or those who want to learn as much as possible, have swiftly embraced *The Sibley Guide to Birds,* published under the auspices of the National Audubon Society. But there's a whole shelf of field guides from which you can choose. Page through them all, and pick the one you like best. One tip: A guide that has range maps on the same page as the picture of the bird is easier to use, since you can see at a glance which species are probable in your area.

have wide ranges, many of us share "our" birds with other regions of the country. But in some cases, bird species are restricted to a smaller area.

As you'll see in this section, the natural conditions of a region determine which birds are most at home there.

Lots of birds adapt to a wide range of climate and conditions. In this section, you'll discover how climate and habitat affect the particular birds you'll find in each region of the country. You'll learn how those natural conditions can affect which birds you see in your backyard, and how to plan your yard to take advantage of them.

The lists in this section will give you a sampling of special birds that are at home (some in summer, some in winter, some year-round) in each region. These are the birds that are adapted to the natural conditions of that region—and generally not to other areas.

When you check a field guide or walk around your yard, you'll notice many other species that

aren't listed in the regional highlights. Hundreds of bird species have ranges that cover much wider areas, and most of them aren't included (except for bluebirds, which hold perennial bragging rights). But if you want to make a birdwatcher from another part of the country drool, just mention one of these regional highlights.

Any of these mouthwatering birds may show up in your yard, if you live in that region. Well, maybe not quite all—that ivory-billed woodpecker of the Midwest seems to be sticking to its "Big Woods."

The Northeast: Moderate Climate, Mature Trees

Long settled, the Northeast includes huge cities such as New York, Boston, and Philadelphia, plus plenty of smaller cities and many towns and suburbs. Yet there's still a good amount of countryside. Ancient mountain ranges run through this

Highlights of the Northeast

Blackburnian warbler
Black-capped chickadee
Cardinal
Eastern bluebird
Fox sparrow
Golden-winged warbler
Great crested flycatcher
Nashville warbler

Northern oriole, Baltimore race
Purple finch
Rose-breasted grosbeak
Ruby-throated hummingbird
Scarlet tanager
White-throated sparrow
Wood thrush

area, and water is usually abundant in all seasons. The woods are a mix of mostly deciduous trees with some conifers. Farmland may be fast disappearing as the population expands, but there are still plenty of open meadows, pastures, and cropland. Mature shade trees and street trees are common in older neighborhoods, although there are plenty of just-getting-started suburban plantings.

The climate has four distinct seasons, with temperatures dropping well below freezing in winter. This is the area that runs closest to the calendar dates of the seasons; they're roughly equal in most parts of this region. (Sorry, New England, you get a longer stretch of winter.)

Summers are hot and usually humid. Occasional droughts occur, but usually every month of the year brings a good dose of precipitation.

Because of abundant cover and water, this region is ideal for many bird species. Many of them cover large ranges that aren't limited to this region, as you can see on the maps in field guides. The entire eastern half of the country is home ground for lots of species.

Here are the types of birds you can expect in the Northeast's geography and climate:

- Well-established yards and parks with mature trees encourage migrants to stop.
- Old trees in city neighborhoods encourage nuthatches, titmice, and woodpeckers, even in the heart of downtown.

The black-throated green warbler isn't just a migration treat in the Northeast—it's a nesting bird.

The forests of the Northeast are a haven for the wood thrush, a fabled songbird whose rich, fluting notes are heard at dawn and dusk.

- Migrants and resident birds can easily travel from yard to yard, even in cities, by using the plentiful trees and shrubs as a corridor.
- Shade trees and mature shrubs provide good nesting sites for orioles, scarlet tanagers, robins, blue jays, vireos, brown thrashers, and other birds. Lilacs (*Syringa vulgaris*) thrive here and are popular nest sites.
- Patches of open countryside make ideal eastern bluebird habitat. Draw bluebirds to your yard with berry bushes, such as winterberry (*Ilex verticillata*), spicebush (*Lindera benzoin*), and native viburnums (*Viburnum dentatum* and other spp.).
- Moderate climate has encouraged the spread of Carolina wrens, brown thrashers, and catbirds, which may winter over as well as nest.
- Flower gardens are plentiful in this region, and so are ruby-throated hummingbirds.

- Late spring freezes can endanger bluebirds and other vulnerable species; stock up on insect feeder foods in very early spring so that you're prepared if assistance is needed.
- Plant plenty of sunflowers (*Helianthus annuus*), zinnias (*Zinnia* cultivars), cosmos (*Cosmos binpinnatus*), and other flowers in your yard, to supply seeds for winter birds.

The Far North: Conifers and Cold Winters

The North has fewer people and more forests than many other areas. Conifers are abundant in this region. Large and small forests are heavily coniferous, with a good number of deciduous trees, such as maples and birches, mixed in. Abundant natural lakes and other water sources fill the area. Dairy farms dot this region, with contented cows grazing in lush pastures.

Long, cold winters, usually with plenty of snow, are the hallmark of this area. Temperatures often fall well below zero. Summers are usually cool.

Thanks to all that water, this area is overflowing with insects. That may be why it's such a haven for many migrant birds, particularly insect-dependent wood warblers. Unlike heavily farmed regions or densely populated areas, where pesticide use is prolific, the insect populations of the Far North are thriving.

Here are the types of birds you can expect in the Far North's geography and climate:

- Cold-hardy birds, such as Canada jays and boreal chickadees, are well-adapted to this climate.

Highlights of the Far North

Ader flycatcher
Bay-breasted warbler
Black-backed woodpecker
Blackburnian warbler
Black-throated green warbler
Blue-headed vireo
Bobolink
Bohemian waxwing
Boreal chickadee
Canada warbler
Cape May warbler

Clay-colored sparrow
Connecticut warbler
Crossbills
Evening grosbeak
Gray jay
Mourning warbler
Philadelphia vireo
Pine grosbeak
Redpolls
Veery

· Birds that eat the seeds of pinecones, including crossbills and nuthatches, are right at home in this conifer-rich region.

· This is the southern part of the range for species of the North, including evening and pine grosbeaks, Bohemian waxwings, and redpolls.

· Birds that scour insects from foliage and bark, such as nuthatches, kinglets, and warblers, find abundant opportunities here.

· Pinecones and other seeds on trees are vital in wintertime, because they don't get buried in snow. Add native maples (*Acer* spp.), birches (*Betula* spp.), and conifers, if you don't already have them.

· Spring migrants arrive later than in other regions; fall migrants depart earlier.

· This is the destination for many wood warblers; abundant cover and insect food will draw them in on migration or perhaps as residents.

· Evergreens are vital for shelter in snow and cold.

· In wintertime, high-fat foods at the feeder will draw just about every bird species around.

The Midwest: Far-Reaching Fields and Oh, What Weather

This region marks a dramatic change in the geography of the country. Rolling hills of the East gradually give way to flatlands, where the only landmark on the horizon is endless cropland and the sky itself. Forests become smaller and are mostly deciduous. Eastern redcedar (*Juniperus virginiana*) is the main evergreen, dotting open pastures and roadsides. The woods soon peter out, and grasslands take over. This region has its share of cities, towns, and suburbs. But it also has huge farms, once the prairie, where thousands of acres of wheat, corn, and other crops are raised.

Wind is a constant presence on many days in much of this region, because there's nothing to break its force in these flatlands. And because this happens to be where cold air from the north meets warm air from the south, thunderstorms and even more violent weather, including hail, is common. Winters may or may not bring deep snow or blizzards, and ice storms occasionally occur. Temperatures can be bone-chilling in winter, dropping below zero. Spring and fall are often rainy. Summers are hot and humid, and droughts often occur.

Here are the types of birds you can expect in the Midwest's geography and climate:

Rainbow bird? If you live in the lower middle of the country, including Texas, look for the painted bunting. In winter, it moves to Florida.

- Large expanses of open land encourage grassland birds, such as meadowlarks, dicksissels, scissor-tailed flycatchers, buntings, and kingbirds.
- Seed eaters such as blackbirds and native sparrows are in heaven in this region, with its bounty of grasses, prairie wildflowers, and grain crops. Include these seeds in your yard by planting a garden of sunflowers (*Helianthus annuus*), coneflowers (*Echinacea* spp. and cultivars), and millet or other birdseed.
- Birds may be swept off course during strong storms, showing up in areas outside their usual range or habitat.
- Nests can be dislodged from trees in summer storms, a sad but natural part of bird life.

- Deciduous trees in yards or along rivers make an appealing site for oriole nests.
- Planting a windbreak can make your yard a more pleasant place by sheltering it from the wind.
- Include evergreens in your yard, for shelter in unpredictable weather.
- Summer water will bring in birds.
- Adding fall and winter fruits and berries, such as sumacs (*Rhus* spp.), Virginia creeper

Highlights of the Midwest

Cardinal
Dicksissel
Eastern bluebird
Harris's sparrow
Indigo bunting
Ivory-billed woodpecker!
Lark bunting

Meadowlarks
Northern oriole, Baltimore race
Painted bunting
Red-bellied woodpecker
Red-headed woodpecker
Scissor-tailed flycatcher

(*Parthenocissus quinquefolia*), and hackberry tree (*Celtis occidentalis*), can attract birds from a variety of habitats.

- Feeders can be a lifesaver in winter, especially after ice storms.

The Southeast and South: Long, Steamy Summers, Mild Winters, and Plenty of Trees

This region has a mix of habitats, from fantastic swamps, coastal wetlands, and mountain forests to open fields, pine woods, and deciduous forests. Cities and towns dot the region, but there are plenty of farms, too. Rivers, swamps, and wetlands are abundant. The southern Appalachian Mountains cross this region, providing homes for forest birds.

While the habitat varies, the climate is pretty much the same: hot and steamy, with abundant rainfall and mild winters. The farther south, the more extreme the steam heat, until it becomes subtropical—yep, like a jungle. Winters are usually mild, and in some parts flowers bloom year-round. Occasional ice storms or strong summer storms can sweep in, and drenching rains are common.

Plants grow like mad in this kind of climate, which is great news for gardeners and birds. Insects flourish spectacularly well, too, which is another boon to birds.

Here are the types of birds you can expect in the South's geography and climate:

- Many species live year-round here or retreat to this region from the north in winter.

Destination: Deep South

I once met a couple of friendly folks in a Louisiana campground who were proud to call themselves "snowbirds." In autumn, they loaded up the RV and left their northern Illinois home behind; in spring, they returned.

"We're just like the birds," said the woman that December day. "In fall, we go south; in spring, we come back."

Her husband turned from tinkering with their RV to chime in. "Some years, we even beat the hummingbirds," he said. Then he reached into the camper and pulled out a nectar feeder. "See? We're ready for them."

His wife laughed. "Sometimes I wonder if we're feeding the same hummingbirds we have at home, way down here."

Could be!

The southern tier of states, and especially the very farthest south, are wintering grounds for many beloved birds. While other species or others of their own kind keep going into Central and South America, these birds seem to say, "Hey, that's far enough." Here are some of those familiar friends that northern snowbirds of the human kind may encounter in the southern states:

American robin	Hummingbirds
Brown thrasher	Many native sparrows
Eastern bluebird	Orioles
Gray catbird	Tree swallow

The name "red-cockaded woodpecker" sounds a lot more impressive than the bird looks. But it's a coup for the South, the only place the bird lives.

- Hummingbirds may be a year-round presence, so bolster your yard with plenty of their favorite flowers. Be ready for the waves of fall hummers with late-blooming flowers, such as scarlet sage and Texas sage (*Salvia splendens, S. coccinea*), trumpet creeper (*Campsis radicans*), cross vine (*Bignonia capreolata*), lantana (*Lantana camara*), and turtlehead (*Chelone gabra*).
- Provide berry and fruit plants for fall migrants, and be sure to include bayberries (*Myrica pensylvanica, M. cerifera*) for tree swallows and yellow-rumped warblers.
- Include broad-leaved evergreens in your yard, such as magnolia (*Magnolia* spp. and cultivars), redbay (*Persea borbonia*), or rhododendron (*Rhododendron* cultivars), for shelter in rainy weather.

- Trees are rich in insects and insect larvae, a real draw for woodpeckers.
- Dense undergrowth of various heights appeals to thrushes, blue grosbeaks, vireos, and sparrows.
- Nearly all migrants swarm through this region on their way to points north in the spring, or when they're retracing their route in fall.

The West: Wide Open Sagebrush and Mile-High Mountains

In the western half of the country, fragrant sagebrush flatland, cut by canyons, leads to the high mountains of the Rockies, Cascades, and Sierras.

Highlights of the Southeast and Deep South

Bachman's sparrow	Prairie warbler
Blue grosbeak	Red-cockaded woodpecker
Boat-tailed grackle	Red-headed woodpecker
Brown-headed nuthatch	Rufous hummingbird
Carolina chickadee	Summer tanager
Eastern bluebird	White-eyed vireo
Florida scrub jay	Yellow-bellied sapsucker
Fox sparrow	

Winters are generally long and harsh here, with blizzards a common occurrence. Summer is relatively cool and short, although it can be hot at times. This is a fairly dry climate. Most of the precipitation occurs in the fall through spring; summers are dry and humidity is low.

Population is mostly centered around the cities here, with occasional towns and many multiacre ranches. Along the rivers and at homesteads, fast-growing cottonwoods form dense groves of tall trees.

Although gardening can be challenging here, birdwatching is excellent, thanks to the many species of birds that are adapted to these rigorous conditions.

Here are the types of birds you can expect in the West's geography and climate:

Bluebird? Nope. This is the lazuli bunting, at home only in the West. Other areas may get an occasional peek, as this species is prone to wander.

- In the sagebrush country, dryland birds such as quail, native sparrows, and thrashers flourish.
- The cool mountains attract many hummingbirds, as well as forest birds such as Steller's jays and mountain chickadees. Explore the possibilities of penstemons (*Penstemon* spp.), native perennial flowers that are magnets for hummingbirds.
- Gardening can be a challenge here; invest in a regional gardening guide for useful suggestions.

Highlights of the West

Black-headed grosbeak
Black-throated sparrow
Canyon wren
Clark's nutcracker
Dark-eyed junco, Oregon race
Golden-crowned sparrow
Hummingbirds: black-chinned; broad-tailed; calliope
Lazuli bunting
Lewis's woodpecker
McGillivray's warbler

Mountain bluebird
Mountain chickadee
Rock wren
Sage sparrow
Sage thrasher
Say's phoebe
Steller's jay
Violet-green swallow
Western tanager
White-headed woodpecker

- Be sure to include several birdbaths, with at least one of them at ground level. Water is a big attraction to birds of this region; a dripper or fountain will draw them in when they hear the irresistible trickle and splash.
- Plant fruits and berries; their water content makes them a real treat for many birds of this area. Explore native possibilities, such as buffaloberry (*Shepherdia argentea*), golden currant (*Ribes aureum*), and wax currant (*R. cereum*), which will need no coddling to grow well.
- Include conifers in your yard to provide shelter in harsh winter weather.
- Keep a metal trash can filled with extra birdseed, in case of deep snow in winter.

The Southwest and California: Desert Beauty with Scant Water and High Heat

The Southwest and central to southern California is like a whole different planet. This is our American desert, a vast area of land that's dry as a bone. Cities bloom on the desert, but because of the lack of water, the population is mostly centered around those areas. Vast expanses of land with nary a house in sight are the rule outside the cities.

Large trees are hard to find in the desert, with the exception of beautiful oaks and imported species, such as eucalyptus, and palms in a few areas. Shrubs and small trees, many of them thorny to ward off foraging animals, are plentiful. These plants are widely scattered, with sweeps of open space between them—an adaptation that assures that each plant gets a fair share of the water. A few mountain ranges break it up, but they're not lush, either; pines, oaks, and junipers are the predominant trees. Along rivers, trees such as willows can gain a foothold.

Cactuses and other nonthirsty plants, such as yucca, are plentiful in the desert. Wildflowers are mostly annuals, which sprout fast and bloom in a hurry after rain. Most of the rain is concentrated in the winter months, but it may begin in late summer, with "monsoon" rains that bring moisture to the parched land. In some areas, especially California, irrigation has allowed farming to flourish.

Scanty water and extreme heat are the defining factors of this area. But there are plenty of fabulous birds that flourish in these conditions. This region holds claim to dozens of specially adapted bird species.

Here are the types of birds and plants you can expect in the geography and climate of the Southwest and California:

- Because large trees are in short supply in much of this area, birds are often near eye level.
- Irrigated farming areas and watercourses attract a bounty of birds, which may spill over into nearby backyards.
- Fall is prime planting time because the rainy season will soon follow.
- Birdbaths are vital; they may attract more customers than a feeding station. Be sure to include a basin of water at ground level for quail, native sparrows, and other low-level birds.
- Native plants are the best pick because you

Highlights of the Southwest and California

Acorn woodpecker
Black phoebe
Bridled titmouse
California thrasher
Crissal's thrasher
Curve-billed thrasher
Dark-eyed junco, pink-sided race
Dark-eyed junco, red-backed race
Gila woodpecker
Gilded flicker
Gray vireo
Hepatic tanager
Hooded oriole

Hummingbirds: Allen's, Anna's, calliope, Costa's
Lawrence's goldfinch
Lesser goldfinch
Oak titmouse
Red-faced warbler
Rufous-crowned sparrow
Scott's oriole
Tri-colored blackbird
Verdin
Vermilion flycatcher
Violet-green swallow
Yellow-billed magpie

won't have to baby them in this tough climate. Nurseries also stock well-adapted plants from other countries that will do well.

- This region includes fabulous flowers, many of them tailored to the needs of hummingbirds. Investigate the possibilities of penstemons (*Penstemon* spp. and cultivars) and salvias (*Salvia* spp. and cultivars); any of them will be a hit with hummingbirds.

- Many plants from Australia and Africa are just as popular with hummingbirds and nectar-seeking orioles as native plants are— and they're just as drought-tolerant. Look for tubular flowers in red or orange, such as those of grevillea (*Grevillea* spp. and cultivars) or red-hot poker (*Kniphofia* spp. and hybrids).

- Juicy fruits and berries are a hit with birds in this dry region. Although the thrashers and woodpeckers here can make do with very little water, they're quick to come to a luscious crop. All natives will get their atten-

With its clown-makeup face and raucous laugh, the acorn woodpecker is a memorable Southwest sighting.

Hot Spots

Certain areas of the country are famed as hot spots for birds, and we're not talking temperature. These spots are prime birdwatching territory.

Sometimes they occur where different habitats meet, resulting in a mix of birds from both habitats. In the mountains of the Southwest, for instance, you'll spot birds from the surrounding desert in this oasis, as well as those that prefer the trees of the cooler mountains.

Often, such places are where birds reach a funneling point along a migration route. If you happen to live near or visit one of those natural bottlenecks, where the stream of birds narrows, you'll get to see a spectacular sight at migration time. Bird lovers flock to Cape May, New Jersey; Point Pelee, Canada; and other places where the migrants become concentrated before crossing a barrier. Often, the bottleneck is created at the edge of a body of water, where birds accumulate before heading off across the Delaware Bay, in the case of Cape May, or before winging across Lake Erie, at Point Pelee. In the Southwest, destinations such as Ramsey Canyon in southern Arizona are famed for their concentrations of hummingbirds.

Sometimes, hot spots occur where ranges overlap. In the case of Brownsville, Texas, at the very tip of the state, Mexican species reach their very northern limit, bringing the possibility of spotting some unusual species that otherwise aren't found in America, such as the green jay.

It's fun to plan trips to such renowned gathering places. But it's just as much fun to get to know the birds of your own backyard, whether they're tanagers and bluebirds or simple brown sparrows.

Bird lovers are a friendly bunch, and it's fun to talk to others who share your passion. What you'll quickly discover is the truth in that old saying about the grass being greener on the other side of the fence. While I drool hearing about the vermilion flycatcher that visited someone's New Mexico backyard, she's equally envious about the varied thrush in mine.

---

tion, including toyon or Christmas berry (*Heteromeles arbutifolia*) and hollyleaf cherry (*Prunus ilicifolia*); so will the common landscaping shrub pyracantha or firethorn (*Pyracantha* spp. and cultivars), whose spiny branches also offer protective cover.

• Many birds blend in with the subtle colors of the landscape; listen and look hard to spot them.

The Northwest: Mild, Rainy Winters and Miles of Conifers

Deep, dark conifer forests draped in moss and drenched with rain are the distinguishing feature of the Northwest. In spite of centuries of logging, plenty of trees remain, both in natural forests and on replanted tree farms. Beneath those trees is an understory of waist-high ferns and mostly evergreen shrubs. The forests are almost entirely coniferous, but at sunnier openings, deciduous trees hold their own. Alders (*Alnus* spp.), bigleaf maples (*Acer macrophyllum*), plus a smattering of other species, and cottonwoods along the rivers, are the main deciduous trees. Huckleberries (*Vaccinium* spp.), currants (*Ribes* spp.), and blackberries gone wild provide abundant fruits for birds of this area.

The Cascade Mountains and Coast Range, with their vast stretches of conifer forests, dominate the landscape in this area. Valleys can be wide and sunny; the wider valleys are used for farming or for growing grass seed, a top crop in the Northwest. A few large cities, plus countless small towns, are in this region; suburbs are spreading, but there are still large amounts of open space with widely scattered homes.

Rain, rain, and more rain is commonly associated with this area, but the climate is actually more half-and-half: Half rainy season, and half nearly bone-dry. Rain falls from about October to April without much sun breaking through; sunny skies are the rule from May through September. Winters are mild, and in many places, flowers can be found all year.

Here are the types of birds you can expect in the Northwest's geography and climate:

Moss grows everywhere in the Pacific Northwest, including on house roofs. The chestnut-backed chickadee often investigates it in search of insects.

- Most bird species that are particular to this region fall into one of two categories: birds of the trees, such as tanagers, nuthatches, and kinglets; and birds of the dense, shady understory, such as thrushes and winter wrens.
- Because cover is so important to many birds of this area, you'll want to plant trees and groups of shrubs or hedges in your yard to make them feel at home.
- Large numbers of native sparrows are a usual occurrence from fall through spring. Plant plenty of seed-bearing flowers and grasses for these birds, or sow finch mix in a sunny spot.
- Allow the dead stems in your flower gardens to stand until early spring, to provide cover for birds that forage at low levels.

Highlights of the Northwest

Anna's hummingbird
Chestnut-backed chickadee
Golden-crowned sparrow
Hermit thrush
Red-breasted nuthatch
Red-breasted sapsucker
Rufous hummingbird

Steller's jay
Townsend's warbler
Varied thrush
Violet-green swallow
Wilson's warbler
Winter wren

- Add fruit and berry plants to your yard. Many Northwest birds enjoy soft foods, and they will flock to the plantings. Sweet cherries (*Prunus* cultivars) grow particularly well here and are irresistible to birds; if you buy a young tree with flower buds, you'll have cherries the first year you plant it.
- Hummingbirds live year-round in much of this region. Plan a garden with hummingbird flowers for all four seasons. Native salal (*Gaultheria shallon*) blooms off and on through winter; bearberry or kinnikinick (*Arctostaphylos uva-ursi*) begins to flower in late winter. Include a hardy fuchsia shrub (*Fuchsia magellanica*) for continuous bloom well into winter.
- Keep your birdbath freshly filled in summer, when rains are scarce. Hummingbirds and many other birds will be thrilled with a mister device above the bath.

Migration time is full of surprises, like this batch of American robins. Many songbirds travel at night, coming down to feed and rest during daylight hours.

Surprises

A big part of the pleasure of watching birds is the occasional surprise that shows up: the bird that's not supposed to be there, or the bird you never even considered might appear in your backyard.

During migration, you'll discover delightful birds that you hadn't realized were a possibility in your yard. They may be just passing through, but it's still a treat to see them.

Since birds live just about everywhere, that means migrants can also show up just about everywhere.

Most songbirds travel as individuals who happen to be moving north or south at the same time. Although it may seem like a whole flock of hummingbirds has suddenly shown up in your yard, in reality each of these tiny birds made its own way there.

Swallows and blackbirds travel as flocks, but most other backyard birds move along in loose groups of individuals spread out over a wide area.

One of my most memorable "birding trips" was a ferry ride from Cape May, New Jersey, to Lewes, Delaware. It's a 17-mile trip that takes about an hour and a half by ferry, but there was a stiff wind blowing. Warblers, hummingbirds, flickers, and other birds, plus countless monarch butterflies, were crossing the bay at the same time we were, and their wings were working hard against the wind. Several of them, perhaps exhausted after fighting the wind—or maybe just smart!—alighted on the boat when they needed a break.

Now You See 'em, Now You Don't

Just because migrant birds travel as individuals instead of in a tight flock, that doesn't mean you won't see a big bunch of them in your yard at the same time. Birds of the same species migrate at the same time, often on the same day or within a span of a few days. That's why all those juncos at your feeder seem to disappear overnight: It was time for them to go.

Many migrants travel at night. I used to think it was to avoid hawks, which fly during the day, and maybe that's part of the reason. But more likely it's because many migrants navigate by the stars, a romantic notion that's been proved in scientific experiments.

When dawn arrives, the loose flocks of birds drop down from the sky to a hospitable location with plenty of food and cover. That could very well be your yard.

Waking up to find migrants in your yard is one of the biggest thrills of the year. The thrushes or native sparrows or whatever has landed may not stay very long. Even in daytime, many migrants keep moving in the general direction of their

In winter, the white-winged crossbill and its cousin, the red crossbill, travel irregularly across the country. They're a thrill to watch, wherever they land.

journey. Watch the birds as they forage, and you may see them gradually moving northward in spring, southward in fall.

I've tried many times to catch the travelers in the act of coming down from the sky, but I've never quite made it. I've heard their calls overhead during the night and just before dawn. But by the time the light brightens enough to see who's in my yard, the birds are already busily eating.

Change Is a Constant

Mockingbirds were once a treat only for the South; now you can find the birds all the way up into Maine. Bluebirds, Carolina wrens, and gray catbirds have also gone into expansion mode over the years, and more recently, cardinals and blue jays are seeking new frontiers to the west of their traditional range.

We're noticing changing patterns in migration, too, with some species, hummingbirds in particular, becoming regulars thousands of miles from their usual range.

Gardening and bird feeding also have big effects on birds. Global warming is fact, not fiction, and its effects are very likely to affect the habits of birds. As wildflowers bloom earlier in the year—more than 2 weeks earlier, say some reports—birds may soon speed up their schedules too. It's one big interconnected system: flowers, insects, birds, and other living creatures. When one changes, the others eventually will, too.

What does it all mean to us backyard birdwatchers? Keep an eye out for the unexpected. The times are changing, and the birds in our backyards are bound to show the effects.

Resources

Visit Sally Roth at www.sallyroth.com for more of her resourceful ideas.

Feeders

Look for well-made, sturdy feeders that are easy to refill and easy to mount. You can find them at discount stores, bird supply shops, and through mail-order sources, such as these:

Duncraft
102 Fisherville Rd.
Concord, NH 03303
888-879-5095
www.duncraft.com

BestNest
4750 Lake Forest Drive, Suite 132
Cincinnati, OH 45242
877-562-1818 or 513-232-4225
www.bestnest.com

WildBirdingWorld
The Kayes Group
PO Box 3326
Mesquite, NV 89027
866-205-9917, PIN 2764
www.wildbirdingworld.com

Starling-Proof Feeders

Duncraft
102 Fisherville Rd.
Concord, NH 03303
888-879-5095
www.duncraft.com

RollerFeeder
St. Paul, MN 55108
800-432-3602
www.rollerfeeder.com

WildBirds Etc.
www.wildbirdsetc.com

Insect Feeder Foods

To find mealworms, waxworms, insect-containing suet, and other delectable insect foods, check your local bird supply shop. (You can buy live mealworms very reasonably at a fishing bait shop, as well.) You can also find insect feeder foods, including those that are packaged to minimize the "Eww" factor, at mail-order sources, such as these:

Duncraft
102 Fisherville Rd.
Concord, NH 03303
888-879-5095
www.duncraft.com

Worm Man
Worm Man's Worm Farm
PO Box 6947
Monroe Township, NJ 08831
732-521-8241 (for orders) or 732-656-0369
   (to report problems)
www.wormman.com

The Super Worm Farm
PO Box 25
601 Mountain Rd.
Kempton, PA 19529
866-680-2030
www.superwormfarm.com

Birdbaths and Accessories

Birdbaths are widely available at discount stores, garden centers, concrete yard ornament shops, and wild bird supply stores. To find misters, solar fountains, drip tubes, "water wigglers," and other devices that cause the water in the basin to splash or gurgle, check the offerings at water garden shops, wild bird supply stores, and some nurseries or garden centers. Or you can shop by mail or online, at suppliers such as these:

Duncraft
102 Fisherville Rd.
Concord, NH 03303
888-879-5095
www.duncraft.com

BestNest
4750 Lake Forest Drive, Suite 132
Cincinnati, OH 45242
877-562-1818 or 513-232-4225
www.bestnest.com

BirdBaths.com
NetShops, Corporate Office
12000 I St., Suite 20-200
Omaha, NE 68137
800-590-3752
www.birdbaths.com

Motion-Activated Cat Chasers

To find a device that hooks up to your hose to deter cats and other trespassers with a sudden blast of water, check bird supply stores, well-stocked garden centers, or suppliers such as these:

SafePetProducts.com
Rockwell Products, LLC
150 Stanford Ave.
Medford, OR 97504
877-231-1426
www.safepetproducts.com

Biocontrol Network
5116 Williamsburg Rd.
Brentwood, TN 37027
800-441-2847
www.biconet.com

Native Plants

It's much easier to find native plants these days than it once was. Start by asking for them at your local nursery. If you have a nursery that specializes in native plants in your area, check it out. Ask for whatever it is you want; if it's not in stock, the owners may be able to acquire it.

Independently owned nurseries are the best bet. Native plants—the same plants that are common as dirt in

wild places—are often hard to find at large garden centers. When I do manage to find a few, they're often priced higher than common ornamentals, probably because there's a smaller demand for them. But even the garden centers of big-box stores are beginning to stock some native species—and the more often native plants are requested by their customers, the more likely that stock will increase.

Another good place to find natives is at plant sales. I also keep an eye on my newspaper in spring, looking for plant sales by garden clubs, plant conservation groups, native plant societies, and other organizations that may have interesting native plants for sale—usually at bargain prices.

The Internet has been a boon for finding mail-order sources for unusual plants. Not so long ago, only a handful of nurseries specialized in native plants; today, there are scores of them, in every area of the country. Just do a search for "native plant nursery [your state]" and see what turns up.

Plants

You can find an excellent selection of native plants and other bird-appealing plants, including wildflowers, grasses, shrubs, trees, and vines, at trustworthy mail-order suppliers and native plant nurseries. Here's a very small sampling to whet your appetite:

Tripple Brook Farm
37 Middle Rd.
Southampton, MA 01073
413-527-4626
www.tripplebrookfarm.com
Hundreds of fabulous plants—I need a bigger yard!—including native viburnums and many, many other natives.

Blake Nursery
316 Otter Creek Rd.
Big Timber, MT 59011
406-932-4195
www.blakenursery.com
Specializes in plants for western gardens, including a terrific selection of hardy Montana natives that will thrive elsewhere in the West, too—or give that western touch to an eastern garden.

Forestfarm
990 Tetherow Rd.
Williams, OR 97544-9599
541-846-7269
www.forestfarm.com

Plant addicts, beware: One look at this chunky, jam-packed catalog and you'll be hooked. An unbelievably vast selection of thousands of plants, including natives from across America. Lots of favorite plants in my gardens have come from Forestfarm over the years, and I've been thrilled every time with their superior size and vigor.

Woodlanders
1128 Colleton Ave.
Aiken, SC 29801
803-648-7522
www.woodlanders.net

One of the older native plant specialists (since 1979), Woodlanders offers mouthwatering natives for the Southeast. Call for a catalog; no online shopping—yet.

Hamilton's Native Nursery & Seed Farm
16786 Brown Rd.
Elk Creek, MO 65464
417-967-2190 or 888-967-2190
www.hamiltonseed.com

Seeds and plants for native grasses, prairie flowers, native shrubs and trees, and other great finds.

Prairie Nursery
PO Box 306
Westfield, WI 53964
800-476-9453
www.prairienursery.com

Prairie plants are tough and adaptable, and this company has supplied many of those in my gardens. Reasonable prices and a super informative catalog chock-full of beautiful grasses, coneflowers, perennial sunflowers, and other wildflowers.

Raintree Nursery
391 Butts Rd.
Morton, WA 98356
360-496-6400
www.raintreenursery.com

Terrific fruit trees and bushes for people—and birds! It's a treat to open a well-packed box from this company and find big, healthy, high-quality plants rarin' to go. You'll discover all of the usual fruits and berries, plus a great selection of varieties that are hard to find elsewhere, such as mulberries and native fruits.

Digging Dog Nursery
PO Box 471
Albion, CA 95410
707-937-1130
www.diggingdog.com

Get ready to fall in love with hummingbirds—this catalog has so many plants that hummers adore, you can fill your yard *and* your neighbor's with great finds. You'll also discover other interesting perennials, including native plants for songbirds. Specializes in plants for the Southwest, but many of these beauties will thrive elsewhere, too.

High Country Gardens
2902 Rufina St.
Santa Fe, NM 87507
800-925-9387
www.highcountrygardens.com

Want a nice low water bill? Explore the fabulous drought-tolerant perennials and shrubs in this enticing catalog. Many natives, including a huge variety of penstemons for hummingbirds, plus many other bird-beloved perennials, native grasses, and shrubs.

Las Pilitas Nursery
8331 Nelson Way
Escondido, CA 92026
760-749-5930
3232 Las Pilitas Rd.
Santa Margarita, CA 93453
www.laspilitas.com

Discover wildflowers, shrubs, and trees for Southern California, many of them natives. This company emphasizes gardening for butterflies, birds, hummingbirds, and other wildlife, and you'll turn up all kinds of must-have plants. If you can't visit in person, you can browse and order online.

All Native Garden Center
300 Center Rd.
Fort Myers, FL 33907
239-939-9663
www.nolawn.com

Fabulous plants with tropical flair, and natives that can take the heat and dry spells. More than 200 native Florida species of plants, many of them superb for hummingbirds and songbirds. No mail-order services currently, but worth the drive; the staff includes two National Wildlife Federation Backyard Wildlife Habitat Stewards, so you'll find plenty of information just for the asking.

Seeds

Planting a few handfuls of birdseed from your feeder is the simple way to start a birdseed garden. But lots of other plants supply excellent seeds for birds. You can find seeds for zinnias, sunflowers, cosmos and other bird favorites on local seed racks. Or you can discover the wider world of bird seeds in mail-order catalogs and Web sites. Look for grains in the vegetable section of catalogs. If you have a big yard, check out prices for seeds in bulk. Here are just a few of my favorites; you'll find dozens of others online; most sources for prairie plants also sell seeds.

Shop Smart

When you shop in person, you can be sure you're buying healthy, vigorous, good-size plants. To avoid disappointment when you shop by mail, try these tips:

- If the catalog doesn't prominently tell you, in plain English, how big of a plant you'll get, you may want to shop elsewhere. How big is a "#1 plant"? I have no idea. But a gallon pot, or a 2¼" pot, now, that's my language.

- Before you buy, take a minute to read the fine print about shipping schedules and costs. Shipping costs are usually lowest if the source is near your home, and the plants from a nursery in your region may be better suited to your climate than those that originate far away.

- Look for a money-back guarantee, or at the very least, an offer to replace unsatisfactory plants. A reputable company will replace plants without requiring you to ship the plants back to them.

- Make your first purchase a small one. Wait until you see what kind of plants and service you get, before you spend a lot of money.

- I'm usually very happy with plants from mail-order nurseries whose catalogs I have to ask for, or which I find online. Makes sense: Those companies depend on the repeat business of satisfied customers.

- When I order from the companies whose catalogs seem to arrive in my mailbox every few months—catalogs I never asked for in the first place—the plants have been outrageously small, sickly, or just plain dead. Now I toss those catalogs on the recycling pile right away, so that their low prices can't seduce my cheapskate side. Makes me wonder if companies that do mass mailings of unsolicited catalogs attract so many buyers that they can get away with selling poor quality plants—it doesn't matter whether I buy from that company again, because someone else will.

- To find out what kind of experiences others have had with the company you're considering buying from, you can read the reviews by actual customers on the Web site "Garden Watchdog," davesgarden.com/gwd/. This site provides a great service, acting as a sort of Better Business Bureau for mail-order gardeners.

Native Seeds/SEARCH
526 N. 4th Ave.
Tucson, AZ 85705-8450
520-622-5561
www.nativeseeds.org

This fantastic small company offers a catalog of about 350 types of seeds, every single one of them suitable for farming in arid lands, and many of them great for birds in any garden. From grasses to grains to sunflowers, these seeds will make birds drool. All are heritage types, handed down through the generations, including Native American varieties of corn and sunflowers, not to mention amaranth, millet, and others that are perfect for a birdseed garden—or a loaf of bread. Simply reading the catalog is an education.

Abundant Life Seeds
PO Box 157
Saginaw, OR 97472
541-767-9606
www.abundantlifeseeds.com

Abundant Life Seed Foundation is famed for its collection of all-organic heritage seeds from around the world, many of them painstakingly gathered from gardeners who shared their own personal stock. Unfortunately, a devastating fire hit the warehouse in Port Townsend, WA, a few years ago. To help out this worthy cause, Territorial Seed (see below) of Oregon has taken over the mail-order catalog, so you can still find that wonderful selection of grains, grasses, sunflowers, Indian corn, flowers, and all the other treasures for which Abundant Life is known. Enjoy and support a good cause—the seeds that link us to gardeners of generations before.

Territorial Seed
PO Box 158
Cottage Grove, OR 97424
800-626-0866
www.territorial-seed.com

You'll find a mix of interesting vegetables and bird-beloved annuals in this delectable catalog, including an unbelievable array of sunflowers. Look for grains and corn, too, including Native American varieties.

American Meadows
223 Avenue D, Suite 30
Williston, VT 05495
802-951-5812 or 877-309-7333
www.americanmeadows.com

One of the very few companies that sells all-native mixes of wildflowers, instead of fattening the mix with inexpensive "filler" seeds. Also stocks many common annual flowers and wildflowers, plus regional mixes, both in small quantities and in bulk. Extremely reasonable prices—how about a pound of blue bachelor's button seeds (*Centaurea cyanus*) for less than $10?

Wildseed Farms
425 Wildflower Hills
PO Box 3000
Fredericksburg, TX 78624
800-848-0078
www.wildseedfarms.com

A good source for fast-growing annual flowers with seeds that birds adore. Look for cosmos, zinnias, and many others, in packets or in bulk. You'll find low-priced wild-flower mixes, too, but not entirely native. Personally, I don't mind red Flanders poppies (*Papaver rhoeas*) adding some zing to my flower beds, but if you prefer natives only, you can make your own mix by buying seeds of individual plants.

Pinetree Garden Seeds
PO Box 300
New Gloucester, ME 04260
207-926-3400
www.superseeds.com

The first company I ever bought mail-order seeds from, and still going strong decades later. This family company offers a huge selection of interesting annual flowers at reasonable prices. You'll also discover a great collection of sunflower varieties at prices cheap enough to try them all, plus graceful millets, wheat, corn, and other grains for birds.

Acknowledgments

This book has been in the making for decades. Every plant I helped my mother haul home from the woods, every pocketful of seeds I collected on a walk, every moment I stopped to watch what a bird or a bug was doing, every time I got my bearings in a new part of the country by figuring out what was growing around me and who that was singing in the trees and how they all fit together—every day of my life, I've been learning about birds, insects, plants, and everything else under the sun.

My house is lined with bookshelves, but the real education comes from doing it myself. Books help me put names to what I see, and I love to read about how others' observations compare with my own. But watching shows me how everything is connected. And gardening teaches me what works—and what doesn't.

Of course, a lifelong obsession is way too much to cram into one book, which is why I'm grateful to Christine Bucks, the skilled and astute editor of this book. Chris helped me think out what should go in these pages, and how it was best presented. With good grace and plenty of humor, she gently kept me on course.

Chris polished my words with a sensitive touch. But being an editor requires a lot more than being good with the language. It's more like being a hairstylist or a bartender—you get to hear it all. Many a time, I was grateful for Chris's warm heart and listening ear. And I know she'll never reveal all those true confessions she heard along the way, like how I accidentally ate a ladybug.

Thanks to editor Karen Bolesta, too, who later picked up the reins on this book. Her finesse and her funny bone made the finishing touches a breeze.

I'm grateful, too, to Nancy Bailey, the project manager of this book. Nancy has a knack for keeping a dozen balls in the air at once—and smiling while she does it. I think of her every time I try to find the right scrap of scribbled notes in the teetering piles on my desk.

Speaking of organization, my research assistant, David Roth-Mark, proved invaluable. He checked scientific names, organized lists as I brainstormed, and did any other detail work I needed, fast and accurately. It's vital to have an assistant whose work you can trust, and David does it right the first time.

Susannah Hogendorn, copy editor, kept an eagle eye out for typos and made sure my commas didn't get out of line. Or my periods, semicolons, run-on sentences, or any other transgressions of the language that occurred when I was so excited about what I was writing, the rules went right out the window.

Designer Joanna Williams made this book look good inside and out. I think of her as choosing just the right pieces of jewelry to go with an outfit—the dress would look mighty plain and boring without her magic touch.

And finally, since this book is all about families, a word about my own. I was the baby of the family, and my sisters and brother were often my guides and playmates. Thank you to my brother, Paul Roth, and my sisters, Marie Bedics, Pat Benner, Carole Mehrkam Roth, and Mary Dech. All those long-ago years of catching tadpoles, or finding seashells, or picking fistfuls of violets, or standing at the very edge of Big Rock—with a reassuring hand to hold—are still with me.

Photo Credits

© Gay Bumgarner/Alamy: pages 28, 338-339

© Rebecca Erol/Alamy: page 72 (bottom)

© Holt Studios International Ltd./Alamy: page 336 (top)

© Superstock/Alamy: page 335

© Bill Beatty: page 349

© Robin Fritz: page 230 (bottom)

© Christi Carter/Garden Picture Library: page 144 (bottom)

© Neil Holmes/Garden Picture Library: page 344

© Michele Lamontagne/Garden Picture Library: page 105 (top)

© J. S. Sira/Garden Picture Library: page 23

© Friedrich Strauss/Garden Picture Library: page 336 (bottom)

© Ron Sutherland/Garden Picture Library: page 293

© Jun Maejima/Amana Images/Getty Images: page iv

© Stockdisc Classic/Getty Images: page v

© Pamela Harper: pages 24, 26, 54, 143, 150, 198, 206, 238, 251 (top), 265, 269, 310 (bottom), 317

© Gay Bumgarner/Index Stock: page 68-69

© Marion Brenner/Botanica/Jupiter Images: page 49

© Ann Cutting/Botanica/Jupiter Images: page 204

© Sandra Ivany/Botanica/Jupiter Images: page 275

© Bob Stefko/Botanica/Jupiter Images: page 316

© Mark Turner/Botanica/Jupiter Images: pages viii–1, 192

© Comstock/PictureQuest/Jupiter Images: page 118 (bottom)

© Rick Mark: pages 19, 20, 22, 32, 39, 61, 75, 102, 103, 116 (bottom), 132, 144 (top), 170 (top), 210 (top), 288 (bottom), 343

© Maslowski Productions: pages 10, 105 (bottom), 348, 370

© G. Armistead/Vireo: pages 163, 185

© G. Bailey/Vireo: page 36 (top)

© P. Bannick/Vireo: page 88

© R. & N. Bowers/Vireo: pages 95 (top), 122, 180, 268 (top), 309 (bottom), 362

© J. Cancalosi/Vireo: pages 267 (top), 327

© R. Crossley/Vireo: pages 195 (top), 224 (bottom), 292 (bottom)

© H. Cruickshank/Vireo: page 342 (bottom)

© J. Culbertson/Vireo: pages 121 (top), 197

© R. & S. Day/Vireo: pages 229, 306, 310 (top), 340

© G. Dremeaux/Vireo: page 213 (bottom)

© J. Fuhrman/Vireo: pages 133, 256

© W. Greene/Vireo: pages 106 (top), 245, 307

© C. H. Greenewalt/Vireo: page 67

© J. Heidecker/Vireo: pages 17 (bottom), 62, 305 (bottom), 345

© B. Henry/Vireo: pages 2, 118 (top), 277

© S. Holt/Vireo: pages 214, 325 (bottom)

© M. Hyett/Vireo: page 91

© A. J. Knystautas/Vireo: page 134

© G. Lasley/Vireo: pages 255, 289 (top), 294

© P. La Tourrette/Vireo: pages 195 (bottom), 337, 365

© S. Maka/Vireo: page 364

© G. McElroy/Vireo: pages 5 (bottom), 70, 147, 161, 241 (top), 267 (bottom), 282, 283 (bottom), 291 (bottom), 296 (top), 371

© A. Morris/Vireo: pages 5 (top), 17 (top), 53, 80, 149, 183, 242, 326 (bottom), 356

© Dr. E. S. Morton/Vireo: page 139

© R. Royse/Vireo: pages 244, 281 (bottom), 326 (top)

© S. S. Rucker/Vireo: pages 311, 342 (top)

© R. Saldino/Vireo: page 158

Index

USDA Plant Hardiness Zone Map

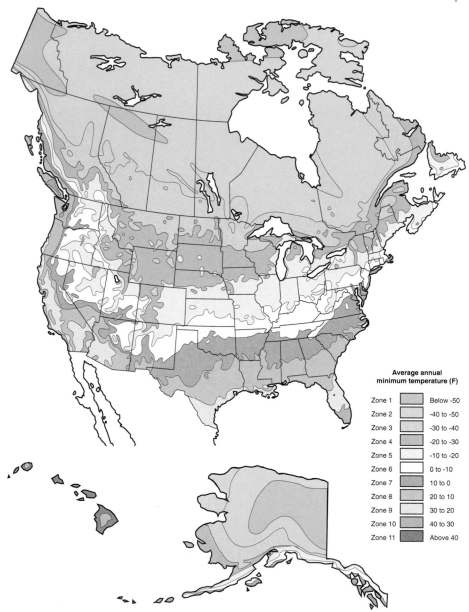

Average annual minimum temperature (F)

Zone 1		Below -50
Zone 2		-40 to -50
Zone 3		-30 to -40
Zone 4		-20 to -30
Zone 5		-10 to -20
Zone 6		0 to -10
Zone 7		10 to 0
Zone 8		20 to 10
Zone 9		30 to 20
Zone 10		40 to 30
Zone 11		Above 40

This map was revised in 1990 and is recognized as the best indicator of minimum temperatures available. Look at the map to find your area, then match its pattern to the key above. When you've found your pattern, the key will tell you what hardiness zone you live in. Remember that the map is a general guide; your particular conditions may vary. *Map courtesy of Agriculture Research Service, USDA.*